LONDON IN PAINT

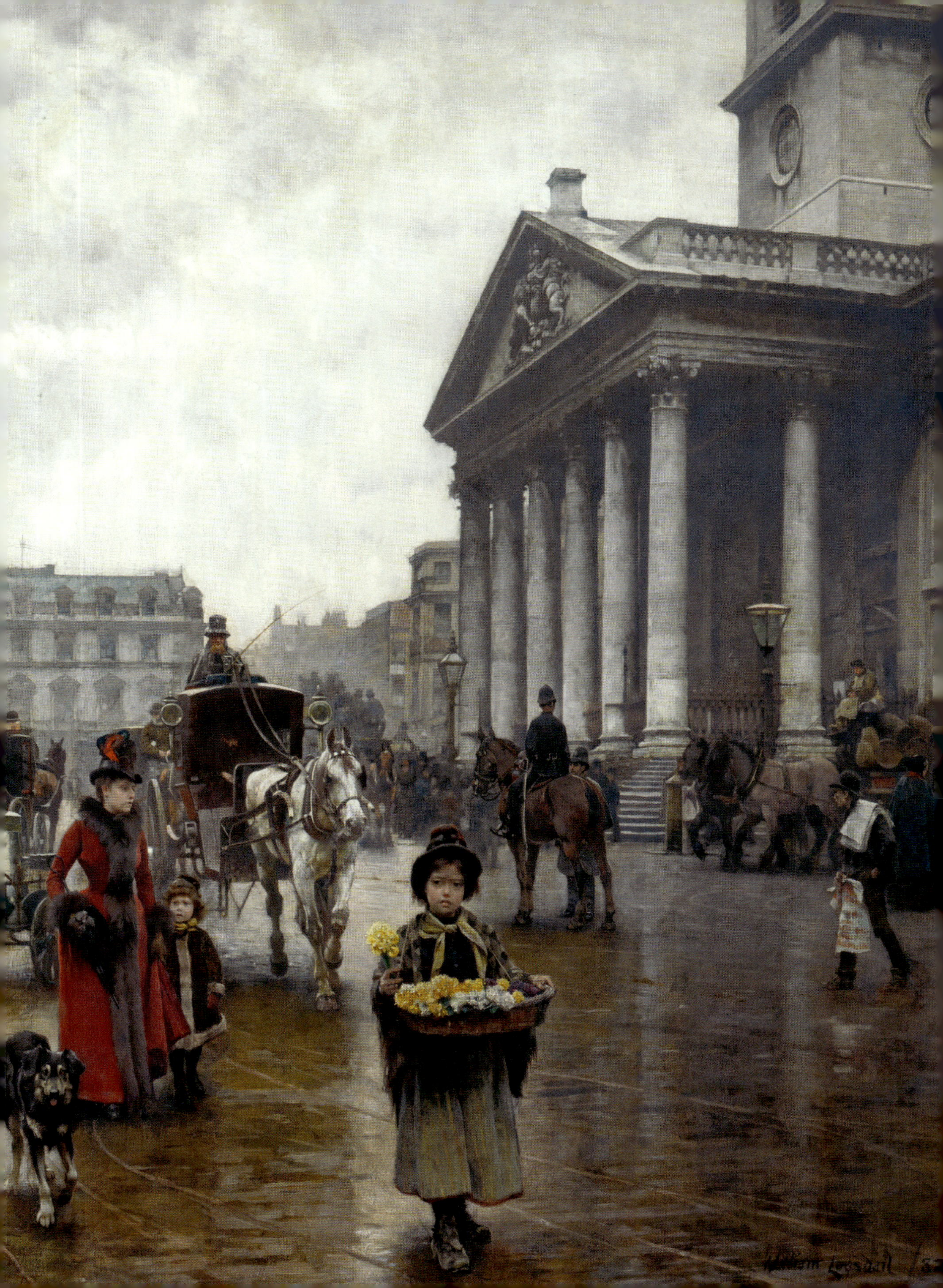

LONDON IN PAINT

LEE CHESHIRE

TATE PUBLISHING

First published 2017 by order of the
Tate Trustees by Tate Publishing,
a division of Tate Enterprises Ltd,
Millbank, London SW1P 4RG
www.tate.org.uk/publishing

A catalogue record for this book is available
from the British Library

ISBN 978-1-84976-501-5

Distributed in the United States and Canada by ABRAMS, New York

Library of Congress Control Number:
applied for

Designed by willwebb.co.uk

Colour reprographics by Altaimage, London

Printed and bound by Litografia Rosés / SYL L'Art Grafic, Spain

Cover: L.S. Lowry *Piccadilly Circus, London* 1960. Oil on canvas 76.2 x 101.6. Private collection. © The Estate of L.S. Lowry. All Rights Reserved, DACS 2017. Photo: © Christie's Images/ Bridgeman Images. See p.71

Frontispiece: William Logsdail *St Martin-in-the-Fields* 1888. Oil on canvas 143.5 x 118.1. Tate. Presented by the Trustees of the Chantrey Bequest 1888. Photo: © Tate 2017. See pp.64–5

Measurements of artworks are given in centimetres, height before width. See pp.182–4

FSC
www.fsc.org
MIX
Paper from
responsible sources
FSC® C109493

CONTENTS

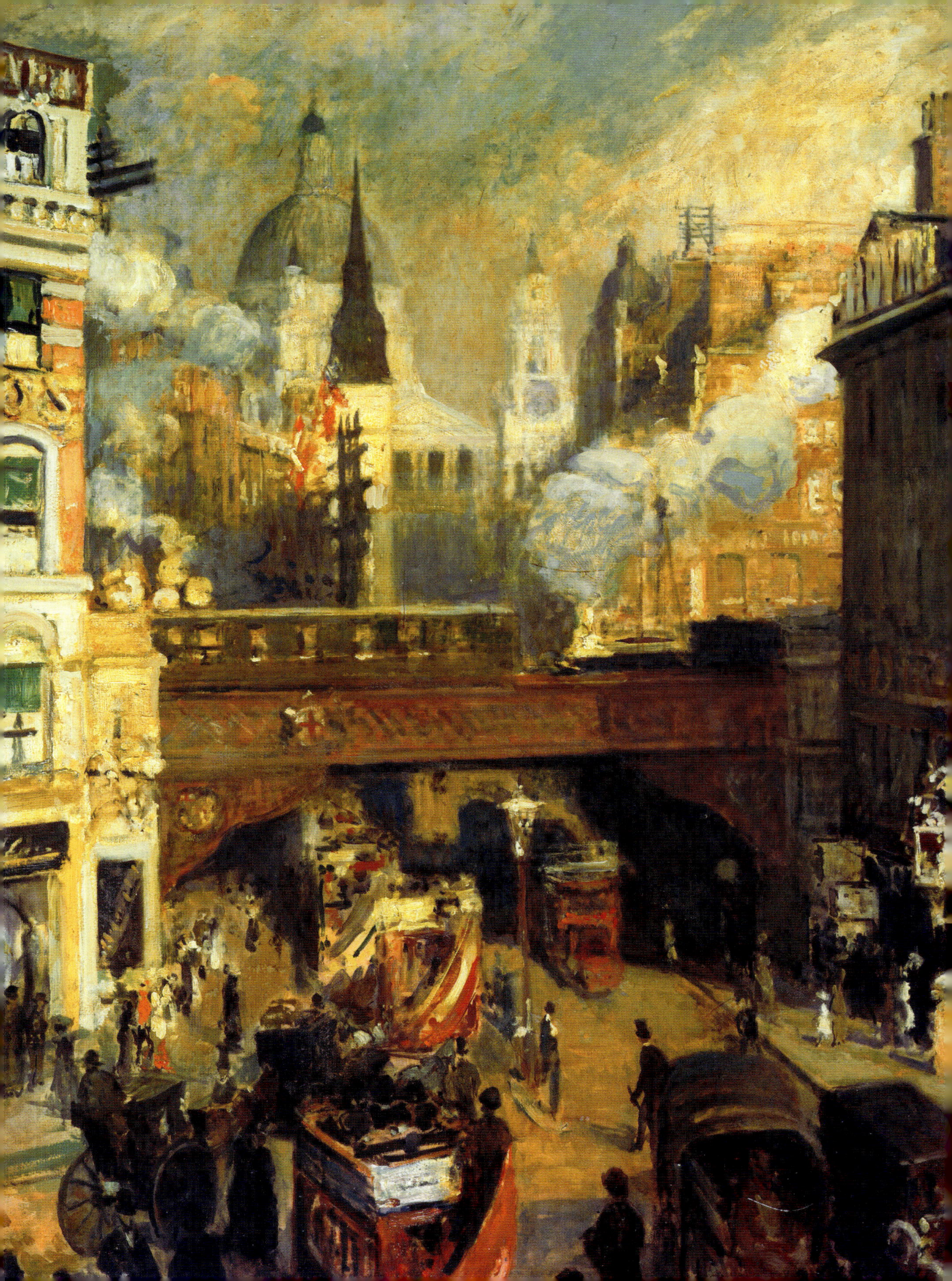

INTRODUCTION

...for those who live in the most wonderful and complex city in the world, the most fruitful course of study lies in a persistent effort to render the magic and poetry they daily see around them.

Walter Sickert, 1889

Many of the artists that feature in this book were not born or raised in London; those that were drawn to the city brought a taste of their home cities with them, and found within London a reflection of themselves. As a result the vision of London that they helped to create and popularise, the idea of 'London' which we all hold in our heads and see reflected in holiday snaps and on picture postcards, is in large part from the perspective of the enthusiastic alien rather than the native. The city's view of itself has always been intermingled with how others view it.

London, arguably, is unique in the way that it resists any easy visual encapsulation. Many first-time visitors find it ugly or underwhelming – it does not have the sublime coherence of Paris, Venice or Bath. It's not hard to find areas that are in need of prettying up, or once-beautiful views that have been spoiled by unsympathetic development.

But the wonderful truth, as most visitors come to realise and treasure, is that London is not a city built in accordance to one theory of beauty. It is a never-ending competition between philosophies of architecture and city design, with no authority powerful enough to dominate. The ever-evolving streets of the metropolis are in constant flux and turmoil. While rivals Paris and New York may feel as if they are on a slow decline from their heyday, London seems as though it is constantly being rebuilt anew.

This cannot be clearer than from the top of the hill outside the Greenwich Observatory in south-east London. There are few places in the world where you can see such a variety of architecture from one vantage point – from the calm classicism of the seventeenth-century Queen's House, to the high-tech folly of the former Millennium Dome. From this viewpoint alone there are dizzying numbers of possible Londons.

So how and where to begin? The first artists to paint the city were from abroad, mainly from the Low Countries: the genre of landscape painting, the technique of using oil paint, and the modern market economy all came of age there in the sixteenth and seventeenth centuries. Painters such as Claude de Jongh (pp.18–21) were drawn across the Channel in search of new subject matter and new clients, and depicted early-modern London as reminiscent of the canal-pierced towns of the lowlands. It was perhaps at this time that the River Thames gained its central importance in London views. While there is plenty of artistic material in London's rural suburbs or the closely knit alleyways of the old city, and many artists in these pages have plundered it, the views of London that painters

Jacques-Emile Blanche
Ludgate Circus: Entrance to the City (November, Midday) c.1910.
Here, the French painter captures this popular view of St Paul's Cathedral from the end of Fleet Street. The picturesque railway viaduct, with its steam locomotive, was demolished in the 1990s.

have returned to again and again over the centuries feature this famous river with its majestic curves. Its bridges regularly star in paintings of the city, and in this era Old London Bridge in particular, with its encrustation of medieval buildings, was a popular subject.

The importance of London's river in art was cemented by the arrival of Canaletto in the 1740s, who adapted his gloriously lit scenes of Venice very little, painting the Thames as if it were simply an even grander Grand Canal. His time here coincided with a new-found wealth and confidence, as London was transitioning into the world's largest city and its de facto capital. He recorded the grand new projects that were transforming the face of the city, including Westminster Bridge, the first new bridge in central London for over a millennium (pp.156–7). Canaletto's visit was a catalyst for the native art scene, which was then based in and around Covent Garden in the rapidly expanding West End. It is at this time that we start seeing works by recognisable London-born artists, such as William Hogarth (1697–1764) and Samuel Scott (1702–72). The former brought a local's eye to his paintings, less interested in the picture postcard views than the drama played out on the city's streets.

The popularity of London as a subject has waxed and waned over the years. Richard Wilson (c.1714–82), J.M.W. Turner (1775–1851) and John Constable (1776–1837) created works that forced people to take pure landscape painting seriously as art, but they made few major paintings of the urban cityscape, instead living and working beyond, in the greener, rural areas such as Twickenham or Hampstead. In the Victorian era, London became the first truly modern city, with public transit, fast communications and widespread electric lighting. It found enthusiastic cheerleaders in a generation of artists keen to sell the fruits of their labours to the growing middle classes. It was, however, spurned as a subject by the era's dominant avant-garde group, the Pre-Raphaelites.

It was the French Impressionists that were to bring London back to art's cutting edge. Interested in showing modern life as they saw it in front of them, as well as exploring the pictorial effects of light and colour, they found unmissable opportunities in London's fog-bound hustle and bustle. James Abbott McNeill Whistler (1834–1903), although not part of the group, was friendly with them and pointed Claude Monet (1840–1926) towards the best views of the Thames when he visited. The results are some of the most astonishing paintings ever made, moving from accurate representation into other-worldly abstraction.

The Impressionists had a profound influence on the next major group of homegrown artists to depict the city, the Camden Town Group, who also aimed to reflect the realities of modern urban life, but just as often created idyllic views of residential squares and streets that were soon to have their peace shattered by the First World War. Walter Sickert (1860–1942), at the forefront of the group, is best known for his sinister paintings of gloomy interiors, but the other artists explored every part of London, or captured intimate views out of their bedroom windows.

With the increasing impact of abstraction and the decline of painting of all types after the war, London has appeared decreasingly in the works of cutting-edge artists. Important exceptions are works by Frank Auerbach (b.1931) and Leon Kossoff (b.1926), who use the city as source material for images which at first glance might seem to be entirely abstract. Others included in this book have done the opposite, recording the city in minute detail that harks back to the great paintings of Canaletto.

All the paintings in this book are topographical in that they depict an identifiable location to a reasonable degree of accuracy. They all show places you could visit today – and potentially stand in the same place the artist did. Some scenes have changed little, even after the passage of time; others show buildings which have long disappeared. The map on pages 180–1 shows the location of the works as far as can be ascertained. This book does not include paintings of generic (and unidentifiable) street scenes or interiors – such as the many works by William Hogarth or Walter Sickert. Nor does it attempt to address the many great watercolours of the city, as these deserve their own consideration.

The following pages contain many extraordinary, important and well-known paintings, but also works by relatively unknown artists – some indeed who remain anonymous. Whether these artists have depicted iconic landmarks, such as the Houses of Parliament or St Paul's Cathedral, recorded scenes of grand occasion or everyday life, or instead focused on evoking the atmosphere or character of London – all of them have attempted to capture a snapshot of this constantly changing, infinitely faceted city, to put their London – in all its splendour, variety and moods – down on canvas.

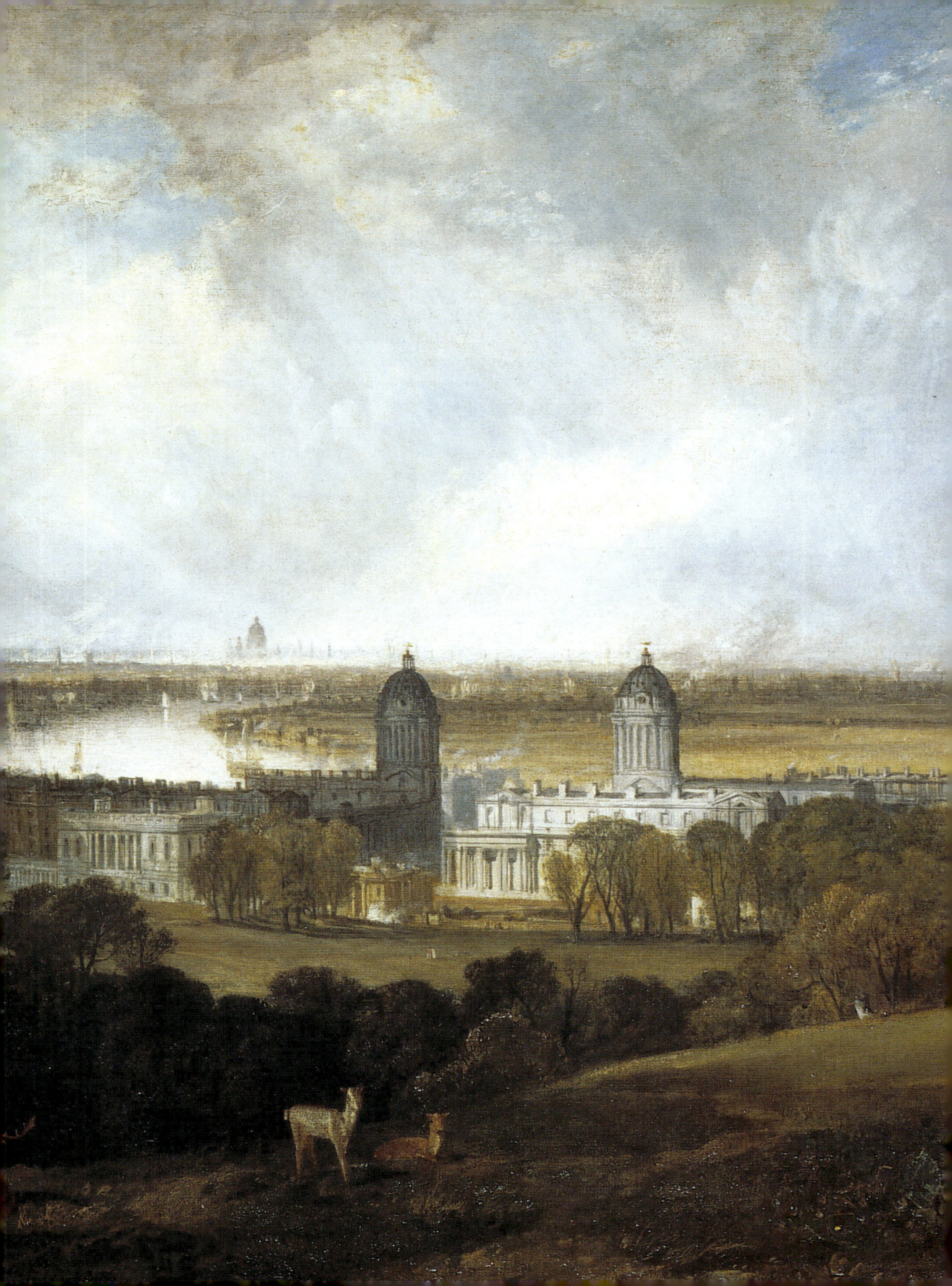

I

VIEWS AND VISTAS

LONDON FIRST APPEARS IN ART in its entirety, in vast bird's-eye panoramas. Today we are used to seeing London this way. We can summon up views from satellites, then turn and examine them as if we hold an infinitely detailed model of the city in our hands. In the sixteenth century these views had to be drawn and painted. The great publication *Civitas orbis terrarum*, begun in 1572, contained over five hundred maps and bird's-eye views of cities all over the world. Typically for the time, its map of Tudor London, spilling over its medieval walls and reaching out to Westminster and Southwark, is adorned with tiny drawings of the houses and people, drawn in semi three-dimensional perspective. As well as fulfilling military and administrative purposes, these maps were valued for aesthetic and symbolic reasons. What better way of showing that you were a man of the world than having the world's greatest cities laid out on your wall?

In the 'long views' by artists such as Anthonis van den Wyngaerde (1525–71), C.J. Visscher (1587–1652) and Wenceslaus Hollar (1607–77), the angle of view becomes lower, emphasising the skyline and illustrating the buildings more realistically. Often picturing London from somewhere above Southwark, these etchers and engravers probably worked from the top of the tower of Southwark Cathedral, then the tallest point south of the river, but used their imagination to show the city from a slightly higher viewpoint further back. With incredible detail and a fair level of topographical accuracy, these images provide a compelling record of the city before it was destroyed by the Great Fire of 1666.

The earliest paintings of London adopted the views established by these etchers. They presented London from afar, from the hills that border the Thames's river valley, or they used the mighty river itself to carve through the densely packed streets. Many of the early landscape artists were Dutch or Flemish and these views resembled the cities of the near Continent, particularly Antwerp – another rich trading city situated on a wide river, which London was just starting to surpass. These paintings were the beginning of a tradition of depicting London as a grand waterside city, establishing standard views that have shaped the work of the many artists who have followed.

J.M.W. Turner *London from Greenwich Park*, exhibited 1809 (detail). See p.23

Charles d'Orleans in the Tower of London

Unknown artist, late fifteenth century

This is probably the earliest painting of a recognisable London. Usually, medieval images of London, such as those in early woodcut prints, tended to use either a familiar icon – such as Old St Paul's Cathedral – to represent the city, or portray a generic huddle of roofs and spires that could be any city. While the unrealistic bend of the river and the oversized people depicted here are medieval in style, this painting is groundbreaking in that it shows an identifiable location.

Part of an illuminated manuscript, the work was produced by a Flemish artist to illustrate an edition of Charles d'Orleans's poems. Charles was a French nobleman who spent twenty-five years as an English prisoner; he is shown here as a captive in the Tower of London. In true medieval tradition, he appears several times: a cut-away shows him writing inside the central keep – known as the White Tower – and above he is pining at a window. Charles can also be seen talking outside the tower and perhaps even on horseback leaving through the gate on the left.

The White Tower has changed little, although it is no longer painted with the whitewash that gave it its name. In the foreground is the infamous Traitors' Gate, the water gate through which Tudor prisoners – including Anne Boleyn – entered the Tower. In the background is Old London Bridge, topped with buildings.

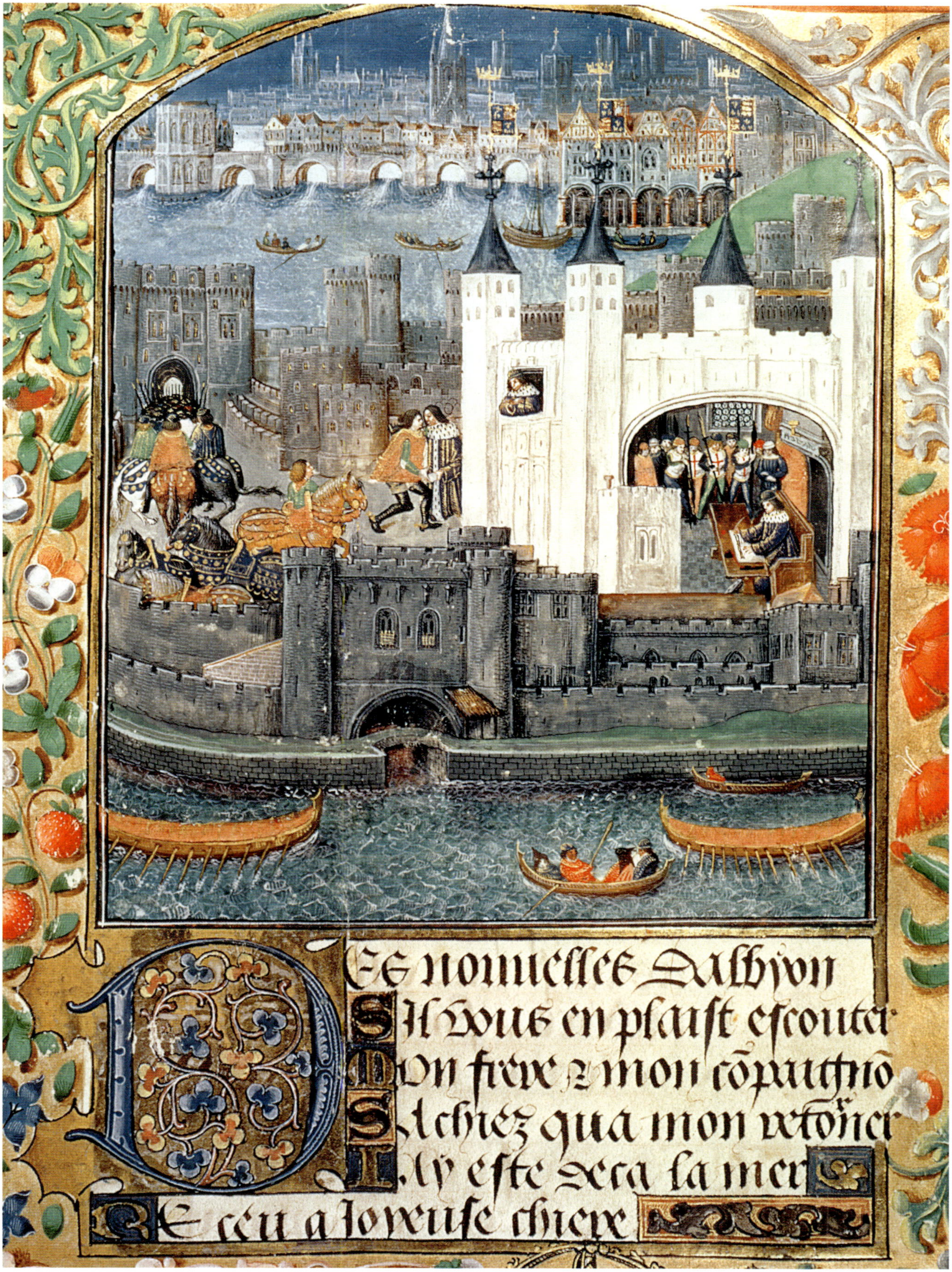
Des nouvelles Dalbyon
Sil vous en plaist escouter
Mon frere z mon cõpaignõ
Sachiez qua mon retõner
Iay este deca la mer
De ceu a joyeuse chiere

Prospect of London and the Thames from above Greenwich

Unknown artist c.1620–30

Although by far the largest city in England by the early seventeenth century, London had not yet expanded far beyond its historical walls. Here it is seen in the distance from the south-east, surrounded by fields and clearly separated from the villages of Deptford, in the middle, and Greenwich on the right.

At this time, the London skyline was dominated by three large churches – Westminster Abbey, Old St Paul's Cathedral and St Mary Overie (now Southwark Cathedral) – and the latter two are clearly visible here. The marshland in the centre of the painting is now the location of Canary Wharf. At the far right is the Duke of Gloucester's Castle, now the site of Greenwich Observatory, and at the foot of the hill is the medieval Greenwich Palace – a favoured home of Henry VIII and Elizabeth I, now the location of the Old Royal Naval College.

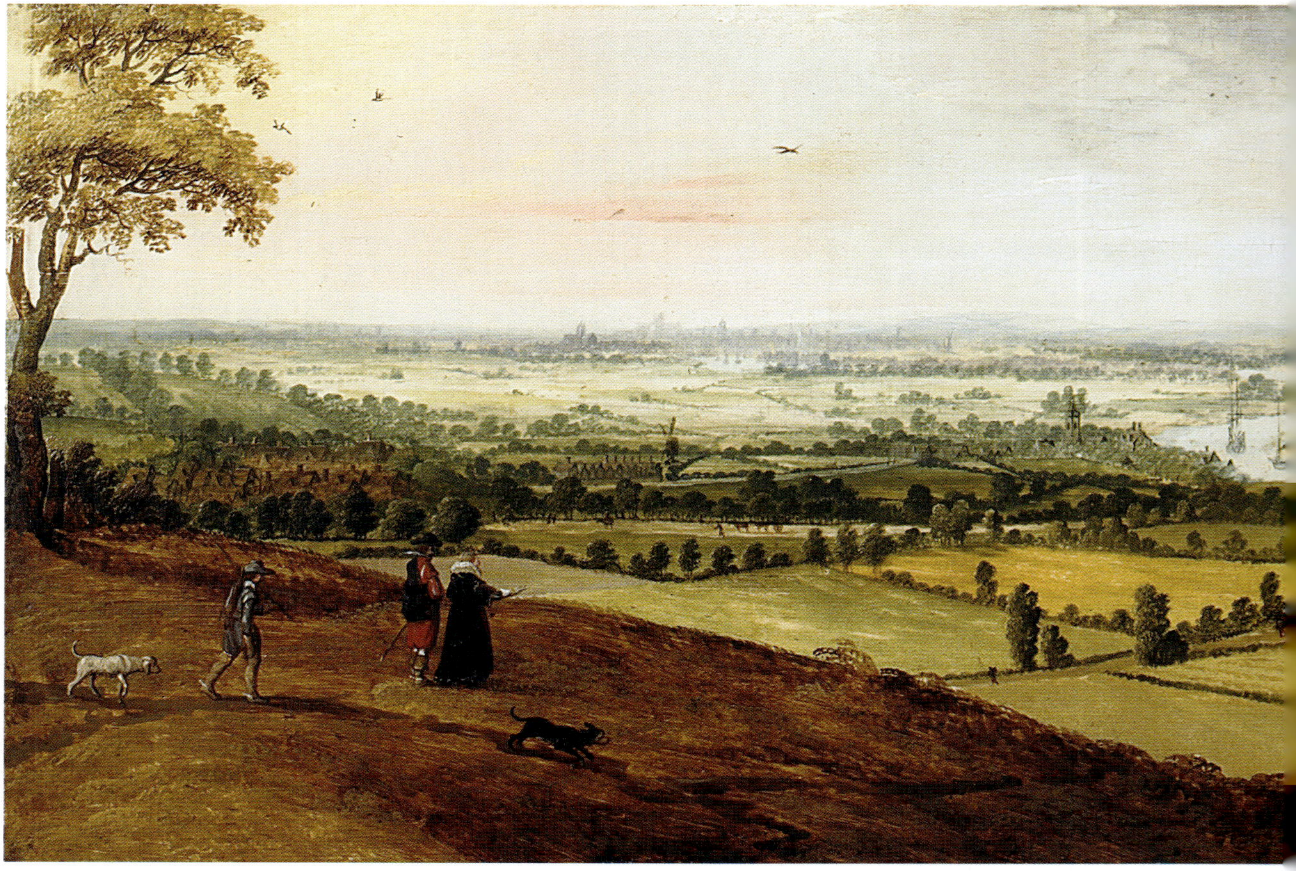

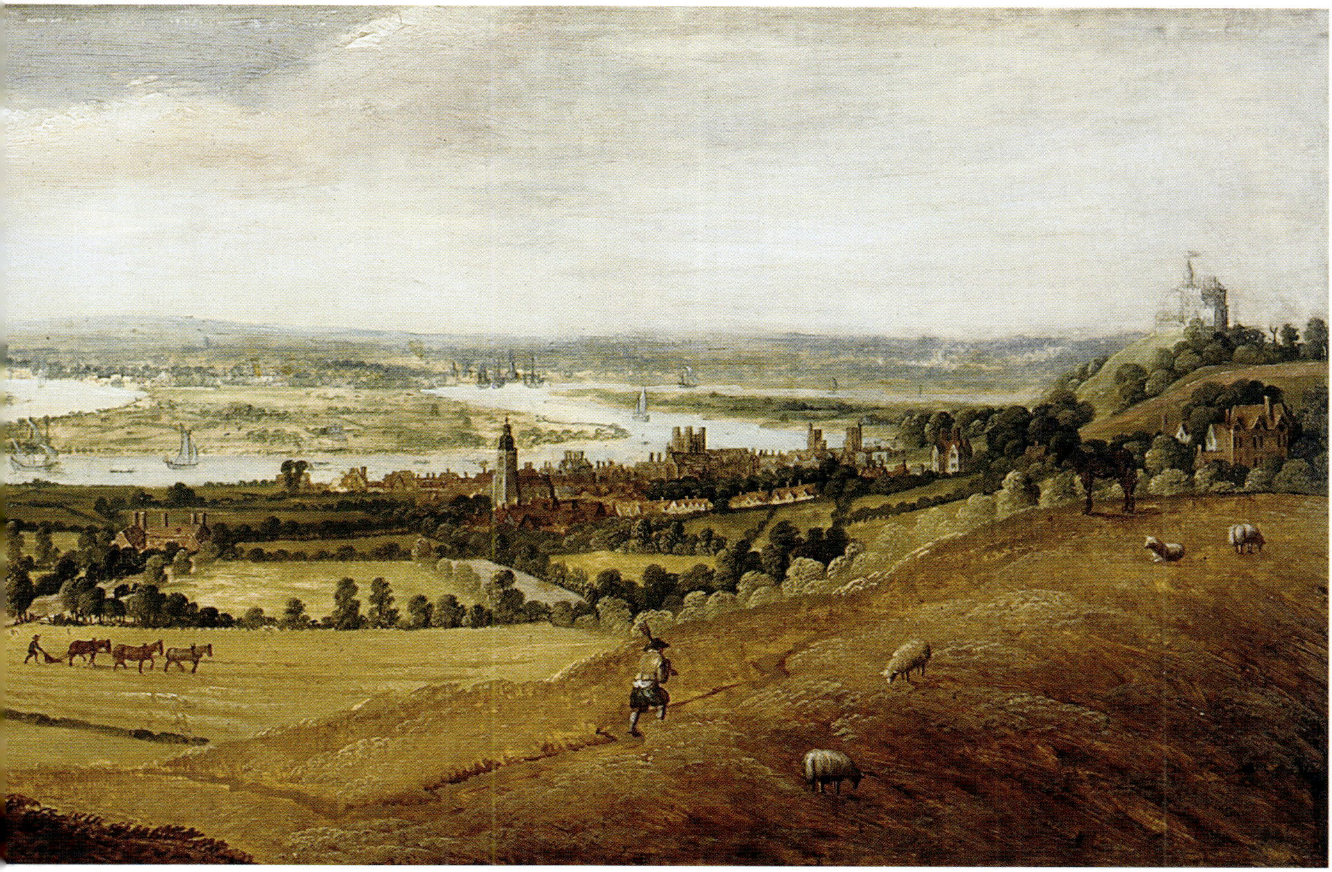

London from Southwark

Unknown artist c.1630

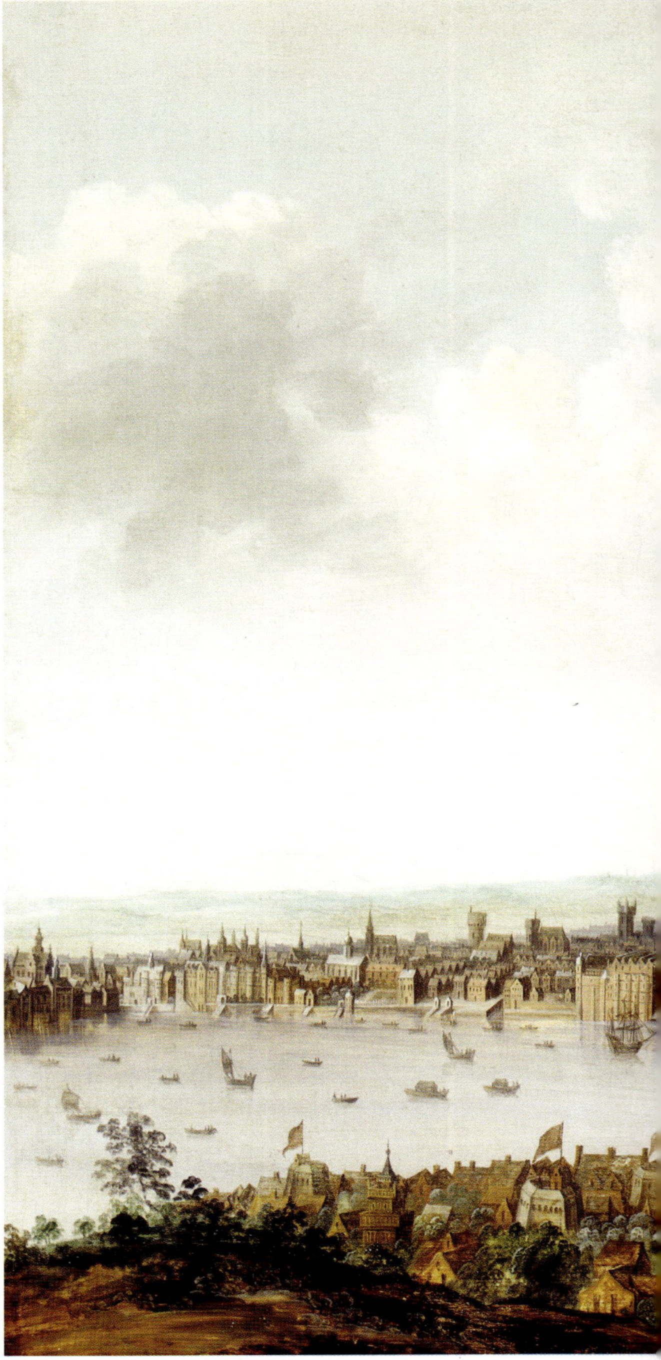

This work translates the 'long view' prints and drawings of Hollar and others into paint, adding colour to the city and positioning it below a vast sky. It is one of a handful of paintings that show London before it was destroyed by the Civil War of 1642–51 and the Great Fire of 1666 – historians have determined that it depicts the city as it was around 1600.

Although compressed, many familiar landmarks can be picked out. The Gothic bulk of Old St Paul's has already lost the spire that made it one of the tallest buildings in the world, and it would soon be burnt to the ground. Old London Bridge – note the heads of executed prisoners on spikes above the gatehouse – is prominent on the right side of the painting. It stands a few metres to the east of the position of the current bridge. Southwark Cathedral, at the lower centre, has survived, as has the Tower of London, on the far right.

This format had the unintended consequence of recording Southwark – then not considered part of the city proper – in great detail in the foreground. It was a disreputable area of taverns and theatres (including Shakespeare's Globe), bull- and bear-baiting pits and several prisons. The road approaching London Bridge at the bottom right was the way to the Channel ports and this would have been the first view of London many foreign artists would have glimpsed.

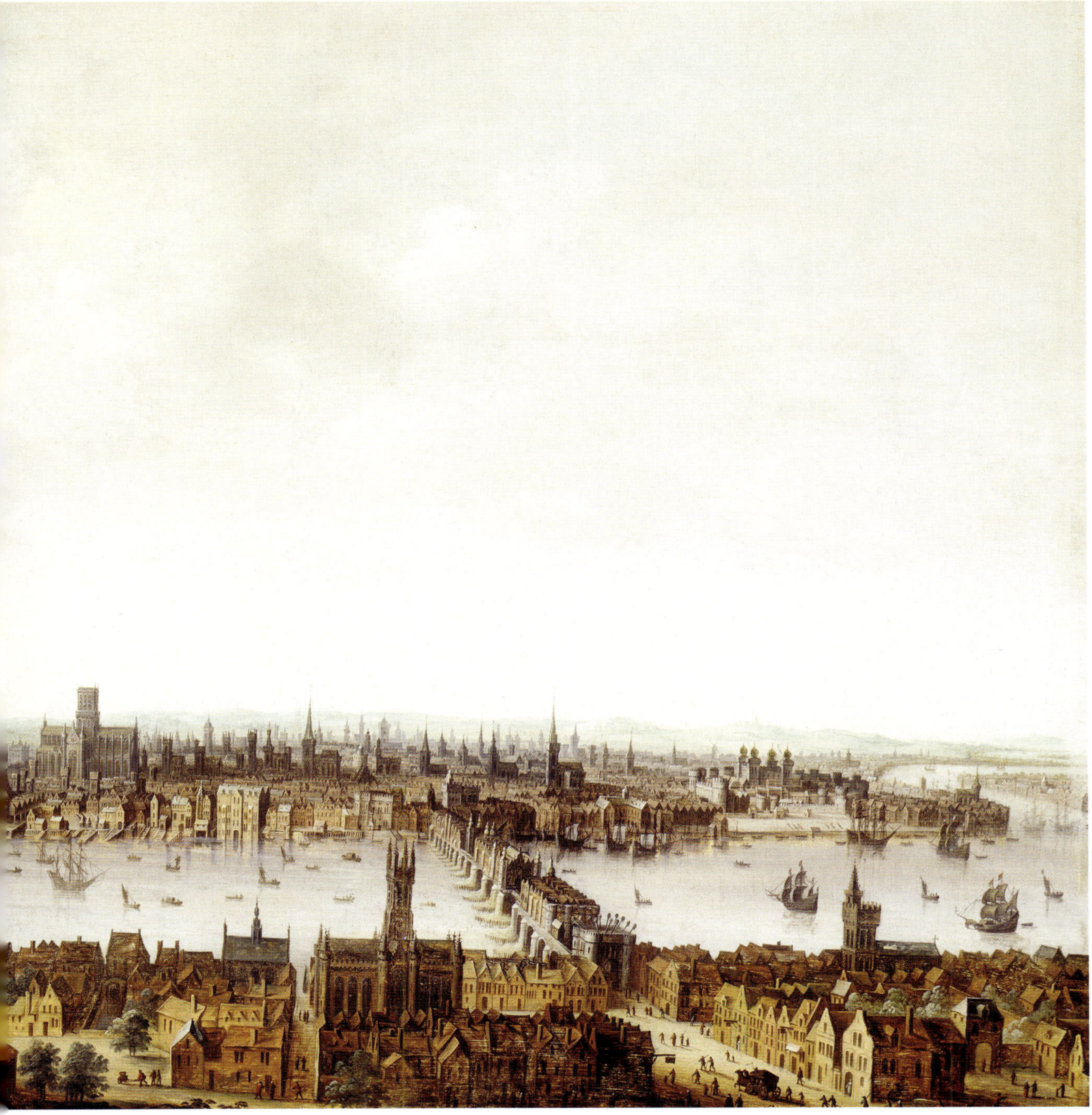

The Thames at Westminster Stairs

Claude de Jongh 1631

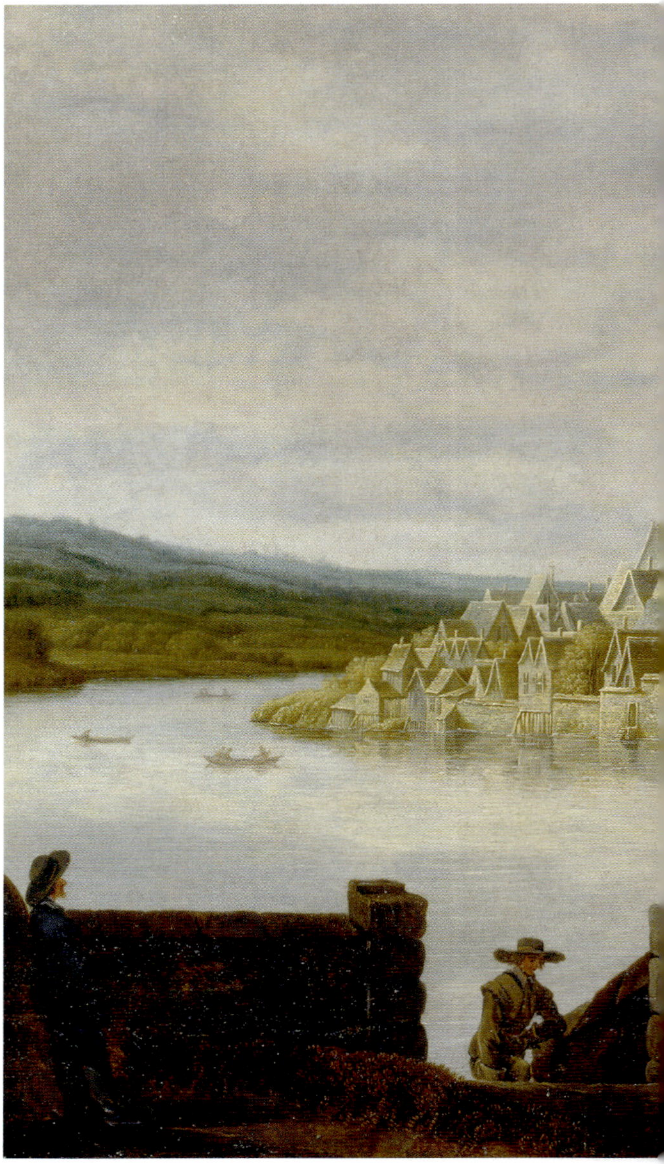

Painted by artists for centuries, this view is still called on to represent London in guidebooks and Hollywood films. This is one of its first appearances, although the cityscape has changed so much it is hard to recognise it as Westminster. Today, this entire waterfront is occupied by the Houses of Parliament.

Claude de Jongh was one of the earliest painters to show London from close-up rather than in wide, map-like panoramas. Born and based in the Netherlands – the world leader in cityscapes – he visited London regularly to sketch, before finishing his paintings at home in Utrecht. Several liberties taken with details suggest that they were intended for Dutch patrons, who were enthusiastic buyers of such subjects and would not have noticed the inaccuracies.

The golden light, rolling hills and picturesque tumble of riverside dwellings show that this scene is a little idealised. But the key buildings are there. At the far right of the painting is Westminster Abbey. To its left is the gable end of Westminster Hall, which survived the burning of the rest of the Palace of Westminster in 1834. The rectangular building in the centre of the painting is St Stephen's Chapel – the original House of Commons. Built by Henry III (r.1216–72) to rival Paris's jewel-like Sainte Chapelle, it became the debating chamber for the Commons in 1547 and its layout influenced that of the modern-day Parliament.

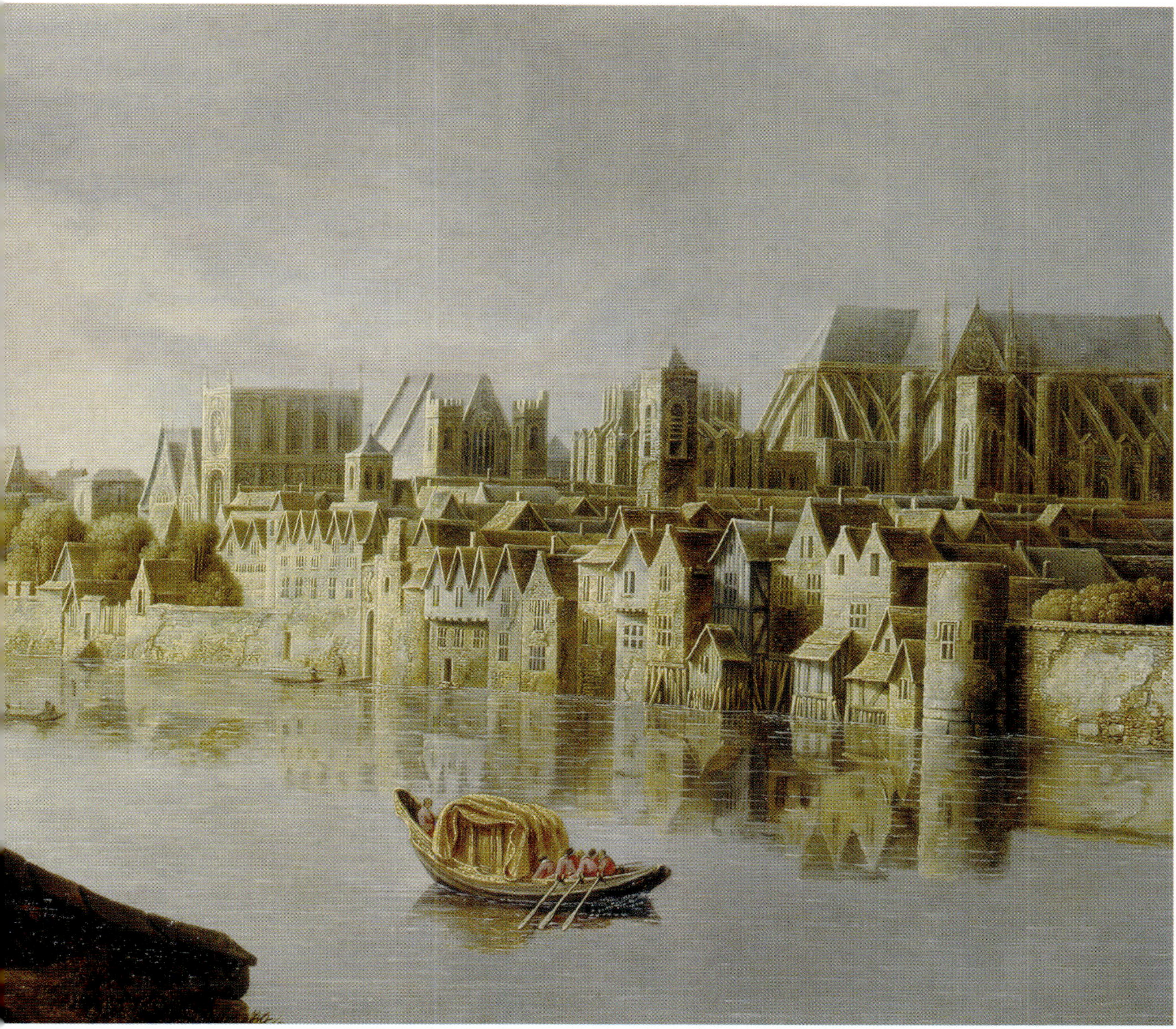

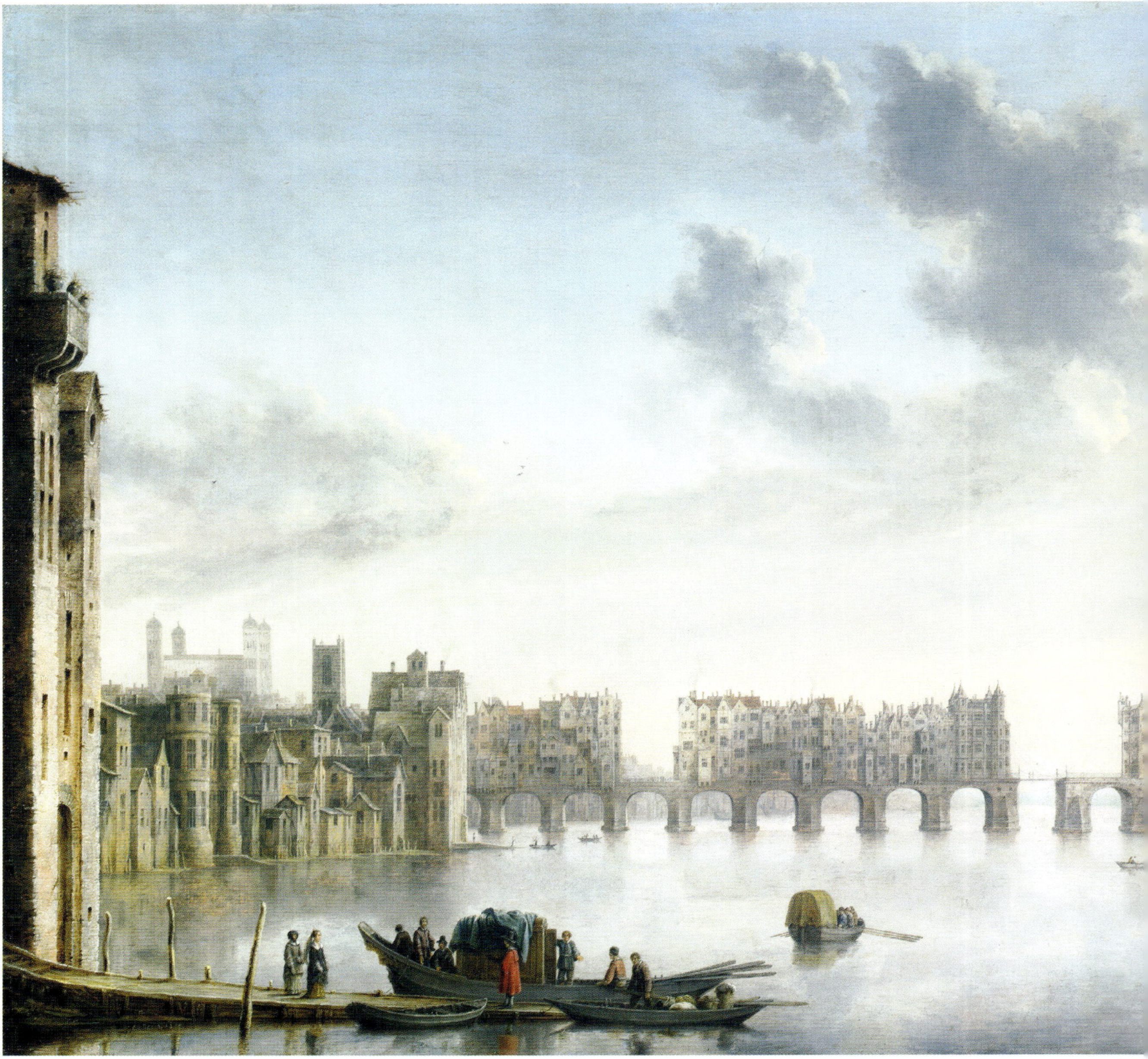

View of Old London Bridge from the West

Claude de Jongh 1650

Old London Bridge was one of the wonders of the medieval world, surpassing rivals such as the Ponte Vecchio in Florence in the number and splendour of the buildings that topped it. At the time of this painting, London Bridge was the only bridge in London to cross the Thames, and had been since the city was established by the Romans in the first century.

The medieval bridge was begun in 1176 and took thirty-three years to complete. By the time Claude de Jongh painted the bridge it supported 200 buildings, up to seven stories high. There were private houses, over a

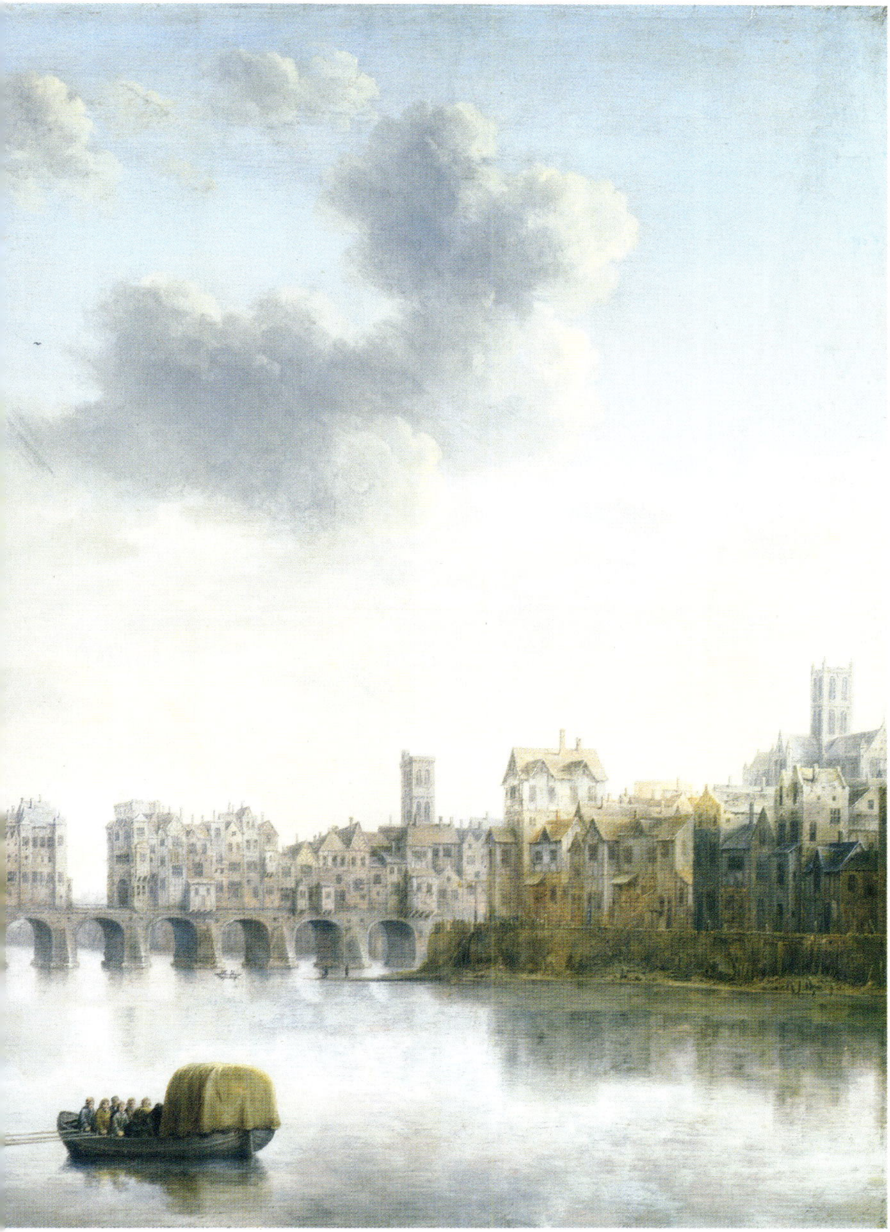

hundred shops and even public toilets which discharged directly into the river. Many of the buildings overhung the road, turning it into a narrow alley that took up to an hour to cross. The biggest was the palatial Nonsuch House, visible here in the centre next to the drawbridge. Built in the Netherlands, it was shipped to England in pieces, the earliest known example of prefabricated construction. The buildings on London Bridge were removed in the eighteenth century to remedy the traffic problems, before the whole bridge was replaced in 1831.

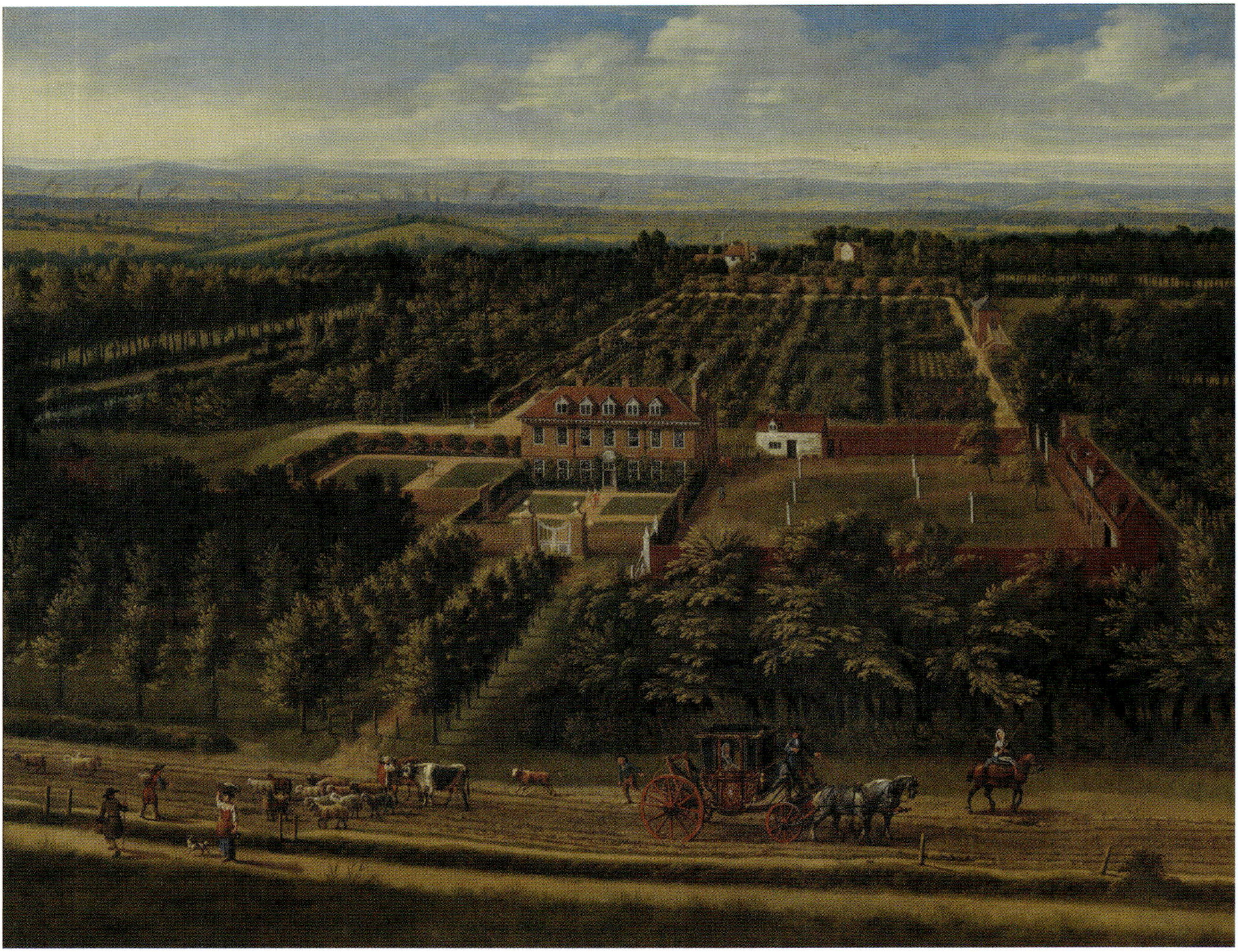

View of a House and its Estate in Belsize, Middlesex

Jan Siberechts 1696

London might not be immediately evident in this painting, but it is there – a thin grey line in the upper left, with smoking chimneys and the outlines of Westminster Abbey just visible. The view is from the north-west (the opposite to the painting from Greenwich illustrated on the facing page, and pp.10–11).

The location is Rosslyn Hill in Belsize Park, now a relatively inner suburb near Hampstead. The grand estate it looks down upon belonged, it is believed, to a goldsmith called John Coggs. He made his money by lending money to his clients, the beginning of the modern banking system. As a wealthy banker, he had his sprawling estate in the country as well as a pad in the city. This painting celebrates and links the two.

Jan Siberechts was another Lowlander and early landscape painter. After a successful career in Antwerp he came to England, where people like Coggs were eager to immortalise their new wealth and status in paint. The country-house portrait was a popular genre in England in the late seventeenth century, and Siberechts was a sought-after practitioner – he also made paintings of top-drawer stately homes such as Longleat House, Wiltshire and Wollaton Hall, Nottingham.

London from Greenwich Park

J.M.W. Turner, exhibited 1809

The irresistibly picturesque view towards London from Greenwich Park has enchanted tourists and painters alike, including one of London's most famous artistic sons. J.M.W. Turner took this view from One Tree Hill, just east of the Royal Observatory. The deer are now confined to a small area at the back of the park, but otherwise the main elements of the view remain unchanged more than two hundred years later. The twin domes of the Old Royal Naval College are mirrored by that of St Paul's in the distance – all by the same architect, Sir Christopher Wren. This view of St Paul's is one of several protected by law, creating a tangle of restricted air space that moulds the positions and shapes of the city of London's skyscrapers.

But the sky is as much the subject of this painting as the city – the glowering, typically Turneresque clouds augmented by smoke pumped out by the chimneys. The ships visible on the glimmer of river connect us to the city and remind us of Greenwich's central role in navigation, and the resulting wealth of London and Britain. Turner did not paint London in oils very often, preferring the accuracy afforded by drawings and watercolours to represent buildings, but when he did he nearly always exploited the potential for reflections and atmospheric effects created by the river.

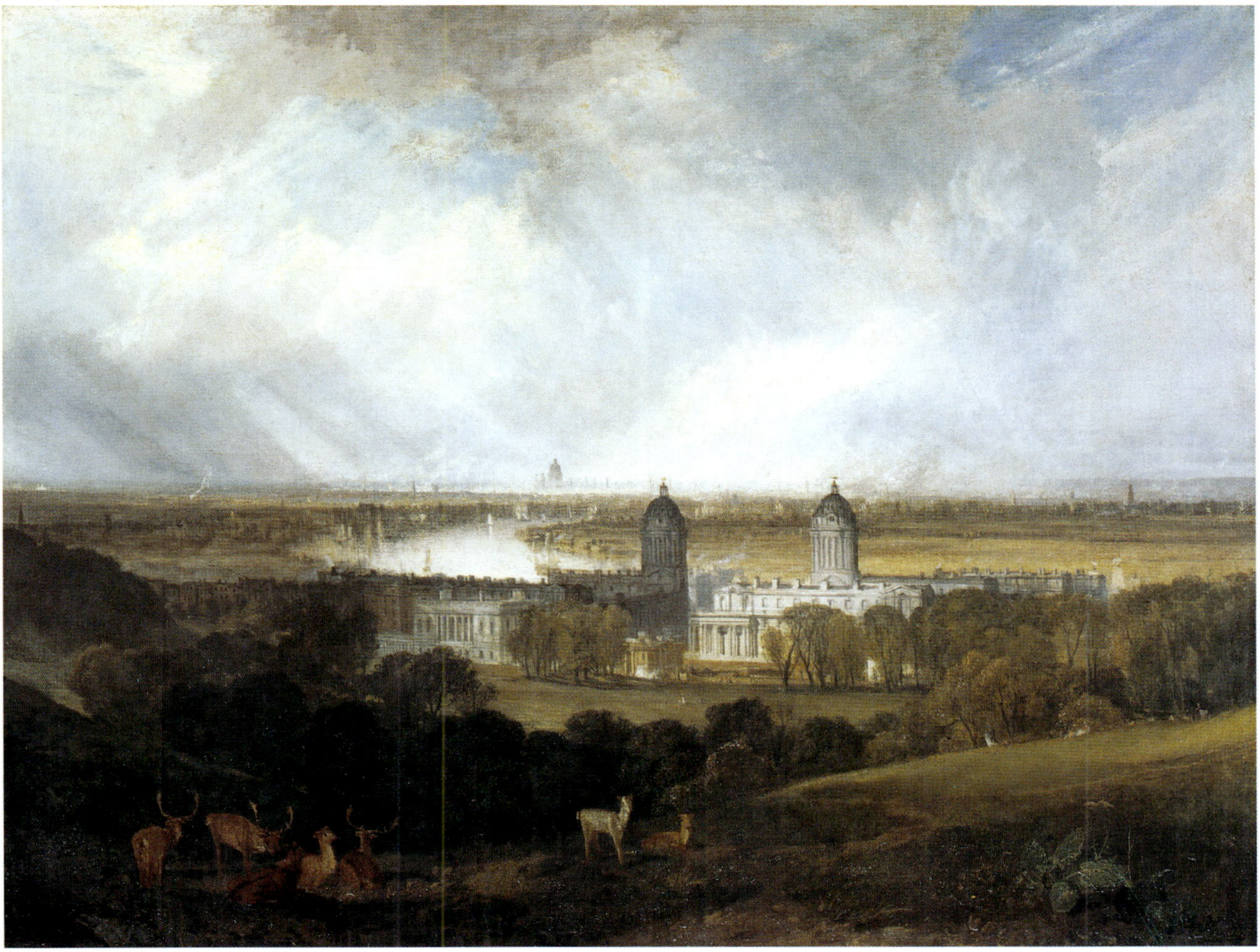

Sir Richard Steele's Cottage, Hampstead

John Constable 1831–2

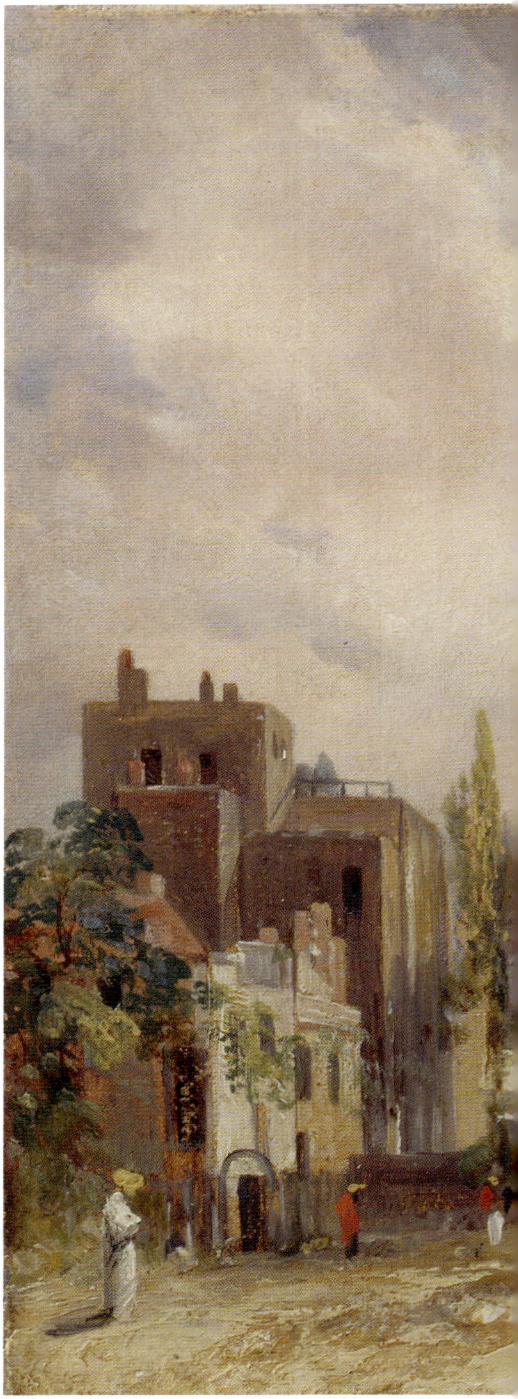

Despite spending a large part of his life living in London, John Constable didn't relish painting it. Unlike his arch-rival Turner – who was born in Covent Garden – Constable was not a city boy at heart, and took a long time to be accepted into the establishment. The majority of his many paintings from Hampstead Heath look out towards the countryside or into the sky, ignoring the metropolis lurking behind. The area was then still semi-rural and allowed Constable to continue to explore the countryside themes he had established early in his career. 'I should paint my own places best,' he once wrote to a friend, referring to his native Suffolk.

This is a rare exception, although you sense that he, like Turner, is most interested in the foreboding clouds. The view is from Haverstock Hill, near Chalk Farm tube station in north London. The cottage mentioned in the title and depicted to the right of the road was the home of the co-founder of the *Spectator* magazine. It is no longer there but Steele is commemorated by a nearby pub.

This view of London would have been similar to that enjoyed from Constable's home on Well Walk in Hampstead Village. He once boasted to a friend: 'Our little drawing room commands a view unequalled in all of Europe.'

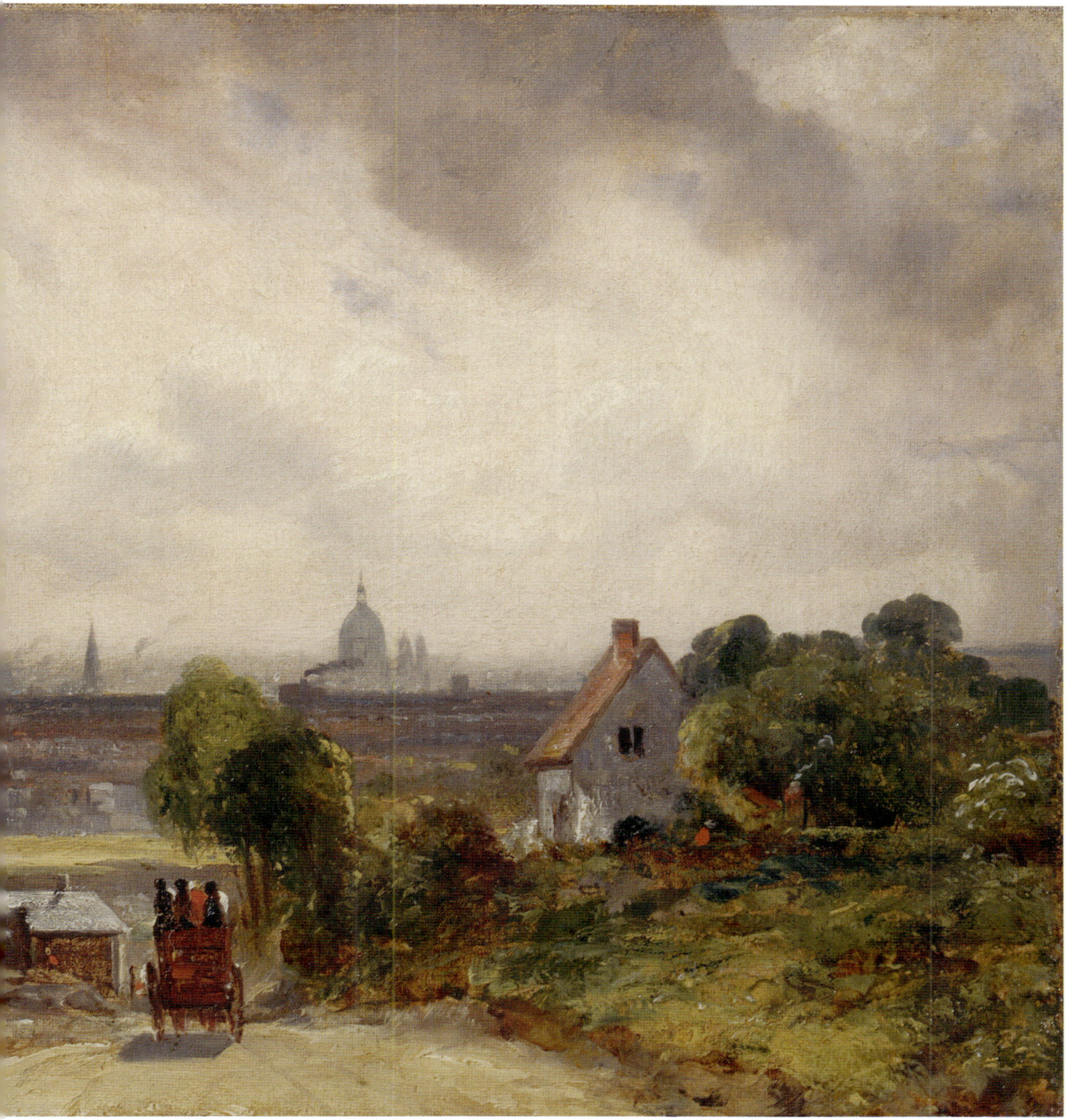

The Heart of the Empire

Niels Møller Lund 1904

The traditional centre of London is Charing Cross. The geographic centre of contemporary London is a back street near Waterloo station, according to a study by the *Londonist* website. Claims might also be made for Westminster or Trafalgar Squares. But this painting says something different – at the time of its creation, this junction above Bank tube station, with Mansion House to the left and the Bank of England peeking in at the right, was the centre of the British Empire when it was almost at its peak. It recognises that what gives London its power is not politics or culture or even the military, but the might of commerce and capitalism. The empire is now long gone, but the City of London is still the axis of the financial world.

This enormous canvas presents a detailed panorama, with the spires of the City churches and, in the far distance on the left, the Palace of Westminster, all distinguishable. The view is from the top of the Royal Exchange (the opposite angle to the painting on pages 174–5). The painting became well known in the 1970s when there was a controversy about how to replace the Mappin & Webb shop in the centre – James Stirling's postmodern No 1 Poultry was the result, its cylindrical prow deliberately echoing the building it replaced.

Born in Denmark but raised in Newcastle-upon-Tyne, Lund painted impressionistic paintings of London and the north-east, and this is his best-known work.

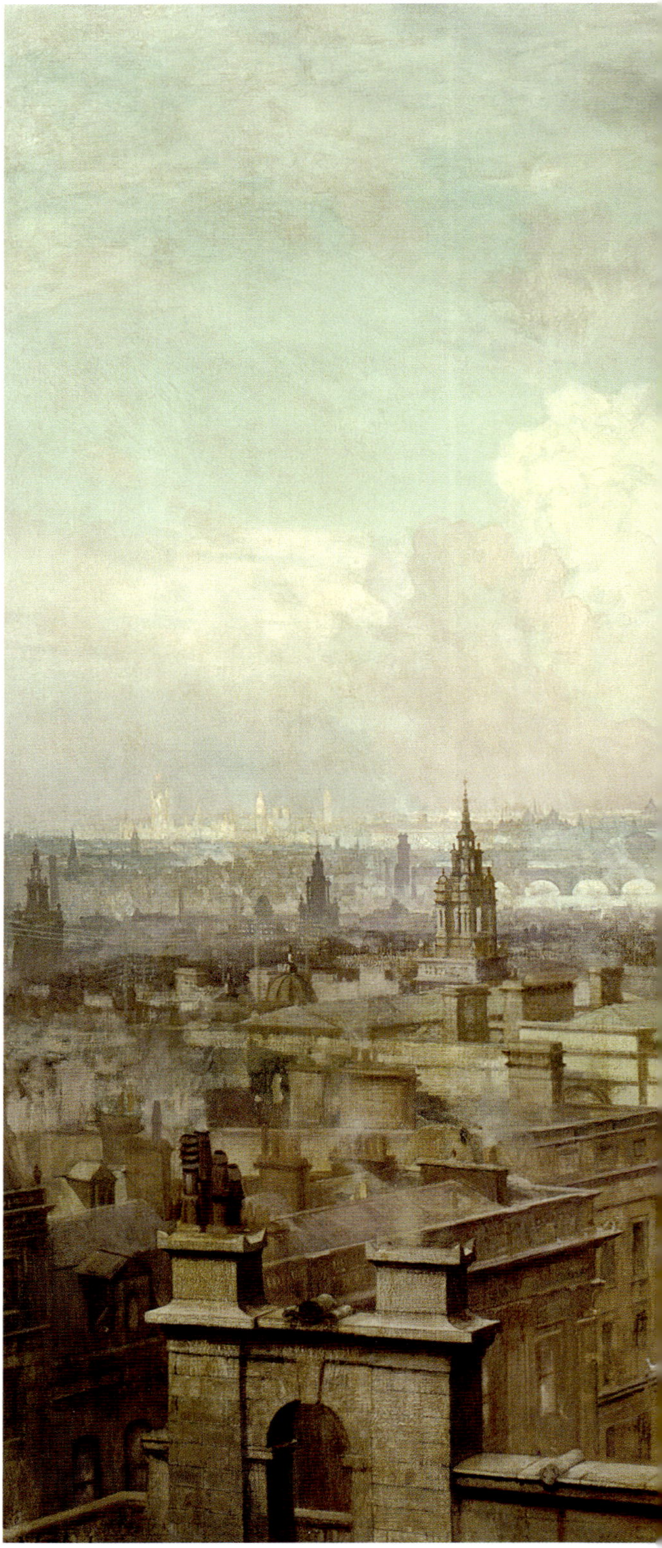

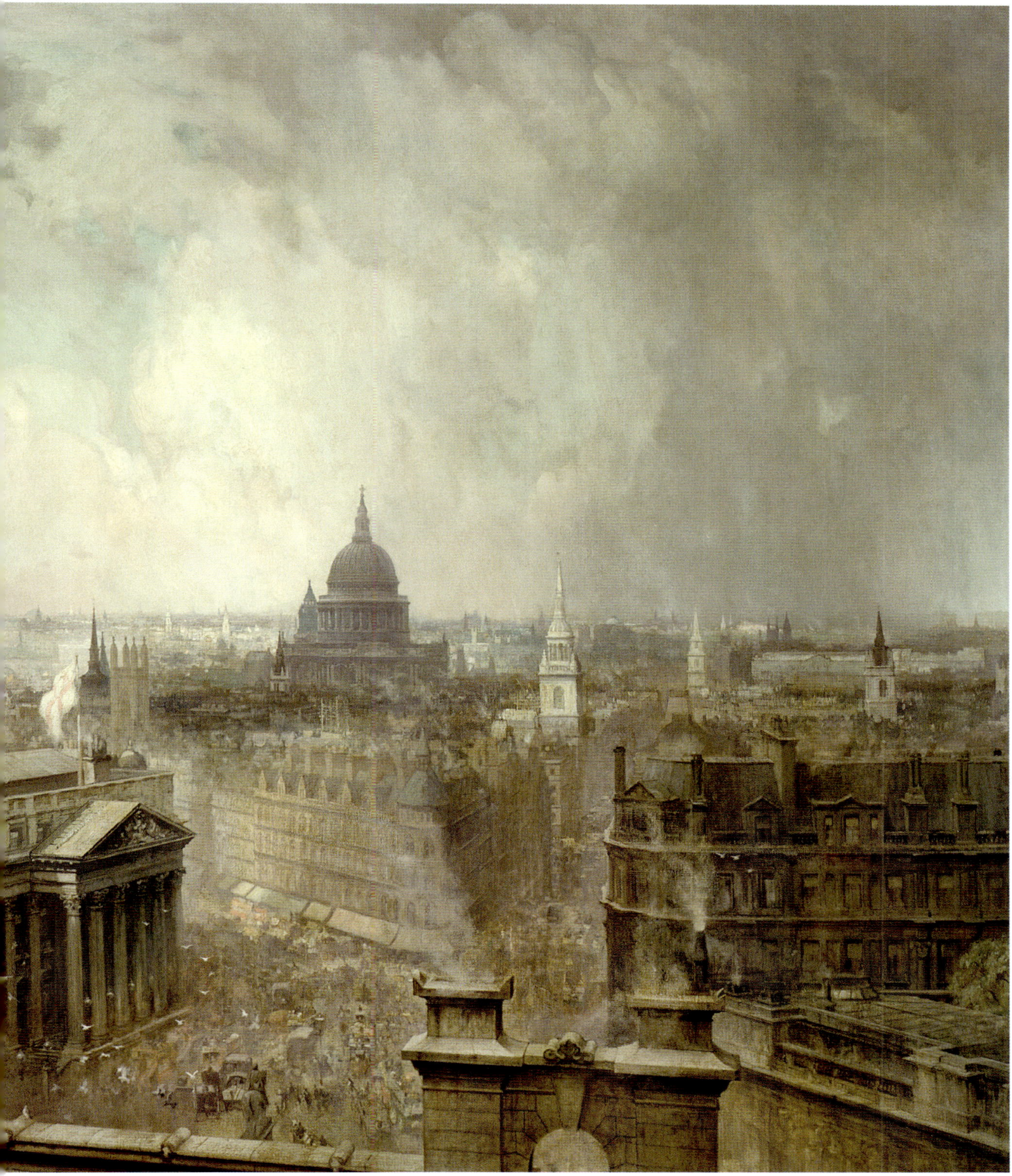

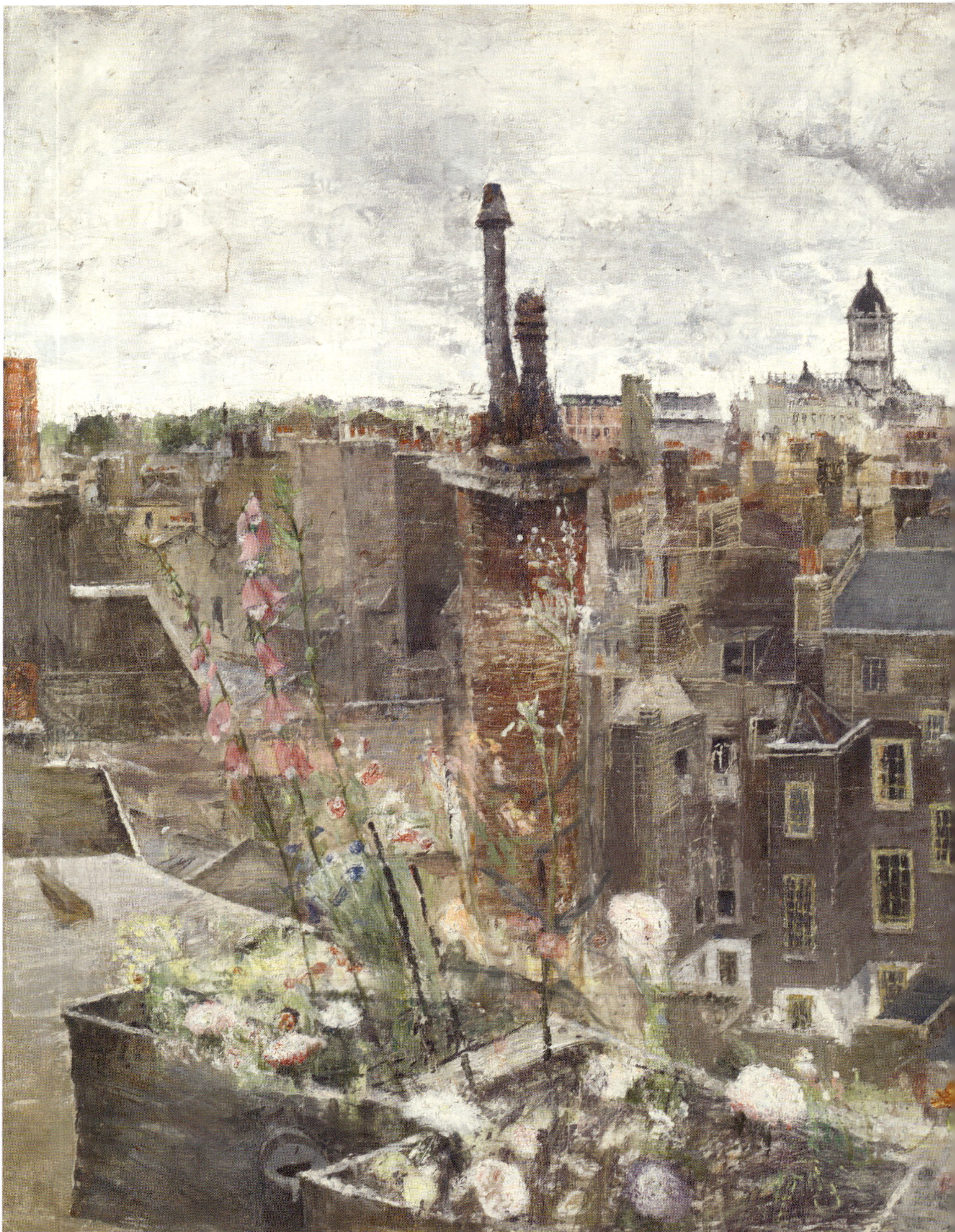

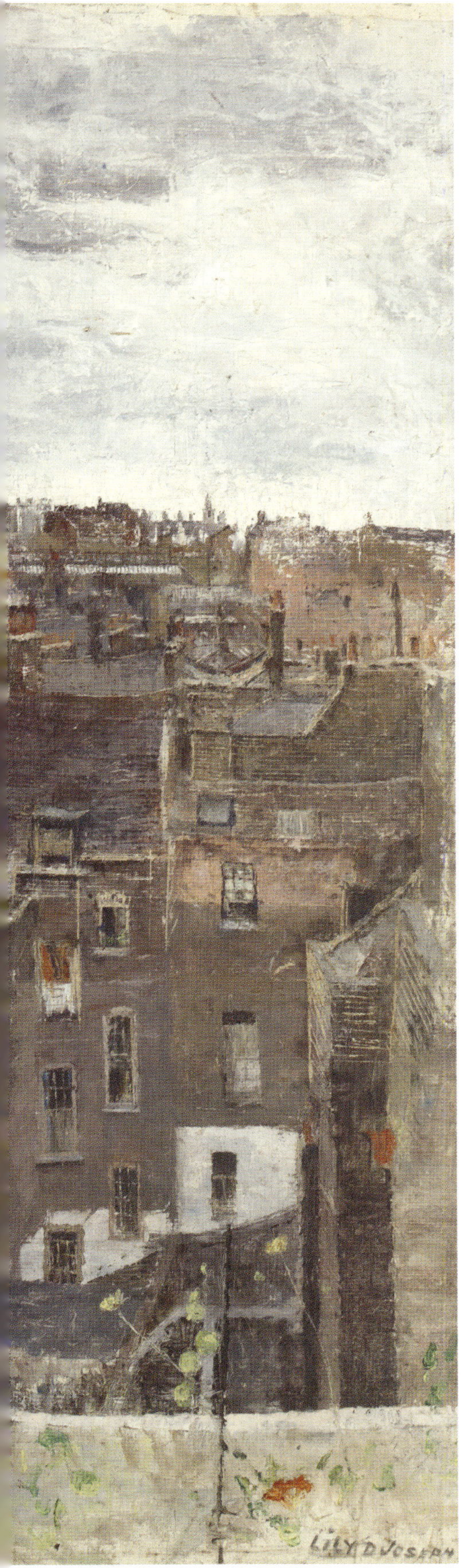

Roofs, High Holborn

Lily D. Joseph c.1937

The rooftops of London will forever be associated visually with two things: Gustave Doré's engraving showing a never-ending city of hell, and Dick van Dyke dancing around the smoke-enveloped chimneys in the film *Mary Poppins*. Lily D. Joseph – a London-born painter and critic – finds a warmer colour and delicacy in the view from her studio window. The painting takes in the backs of terraces on Bedford Row, Bloomsbury, looking towards a grand belle époque building on High Holborn that is now home to a luxury hotel.

Joseph was a formidable figure. She came from a wealthy, cultured family and her brother was the painter Solomon J. Solomon, only the second Jewish man to be elected a Royal Academician. She was heavily involved in the women's suffrage movement and as a result once missed a private view of her own exhibition because she had been 'detained in Holloway Gaol'. She was one of the first women to own and drive a car and learnt to fly aeroplanes in her late fifties.

View of the Thames

Oskar Kokoschka 1959

Born in Austria, Oskar Kokoschka was an inveterate traveller and made views, especially riverscapes, of many European cities, including Prague, Dresden, Lyon and Salzburg. He first visited London in 1925, painting Tower Bridge, and gained British citizenship in 1946 after fleeing from the Nazis. He did not live in London for long – finding Switzerland a better base for his constant wandering – but returned regularly.

Kokoschka painted over a dozen views of London throughout his life, mostly showing the Thames from different elevated viewpoints. He rhapsodised in his memoirs: 'it stimulates me, like the patriotic dreams that others have in their warm beds. My Thames! Those were the days when the merchandise of the whole world was still shipped up this river, when London was still a mother city ... from which a surplus population spread out all over the world.'

This painting was done from the roof of the Shell Mex building on the Strand, to which he gained access through a contact of the art-book publisher Walter Neurath. The building is situated on a bend of the Thames, providing sweeping prospects up and down the river. Prominent in the foreground is the new Waterloo Bridge, opened in 1945. The angle of the view and the loose handling of the paint recall John Constable's celebration of the opening of the previous bridge (pp.166–7), although this one was painted swiftly on site with no preparatory drawings.

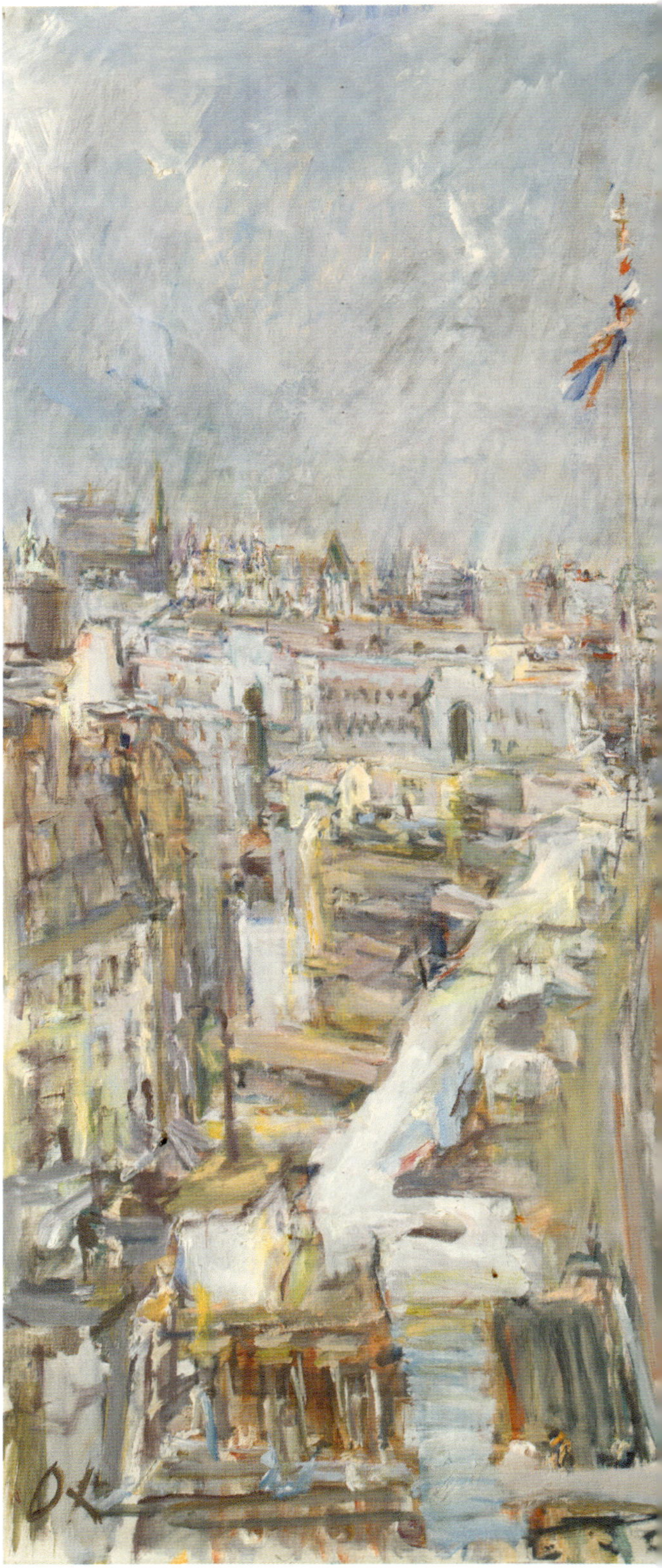

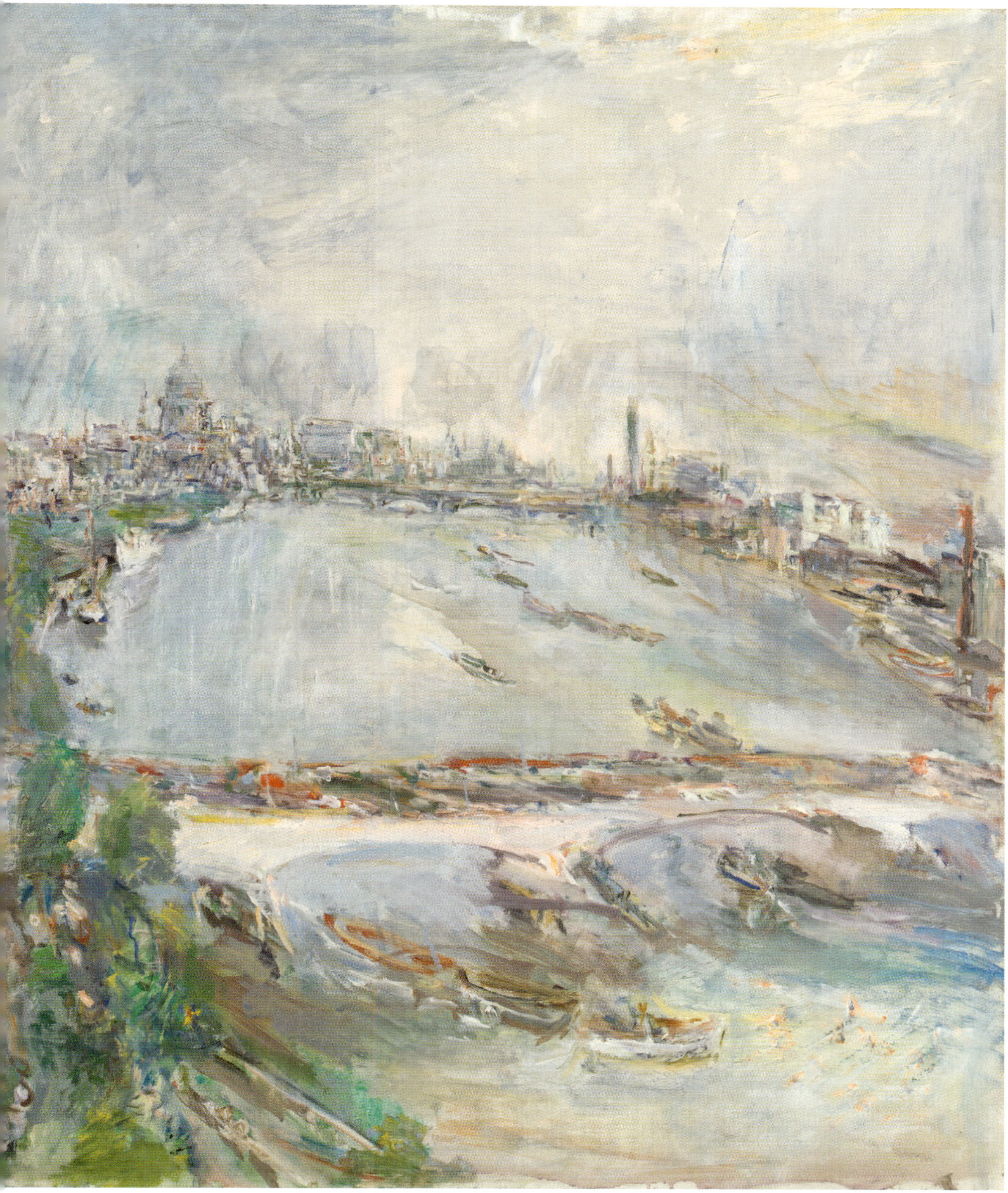

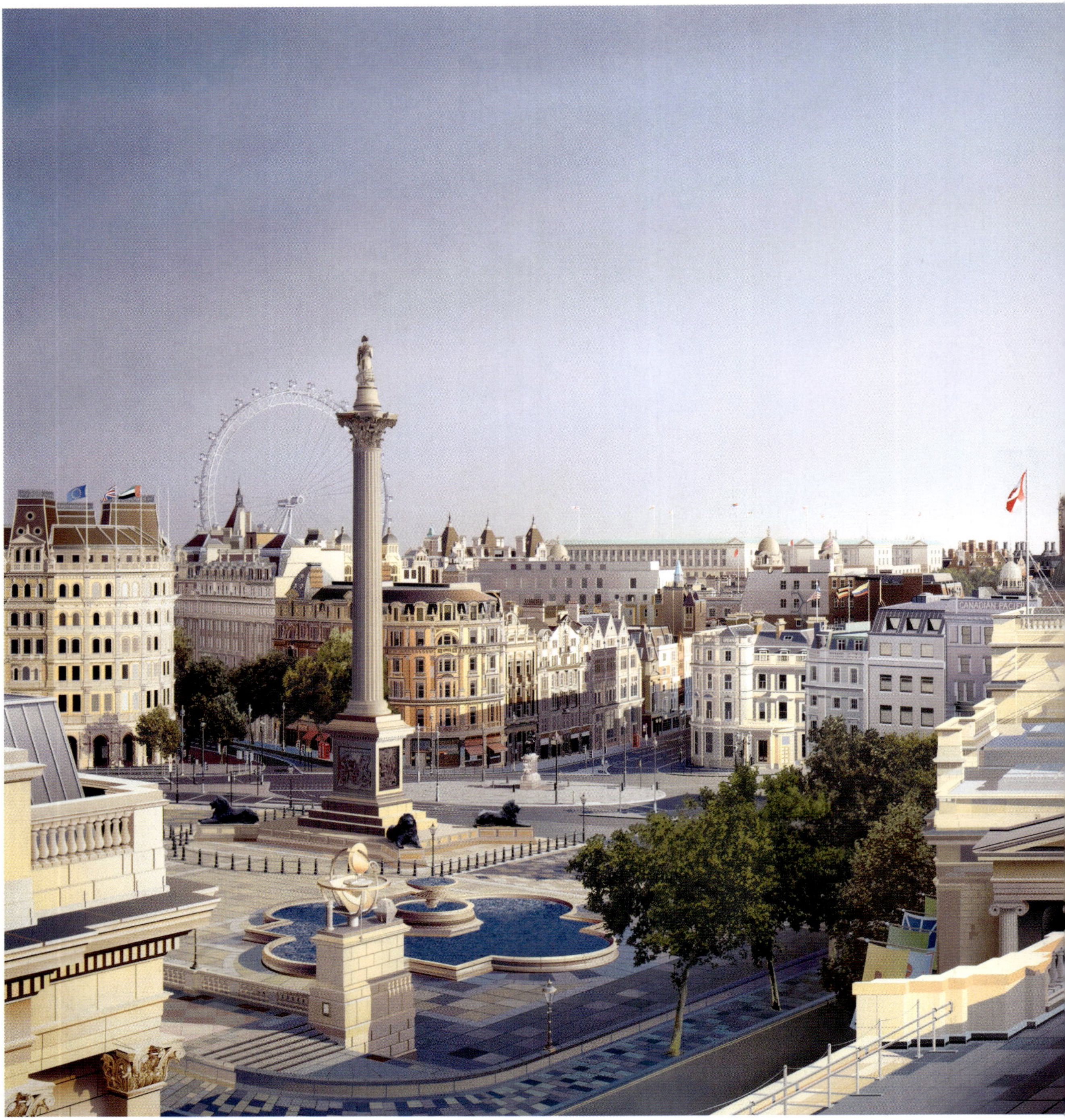

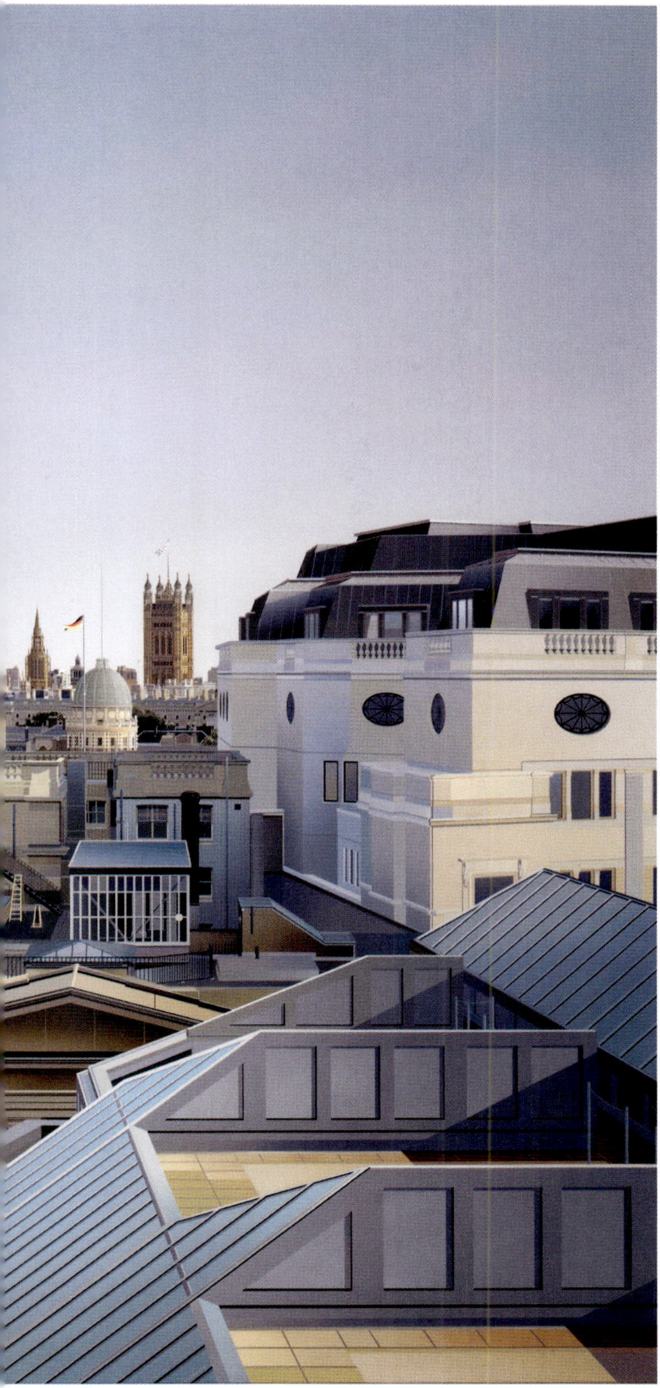

Looking Back to Richmond House

Ben Johnson 2011

Accurate topographical painting has rather fallen out of fashion in the twenty-first century, but there is still something compelling about a complex city shown in minute detail. This nine-foot-wide painting shows London with a crispness and clearness that exists only in our heads and can never be caught on camera. In that it is reminiscent of the beguiling fantasies of Canaletto.

Its composition is actually based on a Canaletto – *The Stonemason's Yard* of about 1725, which hangs in the National Gallery, London. This view is from the gallery's roof and was meticulously put together in one of its public galleries as a special commission. Johnson achieves the distinct separation of his colours by spraying paint through detailed masks created on a computer. He says the long, painstaking process of putting together his paintings divorces him from the reality they depict, until they just become 'paint on canvas'. Born in Wales, Johnson has lived in London since the 1960s. He has created similar panoramas of cities including Liverpool, Hong Kong, Zurich and Jerusalem.

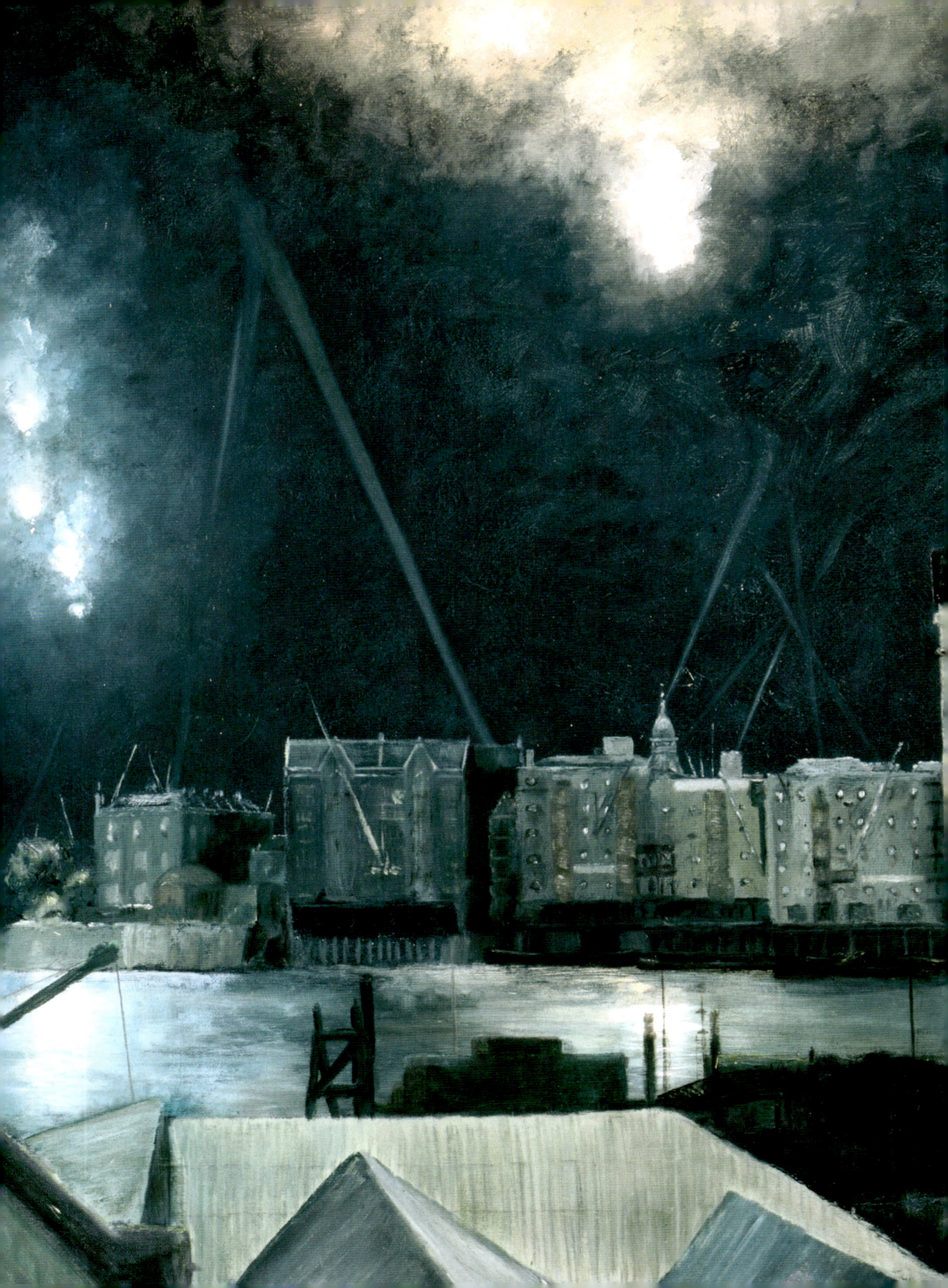

2

DISASTER AND DESTRUCTION

IT IS THE EVENING of 16 October 1834 and excited crowds throng Westminster Bridge. The river is full of small boats, hired or borrowed, everyone trying to get a good view of the devastation taking place before them. The Palace of Westminster, the seat of Parliament and the heart of government, is on fire.

Earlier that day the parliamentary authorities had decided to burn the 'tally sticks', an obsolete way of recording government debts using notched pieces of wood. The fire got out of control and soon the whole building was alight. Accounts differ on whether the crowds stood in respectful silence or oohed and aahed as if they were at a fireworks display. Perhaps the cheer that went up when St Stephen's Chapel collapsed was more akin to the ironic whoops which greet a smashed glass in a British pub, rather than a celebration of the loss of an important piece of heritage. Witnessing the blaze were many artists – including J.M.W. Turner and John Constable – and the event became one of the most depicted of the century.

Londoners have always had a morbid fascination with their city's destruction and it has long been a popular subject for art. The Great Fire of 1666, which razed the historic core of the city to the ground, came at a time when fire and moonlit scenes were in fashion, imported by Dutch painters. Coming just seventeen years after the execution of Charles I (r.1625–49) and immediately after the city had been afflicted by the plague, many people saw the fire as divine retribution for London's wickedness, and some paintings of the fire allude to the biblical destruction of Sodom and Gomorrah. Some had taken to calling London the 'New Troy', but now, like its antique forebear, it looked as if this city too would fall.

The greatest disaster to befall London, however, was the Blitz of 1940–1. This time artists were employed by the state to record the devastation in haunting and memorable works, which are illustrated in the following pages, along with otherwise forgotten blazes which challenged artists to set down their sublime lighting effects and apocalyptic splendour.

Wilfred Stanley Haines *Night Raid over London Docklands* c.1941 (detail). See p.48

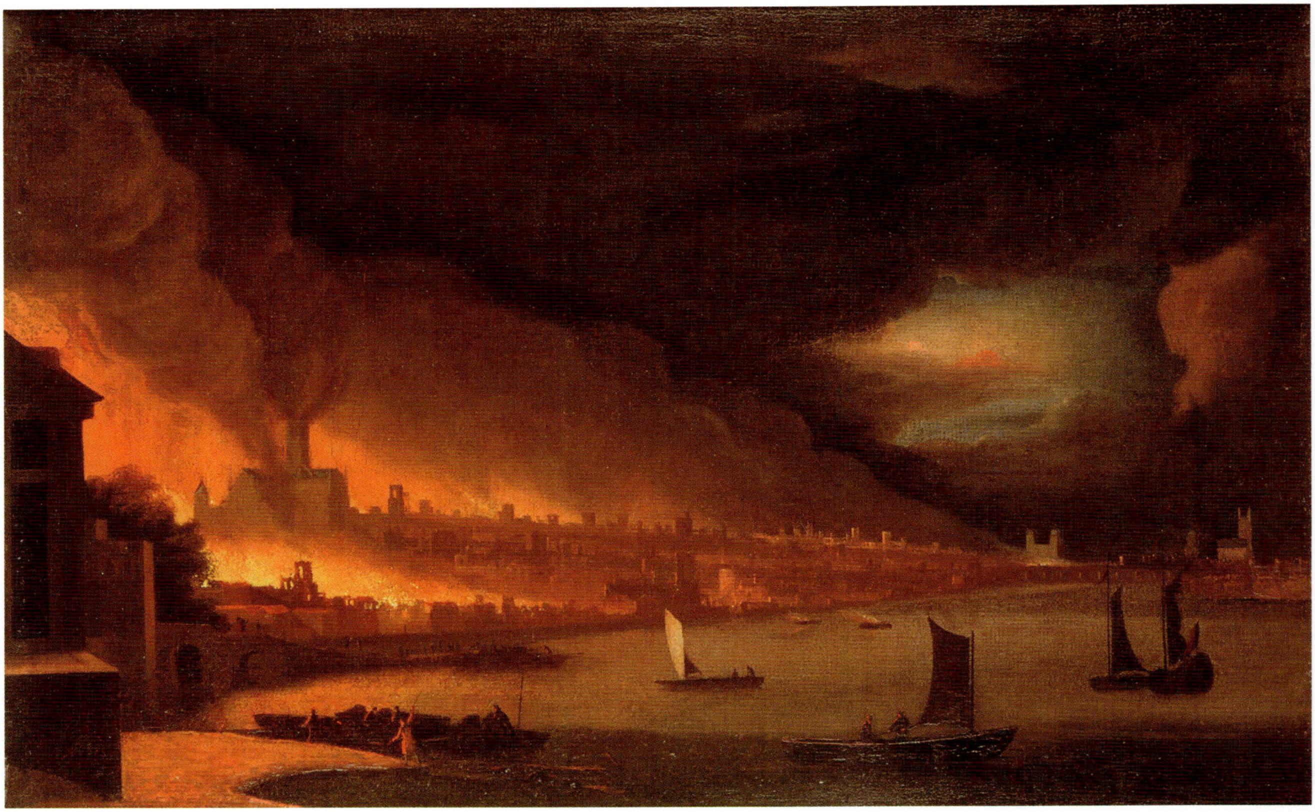

The Great Fire of London

Unknown artist, after Waggoner 1666

Old London was no stranger to fires. Major conflagrations had taken place in 1633, 1212, 1135, 1087, 675 and of course in AD 60 when the Celtic queen Boudica burnt the Roman city to the ground. But the 1666 fire was the first to be comprehensively recorded in paint.

In the rush to make images of the fire, many artists and publishers simply added flames onto existing views of London, particularly the 'long views' from Southwark (pp.16–17). This painting, however, was probably copied from a sketch made at the scene and despite some inaccuracies – the city here seems to be on a hill – it is much more vivid. The world seems to be ending, as if London were caught up in one of Victorian painter John Martin's apocalyptic visions. The Tower of London gleams white at the far right, while in the foreground Old St Paul's sends up a fresh column of smoke. Complicated plans were in place at the time to restore and update the cathedral, and the fire gave Sir Christopher Wren a *tabula rasa* for his masterpiece.

The Great Fire of London

Philip James de Loutherbourg c.1797

The Great Fire was still providing inspiration for painters over a hundred years later. De Loutherbourg specialised in highly dramatic paintings, often with bravura lighting effects, so it is easy to see why this subject attracted him. Showing the fire at night for maximum effect, as nearly every painter did, de Loutherbourg adds a cold dash of moonlight to balance the reds and oranges of the flames. The view is from under an arch of London Bridge, but he seems to have twisted the geography to increase its impact. St Paul's is as yet undamaged, while the Londoners seem torn between fleeing and admiring the spectacle.

De Loutherbourg was born in Strasbourg but settled in Britain. He was best known for his ingenious set designs for the Drury Lane Theatre and his invention of the *Eidophusikon*, a mechanical theatre that wowed audiences with elaborate special effects.

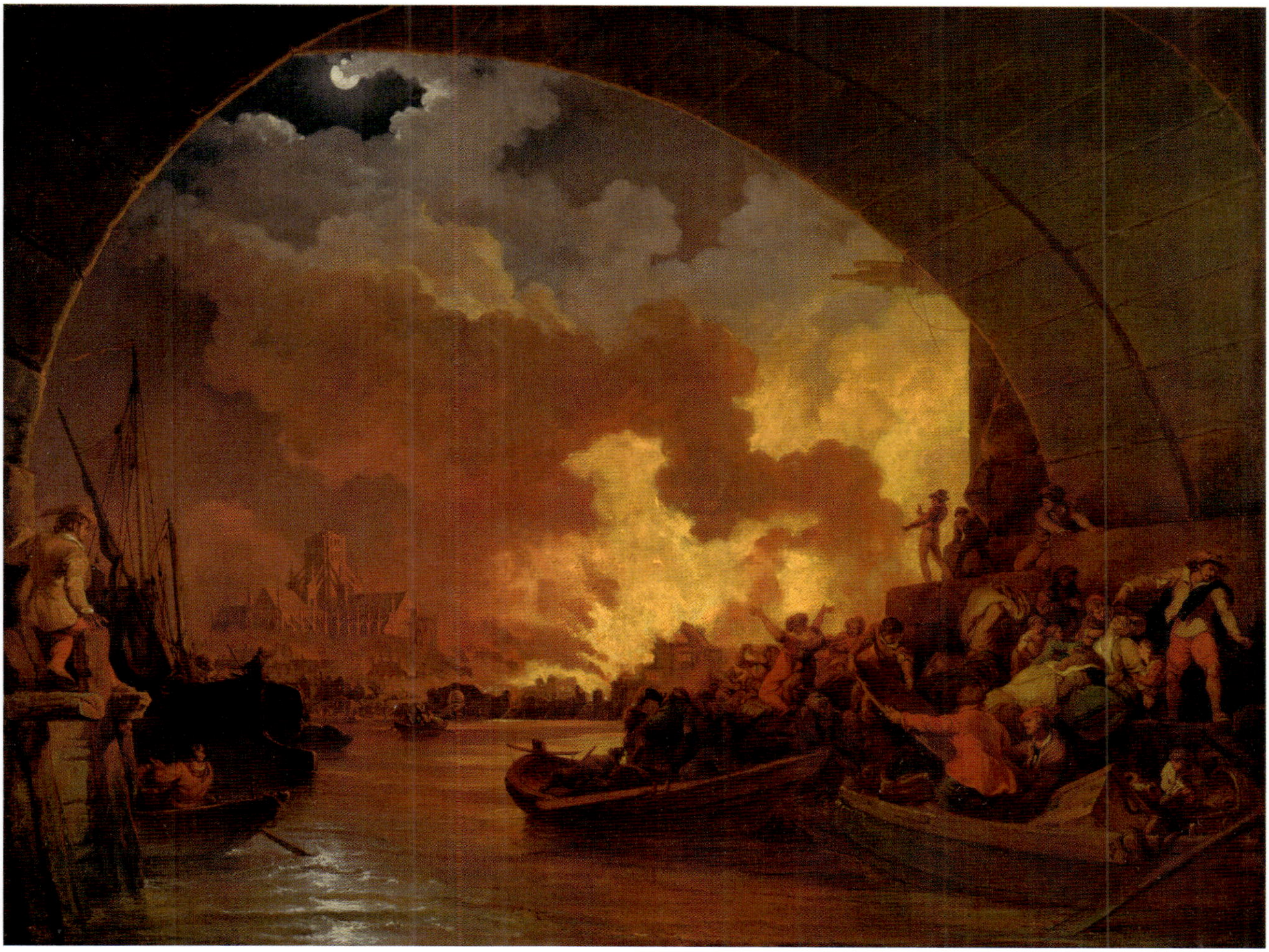

The Inner Temple after the Fire of 4 January 1737

Richard Wilson 1737

Richard Wilson was a pioneer of painting landscapes for their own sake (p.137), but here he turned his attention to reportage. Despite the rebuilding of the city in stone rather than wood after 1666, fires were still regular occurrences in eighteenth-century London – partly because there was no centrally organised fire service. People made do with hand-operated water pumps as seen in the foreground on the left. They had to be filled from the River Thames, which was at low tide when this fire began, hampering relief efforts. In the centre in the light blue coat is Frederick, Prince of Wales, who sent fifty soldiers to help fight the blaze and arrived on the scene to inspect the damage.

The destroyed building is Crown Office Row in the Inner Temple, part of the Inns of Court that form the heart of London's legal profession. Stretching from the river up to Holborn, the Inns are a warren of great halls, chapels, gardens and lawyers' chambers, which feels like a slice of Oxford or Cambridge set down in central London. The area still has a strongly medieval atmosphere despite many of the buildings – including Crown Office Row – having been rebuilt after the Blitz.

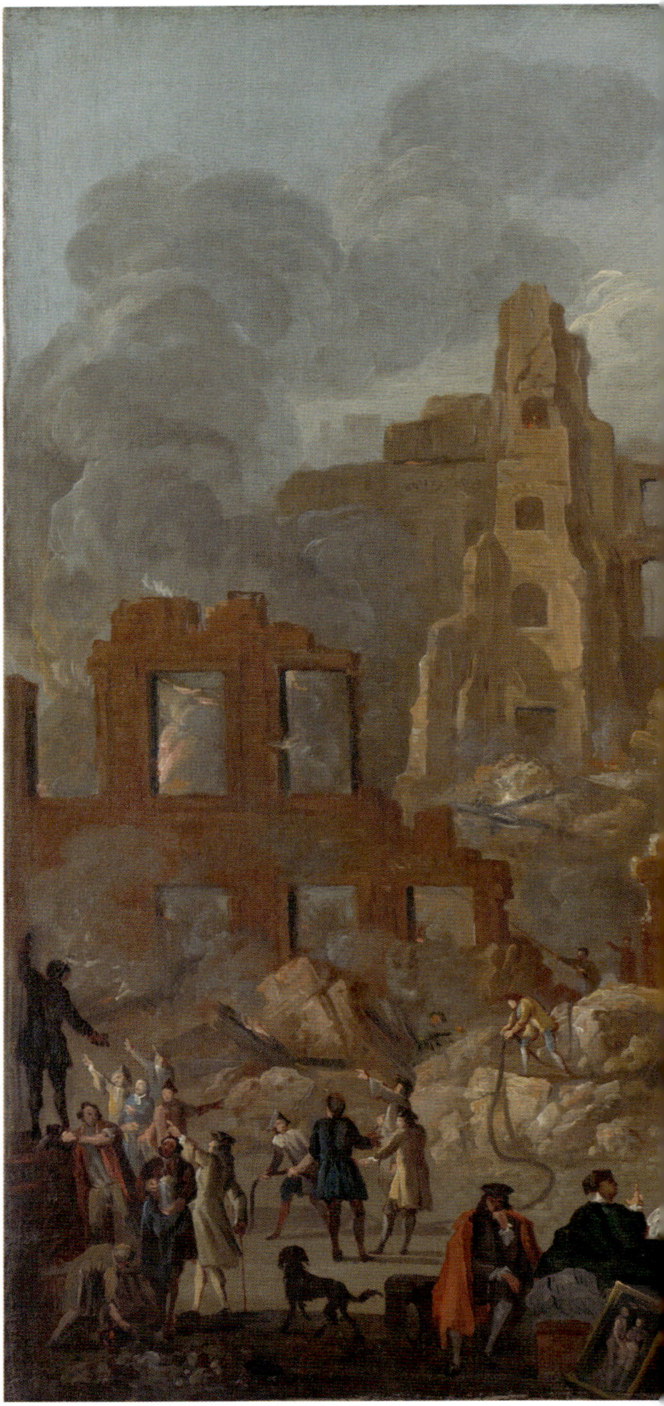

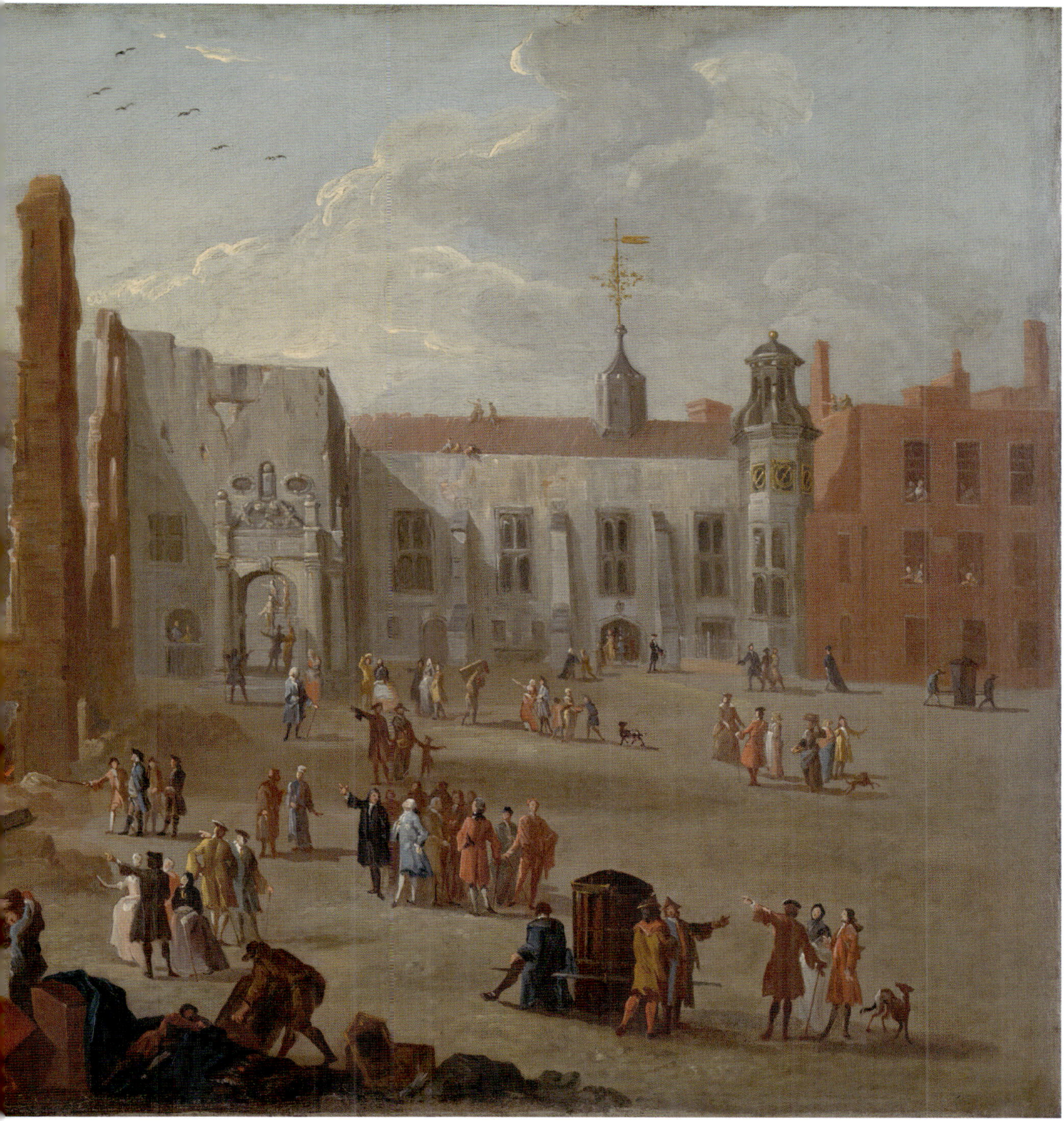

The Burning of the Houses of Lords and Commons, 16 October 1834

J.M.W. Turner 1835

The destruction of the Palace of Westminster resulted in several great works of art. One is Charles Barry and Augustus Pugin's majestic replacement. The others are the two oil paintings J.M.W. Turner made of the event. He was there in person in a rented boat, recording details in his sketchbooks (although watercolours once believed to be of Parliament are now thought to be of a fire at the Tower of London in 1841). The first painting, from the opposite bank, was exhibited at the British Institution a few months after the event. The palace is almost obscured by a thick bank of smoke, the intense heat reflected in the River Thames and the cool stone of Old Westminster Bridge.

This version was shown at the Royal Academy summer exhibition of 1835. The view is from around the point where the London Eye sits today. Turner depicts the masses crowded onto the foreshore and those watching from boats, as well as the towers of Westminster Abbey. But this is an essay in fire and water, the almost abstract exploration of smoke and light in the centre foreshadowing the works that Claude Monet would make from almost the same site seventy years later (p.145).

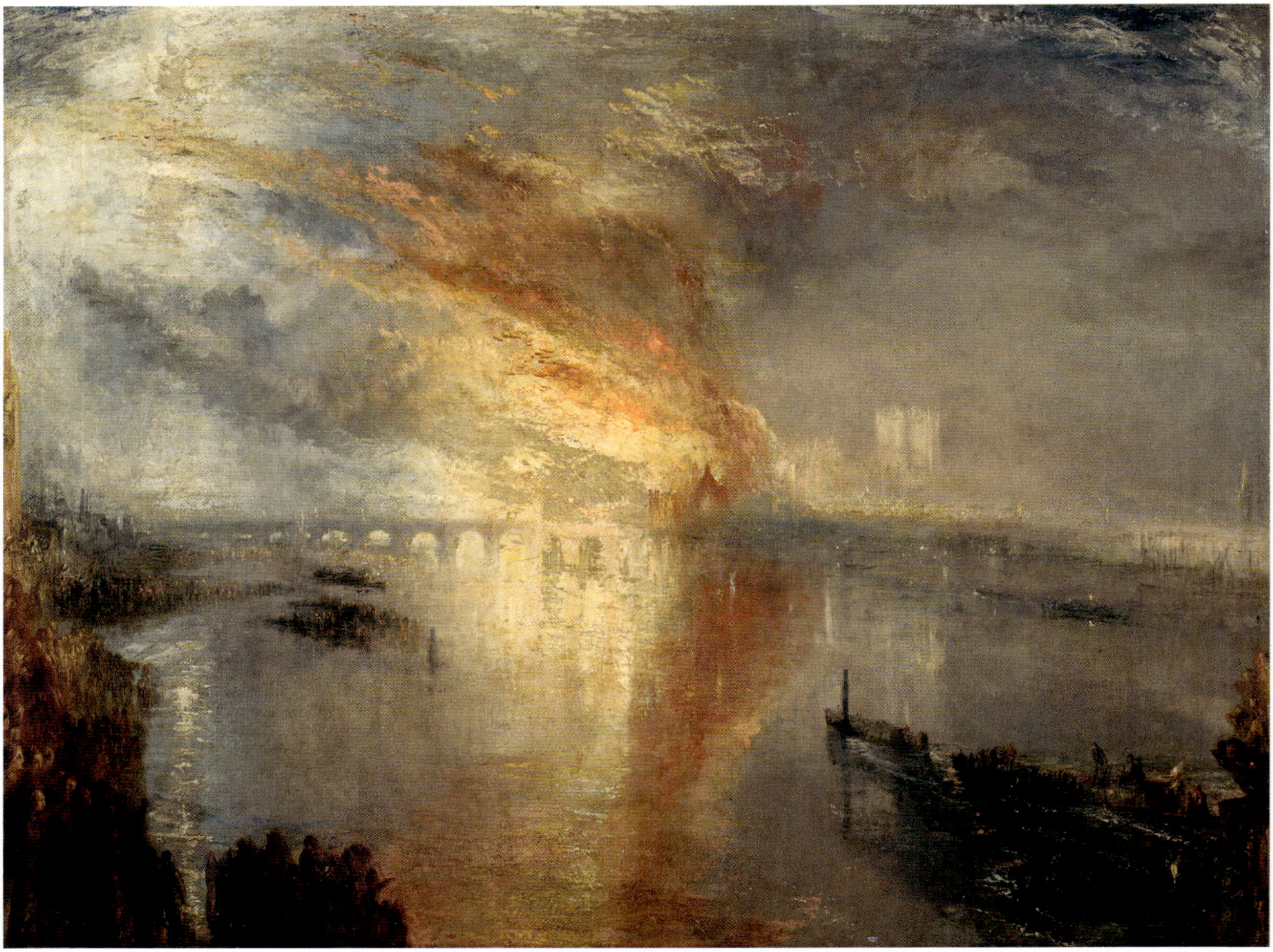

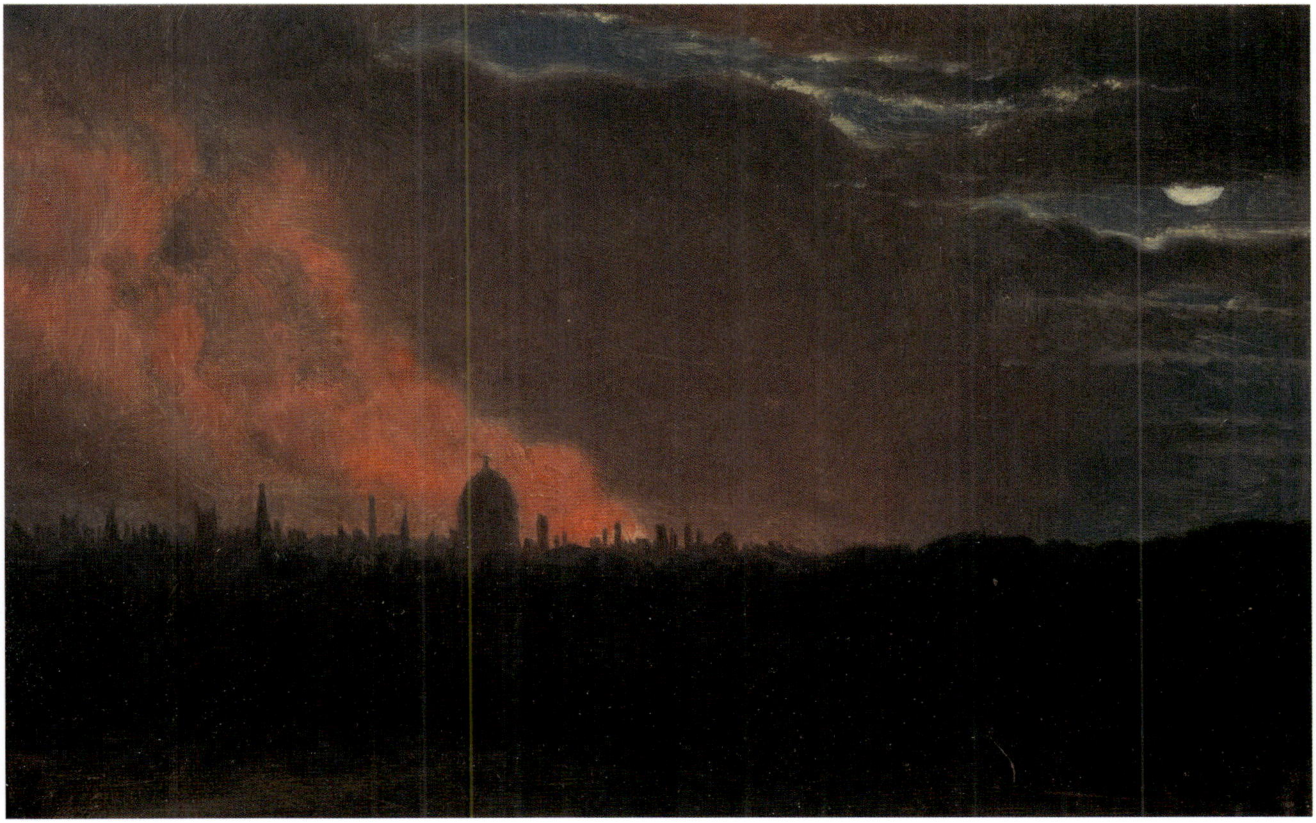

Fire in London, Seen from Hampstead

Attributed to John Constable c.1826

This sketch was once thought to be Constable's version of the fire at Parliament. But the location seems wrong and it might have been painted several years before. Instead it provides a rare glimpse of the London skyline at night, with the windswept flames illuminating the dome of St Paul's and the spires of the City churches. Seen from Constable's favoured Hampstead – perhaps from his house in Well Walk – the painting has a calm, detached approach to the devastation, very different from Turner's evocation of the heat of the moment.

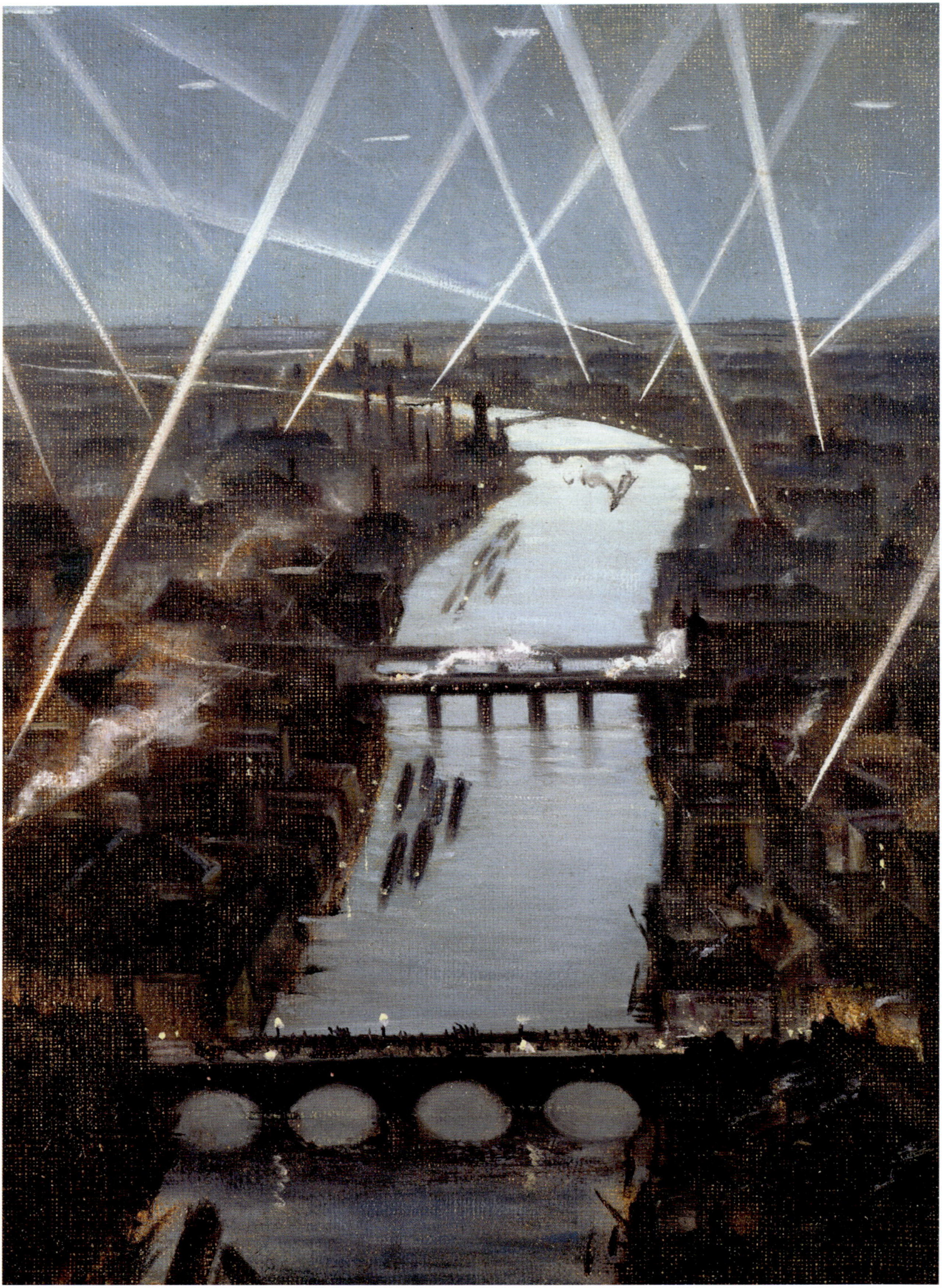

Among the London Searchlights

Christopher Richard Wynne Nevinson 1918

There are not many paintings of London during the First World War. Many working artists were called up to join the army, while the official war artists were concentrated on the frontline. Nevinson was an exception. He joined a voluntary ambulance service that his father, a famous war correspondent, had co-founded. But ill-health forced him to return to London in January 1915. The futurist- and cubist-inspired paintings he did in London of his brief wartime experience made his name (although he later got in trouble for exaggerating his role) and in 1917 he was made an official war artist.

Finding that his avant-garde style was not sufficient to depict the horrors of war, Nevinson moved towards a more realist style. This view was taken from a captured balloon above London Bridge. The city is only lightly abstracted but the criss-crossing of the searchlights shatter the upper half of the painting into facets, a futurist technique he repeated in later paintings of London (pp.176–7).

Blitz: Plane Flying

Clive Branson 1940

A committed socialist who fought voluntarily in the Spanish Civil War, Clive Branson was acutely concerned by the effect of the Second World War on the working people of London. Painted during the eight months of the Blitz, this painting shows ordinary life more or less going on in a suburban Battersea street, possibly the north end of Clapham Manor Street. One house has been destroyed by bombs while a shelter has been built in the road outside another. But then Branson has added in surreal elements, such as the plane – bearing both Nazi and RAF insignia – skimming the rooftops. More subtle but perhaps more disturbing is the large cracked eggshell in the foreground.

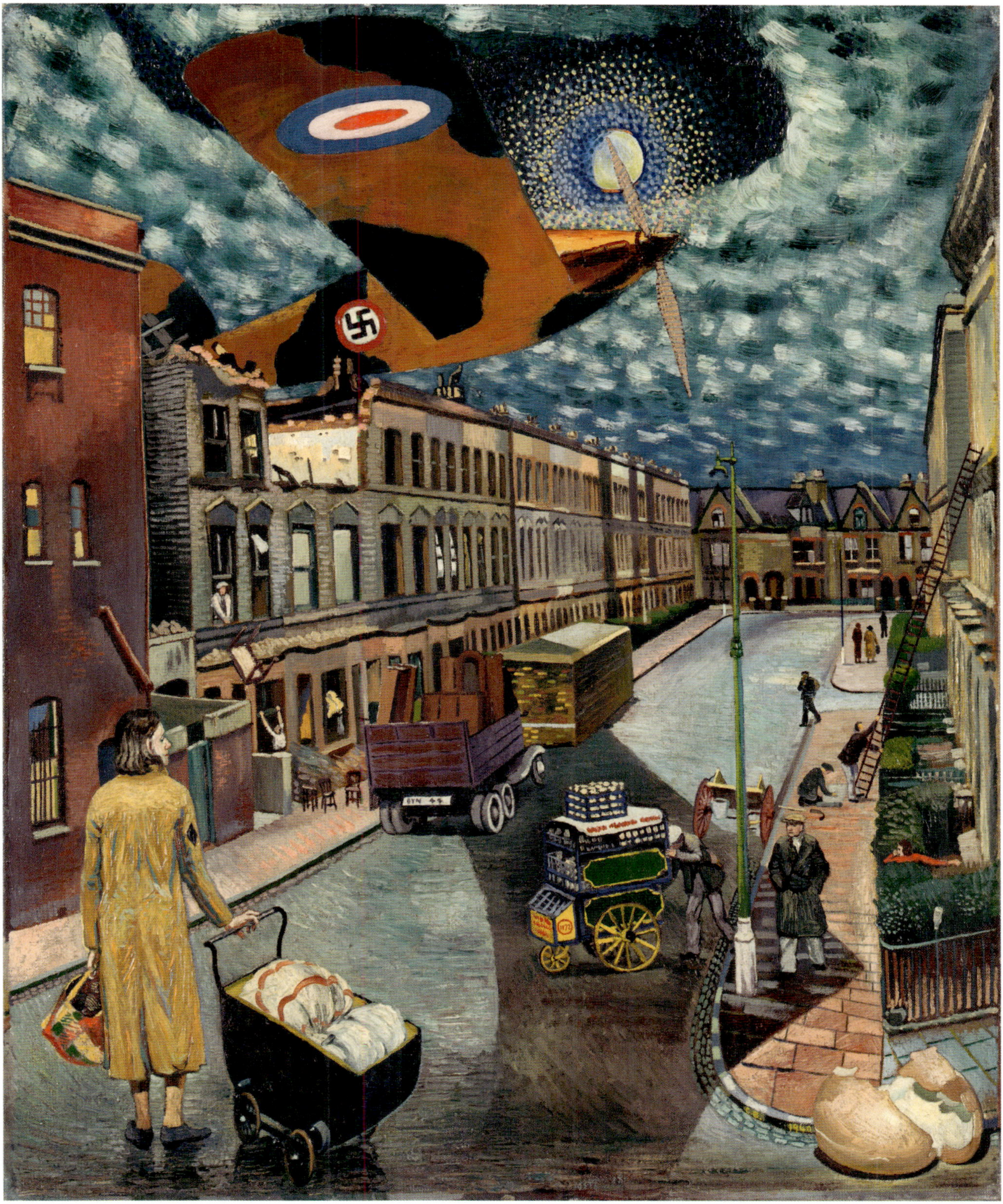

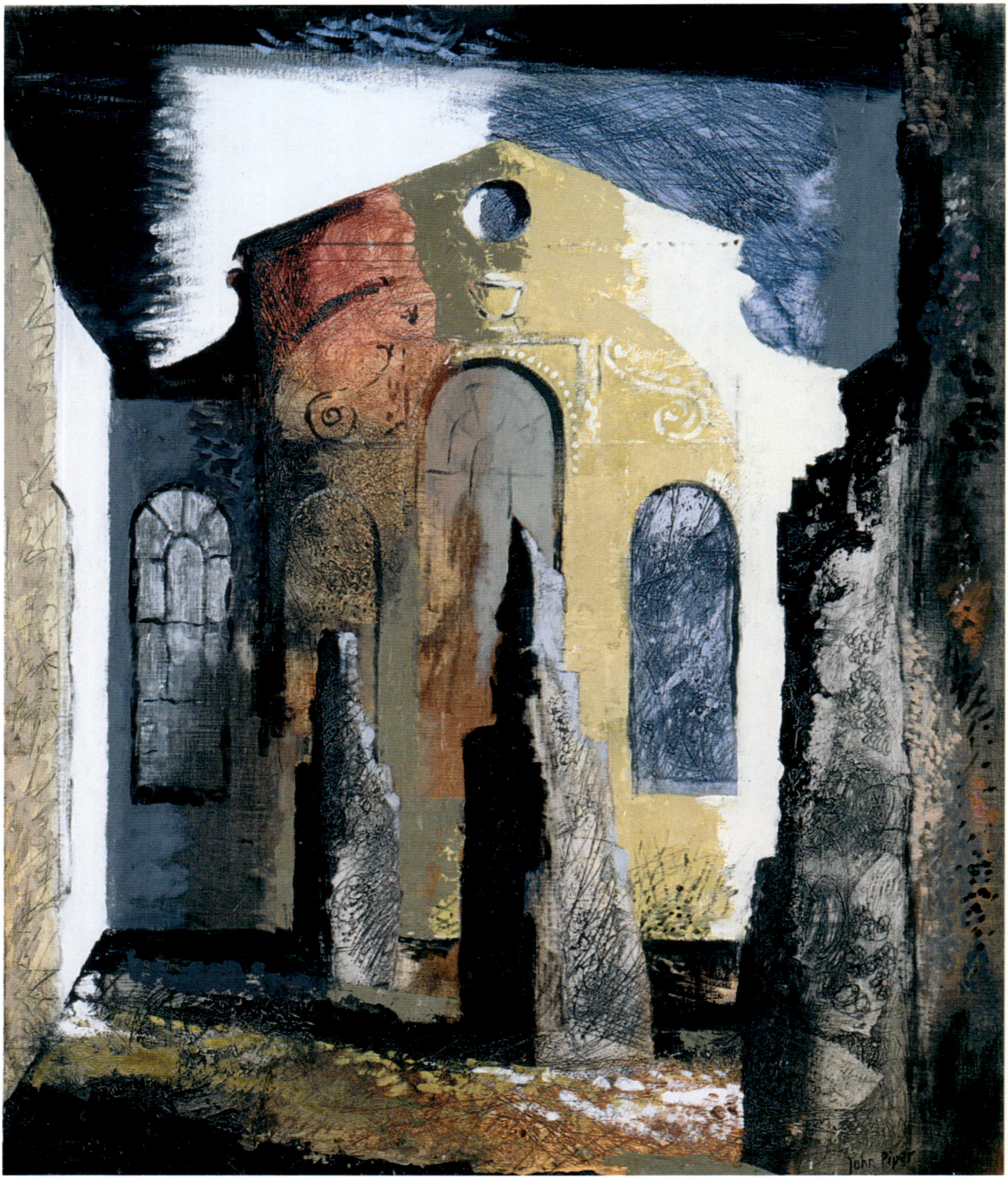
John Piper

Christ Church, Newgate Street

John Piper 1941

The air raid on the night of 29 December 1940 was the most devastating of the Blitz. Tens of thousands of bombs created a firestorm that destroyed an area bigger than the Great Fire, from Islington to the gardens of St Paul's itself, where a special team of firefighters protected the cathedral. The famous photo *St Paul's Survives* was taken the next morning. Many of Sir Christopher Wren's churches were destroyed, including this one, just to the north of St Paul's. The tower remains but the rest of the church was never rebuilt and the ruins are now a public garden.

Before the war, Piper was a prominent avant-garde artist with a particular interest in churches and British heritage. He was the perfect candidate to work for the War Artists Advisory Committee, which was set up by the director of the National Gallery, Sir Kenneth Clark, to provide commissions for artists. Its aim was partly to record landscapes, homes and churches in case they were damaged or destroyed by the war, and partly to save important artists from being killed.

Piper persuaded Clark to let him 'paint pictures of damaged churches' and he was sent to new bombsites as soon as possible, before any clearing up, often arriving the next morning. Like his famous paintings of Coventry Cathedral, this work shows Christ Church without its roof, an empty box open to the sky. Although Piper visited when the destruction was fresh, the stones still hot and the smell of burning in the air, his paintings feel calm and detached, as if they are of ancient ruins. These images were used as propaganda, portraying a sense of stoic defiance.

Night Raid over London Docklands

Wilfred Stanley Haines c.1941

What do firemen do when there are no fires? During the Second World War some of them used the long hours between bombing raids to practise their painting. The rooftop perches they used for fire-watching also gave them a unique perspective on the city. Their work was highly publicised and during the war it was exhibited at the Royal Academy and toured to America, drawing large crowds. It was still dangerous work, though – the painter of this work was killed by a bomb.

An air raid is under way in this painting, one of the many on the extensive network of docks and warehouses that made east London a prime target for German bombers. The location of this view is very close to that of Whistler's nearly a century earlier (pp.96–7), looking north from Bermondsey across the river to Wapping. Falling on the left are parachute flares, used by the bombers for temporary illumination, while searchlights on the right try to pick out the planes for the anti-aircraft guns.

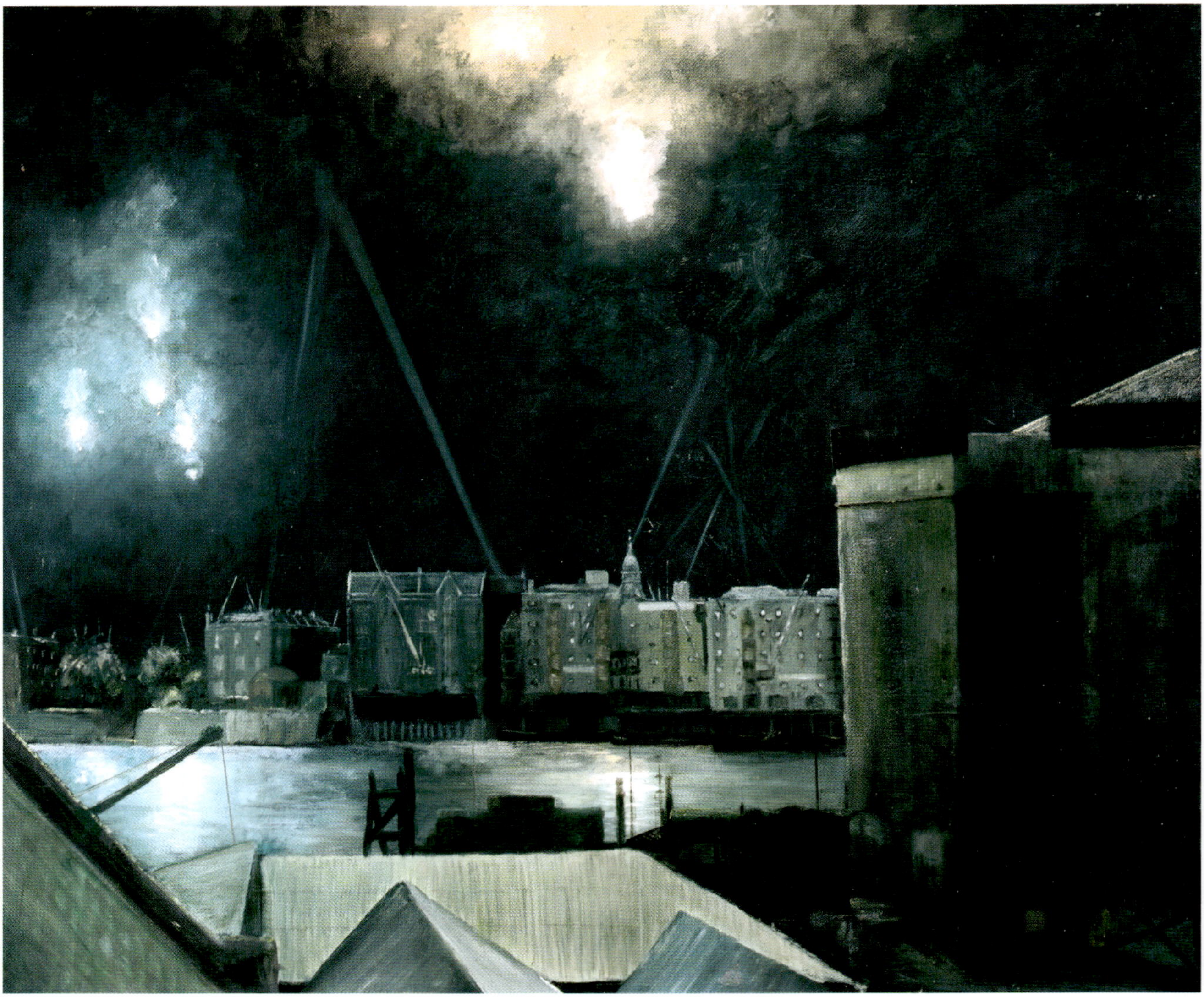

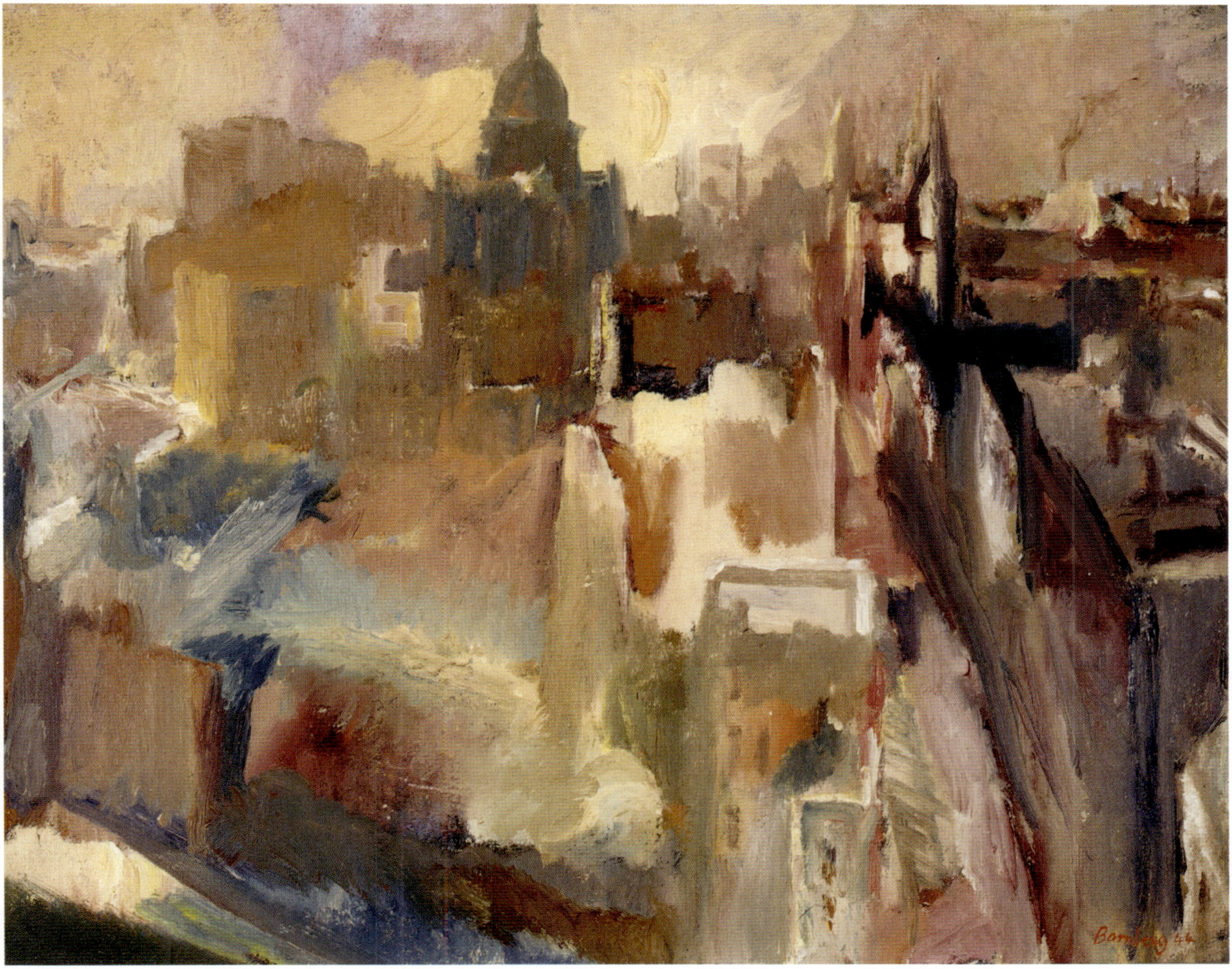

Evening in the City of London

David Bomberg 1944

Although one of the most prominent avant-garde artists in Britain at the time of the First World War, by the late 1930s David Bomberg was feeling forgotten. He desperately wanted to become an official war artist, but his application to the War Artists Advisory Committee was rejected twice, before he received an unsuccessful commission to paint a bomb store in Burton-on-Trent, Staffordshire. He made this work for himself, climbing the tower of St Mary-le-Bow church on Cheapside to take in the shattered city. Echoing the famous photograph, St Paul's is shown standing proud and safe, but the ruined streets are so abstractly presented, and he captures the warm burst of reddish evening light so beautifully, that this painting feels tranquil rather than desolate.

Bomberg connected many of the British painters of the twentieth century, including several in this book. He studied under Walter Sickert, was at the Slade School of Fine Art with Christopher Nevinson, and taught Frank Auerbach (b.1931) and Leon Kossoff (b.1926). He finished his career as a beloved teacher, and a halls of residence at London South Bank University is now named after him.

Battle of Britain: Parachutists from an Enemy Aircraft Brought down in an Apparent Attempt to Bomb Buckingham Palace

Walter Bayes 1942

As a founding member of the Camden Town Group and the London Group, Walter Bayes usually painted serious, austere landscapes, often of coastal scenes. Another of his wartime paintings shows shell-shocked Londoners sheltering from bombs in Elephant & Castle tube station.

But in this one-off commission for the War Artists Advisory Committee, he picks an extraordinary angle to depict an extraordinary event. On 15 September 1940, known as Battle of Britain Day, an RAF pilot was trailing a German bomber he thought was aiming for Buckingham Palace. Having run out of ammunition he rammed the enemy plane, causing it to crash into the forecourt of Victoria Station. This painting shows the German crew bailing out, perhaps from the viewpoint of the British plane, which also went down. Despite these heroics, the bomber somehow let loose its bombs, one of which hit the palace anyway.

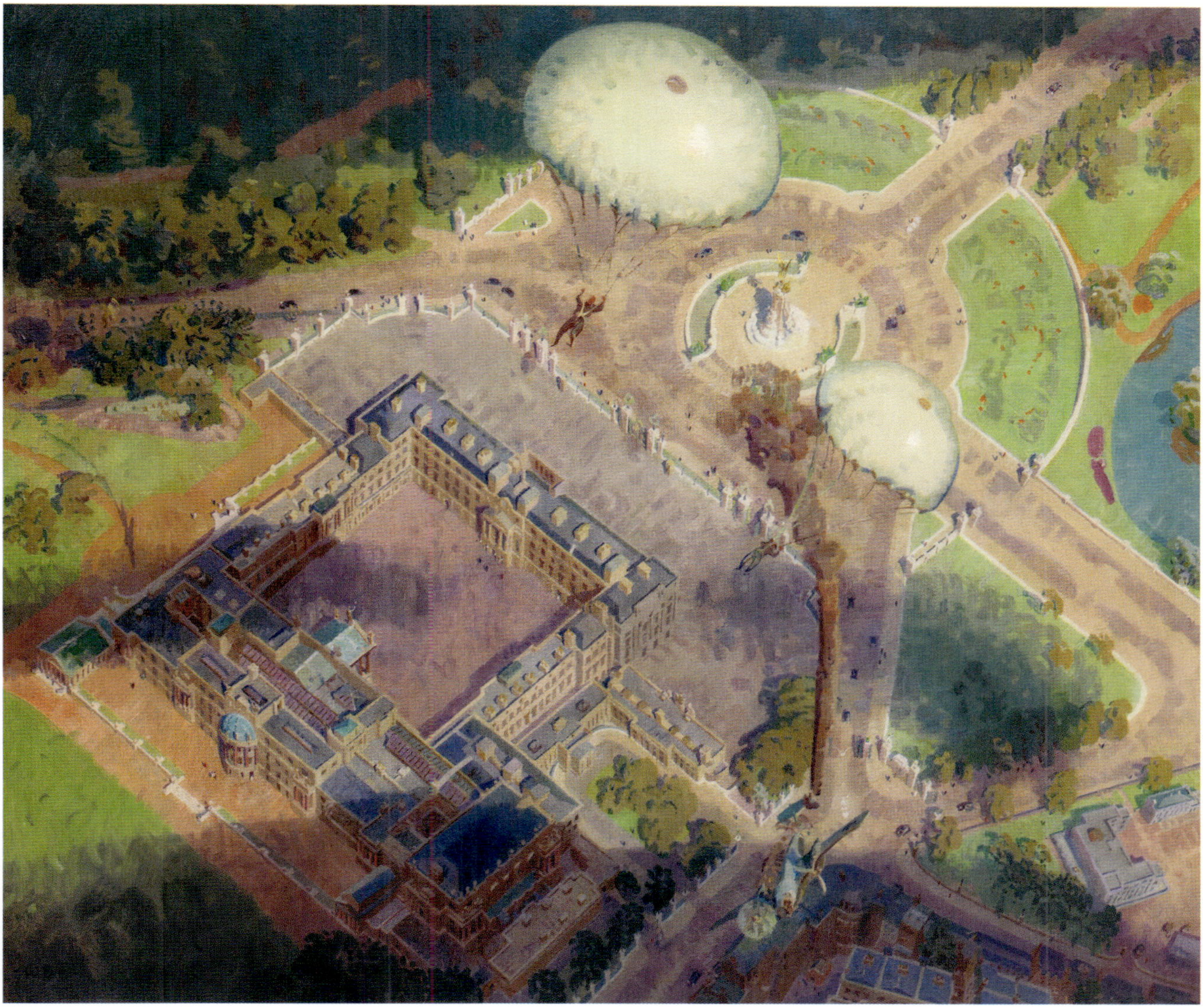

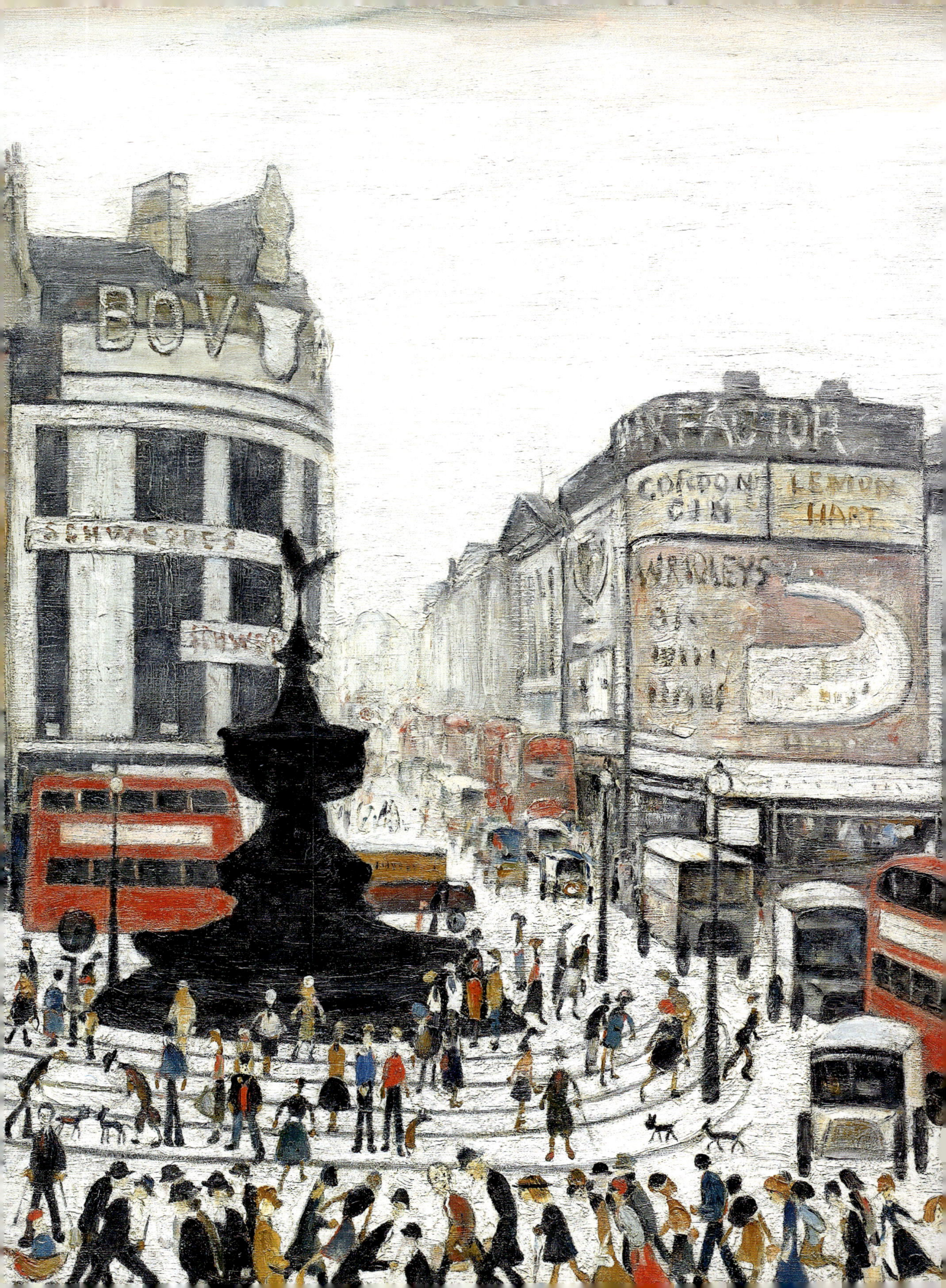
BOV
XFACTOR
LEMON HART

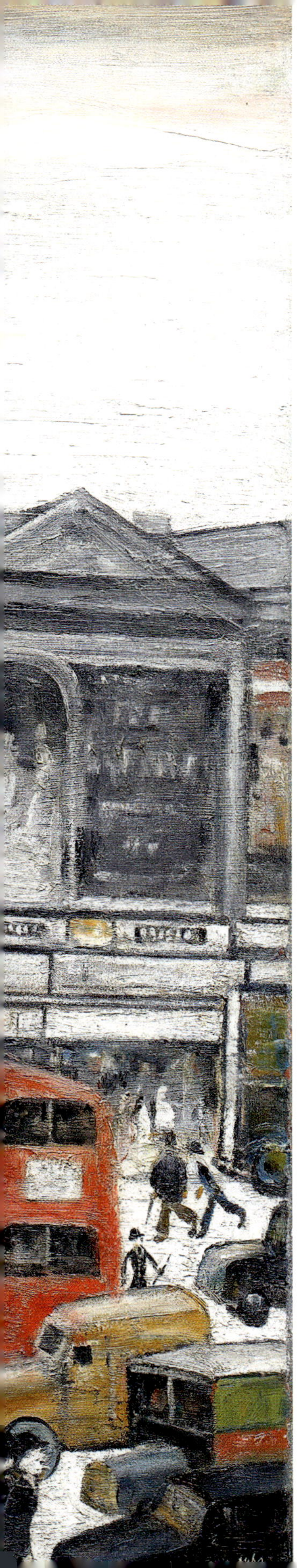

3
TRAVEL AND TRADE

LONDON IS ABOVE ALL a city of commerce. The very presence of most painters in the city is intimately tied up with these systems of exchange – for centuries, artists have come to London to find commissions, to visit their dealers or to exhibit and sell their work.

In the eighteenth century, Covent Garden market was a hub for artists. They picked their way past the stalls, traders and shoppers on their way to visit their upmarket clients, and many recorded the scene in their work. In doing so they established street stereotypes – the flower seller, the street urchin, the middle-class flâneur – which appear again and again in paintings of London.

In the nineteenth century, London developed one of the world's first transit systems to provide workers for its industries: trains, tubes and trams. Mid-Victorian painters glorified these new technologies and the monumental infrastructure they required, whereas the Impressionists and the artists they influenced were fascinated by the new modern ways of living they heralded. Setting down the hectic world of the London rush hour in slow-drying paint proved a harder challenge, and often these works are mysteriously under-occupied, hinting at the alienation and atomisation this transport revolution was believed to have brought in its wake.

After spending a century or so trailing New York, twenty-first century London is again at the hub of the world's economy, despite – or rather, because of – the growth of cities in Asia, Africa and Latin America. Now nearly half of the world's foreign exchange goes through the City of London, and much of the trade in stocks, share and derivatives. But how does a painter begin to set down on canvas this ineffable world of numbers? Some have concentrated on buildings: the glass towers and intimidating facades of international finance. Others have gone back in time to the back-alley beginnings of modern capitalism itself. All give us a sense of a city driven by money and movement.

L.S. Lowry *Piccadilly Circus, London* 1960 (detail). See p.71

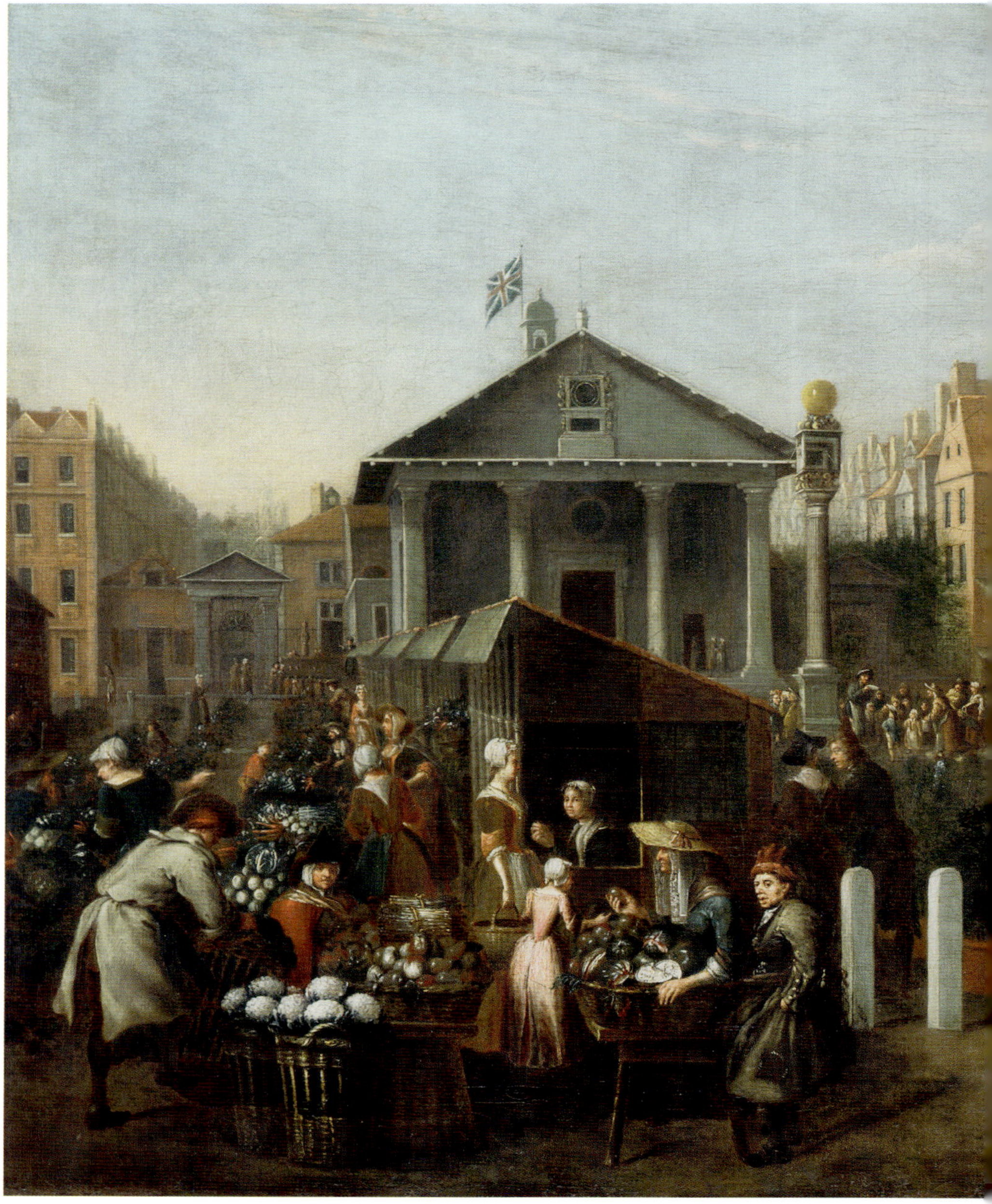

Covent Garden Market

Balthazar Nebot 1737

Before the Bloomsbury Set and the Camden Town Group, there was the Covent Garden Group. This nickname has been given to the artists who lived and worked in, and regularly painted, this area of London in the 1700s.

Built from 1631, Covent Garden was the first London square and an early piece of city planning. It was modelled on Italian piazzas and Paris's Place de Vosges, with regular, classically proportioned houses and covered promenades. The rich and fashionable were attracted to this new development and in their footsteps followed

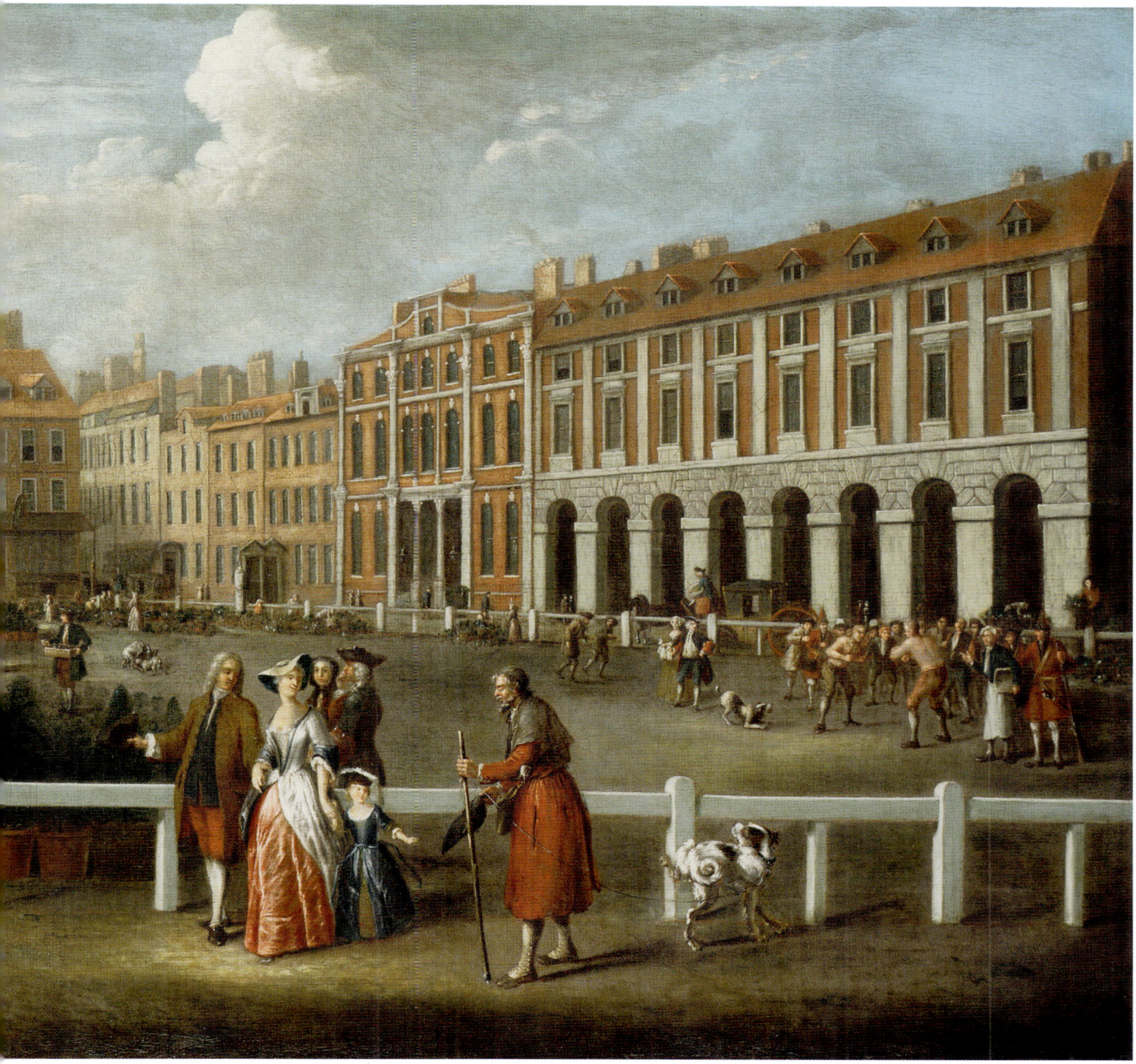

painters who wanted to be close to their patrons. If they were successful enough they hoped to set themselves up in the same high style.

The Covent Garden artists had a promising subject on their doorsteps. Balthazar Nebot was one of those who painted the piazza most often, along with Peter Angelis (1685–1734) and Joseph van Aken (c.1699–1749). The fruit and vegetable market – seen here to the left – provided a counterpoint to the elegance of the architecture. The wooden shacks have now been replaced by upmarket shops, but this painting shows that the character of Covent Garden is not so different today: the spectators of a boxing match to the right are in much the same place where tourists now watch street performers.

Other painters who lived here in the early eighteenth century included William Hogarth, Sir James Thornhill, Richard Wilson and Samuel Scott. The artists were supported by a network of 'colour men' who sold paint and other artists' materials, as well as art schools and print-sellers.

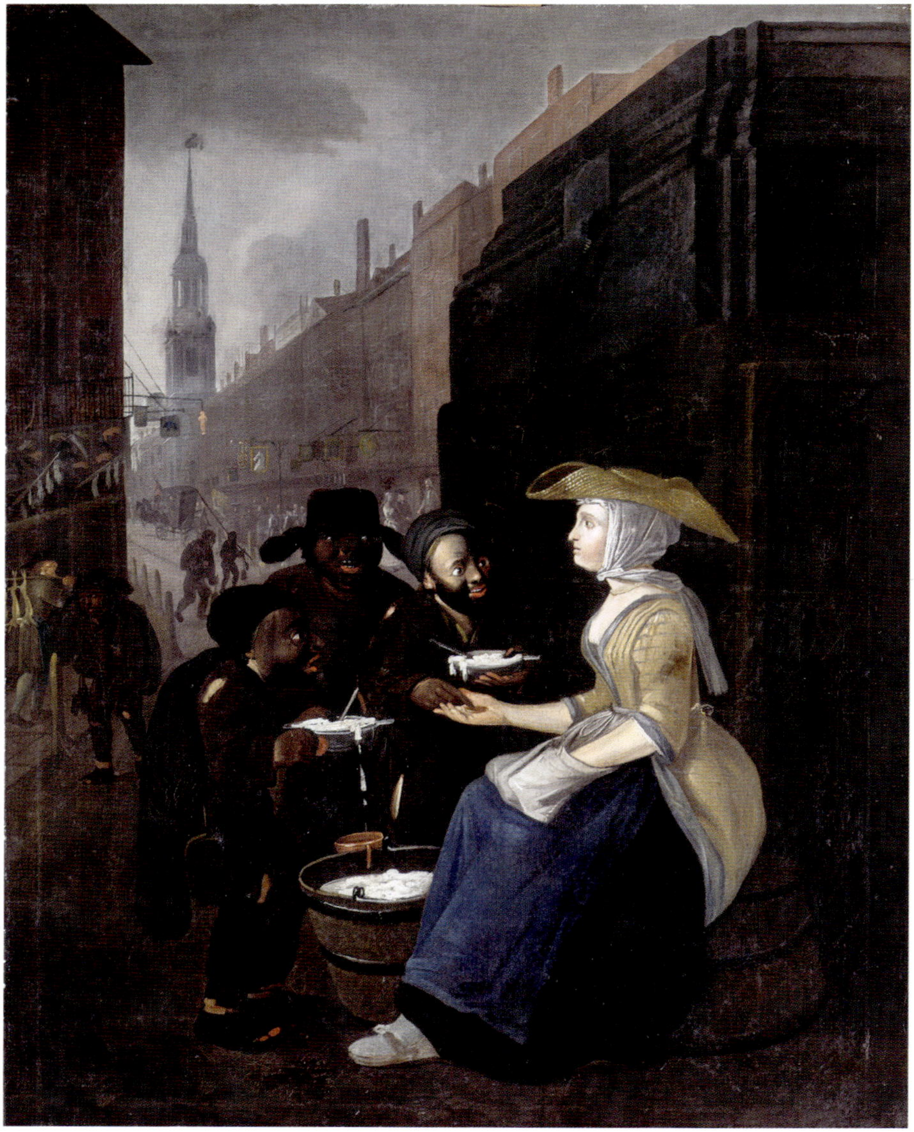

Curds and Whey Seller, Cheapside

British School c.1730

Curds and whey was a popular street food in eighteenth-century London. Here, three impish chimney sweeps – they are the height of children, although one seems to have a beard – buy their lunch from a blind girl. Although other paintings include depictions of street vendors – such as the views of the Frost Fairs or of Covent Garden – this one is unusual in getting close enough to see the money being handed over.

The seller is sitting at the bottom of the Little Conduit, an unfinished water conduit that stood at the western end of Cheapside, not far from St Paul's Cathedral. St Mary-le-Bow stands in the background (compare with p.76).

The Royal Mail Coaches for the North Leaving the Angel, Islington

James Pollard 1827

Mail coaches for Liverpool and Manchester are picking up passengers from outside the Angel Inn in Islington High Street, having started from the City in the early evening. The inn, which gives its name to the nearby tube station and a space on the Monopoly board, had been there since the early sixteenth century. It was rebuilt a few decades before this painting, and again in 1903. Its site is now occupied by a bank, although a new pub continues the name next door.

James Pollard specialised in painting coaching scenes but wasn't to know that this form of transport would soon be obsolete. Euston Station opened 10 years after this painting was made, drastically cutting travel times to the north. Pollard's career trajectory followed that of his subject – successful and prosperous in the 1830s, by the end of his life he was forced to rely on charity.

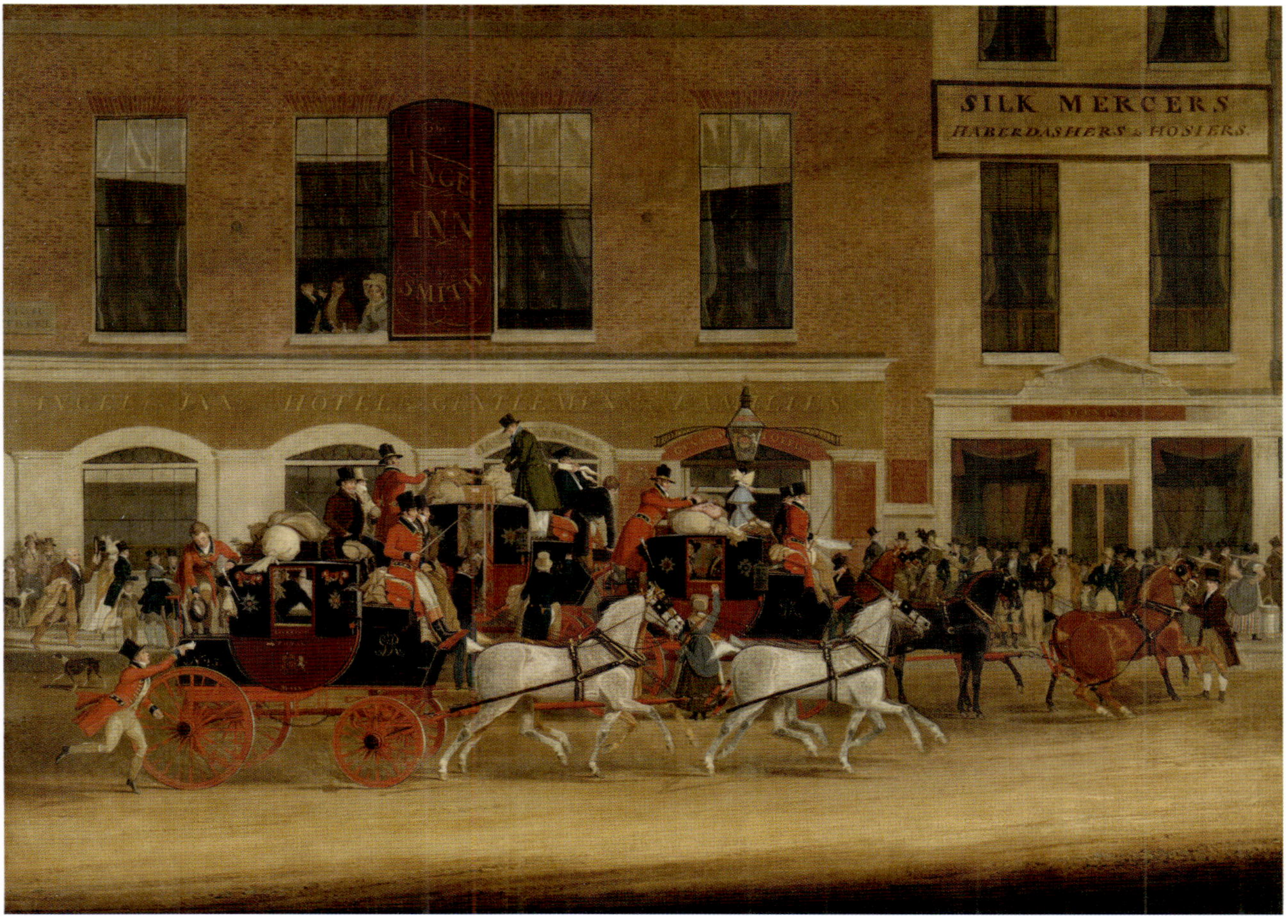

The South Sea Bubble, a Scene in 'Change Alley in 1720

Edward Matthew Ward 1847

Stockbrokers have always had a bad reputation. Expelled from the Royal Exchange in 1698 for rowdiness, they set up business in the coffee houses located in the web of alleyways between Cornhill and Lombard Street in the heart of the City of London. The most famous of these were Garraway's – visible at the back of the painting – and Jonathan's. The latter became the first place that the prices of stocks and commodities were posted, and later became the London Stock Exchange. Traders would pay a penny to work for an unlimited time in the coffee houses, where they could get the latest news from around the world as well as hot beverages.

Ward depicts the famous South Sea mania of the century before: gullible investors are frantically buying shares in soon-to-be-worthless companies. Ward was a successful narrative painter who is now best known for his series of murals in the House of Commons depicting famous scenes from British history. His paintings, according to his wife, all pointed to 'some particular moral'; here he was likely thinking of the similar Railway Mania of his own time.

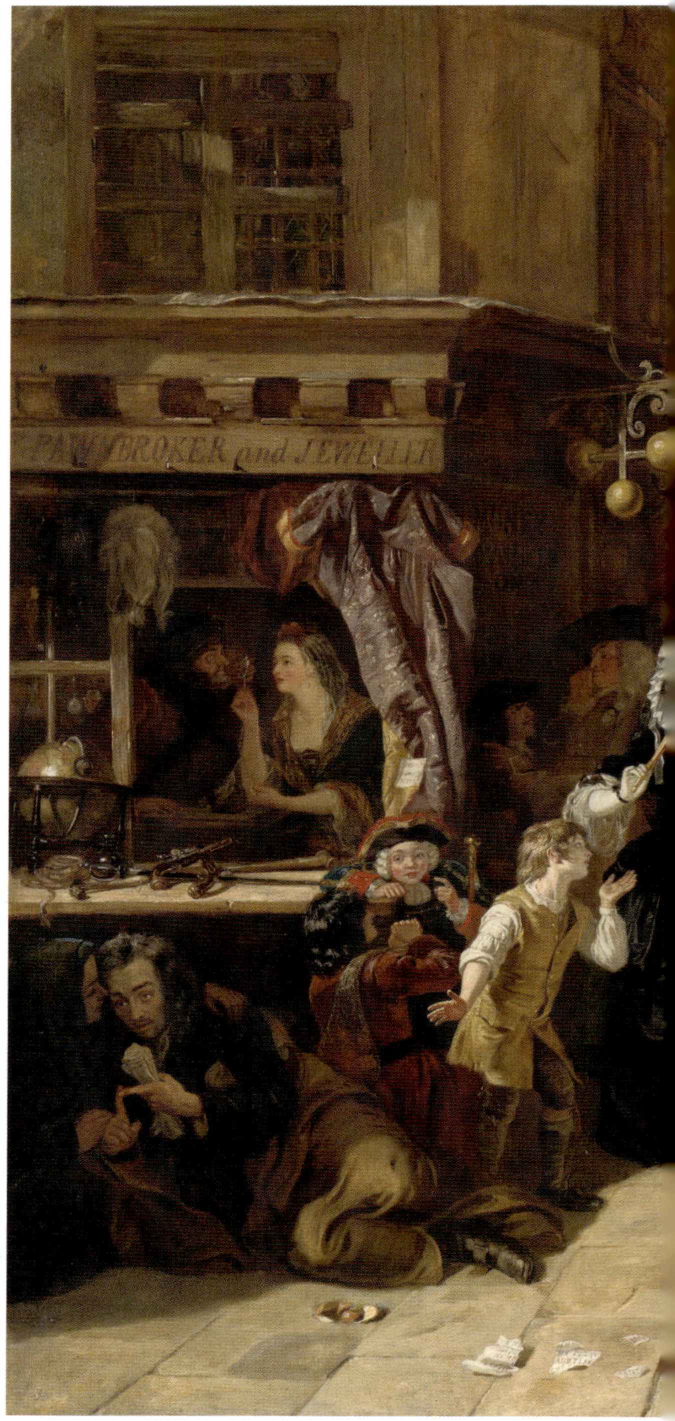

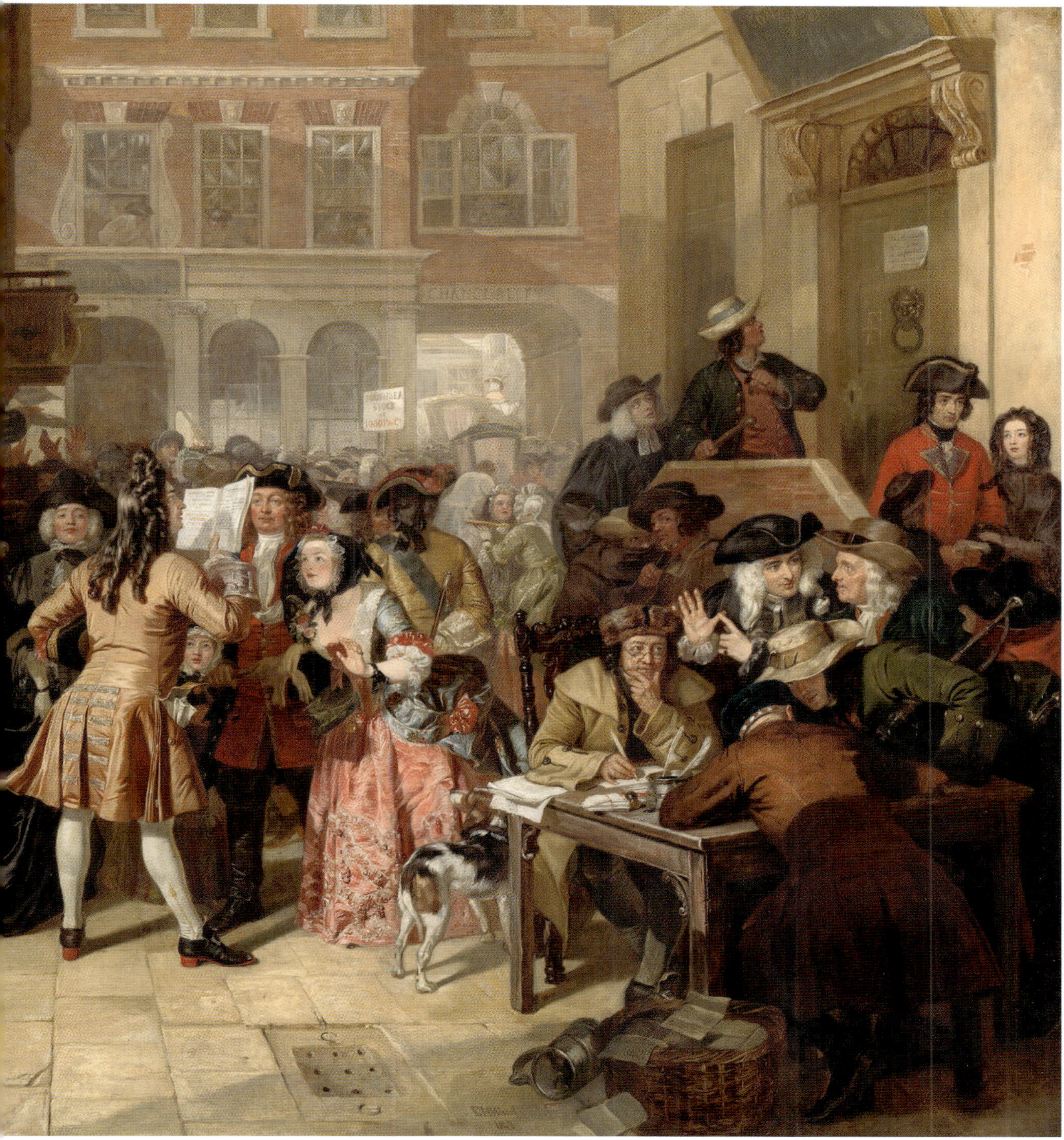

The Railway Station

William Powell Frith 1862

Eight-and-a-half feet long, this painting is a monumental celebration of Victorian modernity. Its subject, Paddington Station, the palatial terminus of Isambard Kingdom Brunel's Great Western Railway, was not yet ten years old.

The architecture depicted here – spindly wrought iron holding aloft a vast expanse of glass – was radically new, letting in light and air. Save for the rather lovely globe gaslights, the view has changed very little today, even down to the filigree ironwork at the end of the platforms.

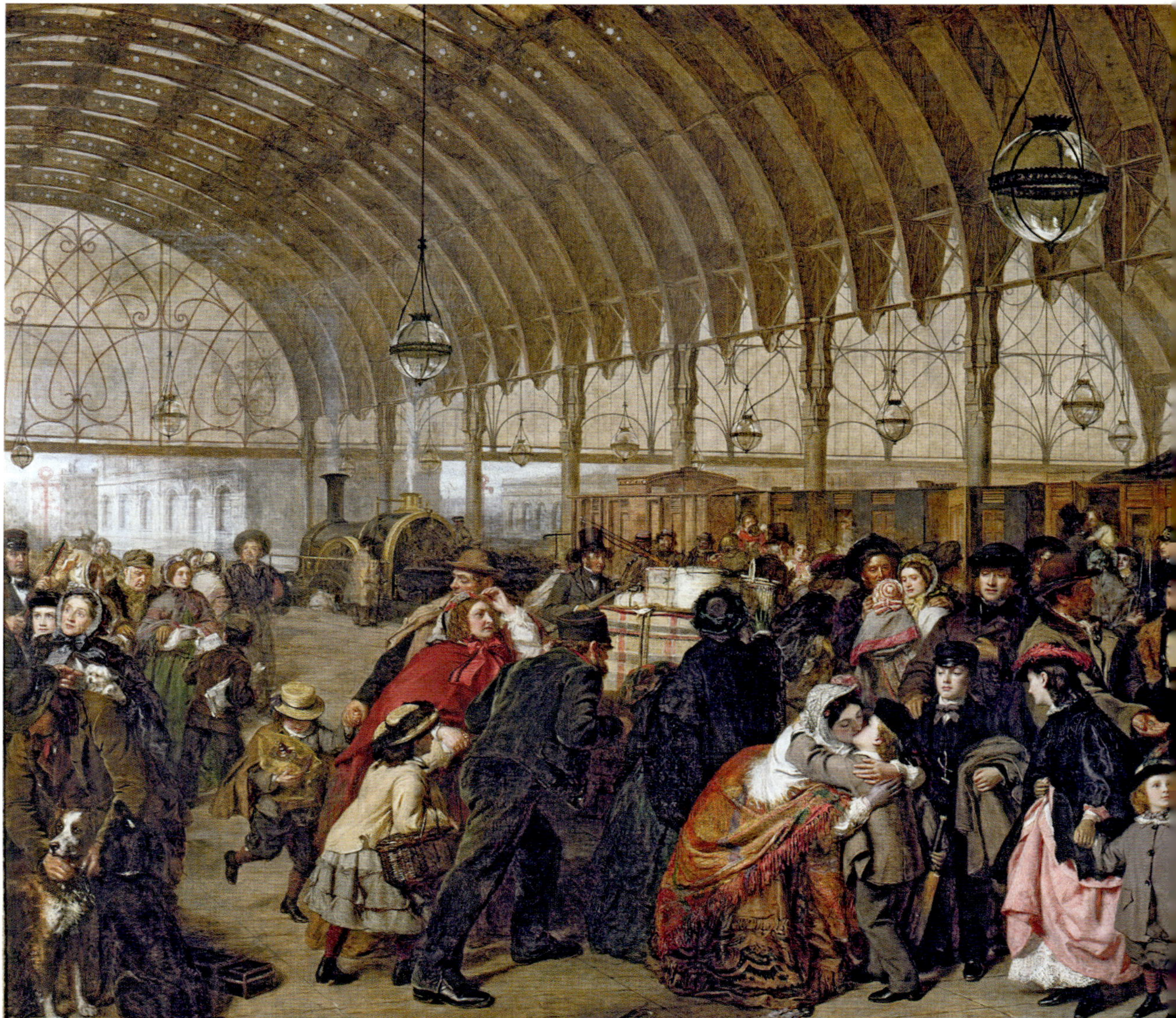

The railways caused a social revolution. They standardised time itself across the country and brought masses of people, as here, together to meet a preordained and precise schedule.

Frith's work, with its interest in crime and class, in comic detail, in the sentimental and sanctimonious, is reminiscent of the great Victorian novel. In the middle stands Frith himself, a proud father sending one of his boys off to school. He was an enthusiastic father – he had twelve children with his wife and seven more with a mistress, Mary, who he maintained near Paddington. Some believe the woman in the pink bonnet and holding a baby, standing to the left of Frith, was modelled on her.

Next to the Frith family, a cab driver hassles a foreign couple for a bigger tip; at the far right, a criminal is apprehended by detectives; and on the far left a man talks to the driver as he gets up steam. All of these incidents were explained in a specially produced pamphlet. The work was not shown at the Royal Academy as was conventional, but presented directly to the public, who paid to visit this one-painting exhibition and file slowly past Frith's masterwork.

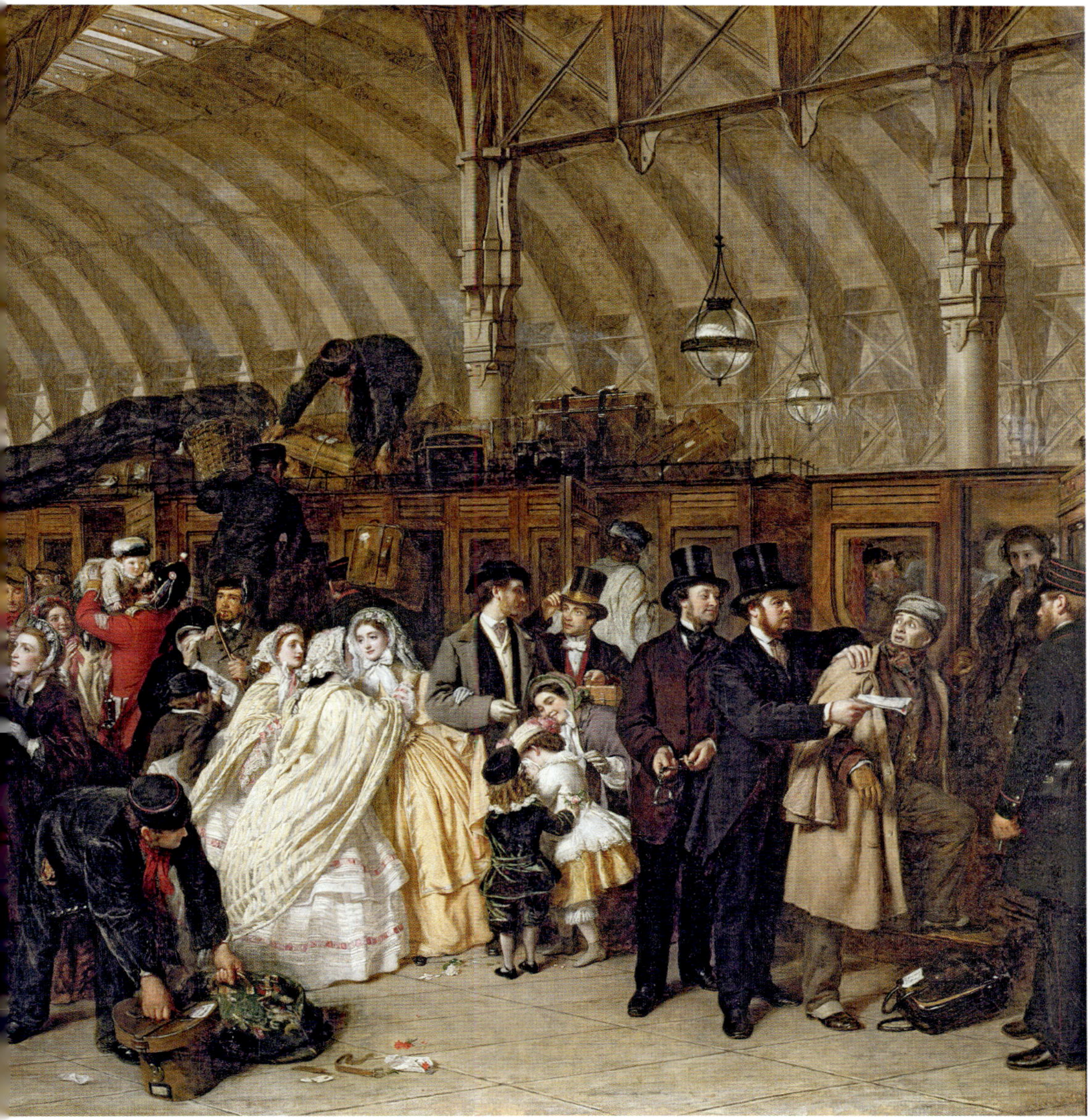

Shaftesbury, or Lost and Found

William Macduff 1862

There is a Dickensian quality to this painting, but the older boy is not training the younger street urchin to become a pickpocket. He is pointing out the benefactor who has enabled him to find work as a shoe-black: Lord Shaftesbury. A vigorous philanthropist, Shaftesbury was responsible for many improvements to the laws affecting children and the poor, including banning children from working as chimney sweeps.

The older boy points to a print of Shaftesbury, based on a painting by Frederick Sandys. They are looking into the window of Henry Graves & Company at 6 Pall Mall, one of London's largest and most successful print shops at the time. All the prints depicted are real and all have a charitable theme.

Shaftesbury gives his name to the nearby Shaftesbury Avenue, created as part of a slum clearance. The statue at the end of it in Piccadilly Circus was also dedicated to him and is called *The Angel of Christian Charity*. Its inappropriately sensuous nature must account for its popular, but incorrect name, Eros.

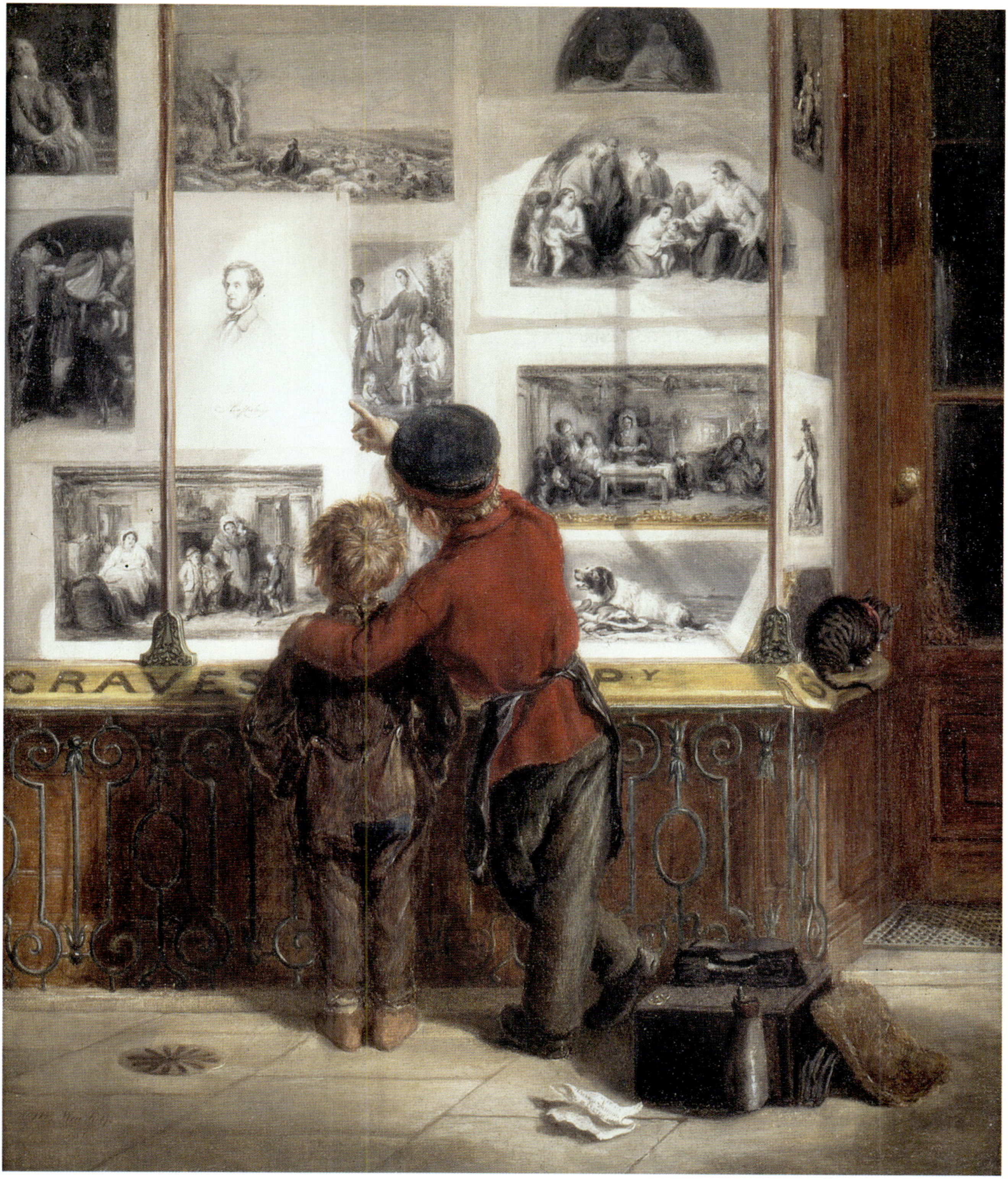
GRAVES

St Martin-in-the-Fields

William Logsdail 1888

The non-committal title of this work belies the urgent political questions it would have raised for contemporary viewers. It was painted on the edge of Trafalgar Square, looking north (compare Tissot's view of the same scene looking east, p.100). Logsdail worked *en plein air*, in the manner of the French Impressionists, sitting in a stationary vehicle for several weeks, his feet under straw to keep them warm.

Trafalgar Square had recently been the site of a brutally suppressed protest against joblessness, and the artist and socialist William Morris (1834–96) was among its leaders. Falling food prices had caused rural unemployment, forcing many to the towns and cities. Flower-selling was a common occupation for girls like the one in the centre of the composition, and for the older ones it sometimes overlapped with prostitution.

Logsdail set out to paint modern London rigorously. This is one of a series of similar views, combining an almost snapshot-like view of the social scene with highly recognisable and accurately depicted landmark buildings. The dominant building is St Martin-in-the-Fields, an early-eighteenth-century church whose combination of classical colonnades and a traditional spire was extremely influential in the United States.

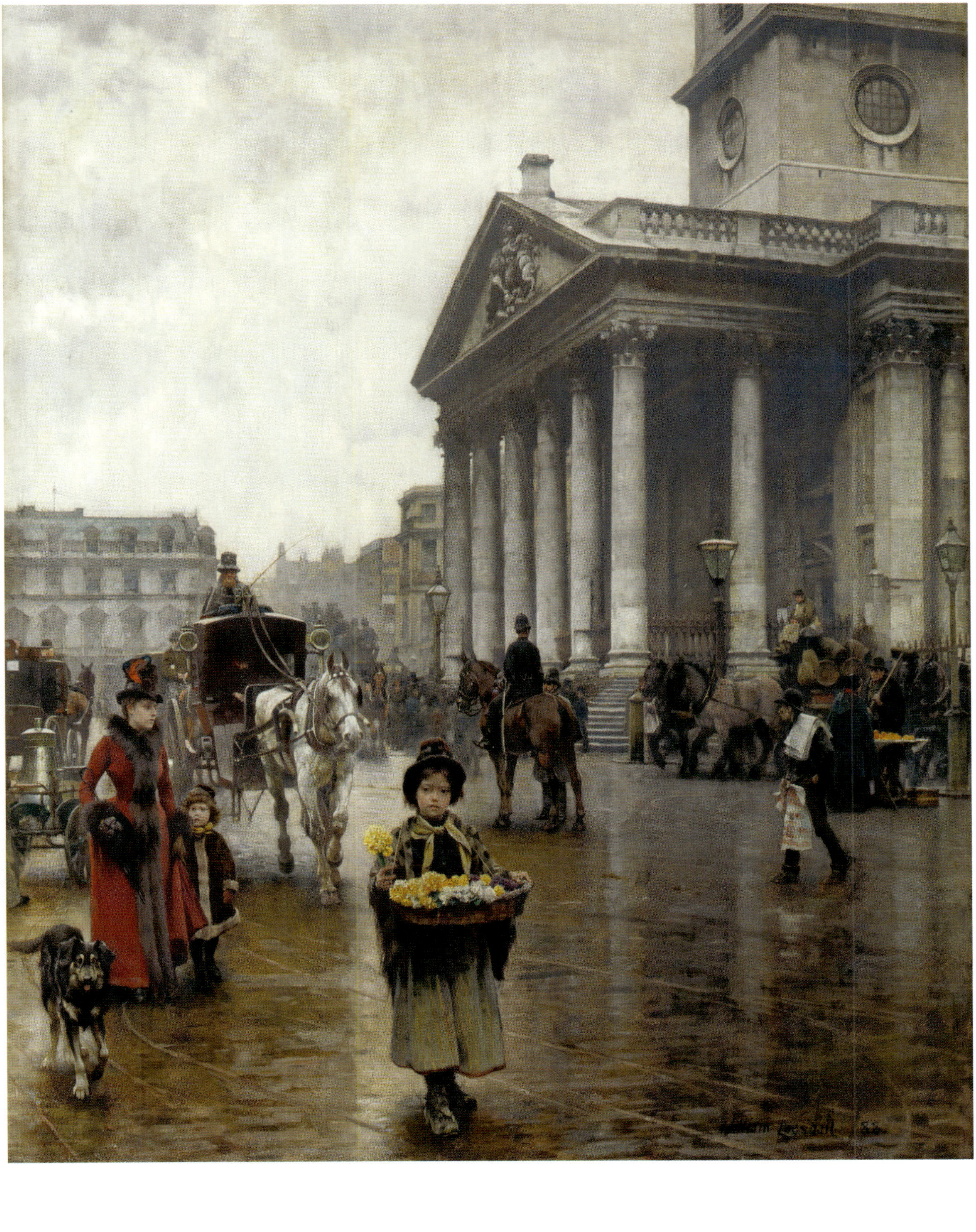

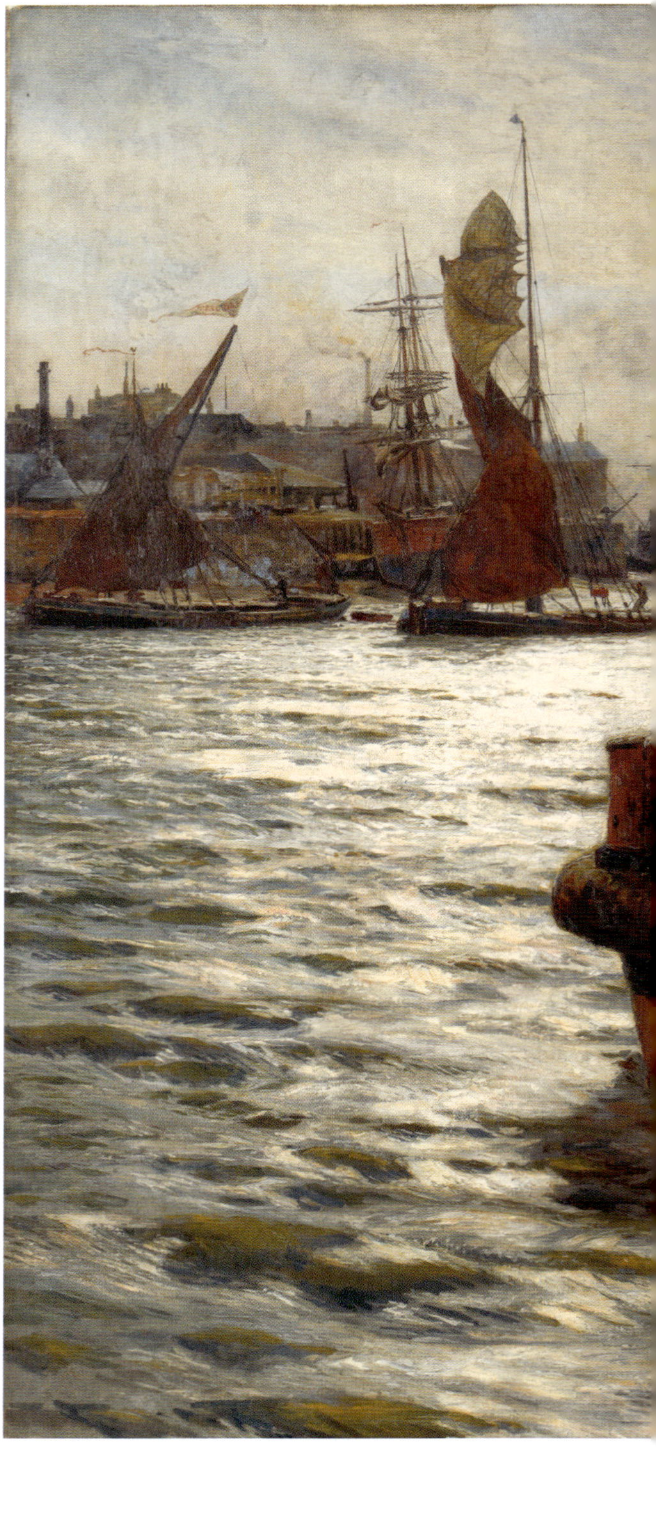

Toil, Glitter, Grime and Wealth on a Flowing Tide

William Lionel Wyllie 1883

In the late nineteenth century you could practically walk along the River Thames, hopping from boat to boat. Wyllie specialised in views of the Thames and took a particular interest in the working river. Here, a tug boat helps to position two lighters full of coal and timber. Behind are sea going ships and to the left are Thames barges, with their distinctive red sails. The location is Greenwich Reach in south-east London, looking towards the domes of the Old Royal Naval College.

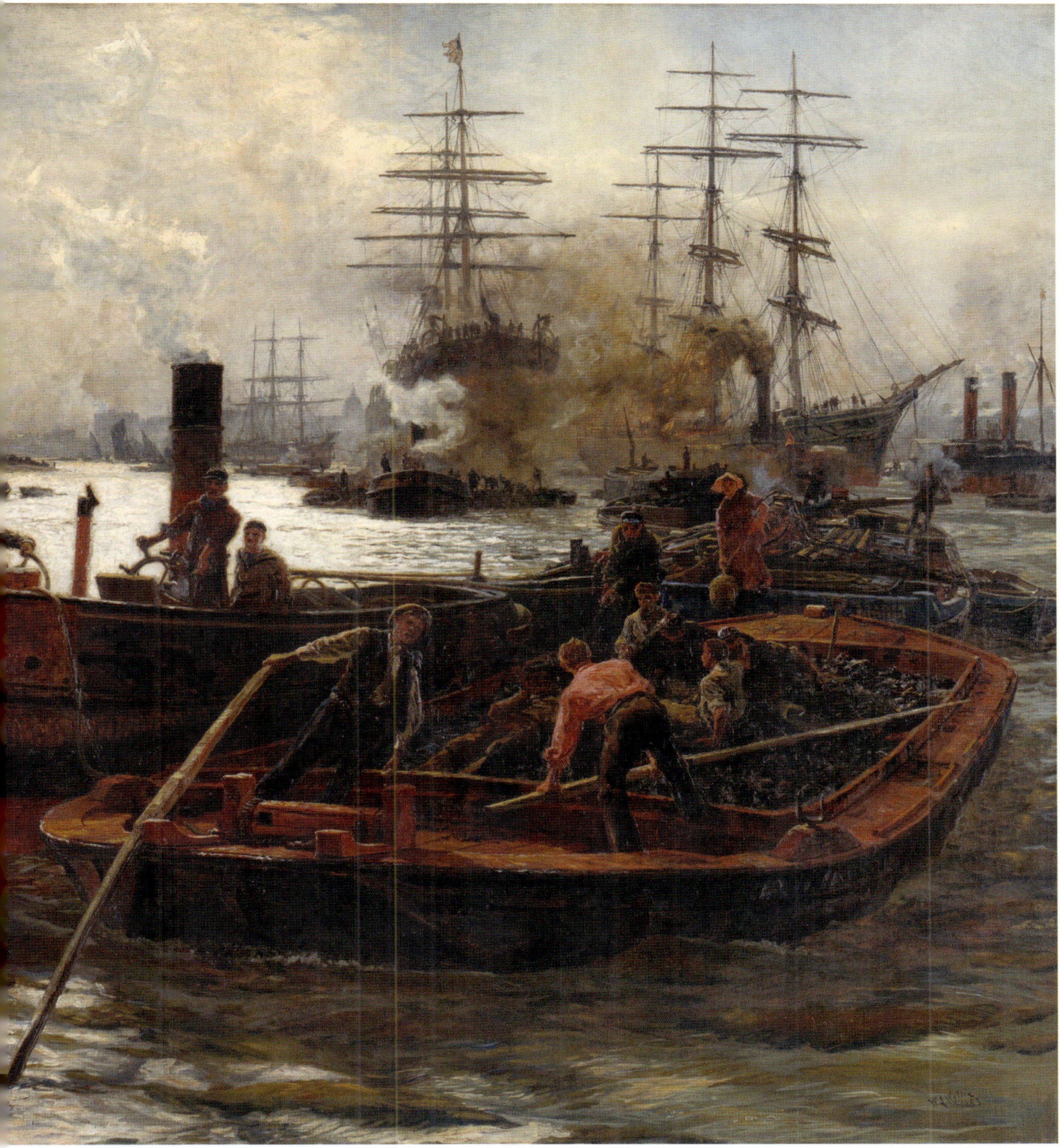

The Pool of London

André Derain 1906

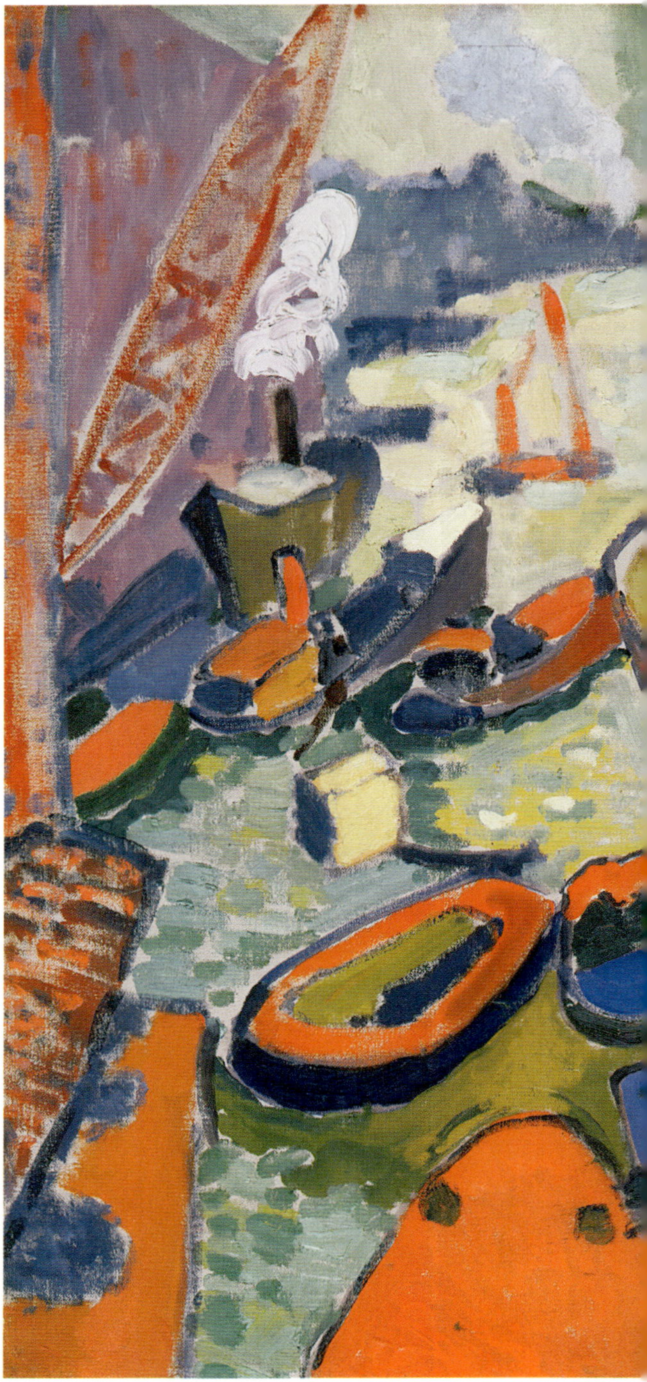

Claude Monet's paintings of the River Thames (pp.144–5) created a stir when they were exhibited in Paris in May–June 1904 and the powerful art dealer Ambroise Vollard despatched the young André Derain across the Channel to capture some more of the 'London atmosphere'. Derain had just made a name for himself at the 1905 Salon d'Automne; the bold, unnatural colours used in his work and that of his friends Henri Matisse (1869–1954) and Maurice de Vlaminck (1876–1958) gained them the title *fauves*, or 'wild beasts'. In March 1906, he arrived in London and made around thirty paintings.

Like Monet, Derain concentrated on scenes of the Thames, but he was inspired by the cosmopolitan hustle and bustle rather than foggy atmospheric effects. The smoky city is lit up by bright, clean light and searing colours. Derain moved to a different spot for each work, but this view across the Pool to Tower Bridge seems to have been a favourite. The location is probably by the old Billingsgate fish market, perhaps painted from London Bridge, which blocked large ships like this going any further. Even with the creation of the Docklands, the Pool was still thriving and busy up until the 1950s.

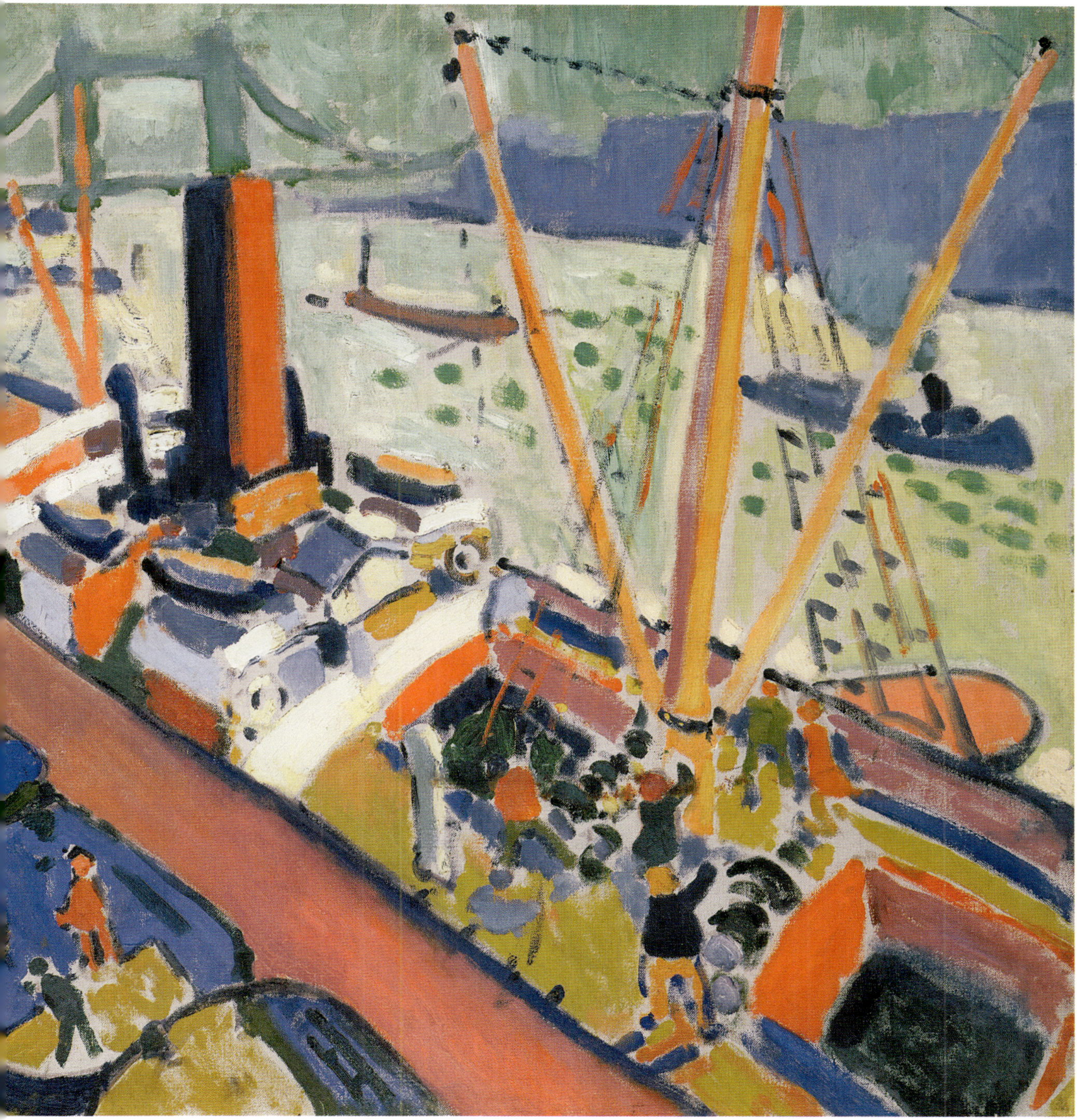

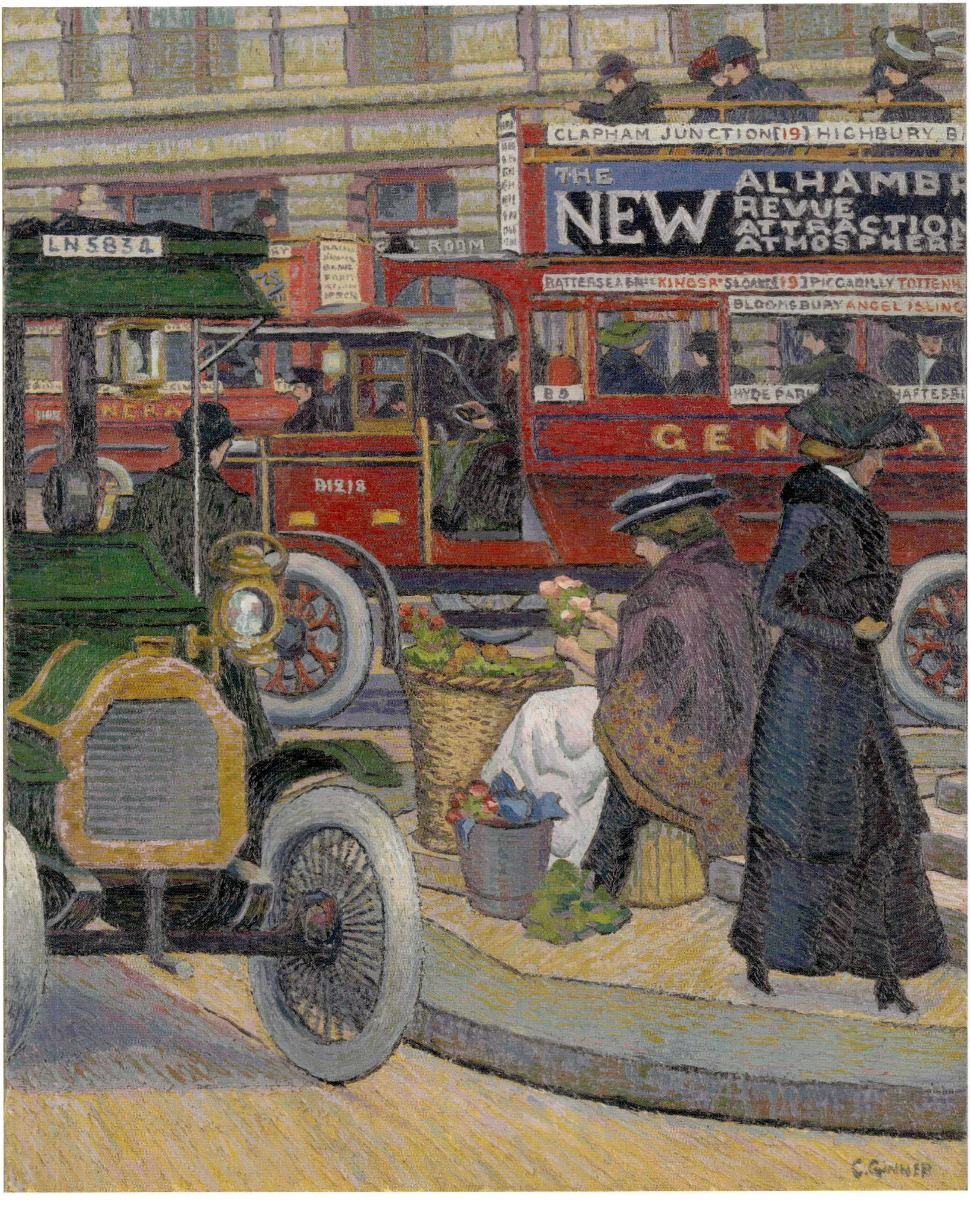
CLAPHAM JUNCTION 19 HIGHBURY
THE NEW
REVUE
LN 5834
D1218
C.GINNER

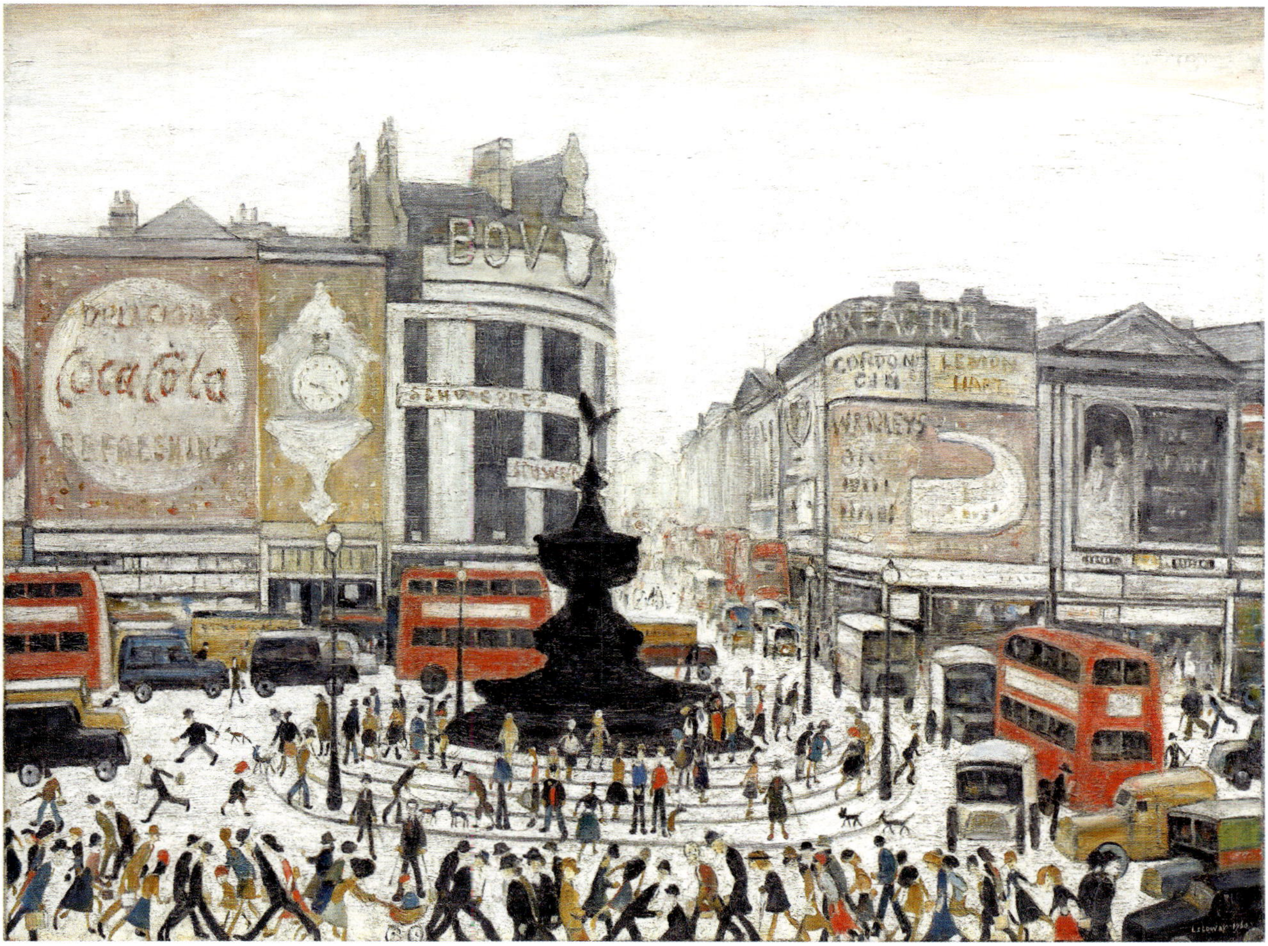

Piccadilly Circus (left)

Charles Ginner 1912

Piccadilly Circus, London

L.S. Lowry 1960

Proverbially busy, Piccadilly Circus has always been a maelstrom of traffic. Charles Ginner painted it just as the engine gained the upper hand over the horse. He crops in close, barely illustrating any of the surrounding buildings, nor an inch of the statue that the flower seller sits alongside. The two buses, a taxi and a car confusingly overlap, and trap the pedestrians between the roads. Newspapers of the day wrung their hands over the increasingly dangerous traffic, much as today's worry about cycle lanes.

Ginner was a member of the Camden Town Group and set out to paint 'modern London' in a determined way that no British artist had done since William Logsdail a generation before. Like the Futurists, he shows an interest in the speed, motion and modernity heralded by the motor car, but is far less celebratory about its impact.

Traffic still plagues Piccadilly half a century later in L.S. Lowry's work. He came to London to visit his gallerist but didn't paint many London views, and when he did they were more faithful to life than his constructed views of northern cities. Here he accurately records the billboards – Coca-Cola has had a spot here since the 1950s; Bovril had the first neon sign; the large clock signified it was 'Guinness Time'. Lowry's mastery at depicting busy streets, his so-called stickmen scurrying to and fro, finds its perfect realisation here.

Queen's Road Station, Bayswater

Walter Sickert c.1916

Despite entreating his fellow painters in the Camden Town Group to get out into London and 'render its magic and poetry', Walter Sickert himself is best known for his paintings of dubious goings-on in cramped and dark interiors. This painting of the underground system retains much of the same atmosphere, with its solitary passenger sitting in half-darkness as he awaits his train. He is hemmed in by the strong verticals and horizontals of the platform and signage – Sickert omits the high arched roof which actually allowed light to stream into this sub-surface station.

On the left can be seen an early version of the iconic London Underground logo. This station was part of the Metropolitan Railway – the world's first underground line – and the red diamond indicated the Railway's independence. The line was eventually absorbed into the wider London Underground system and the logo changed to the familiar roundel with the red circle and blue bar. The sign says 'Queen's Road (Bayswater)' – the station is now known as just Bayswater and is on the District and Circle lines. The advert at the top reads 'Alight here for Whiteley's', then a famous department store, now a shopping centre.

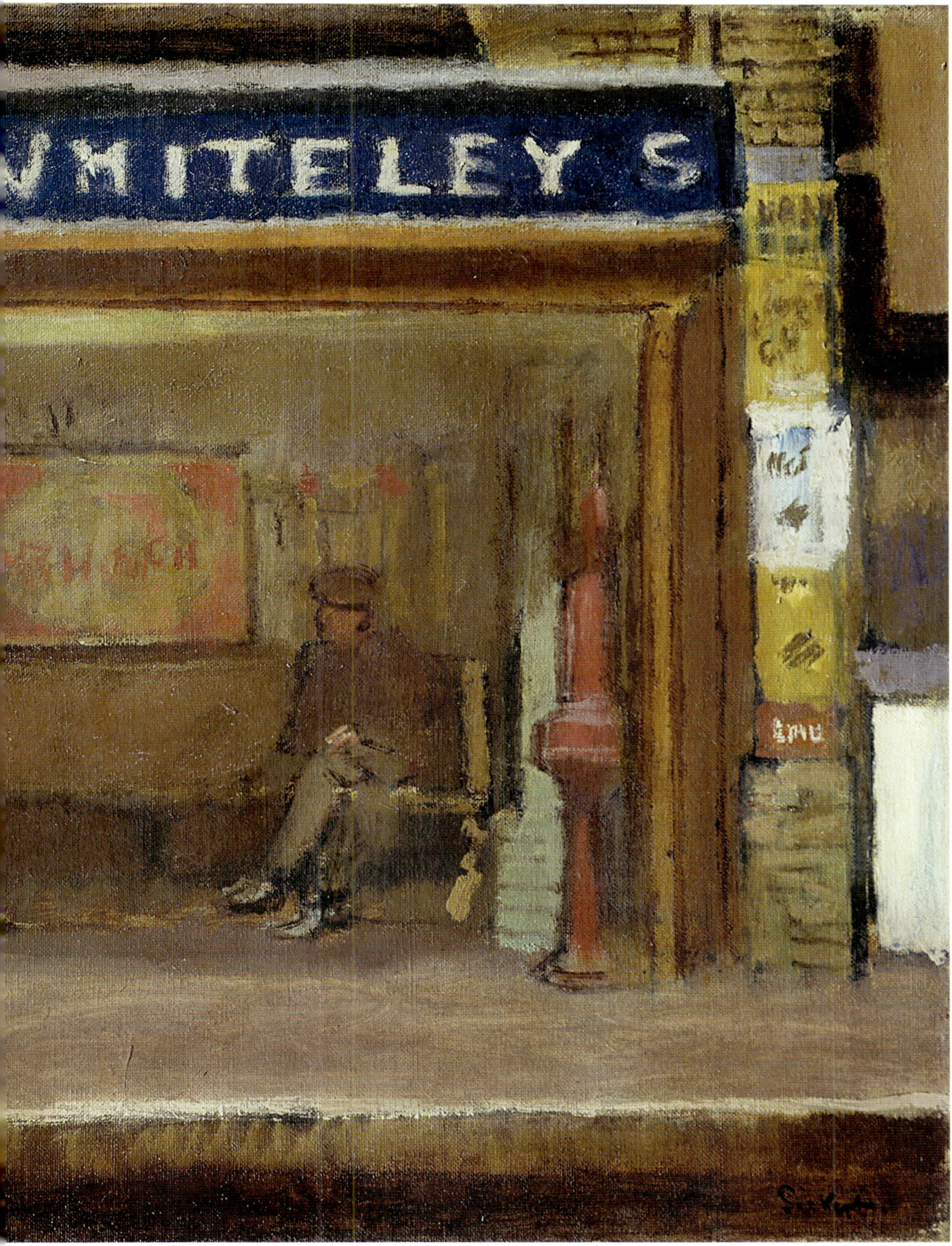
HITELEY S

Selling the 'Daily Worker' outside the Projectile and Engineering Works

Clive Branson 1937

The man and woman selling the communist newspapers in this painting are probably the artist and his wife – the factory was in Battersea, south-west London, close to where the couple lived. Despite the decline in factory employment in London in the twentieth century, this industrial estate still operates. Munitions factories were of especial interest to socialists such as Branson, who realised that the factories' working-class employees were likely to be the main victims if war broke out. Their aprons carry the slogan 'For Unity' against fascism. During the war, Branson died while on service in Burma.

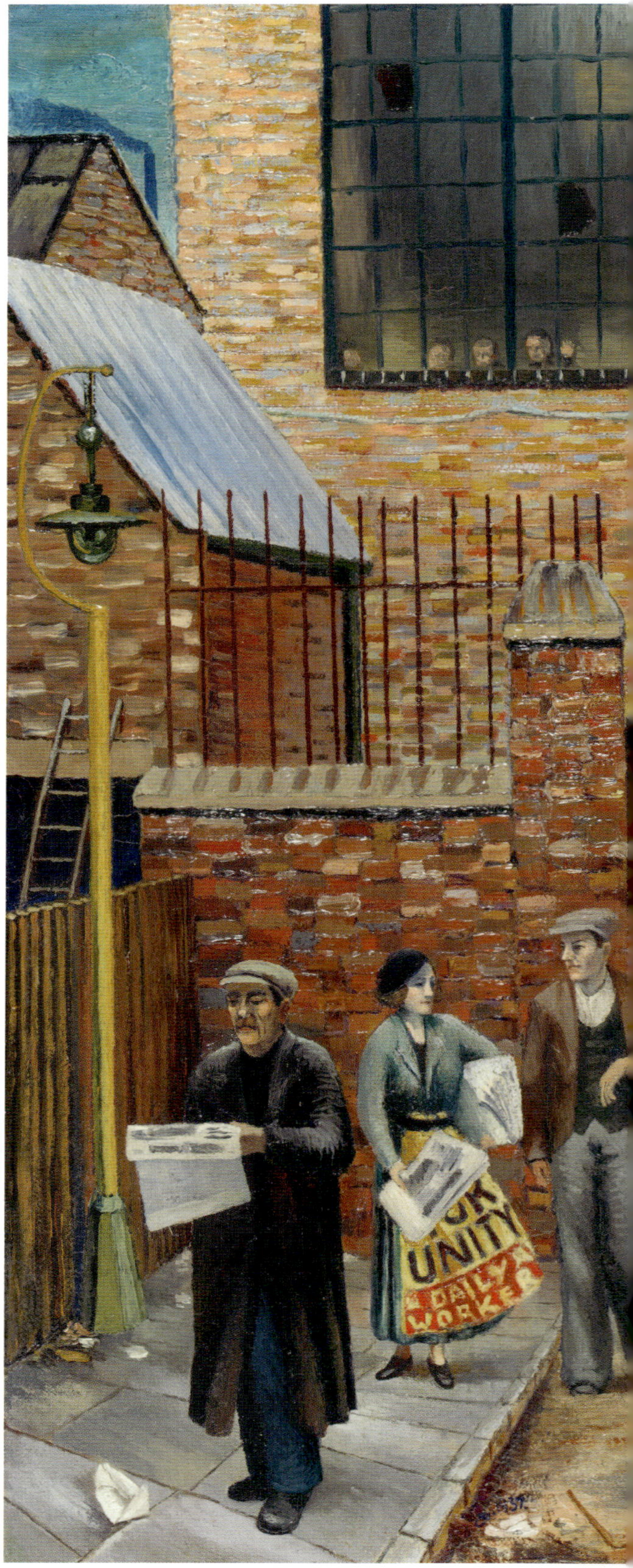

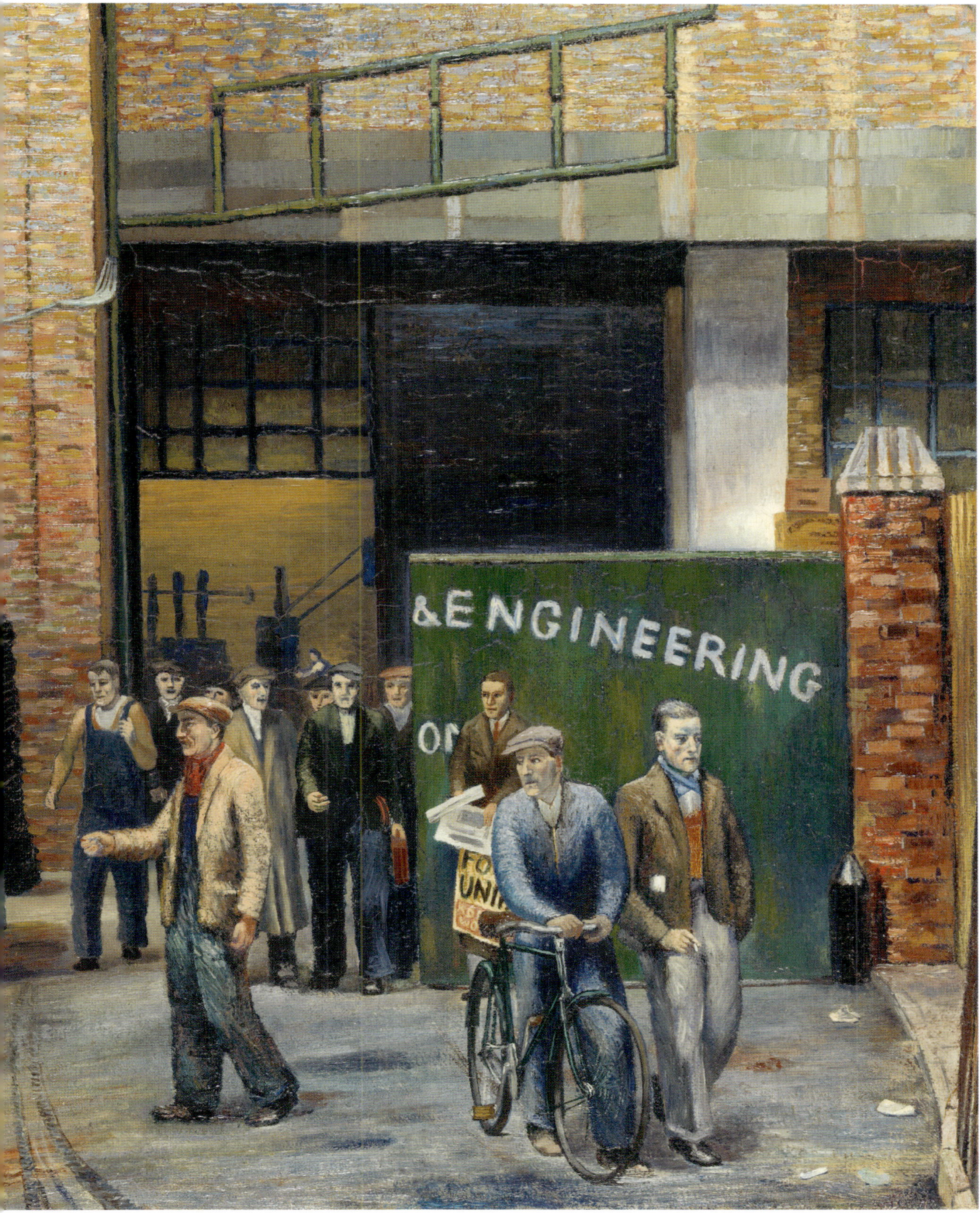
&ENGINEERING

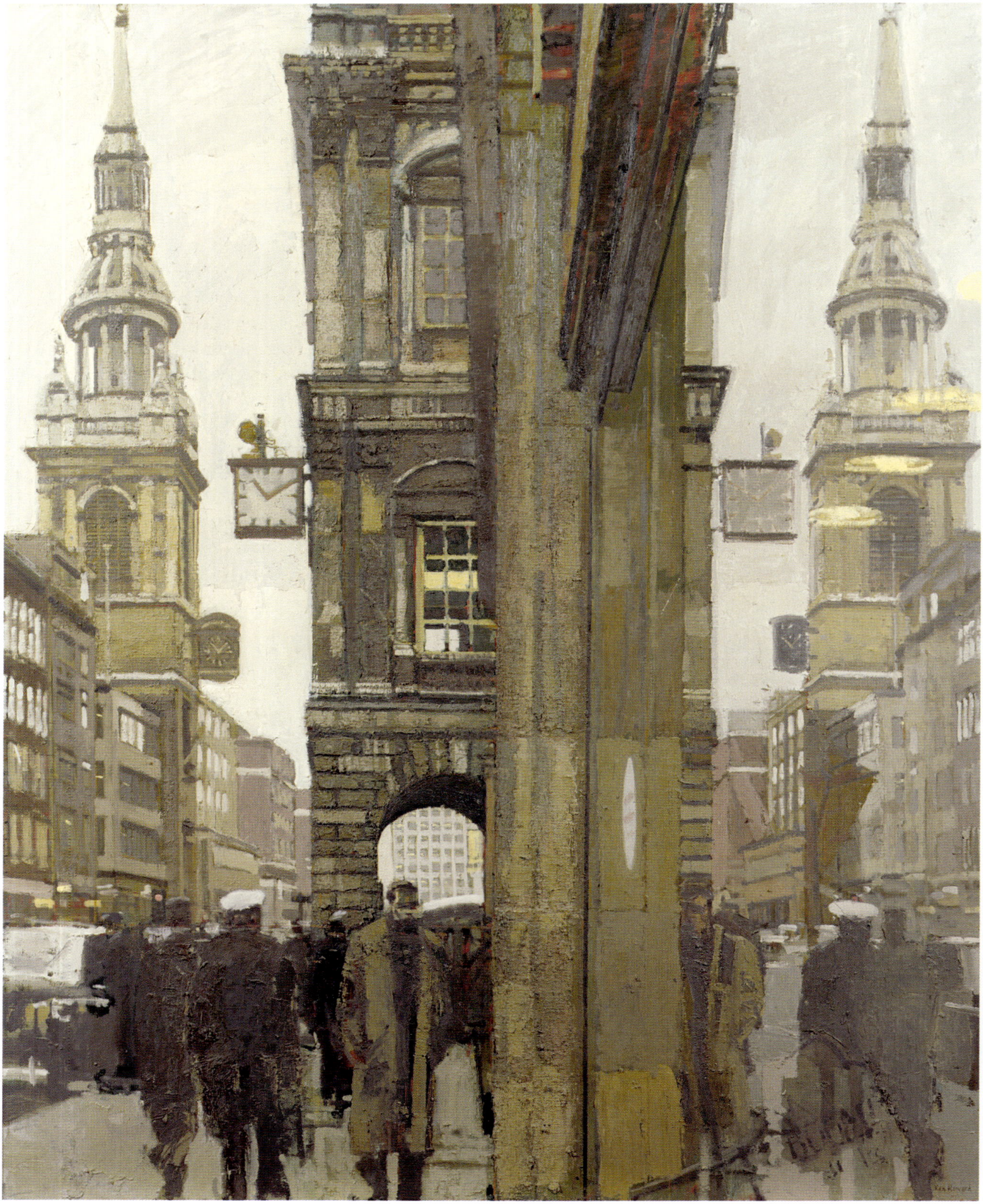

Cheapside 10.10 a.m., 10 February 1970

Ken Howard 1970

Cheapside 'may boast of being the busiest thoroughfare in the world', wrote Charles Dickens Jr in 1879. It is still a shopping street but is no longer particularly well-thronged. Ken Howard catches it on a dank Tuesday morning in winter, a few men in raincoats presumably late for work. Like many before him, Howard is drawn to the cityscapes of London and Venice. He often uses reflections caught in the river or rain-slicked pavements. Here, a sheet-glass storefront mirrors the tower of St Mary-le-Bow.

London, said Howard, is 'exciting in all lights, whether the subtle grey light of winter or the dancing light of summer.' He realised his vocation as painter when working on a picture of a north London railway siding as a young man. A passerby remarked: 'I have walked across this place for many years and this morning for the first time I see that it is beautiful.'

Clapham Junction

Carel Weight 1978

Carel Weight painted the London he was familiar with from his day-to-day life, often, as here, enlivened by casual violence or the drama of the streets.

Famous for being the busiest station in Europe, Clapham Junction in south-west London is nowhere near as visually impressive as that statistic might imply, and is far from the gleaming palace of travel shown in Frith's painting of Paddington (pp.60–1). When Weight painted it, the old booking office had been disused since 1967, lending the area a desolate and dangerous air (it has since been demolished and replaced).

The artist explained: 'I pass it almost every day on the way to my studio and have always been fascinated by the switch-back aspect of the composition which suggests violent movement. It is a district where violence is a frequent feature and where robbery is commonplace.' That eeriness is emphasised by the action: four men are chased by the police. Or perhaps they are fare dodgers fleeing from the station staff. Weight adds staggered outlines to show motion – a technique he took from the Futurists but which is also reminiscent of children's comics.

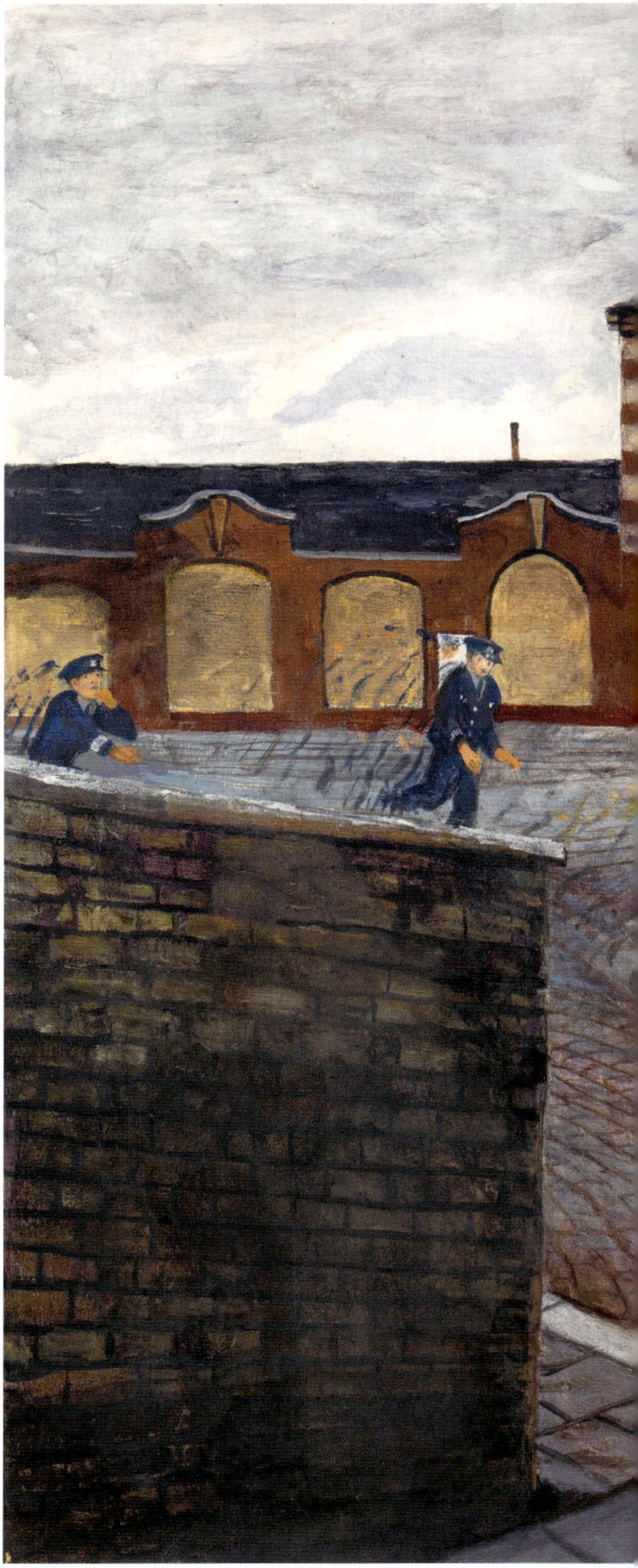

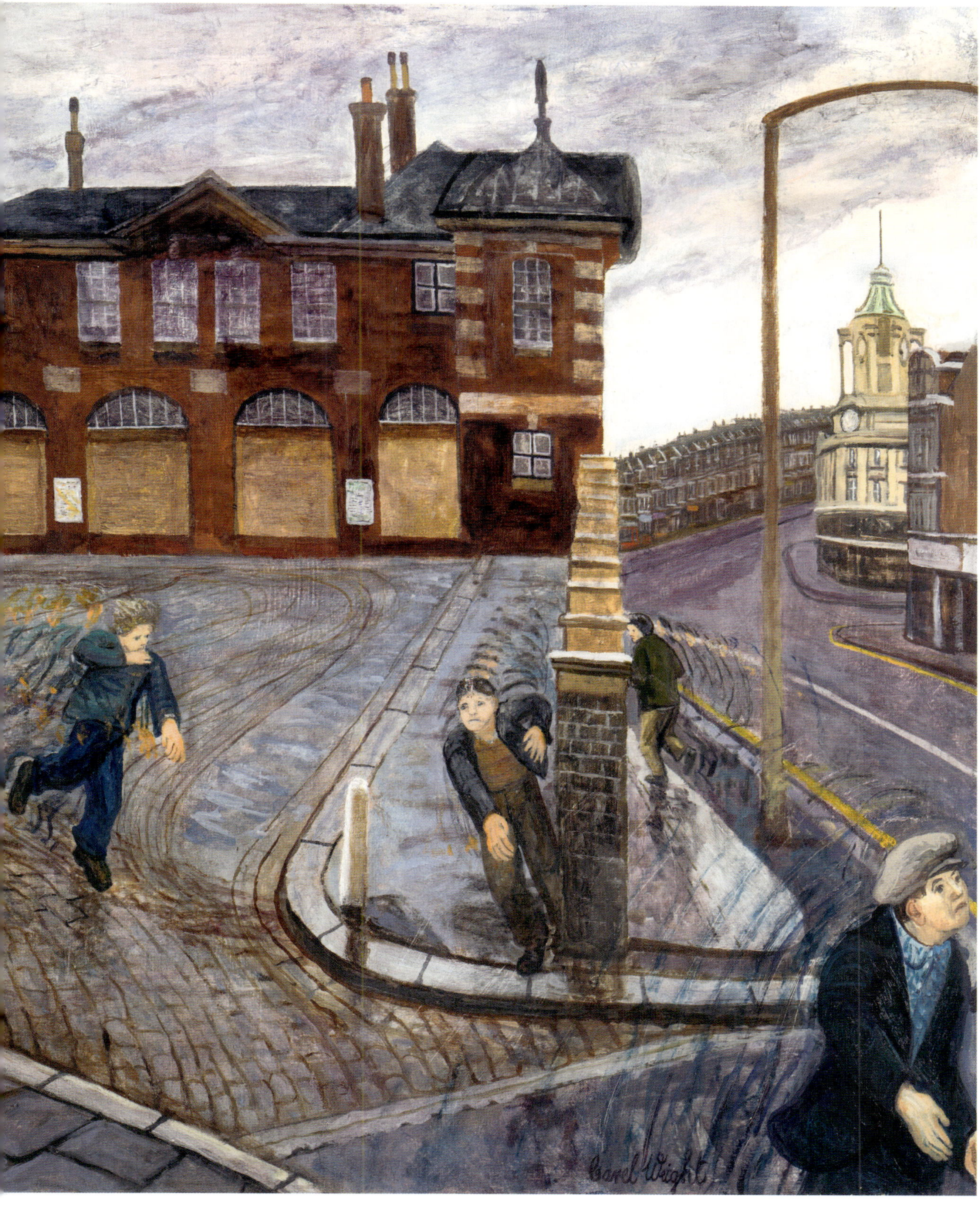

The Flower and Fruit Stalls, Embankment 1995

Leon Kossoff 1995

Leon Kossoff is one of the few artists to take on the challenge of depicting London's rush-hour crowds, his heavily-painted, imprecise style capturing the chaos and confusion. Here he shows the northerly entrance to Embankment station, on the north bank of the Thames close to Trafalgar Square. The York Watergate (shown on pp.162–3) is just out of view to the left. A flower seller – a London street stereotype – makes a modern appearance.

London is prominent in Kossoff's work, as it was in that of his friend Frank Auerbach (p.133). Transport infrastructure appears often – he has made paintings and prints of Kilburn underground station in north London as well as the tangle of lines going into Willesden Junction. This view is one of a series showing the different seasons. In it Kossoff beautifully depicts the hazy light of high summer, capturing the changes in light and emotion.

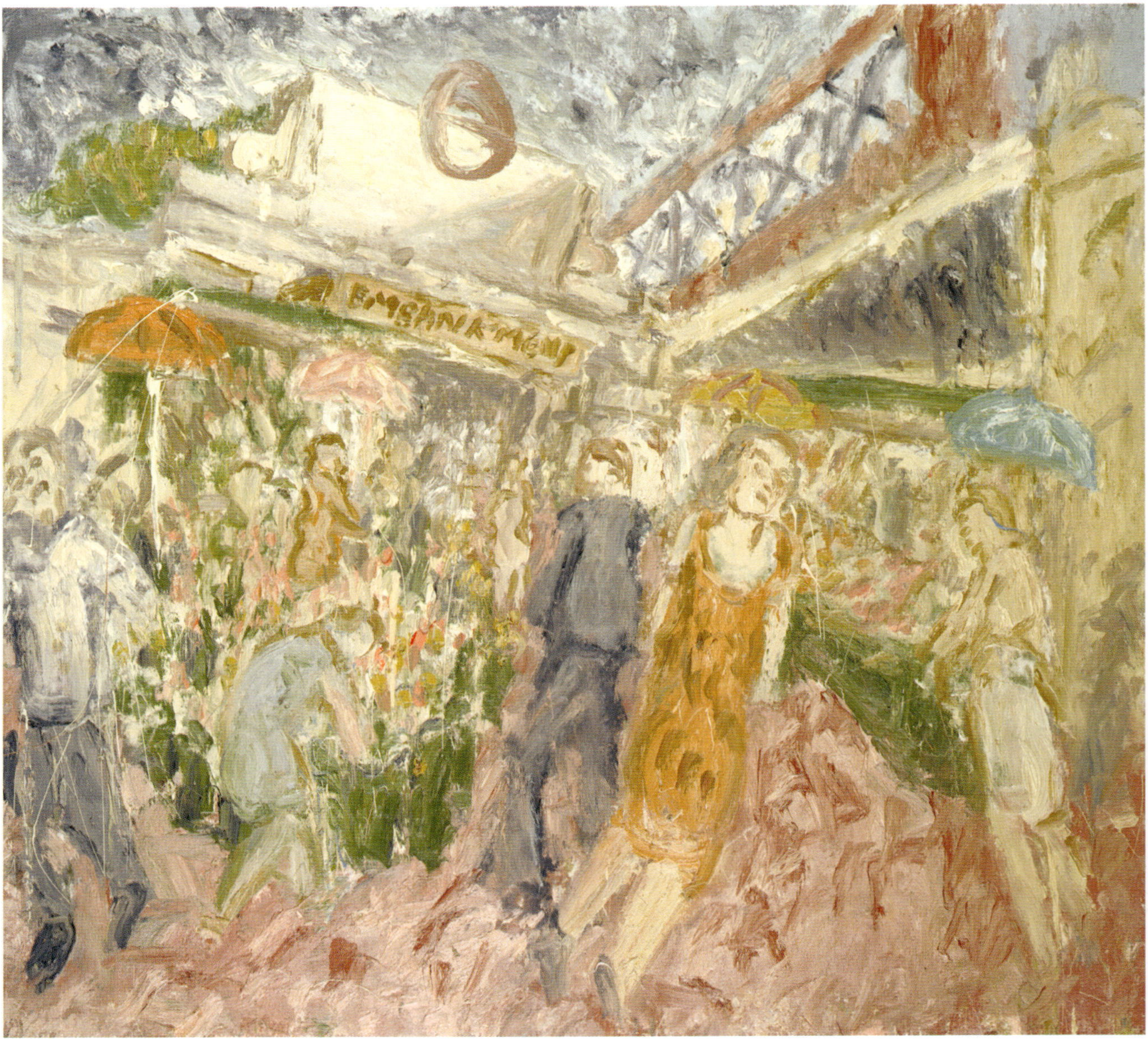

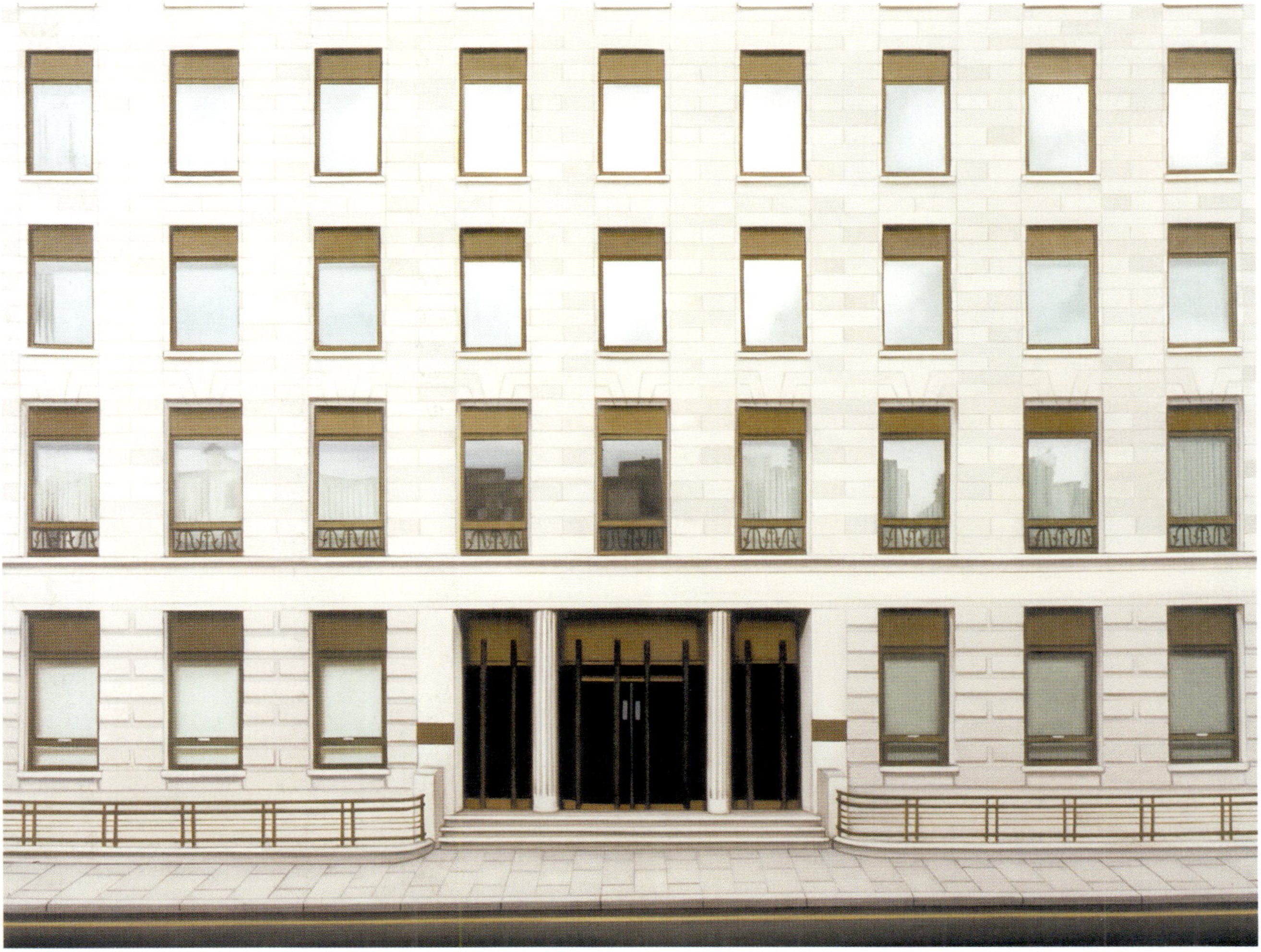

Finsbury Square

Lisa Milroy 1995

Canadian-born artist Lisa Milroy is best known for her paintings of everyday objects – shoes, plates, ribbons – arranged in grids. This fairly unextraordinary 1930s office block in the City of London offers the same pleasures of neatness, order and repetition. She depicts it coolly and objectively, allowing us to appreciate its minimal calmness. Its unpopulated blankness perhaps also reminds us of the corporate nature of many of the City's new buildings, where unknowable activities go on behind inscrutable facades. Interestingly, the building next to this, constructed after Milroy's painting, deliberately plays with the idea of repetition illustrated here, varying its window sizes to subtly break up and enliven its frontage.

Canary Wharf

Carl Laubin 1991

Carl Laubin trained as an architect and began his career making paintings of yet-to-be-realised buildings. He felt that the completion of what was then Europe's tallest building 'deserved the sort of commemorative treatment that was once common [for] great architectural and engineering projects.' However, he was also inspired by the paintings of ruined monuments by the Frenchman Hubert Robert (1733–1808), giving this work a slightly melancholic feel.

This painting shows the tower from the platform of Westferry DLR station. It is surrounded by cranes and tinged blue by protective plastic sheeting at the top. The tower – officially called One Canada Square – stood alone and was not fully used for over a decade. Once seen to be a failure, the arrival of the Jubilee underground line in 1999 re-enlivened the Canary Wharf scheme. There are now more than a dozen skyscrapers, with many more planned.

Laubin now specialises in grand architectural capriccios, combining dozens of famous buildings into one fantastical view.

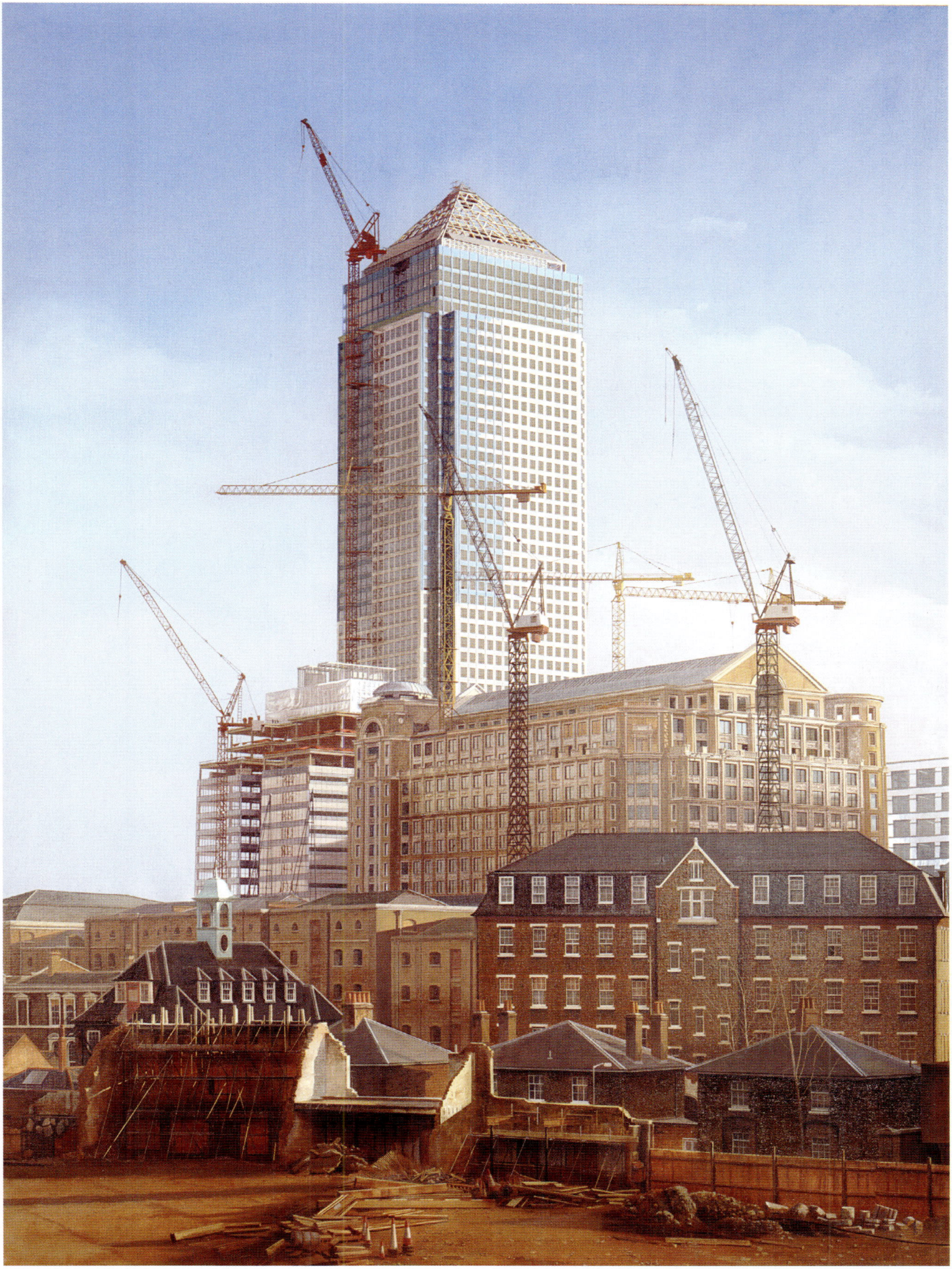

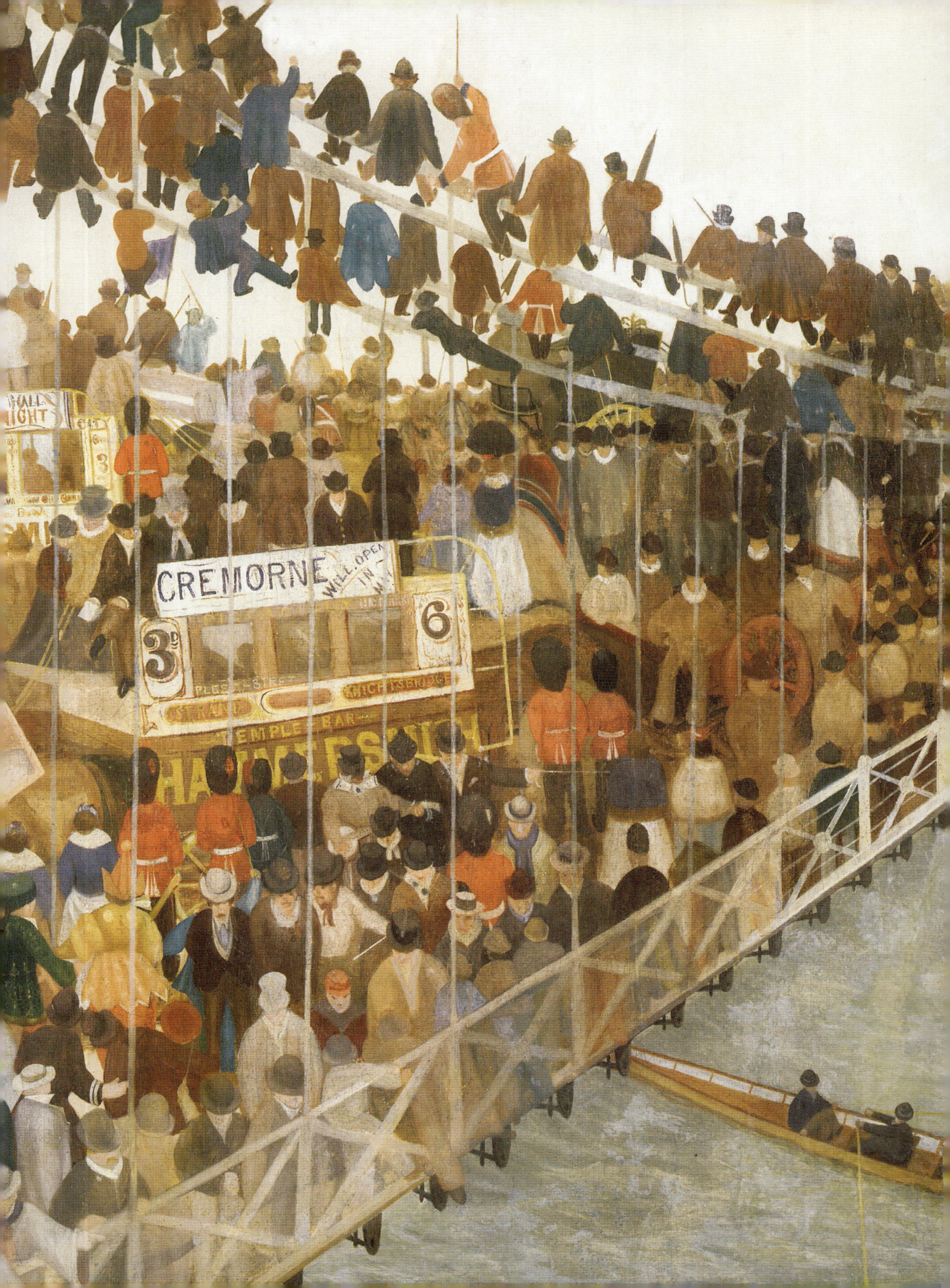
CREMORNE
3d
6
KNIGHTSBRIDGE
STRAND
TEMPLE BAR

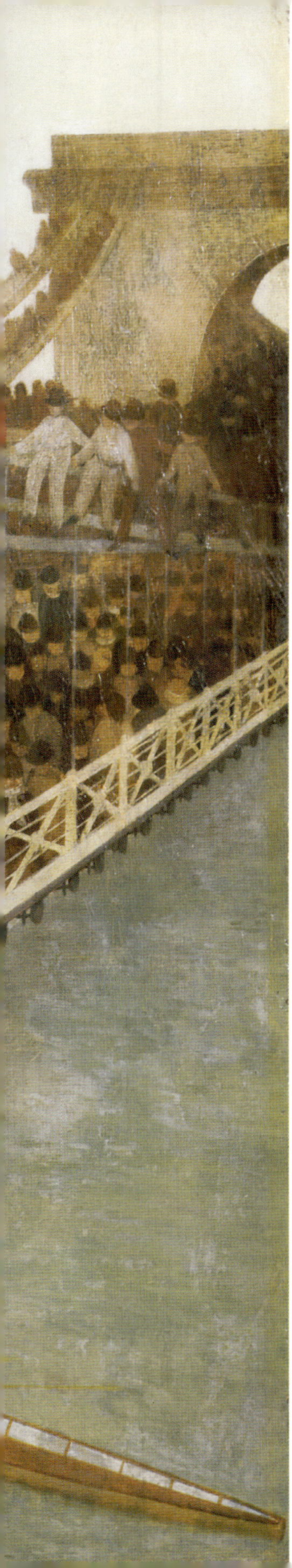

4
THE PLEASURES OF THE METROPOLIS

You feel that the air is heavy with fate, with decisive moments; here Destiny has tightened her web, chosen the halting place of lives. The people confront one another at the little tables; they lean forward, confidentially, bent upon the 'momentary momentousness' of their affairs; and the observer is impressed by beauty, as she laughs, defiant, in the clutch of the effete.

Beatrix Terry, 'As Others See Us', *Art News*, 15 July 1911, p.75

THIS WAS AN ART CRITIC'S REVIEW of a painting of the Café Royal by Charles Ginner (p.103 shows a rival view of the same scene by William Orpen). At the time, this infamous French restaurant and nightspot at the Piccadilly Circus end of Regent Street was the social and intellectual centre of London's art world. On a night there you might see Oscar Wilde (1854–1900), Aubrey Beardsley (1872–98), James Abbott McNeill Whistler (1834–1903), Walter Sickert (1860–1942) or Jacob Epstein (1880–1959).

While artists in the eighteenth and nineteenth centuries had been trying to ape the social graces of their clientele, from the late nineteenth century artists began to gain the hard-drinking, bohemian reputation that persisted to the Young British Artists of the 1990s. With the development of the transport network, there was no longer any need to live cheek by jowl with their patrons or each other. People found common places to meet and socialise – Soho, for example, was synonymous with the art world in the 1950s, despite few artists living there.

Many paintings capture the city's diverse entertainments, whether as mementoes of the artist's social circle or as almost sociological explorations of what makes its inhabitants tick. This chapter regretfully omits the many atmospheric paintings of London pub scenes, simply because the locations are hard to identify. But it does include many other places of entertainment depicted in paint: Sickert's beloved music hall (p.107), or Weight's nostalgic memory of a night at the dogs (pp.112–13).

The nineteenth century also saw the growth of the city's tourist industry, kicked off in earnest by the Great Exhibition of 1851 (p.90). Today, London is the most visited city on earth, drawing millions to its endless sights and entertainments. It has more theatres, more museums, more sports stadia than anywhere else. Unsurprisingly, artists have also been drawn to these attractions, looking at people in the act of looking.

Walter Greaves *Hammersmith Bridge on Boat-race Day* c.1862 (detail). See pp.94–5

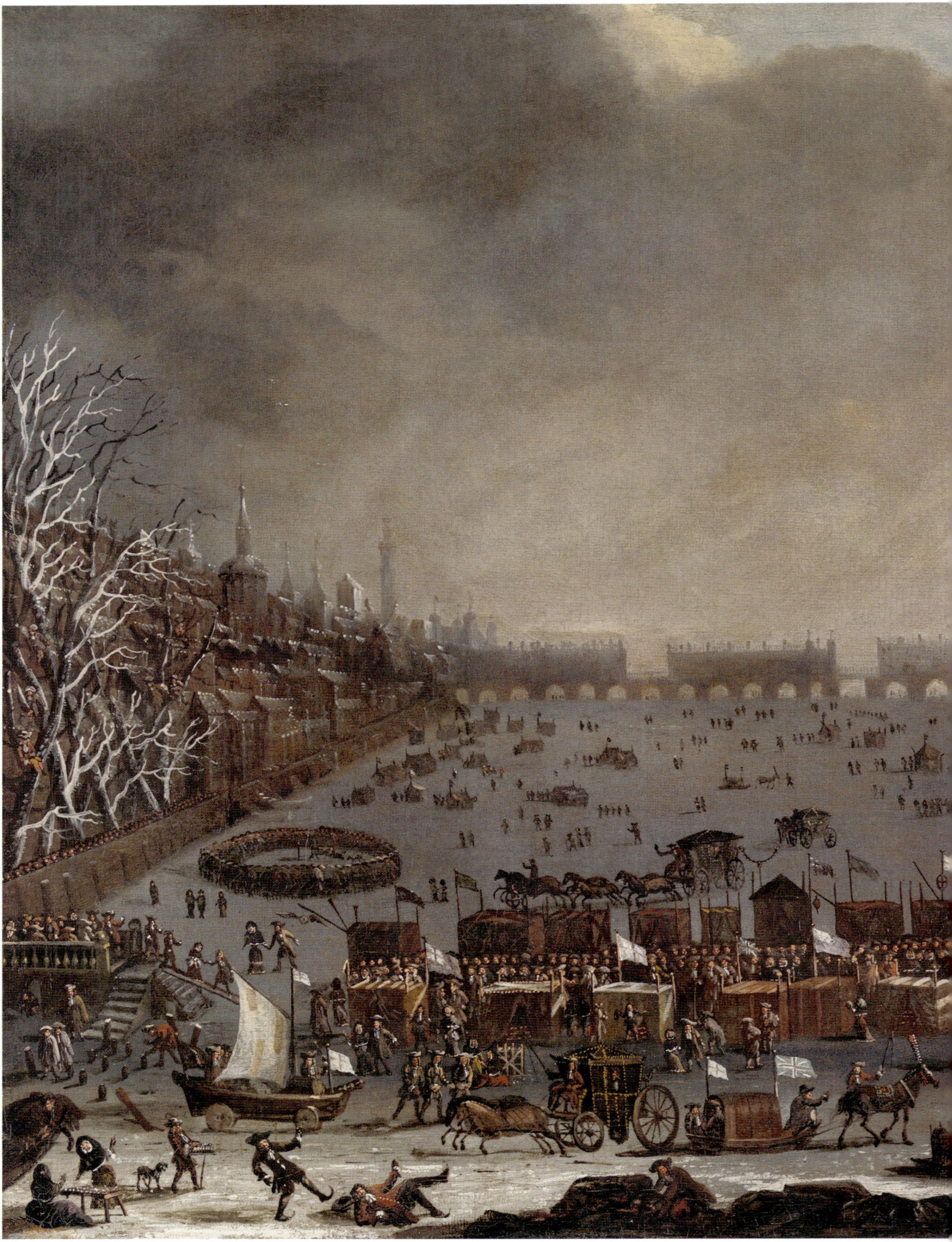

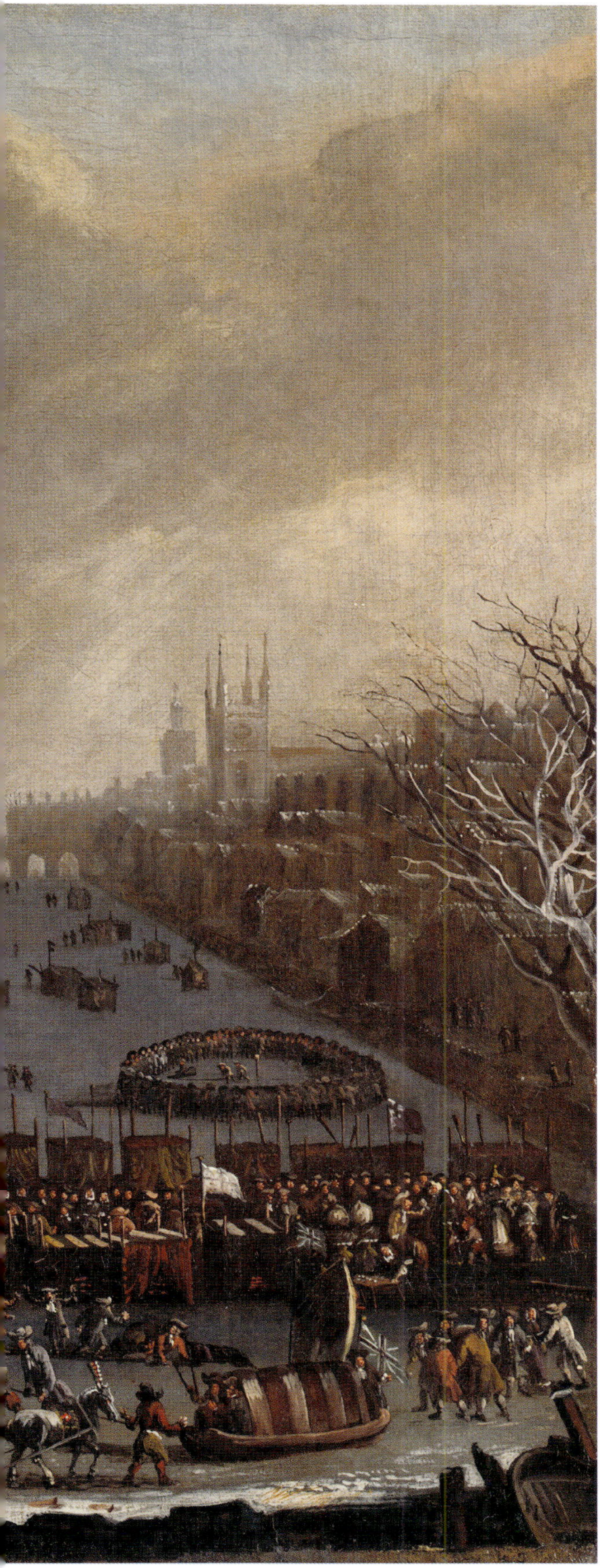

Frost Fair on the Thames, with Old London Bridge in the Distance

Unknown artist c.1685

This picture records the longest and deepest of the Great Frosts that turned the River Thames into solid ice, and the great party that was held on it. Between 1408 and 1814, the Thames froze over twenty-six times – the result of the Little Ice Age and the narrow piers of old London Bridge slowing down the water. Londoners would rush to hold Frost Fairs, often only lasting a couple of days. But the winter of 1683–4 was the worst ever recorded in England, and the Thames remained frozen for two whole months, from December to February.

Diarist John Evelyn wrote: 'Coaches plied from Westminster to the Temple, and from several other stairs to and fro, as in the streets; sleds, sliding with skeetes, a bull-baiting, horse and coach races, puppet plays and interludes, cooks, tipling and other lewd places, so that it seemed to be a bacchanalian triumph, or carnival on the water.'

In the foreground you can see the eccentric forms of transport available, including a coach and horses and a sailboat on wheels. Crowds watch on from the north bank, on the left, and gingerly step onto the ice. The row of shops and food stalls in the centre included a printer, where you could get a card with your name 'printed on the Thames'.

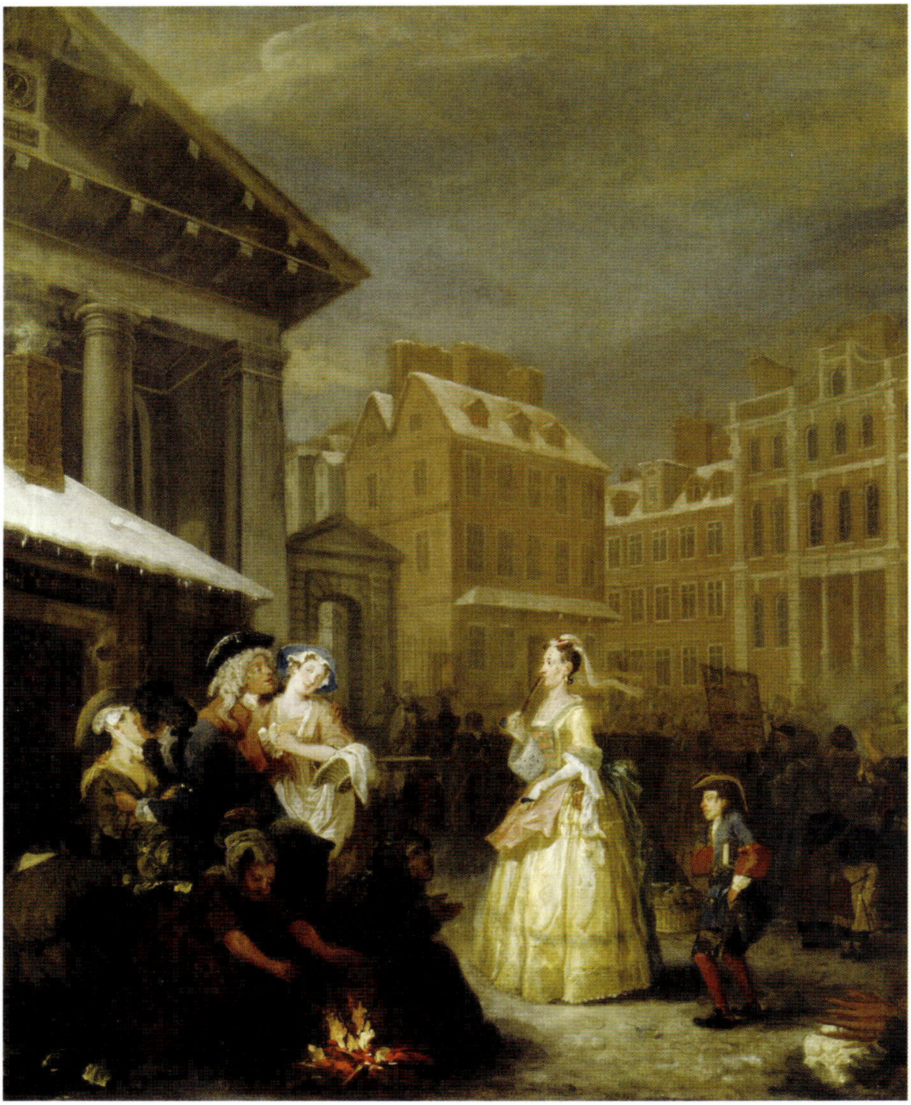

The Four Times of Day: Morning

William Hogarth 1736

At the same time that Canaletto was setting down a minutely observed yet idealised view of the London landscape, one of the city's greatest native painters was popularising his rambunctious take on its street life. Hogarth was not interested in topography but he had an eye for the characters of London's streets. His most famous works, such as *Beer Street* and *Gin Lane* (both 1751) convey a rich sense of London without pinning themselves down as portraits of any specific place.

This scene is an exception – a prudish spinster makes her way to an early morning service at St Paul's church in Covent Garden, trying not to look at the lewd revellers still up from the night before. The painting shows how the dignified piazzas were already becoming known as a place for debauchery. Hogarth had lodged in Covent Garden for a few years with his mentor and father-in-law, Sir James Thornhill. But the rich and fashionable were beginning to depart and Hogarth himself soon moved to the then-upmarket Leicester Square, where he lived until his death.

Punch or May Day

Benjamin Robert Haydon 1829

Two folk traditions come together in this bawdy work. To the left, a crowd watch a Punch and Judy show, performed in the now familiar way with glove puppets in a street booth. An older gentleman, absorbed in the entertainment, is having his pocket picked. To the right, a May Day procession comes through, led by the Jack-in-the-Green – a man, usually a chimney sweep, dressed as a tree. The location is outside Madame Tussauds, looking east to St Marylebone Parish Church.

Haydon himself didn't share the joyous spirit of this work – he was determined to become a serious history painter to rival the Old Masters. He declared himself 'adapted to great national work, to illustrate a national triumph or a moral principle'; however, his attempts to do so drove him to bankruptcy. Haydon had more success with burlesque scenes like this painting, but when even these works failed to sell, he fell into a long fit of paranoia.

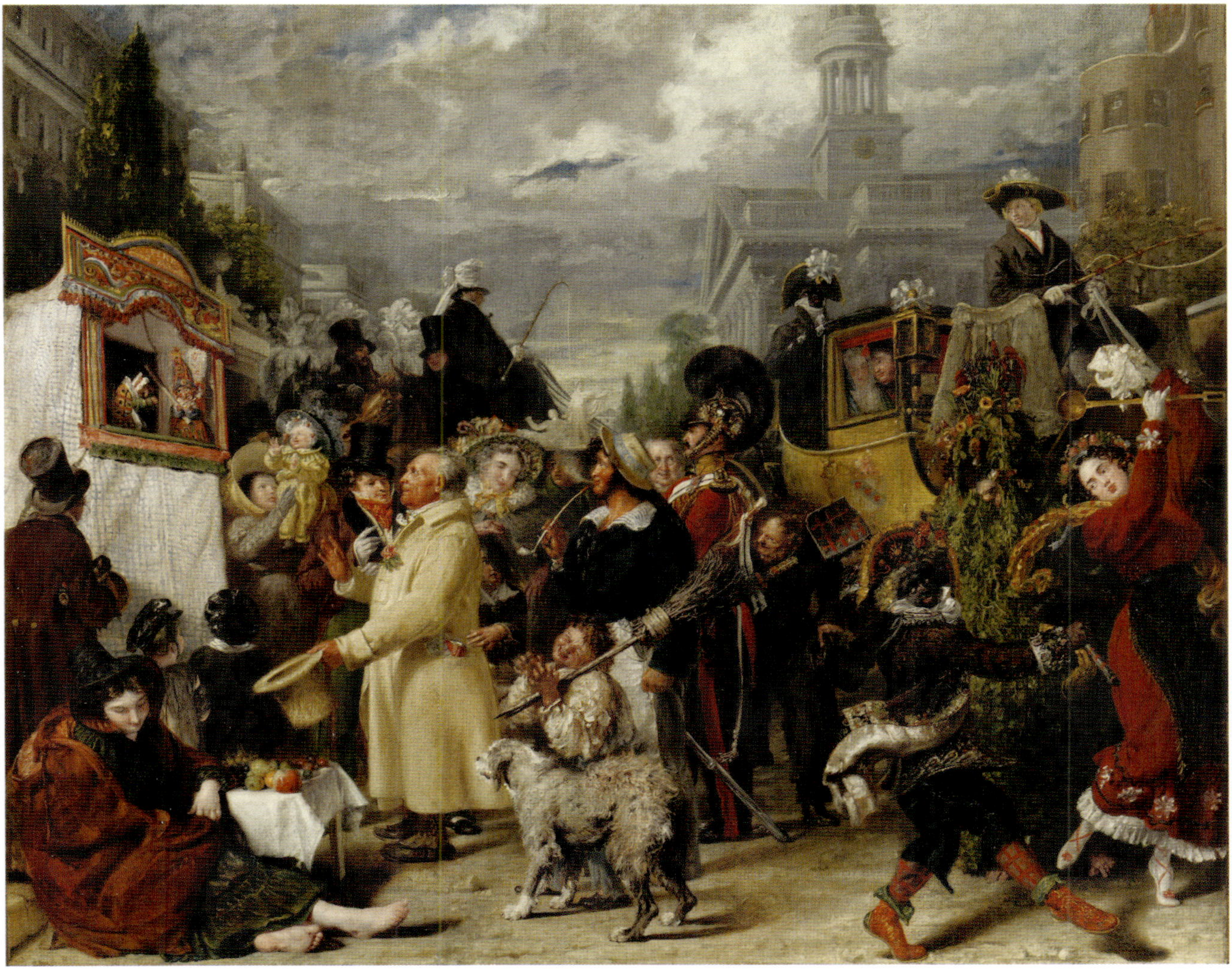

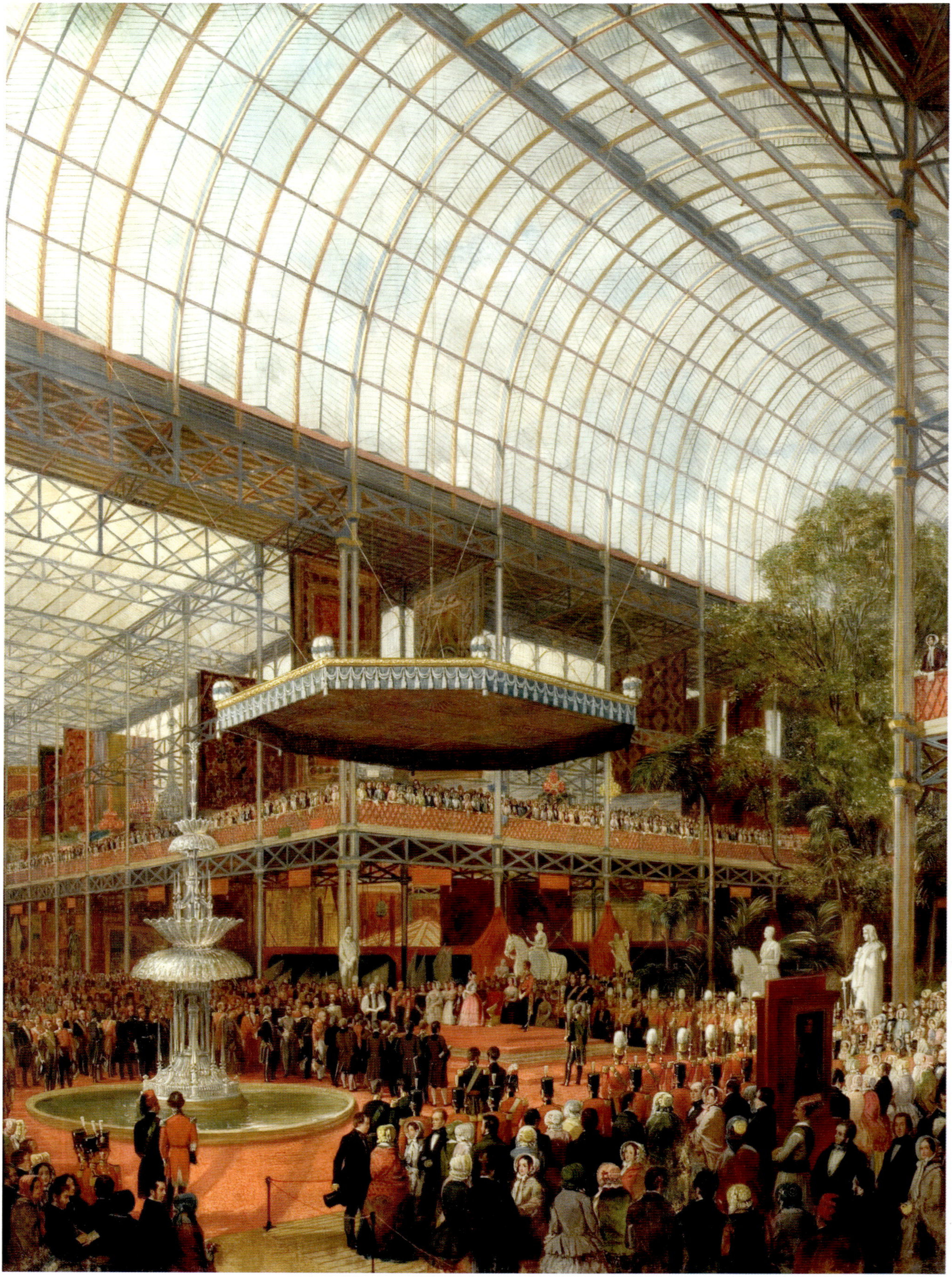

The Opening Ceremony of the Great Exhibition, London

James Digman Wingfield 1851

Constructed for the Great Exhibition of 1851, the scale and ambition of the Crystal Palace is awesome even today. The structure was over half a kilometre long, and the vaulted transept shown here was 30 metres high, easily accommodating three huge elm trees growing on the site in Hyde Park. By far the largest iron and glass building ever conceived at that time, it was designed and constructed in just eight months.

This painting shows Queen Victoria (r.1837–1901) opening the exhibition on 1 May 1851, flanked of course by the project's mastermind, her husband Prince Albert. Over six million people visited during the course of six months – the profits from ticket sales went towards building London's Royal Albert Hall, the Natural History Museum, the Victoria and Albert Museum and others. Many visitors had never been to London before and the event kick-started the capital's tourist industry. The Albert Memorial, which now stands near the site, shows the prince holding the exhibition's mammoth catalogue.

Wingfield was a successful painter of the early nineteenth century, known for his history paintings. He also painted a series of interesting London interiors, including Hampton Court and the Bank of England.

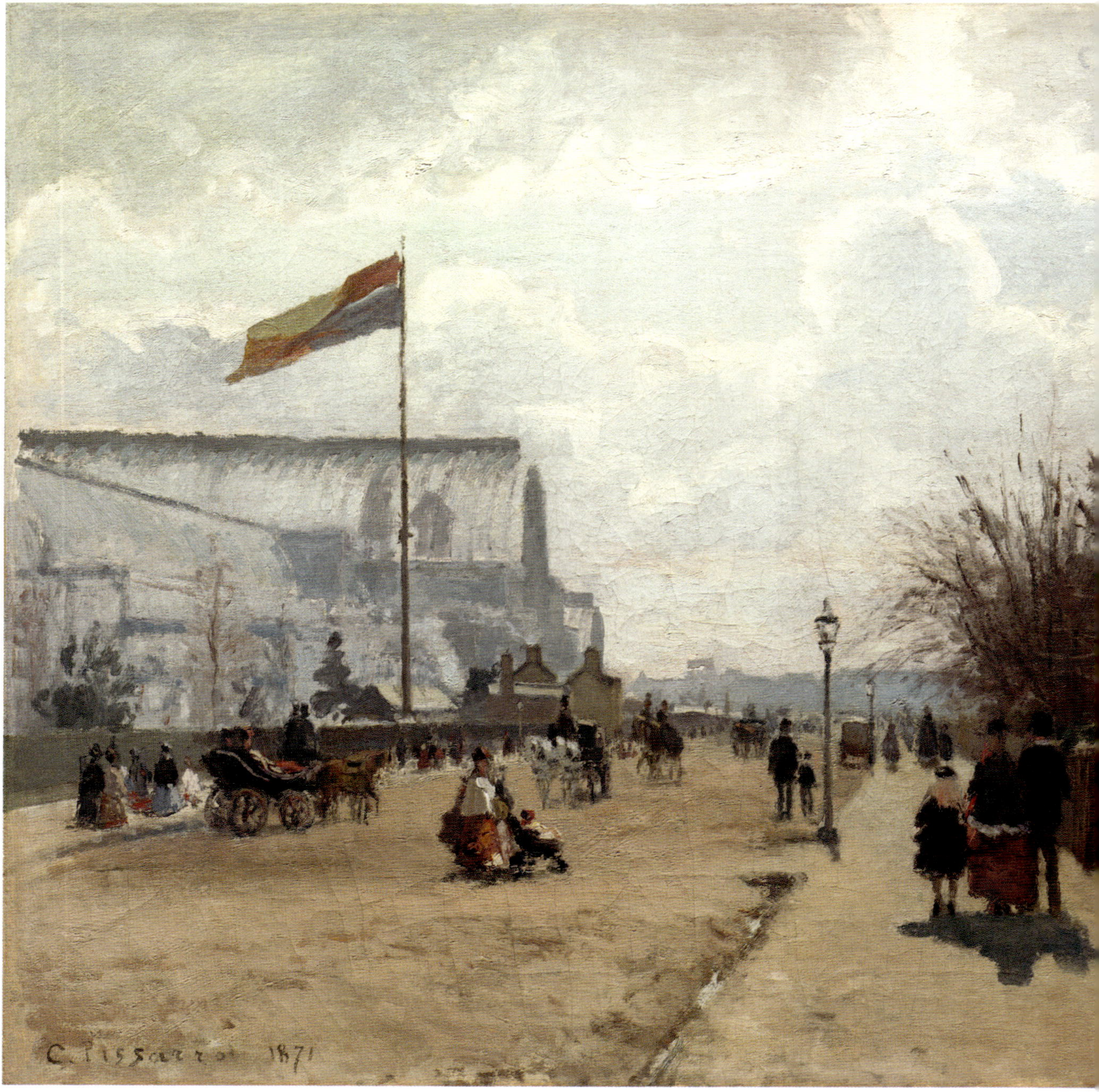

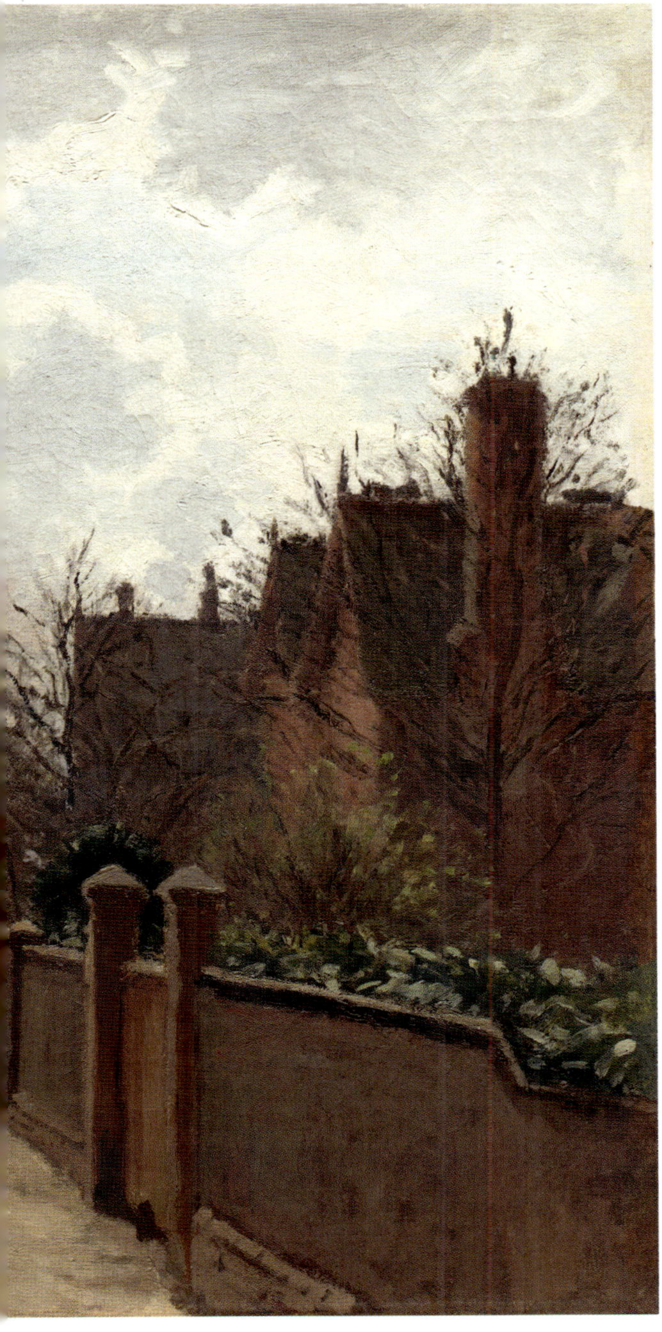

The Crystal Palace, London

Camille Pissarro 1871

Here is the Crystal Palace reconstructed in the south-eastern suburb to which it gave its name.

Camille Pissarro was one of the painters who fled to London to avoid the Franco-Prussian war of 1870. He stayed in Norwood and painted twelve scenes of the area, at that time just beginning to be urbanised. Although he shows some interest in the modern world – such as in the well-known painting of a train pulling out of Lordship Lane station (National Gallery, London) – most of his works have a tranquil, semi-rural feeling to them. The Palace looks incongruous in this otherwise conventional street scene, its ghostly mass picked out in economical strokes of dark blue paint.

Despite Pissarro's interest in British landscape painters such as J.M.W. Turner and John Constable, the British didn't much care for his proto-impressionist works. (Nor did the French or German soldiers who damaged or destroyed hundreds of paintings he had left behind.) Pissarro returned to London in the 1890s, painting better-known spots of central and west London.

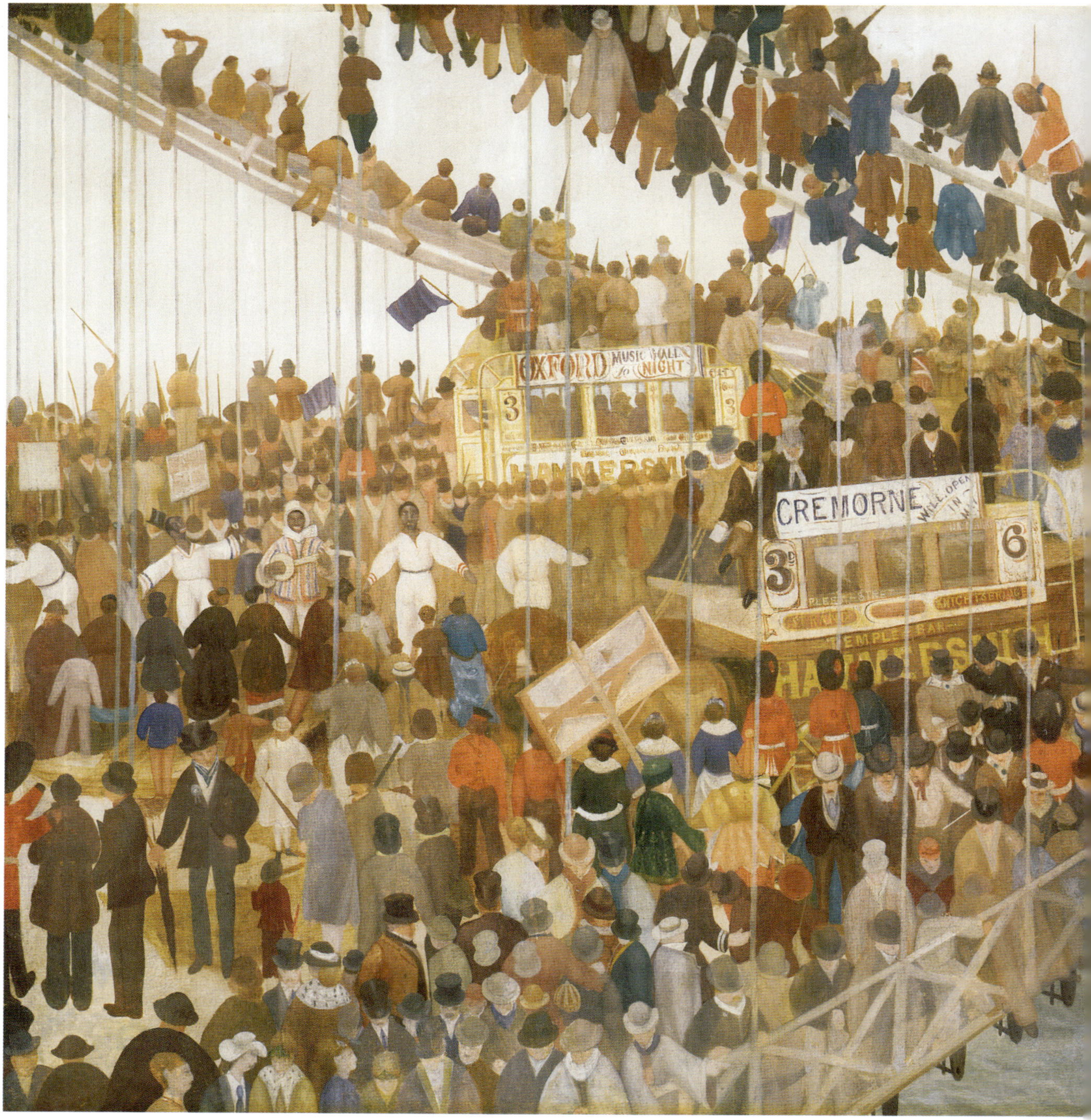
OXFORD
MUSIC HALL
NIGHT
CREMORNE
3d
6

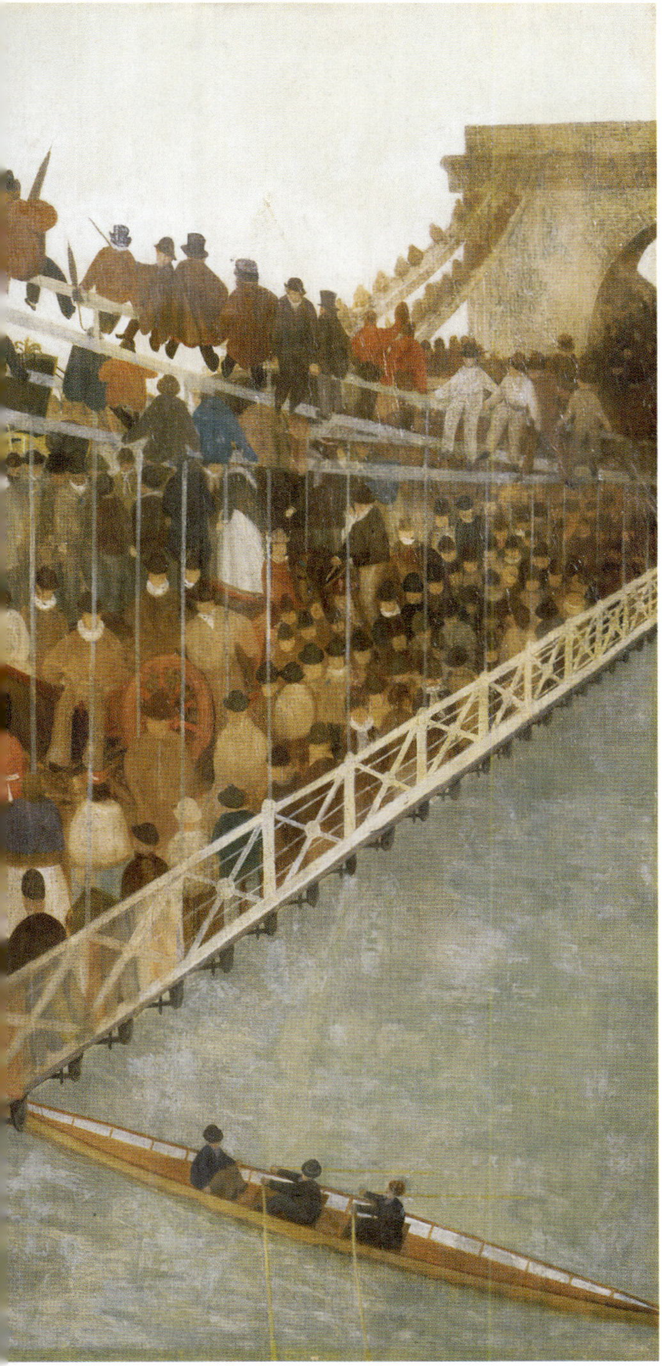

Hammersmith Bridge on Boat-race Day

Walter Greaves c.1862

Charles William Greaves was a Chelsea boat-builder who rowed J.M.W. Turner across the River Thames. His two sons, Walter and Henry, later took up painting and etching and befriended James Abbott McNeill Whistler when he came to live nearby in the 1860s. Walter claims he painted this work at the age of sixteen, before he met Whistler, and the naïve, untutored style certainly doesn't suggest the heavy influence of the older artist.

In this painting Greaves captures all the colour and excitement of the annual Oxford-Cambridge boat race. People crane for a view as a boat passes beneath (not one of the actual competitors as there are only two rowers), and even climb dangerously on to the chains that hold up the suspension bridge. This detail might not have been invented – for the 1870 race around 12,000 people crowded on to the bridge, greatly exceeding its capacity. The worried authorities pulled down the original bridge and rebuilt a stronger structure in 1887.

Wapping

James Abbott McNeill Whistler 1860–4

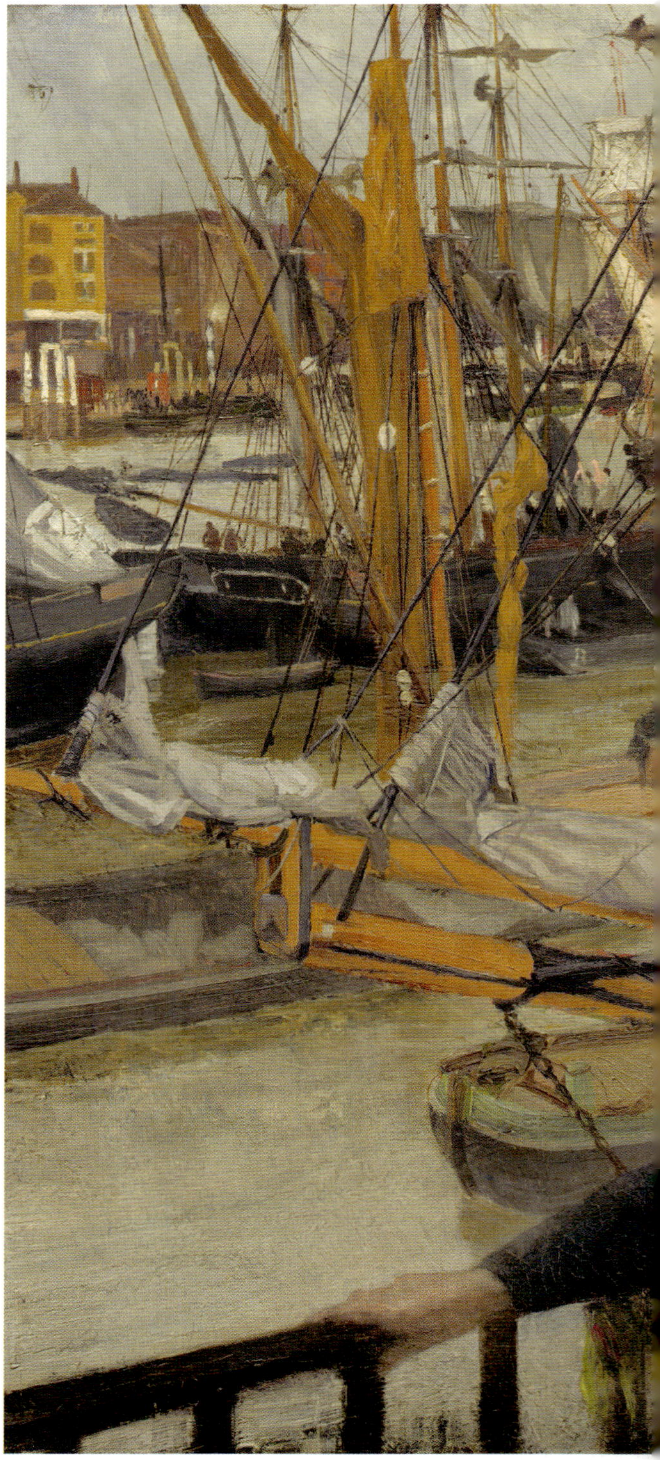

The writer George du Maurier wrote to his mother about his friend Whistler: 'He is working hard and in secret down in Rotherhithe, among a beastly set of cads and every possible annoyance and misery, doing one of the greatest chef d'oeuvres – no difficulty discourages him.' This painting was the work absorbing such toil. Whistler was in his mid twenties and had recently moved to London. He spent much of 1859 working on his career-making series of etchings of the wharves, warehouses, ships and inhabitants of the Lower Pool: a visual tangle of masts, lines, sails, ladders and crumbing brickwork.

As his friend hints, these were rough, working districts, not often frequented by artists – particularly not American-born, French-educated dandies like Whistler. He was determined that his work on this large, ambitious painting was kept secret from his acquaintance Gustave Courbet (1819–77), perhaps because he was trying to emulate the Frenchman's unsentimental depictions of the working man. Here, Whistler refuses to pander to the English taste for narrative – it's impossible to read into the conversation between the three seated figures. He struggled with the woman's head, repainting it three times. The model later became his long-term mistress.

The location is usually cited as the balcony of the Angel pub in Rotherhithe, although there are some slight inaccuracies which might be explained by his obsessive reworking. The pub was restored in the 2000s and offers one of the best views in the city, upriver to Tower Bridge. It might also be the place from which J.M.W. Turner painted his famous *The Fighting Temeraire* 1839.

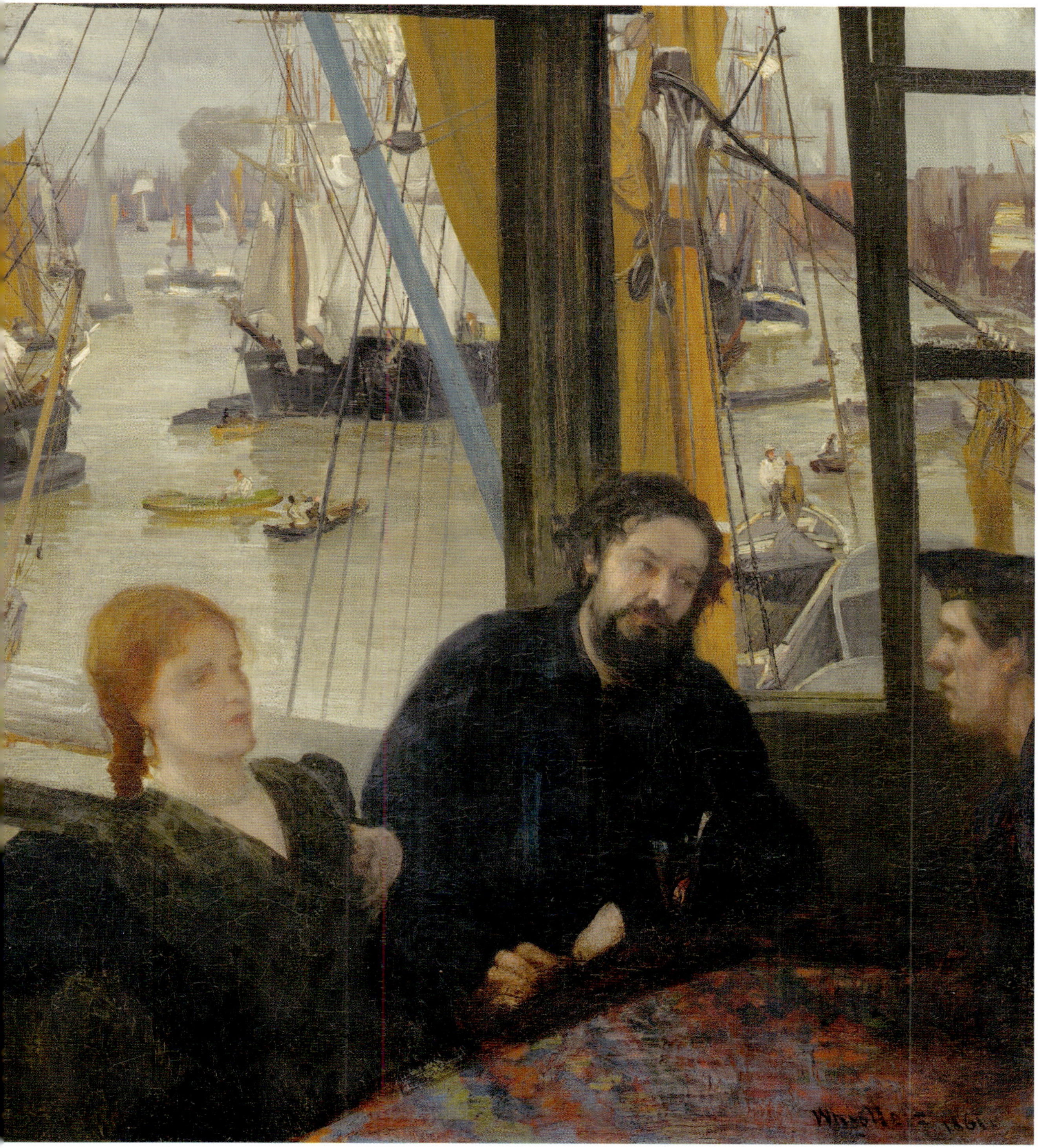

Cremorne Gardens, No 2

James Abbott McNeill Whistler c.1870–80

Cremorne was a popular pleasure garden in the mid nineteenth century, stretching from the River Thames near Chelsea to the King's Road. It was just across the river from the similar but more upmarket Vauxhall. Within the well-laid-out gardens were all kinds of entertainments: music played continuously from the bandstand, there were theatres, a hermit's cave, places to eat and drink, a weekly fireworks display and regular flights in a tethered balloon. People from all layers of society visited during the day, but as the night drew in it became the haunt of drunks and prostitutes. Locals complained about the rowdiness and the gardens closed in 1877.

Whistler lived a short stroll away on Cheyne Walk. He was a regular visitor and painted it several times. This view captures the seedy excitement– the brightly dressed figures are almost ghostlike as they loom out of the twilight. Cremorne was also the site of Whistler's controversial painting *Nocturne in Black and Gold – The Falling Rocket* c.1875, which sparked an infamous libel trial when it was criticised by John Ruskin (1819–1900).

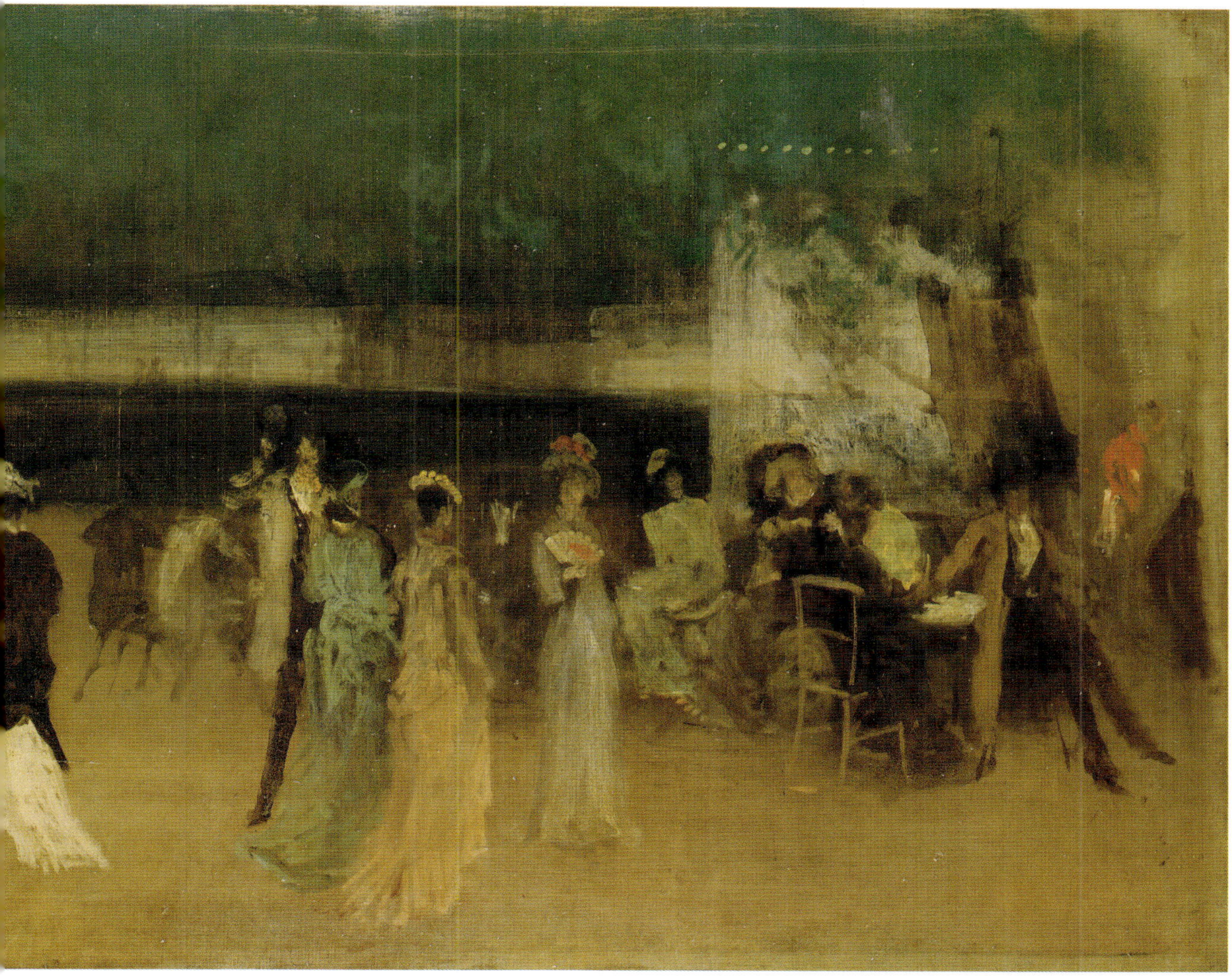

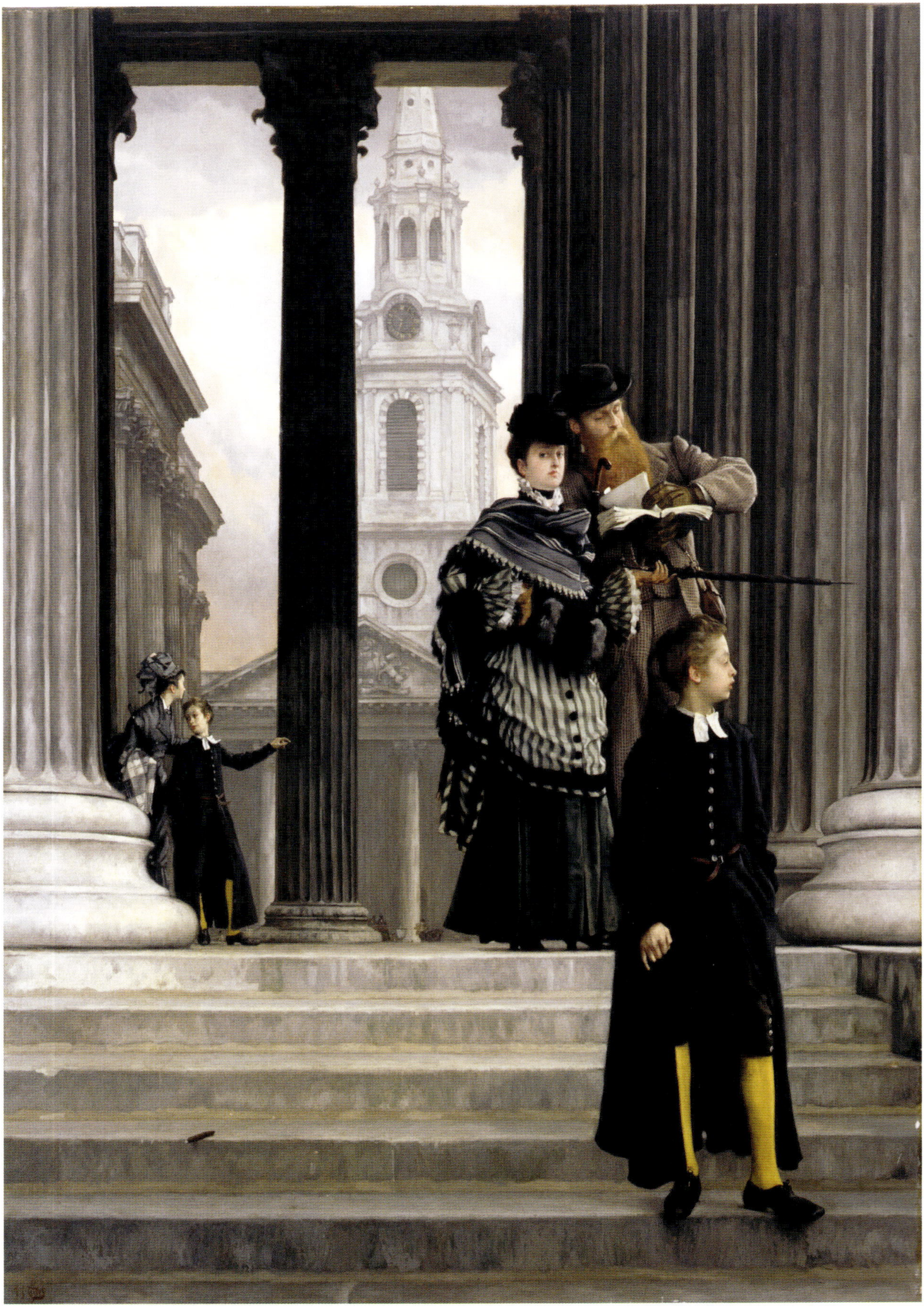

London Visitors

James Tissot c.1874

The view from the porch of the National Gallery is one of the most perfect in the city and a prime sightseeing spot. From here one can take in all manner of landmarks, many fairly new at the time of this painting, including Trafalgar Square, Nelson's Column and the clock tower of the Palace of Westminster.

Unusually, Tissot doesn't show any of this; instead he makes us look at the sightseers themselves. But even they are not experiencing the view – the gentleman is engrossed in his guidebook, while the woman – in contravention of Victorian propriety – stares directly at us. Her look has been interpreted as sexual – is she giving us the come on while her husband fusses with his book? Or is she contemptuously pointing us to the spectacle beyond? She certainly doesn't look very interested in it. The two boys with yellow stockings were pupils at Christ's Hospital school, based in Newgate Street (see John Piper's painting of the bombed-out church, p.46). They earned pocket money by working as tour guides.

This undercurrent of social tension is typical for Tissot, although his work was often dismissed as shallow portraits of upper-class elegance. He was certainly popular with rich and fashionable Londoners – he moved to England after the Franco-Prussian war (1870–1) and was soon making a fortune for commissions. Like his friends the Impressionists, he was interested in the modern city, but never adopted their looser style.

British Museum, Winter

Vilhelm Hammershøi 1906

Like Monet, the Danish painter Hammershøi loved the foggy, smoky air of early twentieth-century London. It suited the muted, almost monochromatic palette he liked to use, and allowed him to imbue this cityscape with the same enigmatic qualities as his better-known interiors. Here, the British Museum glowers in the semi-darkness, with no sign of the six million annual visitors who make it one of the most-visited tourist attractions in the world. It is painted, along with another from a slightly different angle, from the window of Hammershøi's lodgings on Great Russell Street.

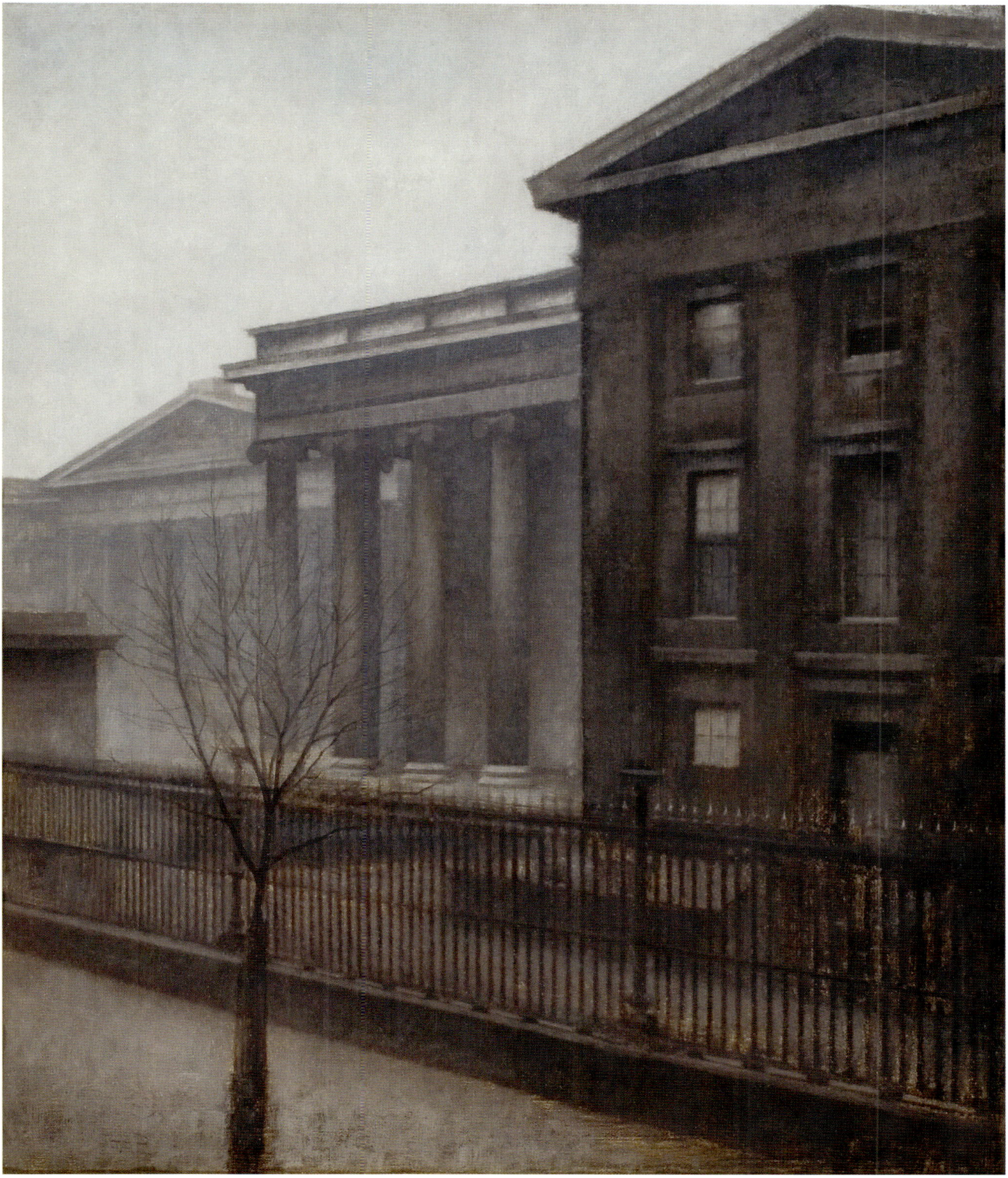

The Café Royal, London

William Orpen 1912

This work by the Irish painter William Orpen captures the bohemian atmosphere and scintillating conversation for which the Café Royal was renowned. The figures in the foreground are probably his artist friends James Pryde (1866–1941) and Augustus John (1878–1961). Around the time of this painting, according to the drama critic Ashley Dukes (1885–1959), 'painters of the general Chelsea or Camden Town Group sat in the part nearest Regent Street, and the circle of T.E. Hulme and the Vorticists sat at the back'. The Café Royal was converted into a hotel in 2008, although the heavily gilded and mirrored dining room that makes this painting such a complex wonder of reflections and lighting effects has been preserved.

At the time of the painting's creation, Orpen was a sought-after portraitist of high society and one of the most famous and financially successful artists working in Britain. The carefree pleasures shown here were brought to an end by the First World War and Orpen then served as a war artist, painting the Western Front in grim detail. His relationships with some of his friends broke down in the following years, and Augustus John publicly criticised Orpen's work and character after his early death in 1931.

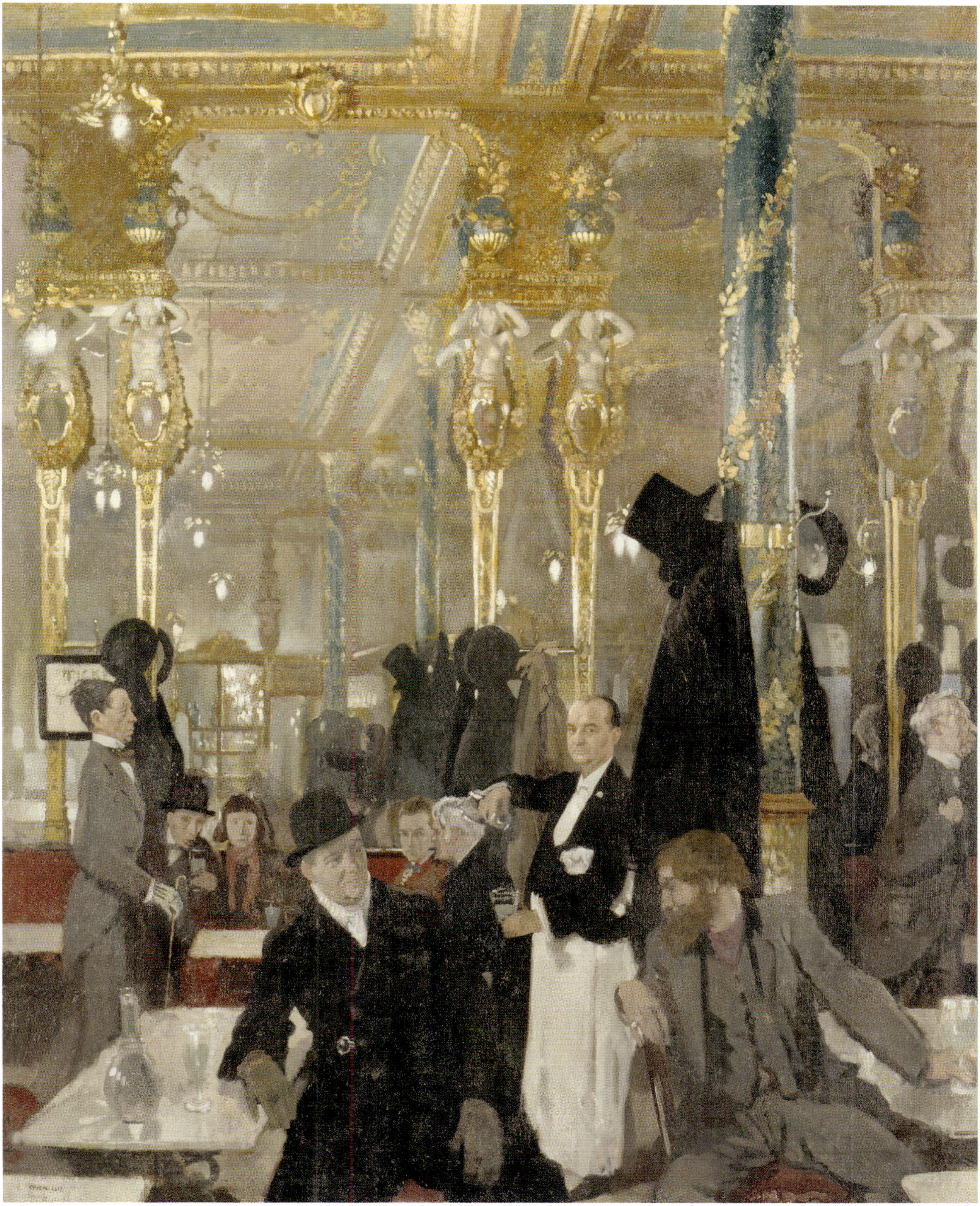

A Wet Night at Piccadilly Circus

Arthur Hacker 1910

Arthur Hacker spent most of his career as a classicist and portrait painter but in 1910, having been elected a Royal Academician, he painted four Whistlerian views of the area around Leicester Square at night. He might have been inspired by the new electric lighting that was setting the West End ablaze. In 1908–10 the first illuminated signs were set up in Piccadilly Circus, and by the 1920s the familiar wall of flashing advertisements was in place.

Hacker doesn't illustrate any of these early billboards here, but plays with the atmospheric effects of the brilliant electric lights (and street gaslights) through a haze of rain. The Eros statue is just to our right, and the grandiloquent Belle Epoque building right in front of us is the London Pavilion, a music hall that set new standards for luxury when it opened in 1885. It is now occupied by another popular attraction, Ripley's Believe it or Not – a museum celebrating the weird and the wonderful.

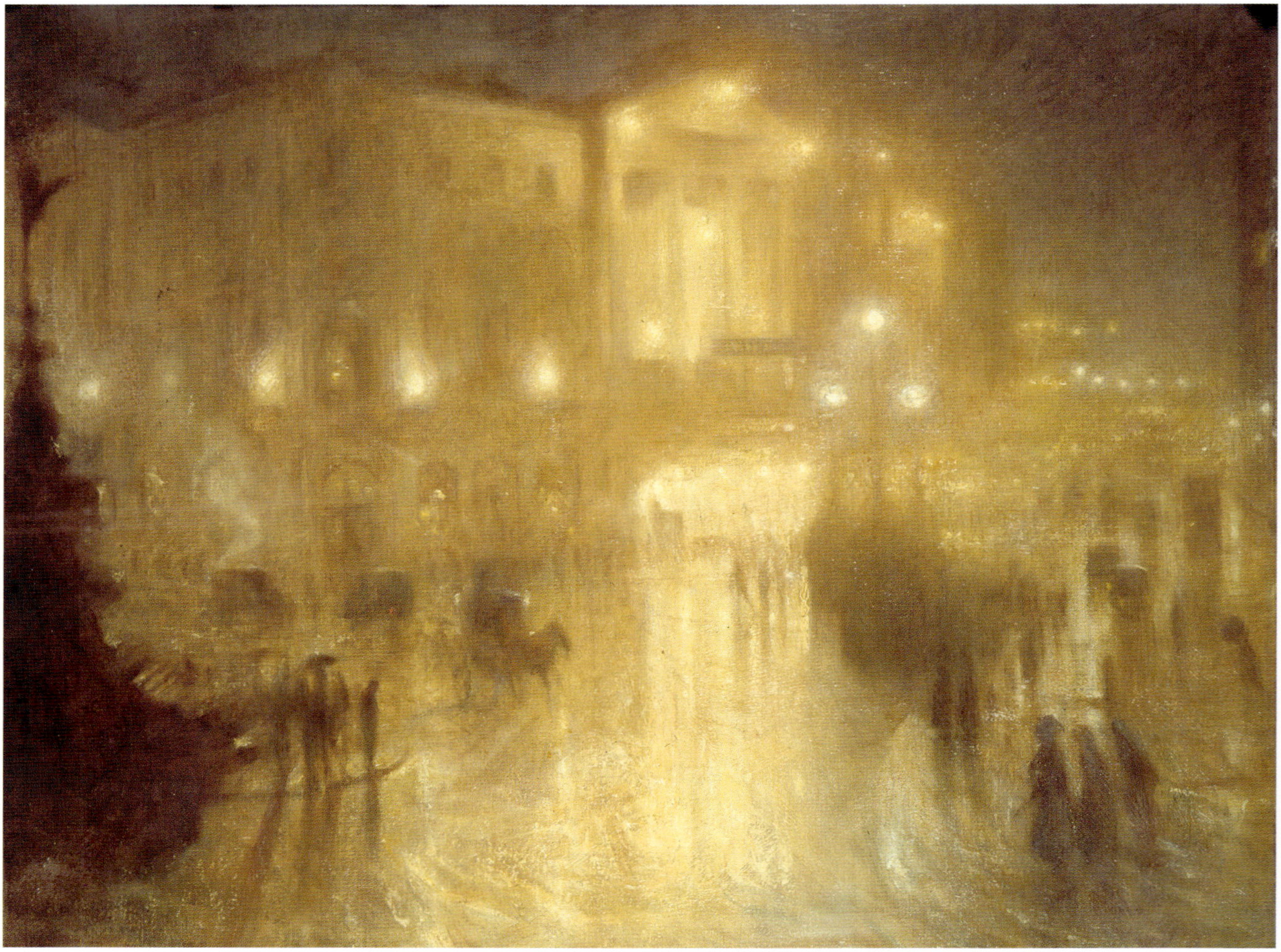

The New Bedford

Walter Sickert c.1914–5

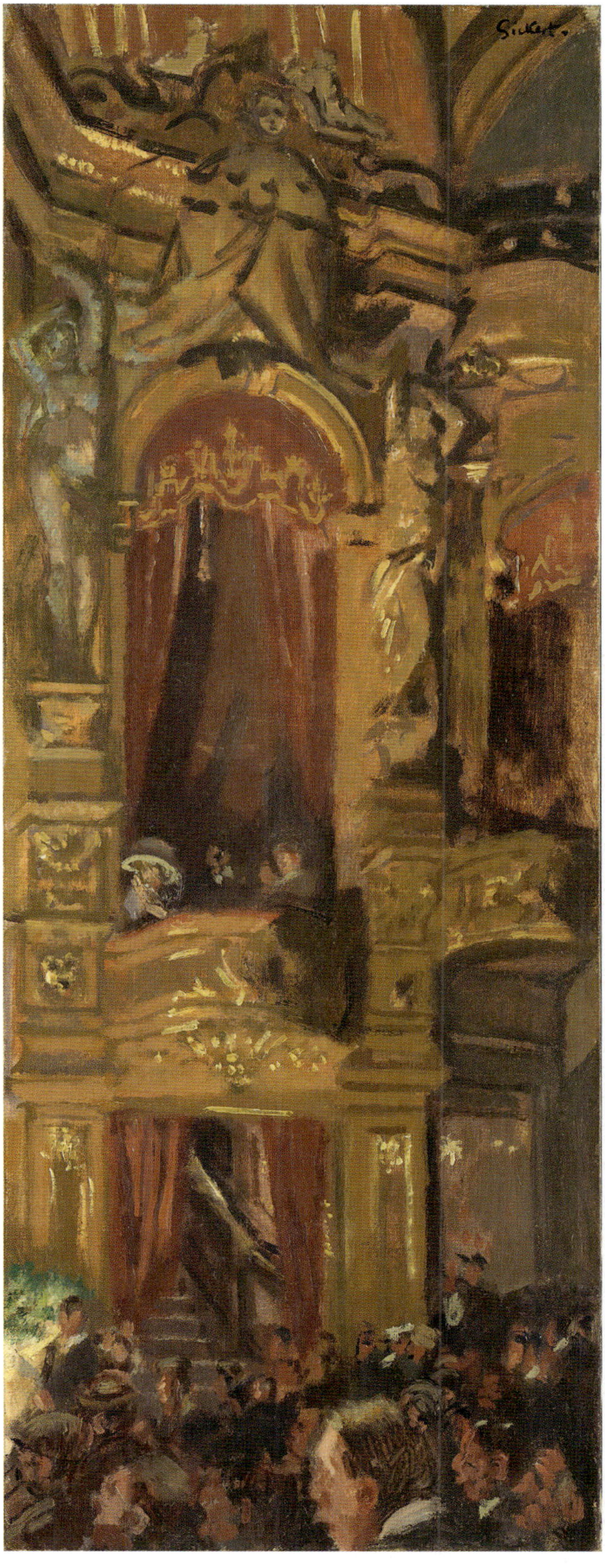

The Bedford music hall in Camden was a favourite haunt of Walter Sickert and his friends in the Camden Town Group, attracted by the rowdy entertainment and working-class bonhomie. It was rebuilt in 1899, newly luxurious in a bid to attract the middle classes. Like the London Pavilion, it had electric lighting and lavish decoration, including the giant golden caryatids shown here flanking the box. Sickert painted music halls many times, sometimes picturing entertainers, such as the child star Little Dot Hetherington. Here he deliberately crops out the stage, allowing us to focus on the audience and architecture, the tall canvas giving a sense of its scale.

The story of the Bedford was typical of London music halls. By 1880, there were seventy-eight large music halls in London, and hundreds of smaller venues. But after the First World War they began to decline as new forms of entertainment became popular. The New Bedford was converted into a cinema, then demolished in 1959.

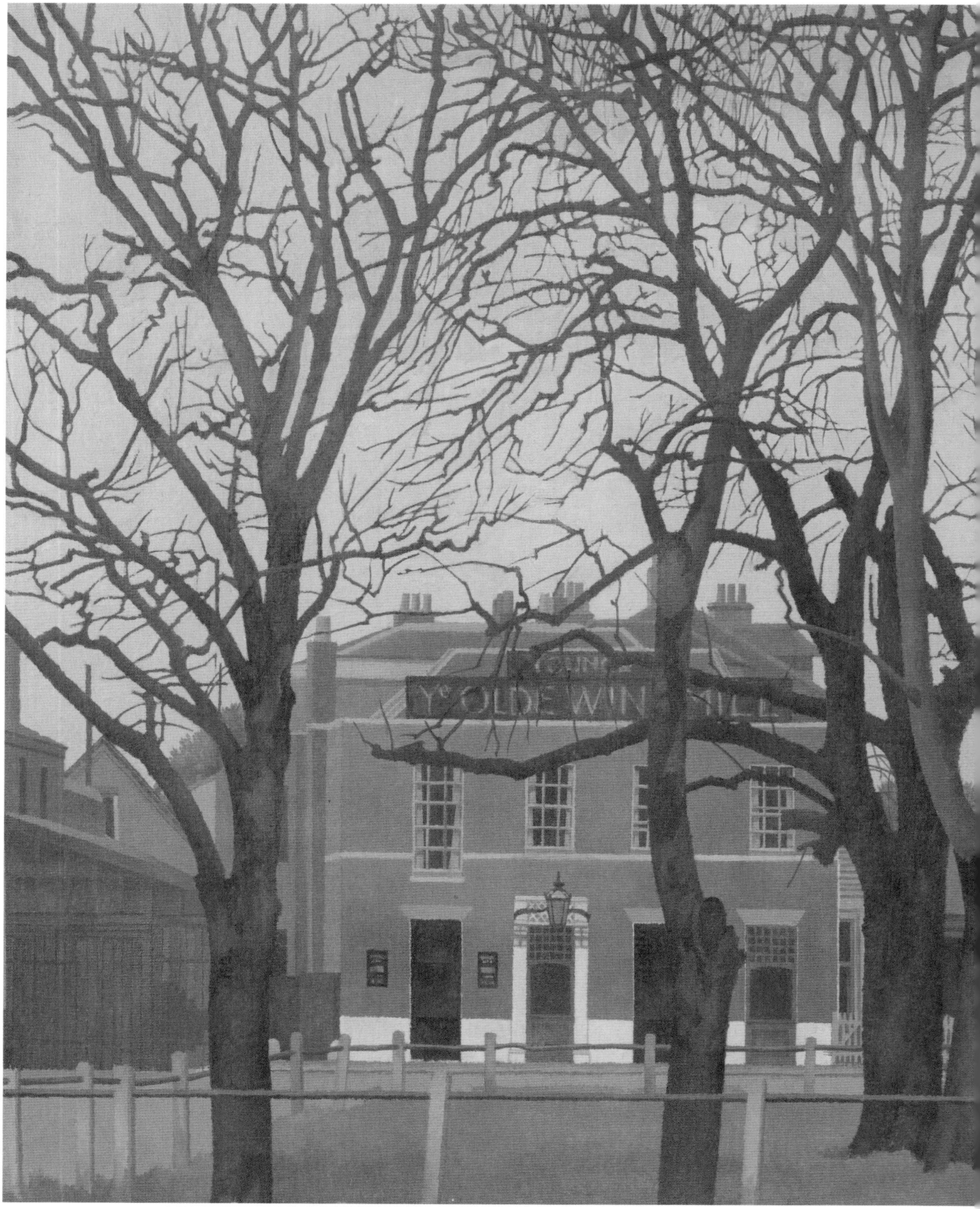
Ye OLDE WIN MILL

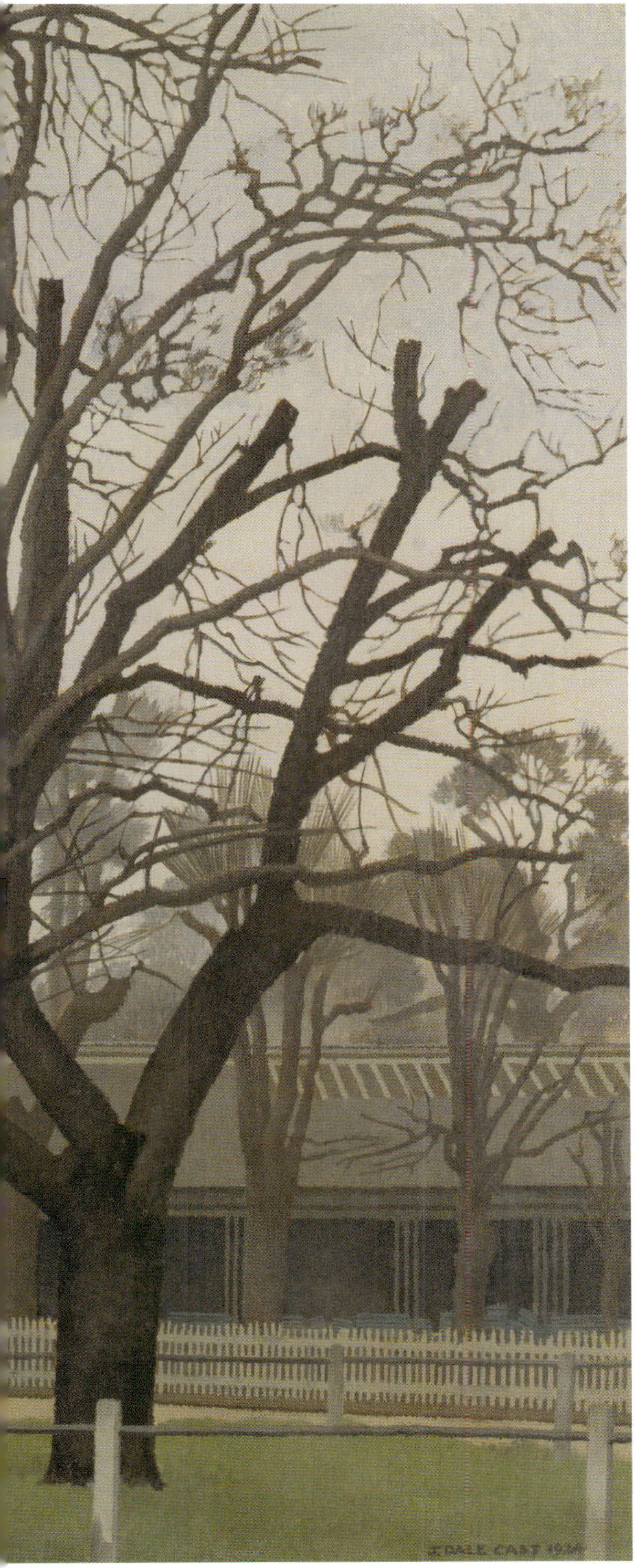

'The Windmill', Clapham Common

Jesse Dale Cast 1934

A surprising number of suburban London pubs have the feel of country inns. The Windmill has been on Clapham Common in south London since the seventeenth century and has been owned by Young's – until recently one of London's two big breweries – since 1848. Today it is a fashionable gastropub and boutique hotel. The appearance is almost unchanged from that presented here.

The artist had a studio facing the pub – this was likely to have been painted looking out of the window. Cast studied at the Slade School of Art in central London in the 1920s, where he learnt a deliberate approach to painting which involved making careful preparatory drawings and sketches, as he did here. His work is very varied in subject matter but includes many London landscapes, including studies of jetties and wharves at Greenwich.

South Bank

William Townsend 1948

Strollers on the Embankment take in the view, although there isn't much to see. The industry-heavy South Bank was left damaged and derelict by the war. At the time of this painting, work had just begun on the Festival of Britain, which would take place on this site in 1951. Townsend was possibly motivated to record the scene before the erection of the space-age buildings – including the extant Royal Festival Hall and the temporary Skylon tower and Dome of Discovery.

The round tower on a square base prominent on the left-hand side was the Lambeth Shot Tower. Used to create gunshot by dropping molten lead from a great height into water, the tower was a Victorian landmark. It was retained for the Festival, equipped with a radio transmitter, but was then demolished to make way for the brutalist Queen Elizabeth Hall.

Despite the drabness of post-war London, with its destroyed fabric and ongoing rationing, there is a sense of contentment and idle enjoyment in Townsend's scene which recalls the Impressionists' paintings of bathers and flâneurs.

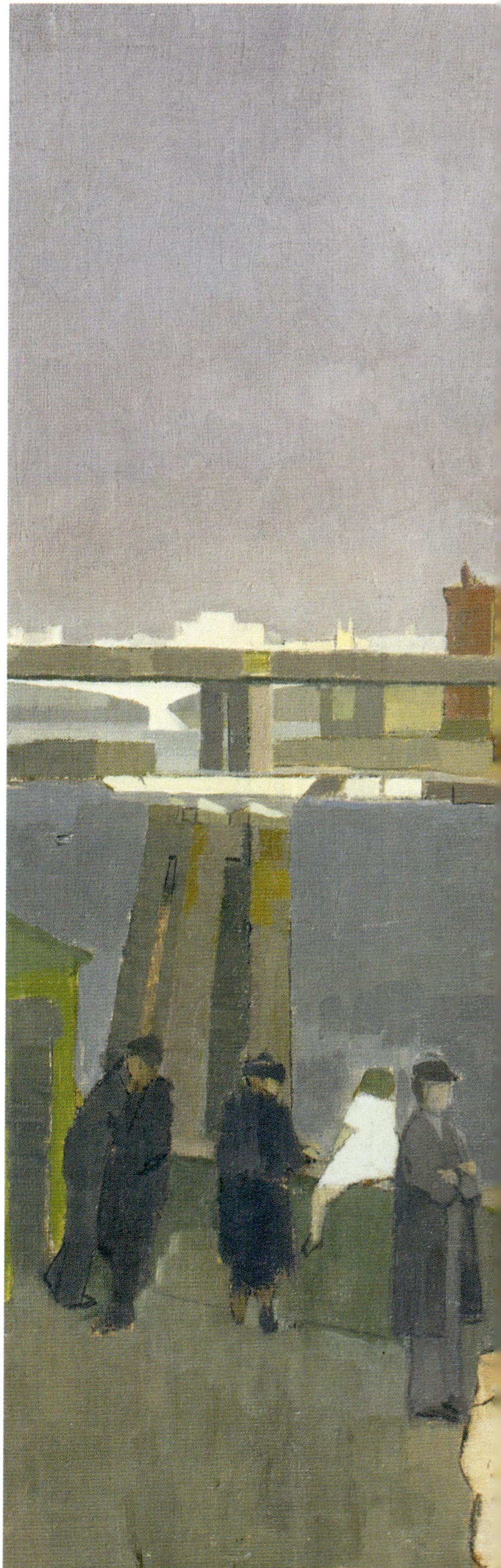

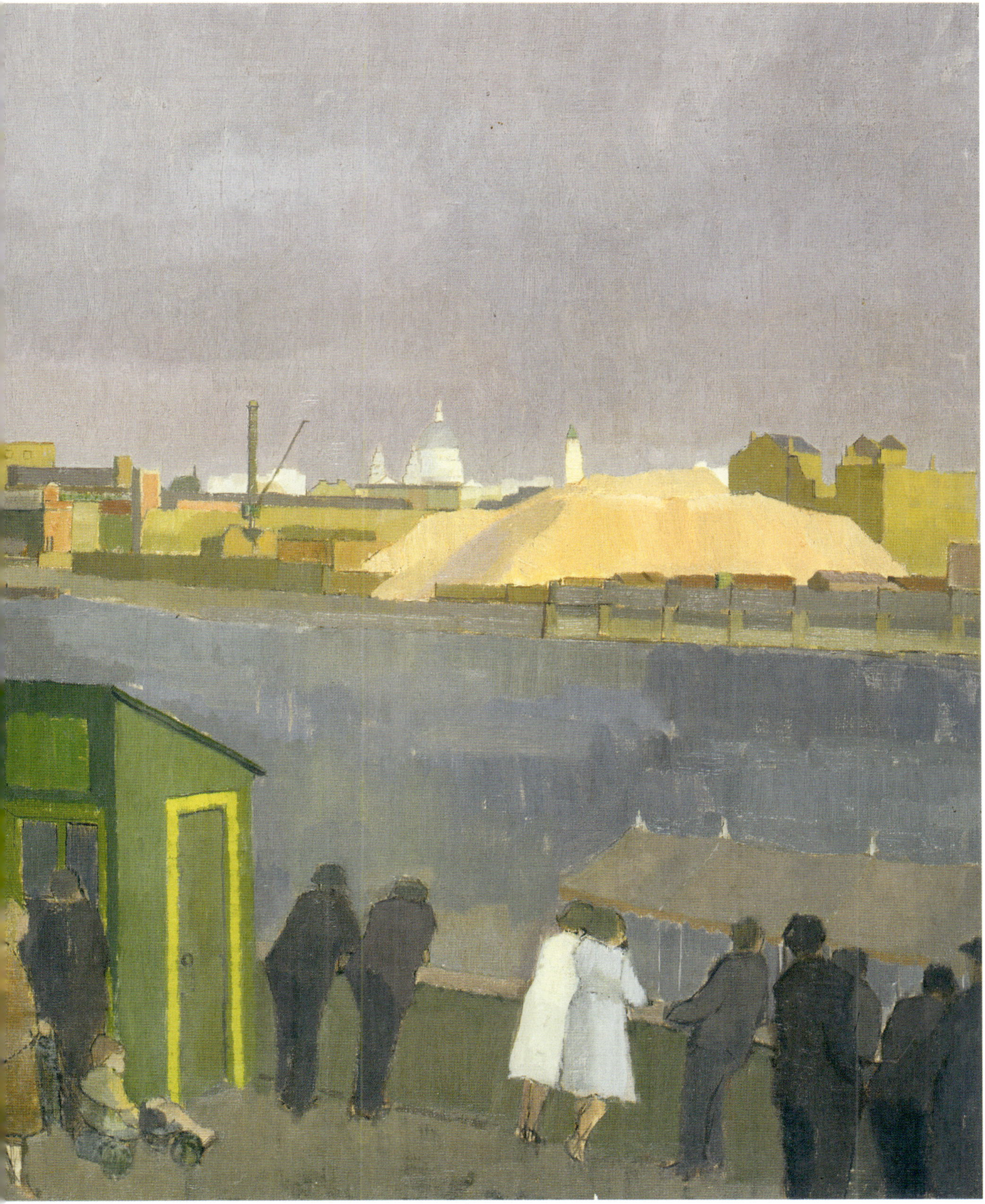

The Dogs

Carel Weight 1955–6

Greyhound racing was at the peak of its popularity when Weight painted this in the mid 1950s. Oval dog tracks with mechanical hares were introduced into Britain from the US in the 1920s. By 1950 there were over thirty tracks in London alone, serving fifty million punters. But the growth of betting shops and the increased value of the land have caused the majority of London's tracks to close down, and now only a couple are left. This painting shows the track which was in Wandsworth, south

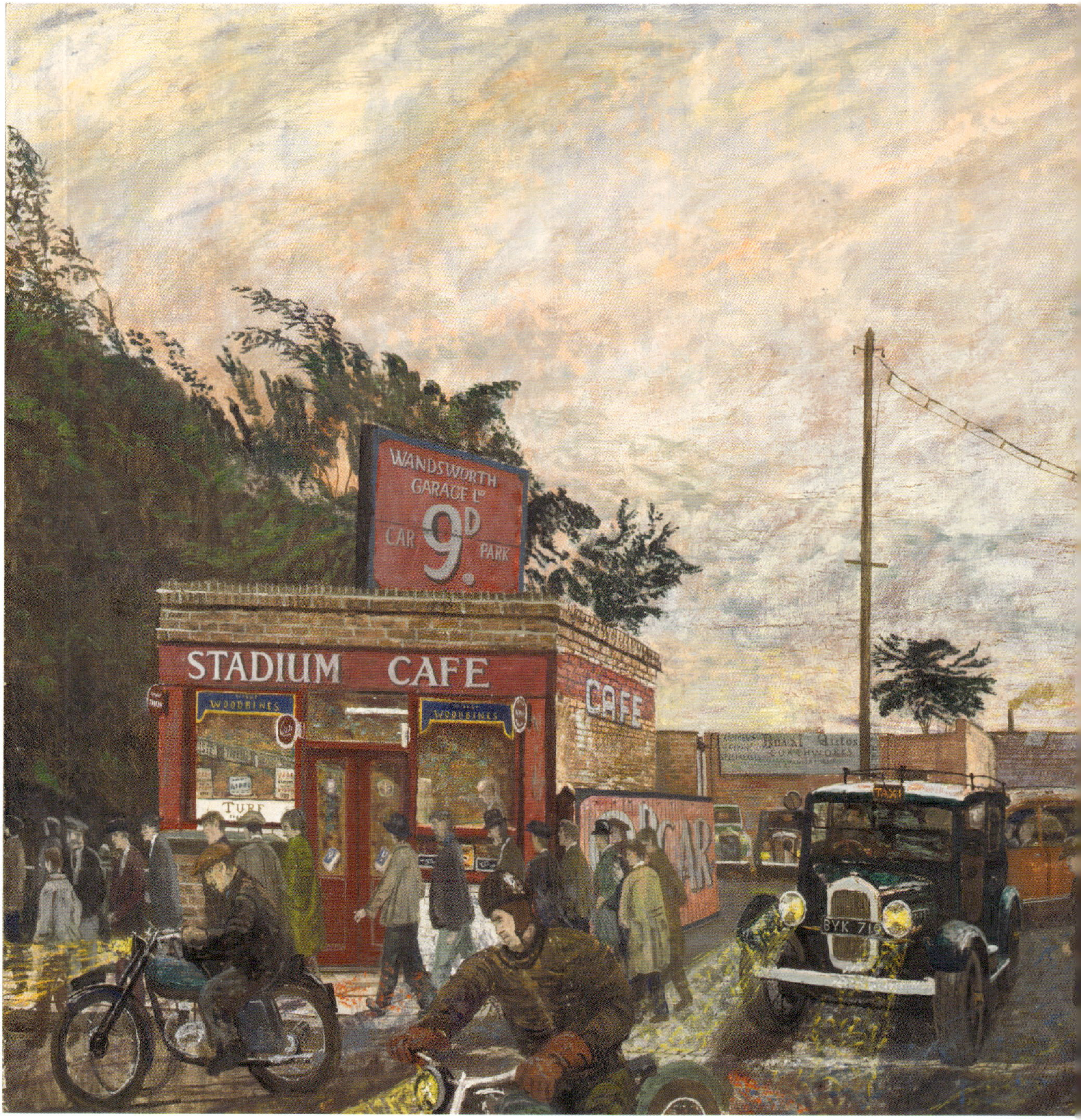

London. It is now the back end of a shopping centre.

Weight's painting is a conscious echo of William Powell Frith's *The Derby Day* 1856–8, in both its mammoth widescreen format and the subject of crowds at a racing event. However, instead of Frith's rather supercilious social satire, with its individual characters and multiple narratives, the people here are a contented mass, spilling out into the warm, bright evening light, heading home on foot, on bike or by car.

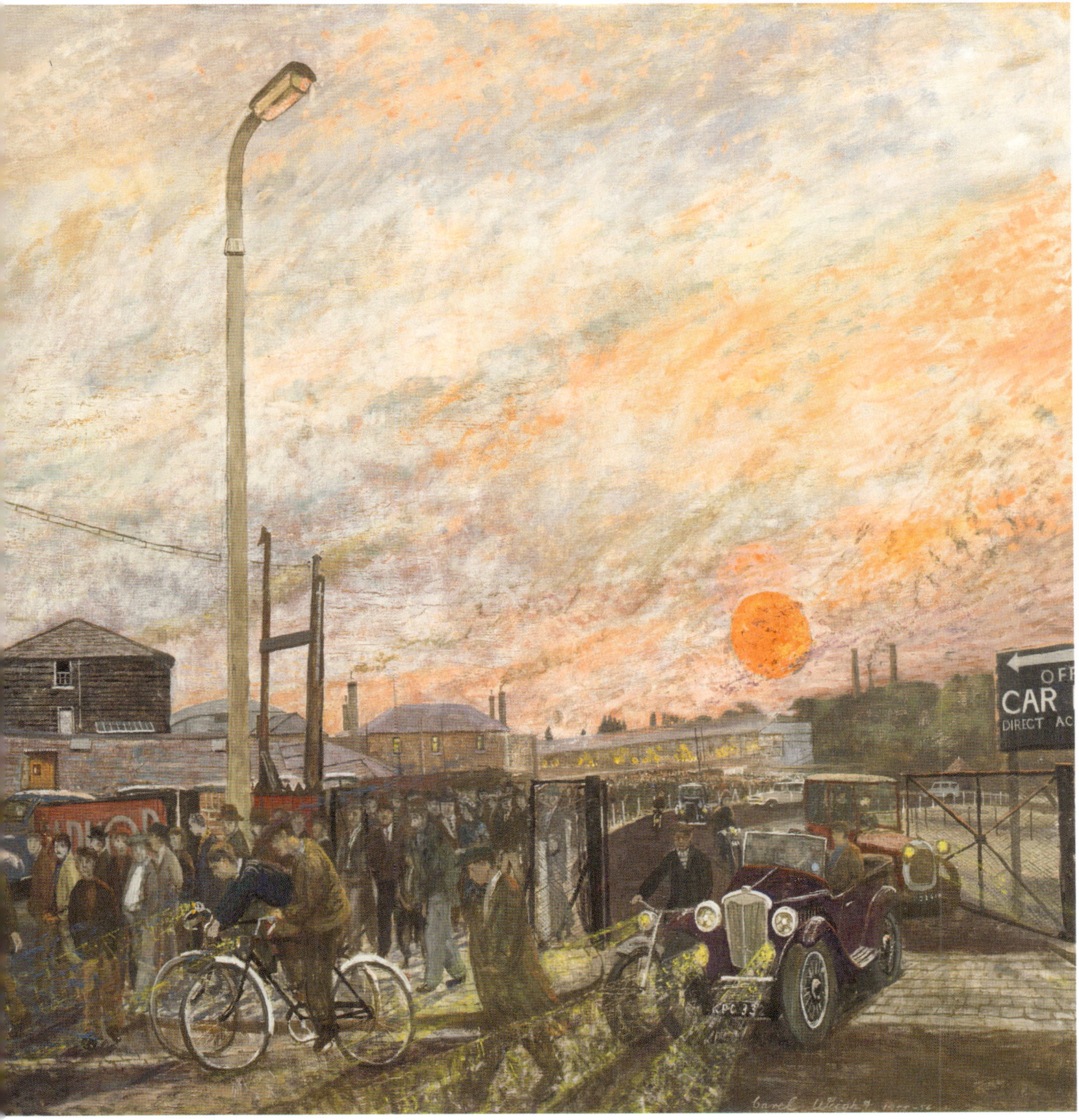

Canal Lovers

Jock McFadyen 1993–4

A catalogue entry for this painting written not long after it was made saw a 'bleak cityscape and cheap love'. A few decades on, it is hard not to see this young couple as two of the hipsters that have colonised this part of east London and dotted its industrial hinterland with fashionable clubs, bars and galleries. Indeed, it was artists like McFadyen who were the pioneers, attracted by the then-cheap rents. McFadyen bought part of an industrial building near London Fields in the 1980s for a studio – once neglected, the area is now expensive and sought after.

This location is by the Grand Union Canal where the train line to Fenchurch Street crosses it; the towpath is popular with cyclists on their way to nearby Victoria Park. It was while walking the towpath that McFadyen found the original inspiration for this work: a homeless glue sniffer. During the development of the painting the downbeat subject changed to this scene of transitory warmth.

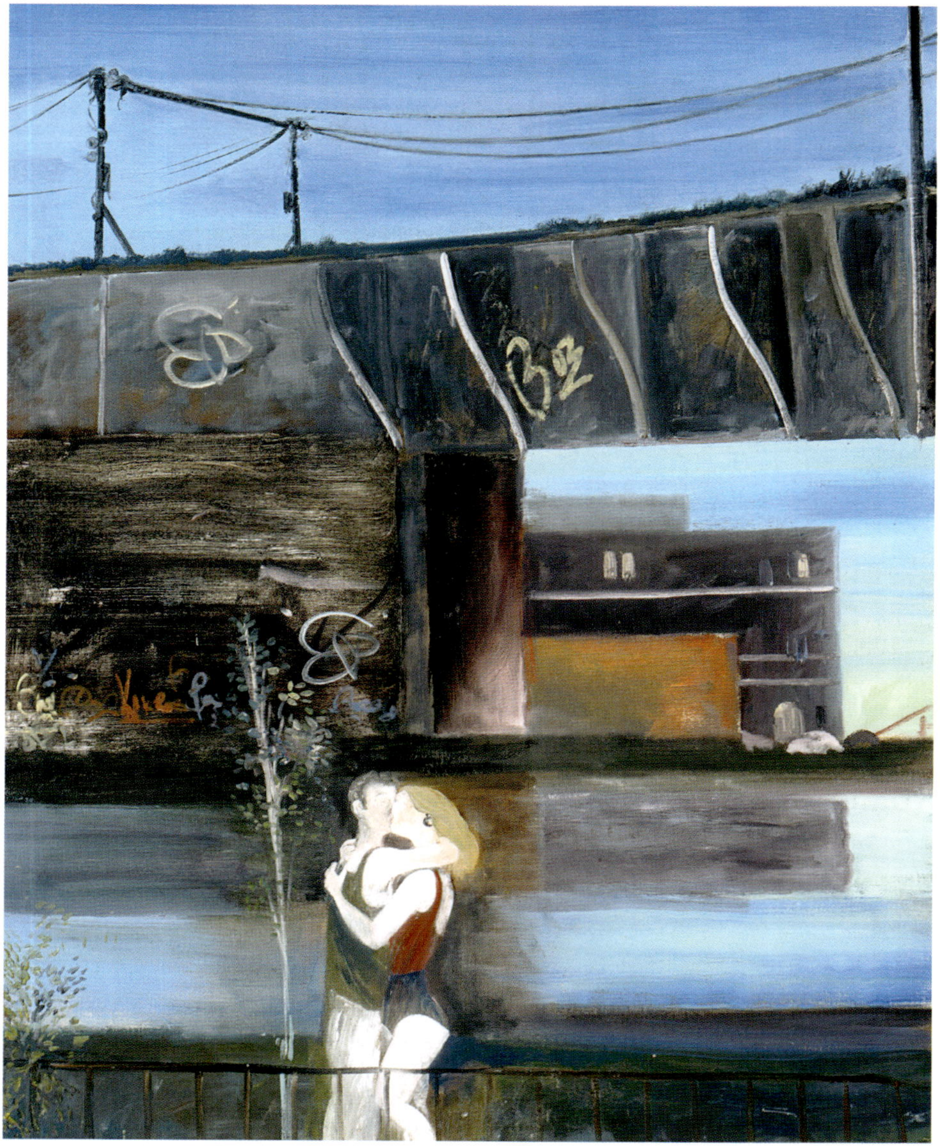

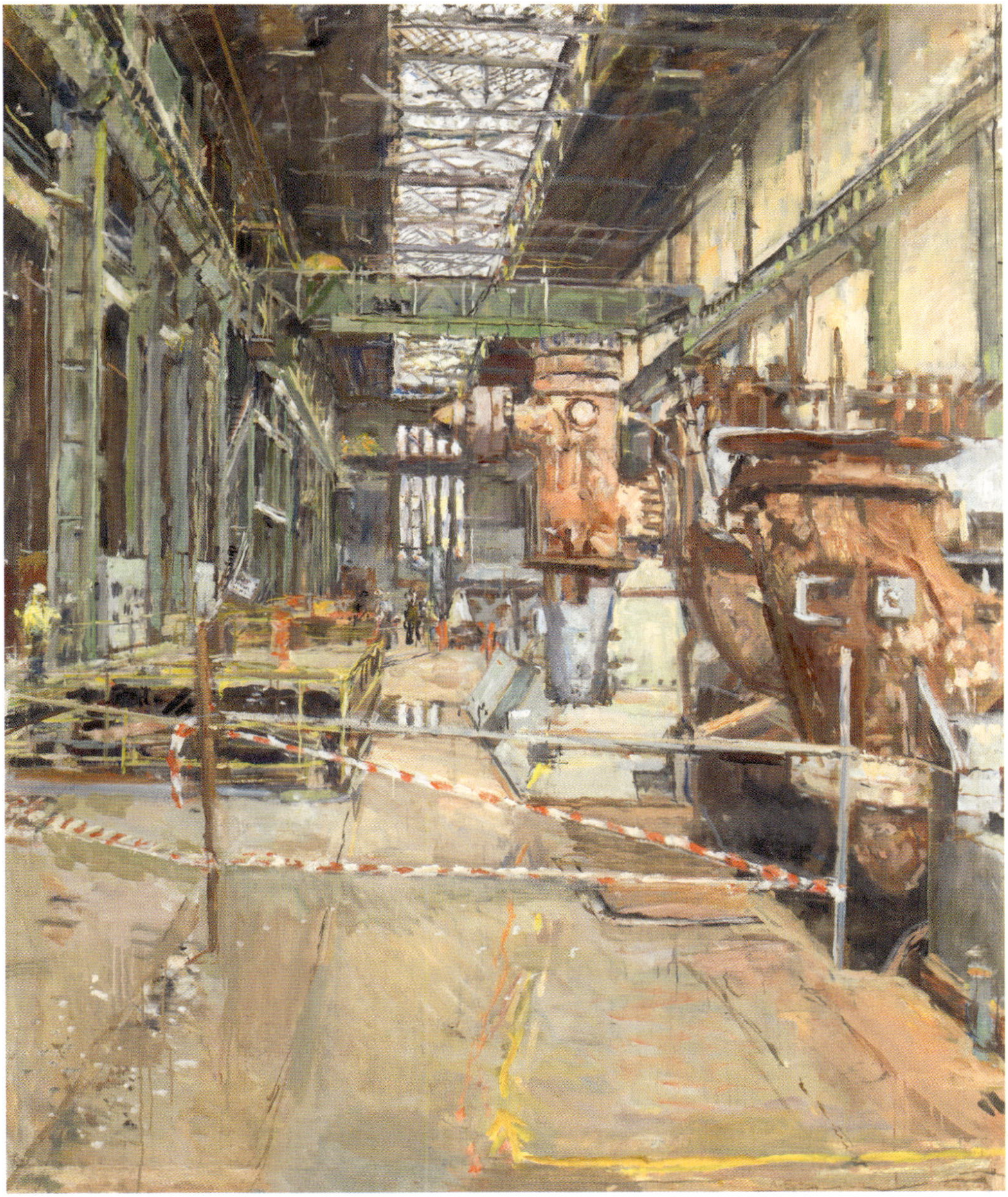

Bankside – The Turbine Hall

Anthony Eyton 1995–6

Whereas the architects of the National Gallery (p.100) and the British Museum (p.103) looked to antiquity to lend their museums an appropriate gravitas, Tate Modern found its home in an existing industrial building, the Bankside Power Station. Anthony Eyton was one of the artists invited to record the interior before construction began. He painted the Turbine Hall, now familiar to millions as the site for monumental artistic commissions. He wrote: 'The machinery looked like modern sculpture and everywhere there were the colours of rust and blue paint.'

Since 1960, Eyton has lived in Brixton, south London and for many years maintained a studio in Spitalfields, on the edge of the City. His paintings of London include rooftop views from his studio window, as well as studies of Liverpool Street and Farringdon stations.

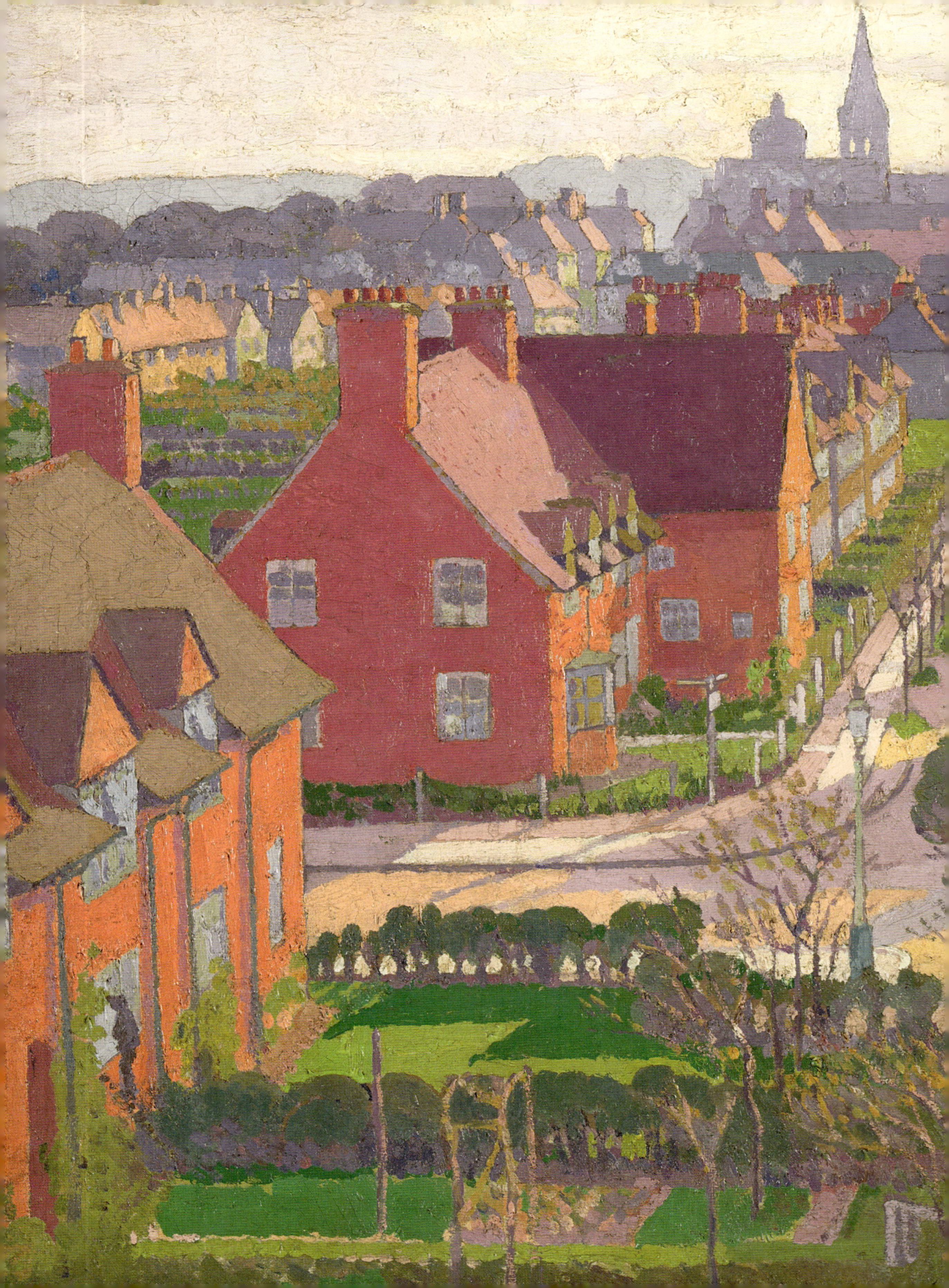

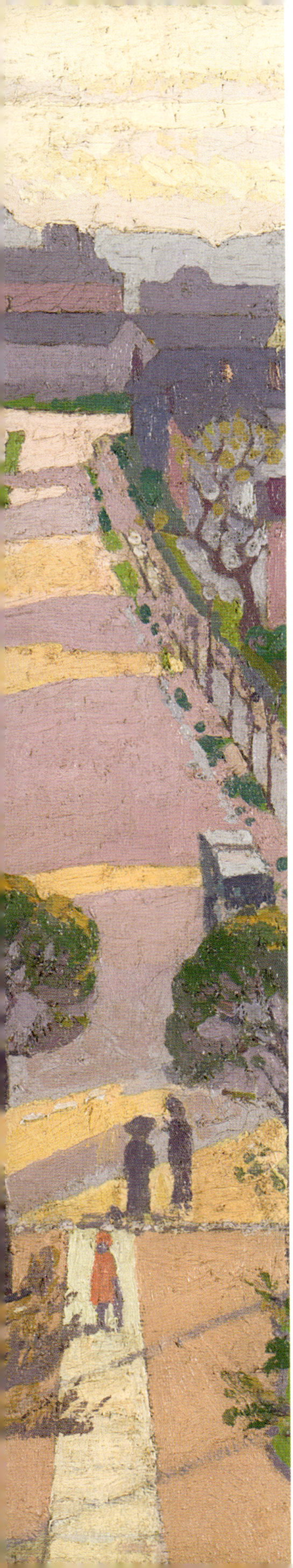

5
A HOME IN THE CITY

WHILE THE FIRST ARTISTS to paint London came from abroad, lured by the prospect of fat commissions and a gap in the market, and later foreign artists came to marvel at the modern metropolis, many artists have painted London for one simple reason – it is where they lived.

In medieval London, many artists were pushed outside the old walls, as only members of the Painter-Stainers' guild were allowed to practise within the City of London itself. This rule excluded the more skilled foreign painters and unfortunately helped to hold back the development of art in England. Forbidden from working in the City, artists congregated in the newly developing West End instead, along Fleet Street, Holborn or in Covent Garden.

It was in Covent Garden that the first modern artists' quarter developed, and artists began painting what was on their doorstep (pp.54–5). However, the influx of hopeful artists seeking commissions did begin to bring down the character of the area. The rich patrons fled further West, to Leicester Square, Soho and north of Oxford Street, and the more successful artists, such as William Hogarth and Benjamin West (1738–1820), followed them.

In the nineteenth century, successful artists established homes in the still-rural villages within easy reach of the centre: Hampstead, Richmond, Twickenham and Chelsea. While for some – such as J.M.W. Turner – this was simply for relaxation and privacy, for others – such as John Constable and James Abbott McNeill Whistler – these new areas became a major presence in their work.

In the early twentieth century, many artists looked nearer and nearer to home for their subjects. They were motivated by a desire to depict the reality of everyday life, but also there is a sense of pragmatism, a compromise between the plein air painting of the Impressionists, which demanded to be executed in front of its motif, and the often inclement London climate. For modern artists like Spencer Gore and Charles Ginner, whose work dissolved the city into forms and colours, the view from their bedroom window served as well as the grandest vista. Frank Auerbach continues this tradition today, exclusively painting subjects within a ten-minute walk of his Camden Town studio. For these artists, their view of London is an intimately personal one.

More recently, artists have been even more influential, if inadvertent, players in London's fearsome property game. Moving to east London in search of cheap studio spaces, artists in the 1990s kick-started a wave of gentrification, which has been spreading across London ever since.

William Ratcliffe *Hampstead Garden Suburb from Willifield Way* c.1914 (detail). See pp.124–5

The Grove, Hampstead

John Constable c.1821–2

This eccentric house on the edge of Hampstead is said to have been home to an equally eccentric resident. At the end of the nineteenth century, Fountain North, a retired navy officer, turned its roof into the quarter deck of a ship from where he was supposed to have fired cannons to salute naval victories. In some versions of the story it is Admiral Matthew Barton, and the house is currently known as the Admiral's House. The story inspired the character of Admiral Boom in *Mary Poppins* and the house in the film resembles this one.

During the 1820s, Constable and his family spent part of every summer in rented lodgings in Hampstead, while maintaining a base and studio in town. Constable's wife had tuberculosis and the country air was expected to aid her health, as well as according with Constable's pastoral instincts. In 1821 he was in Lower Terrace, from which he could probably have seen the Admiral's House from the window. In 1827 he brought a permanent home in Well Walk, though his wife unfortunately died shortly after.

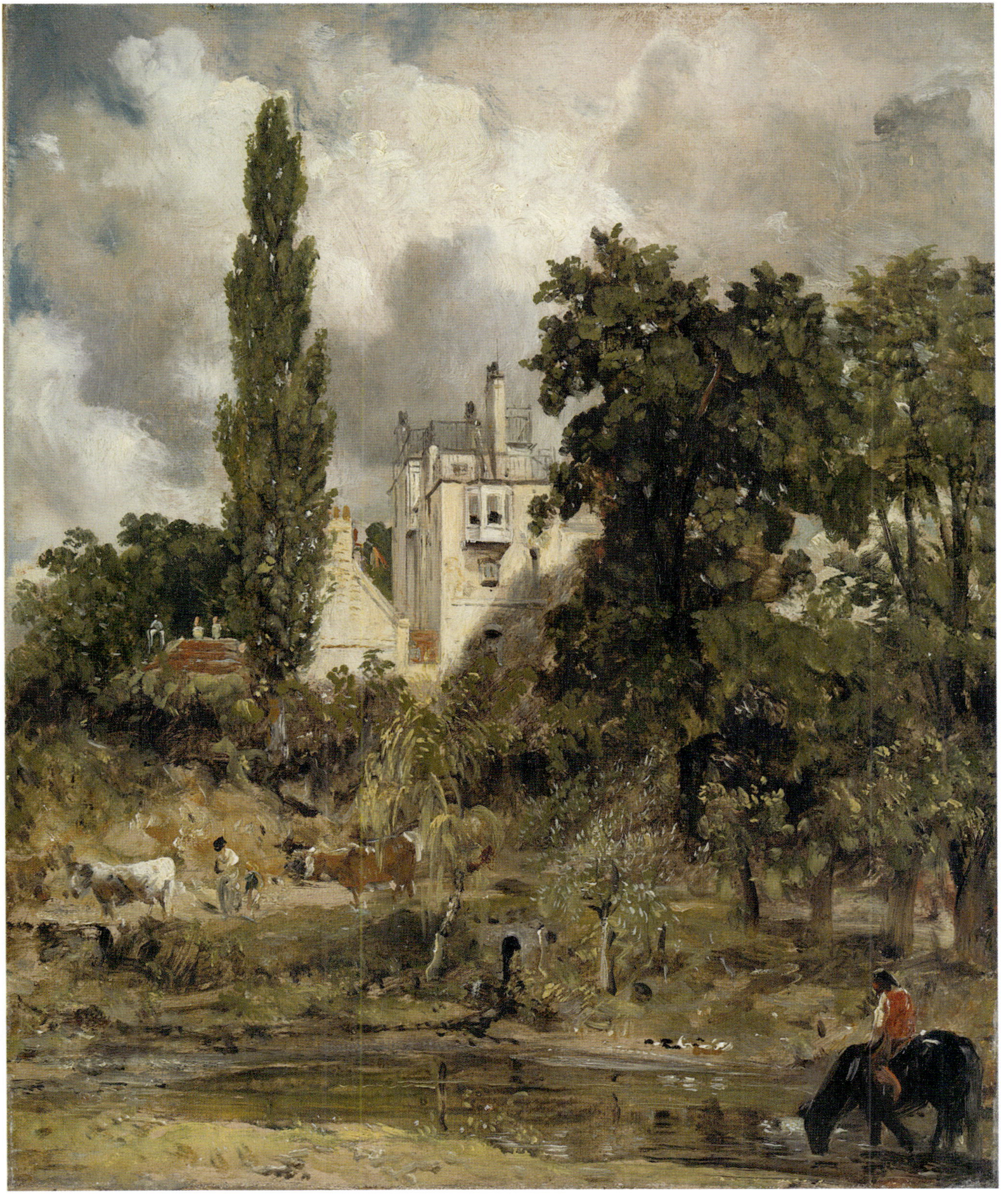

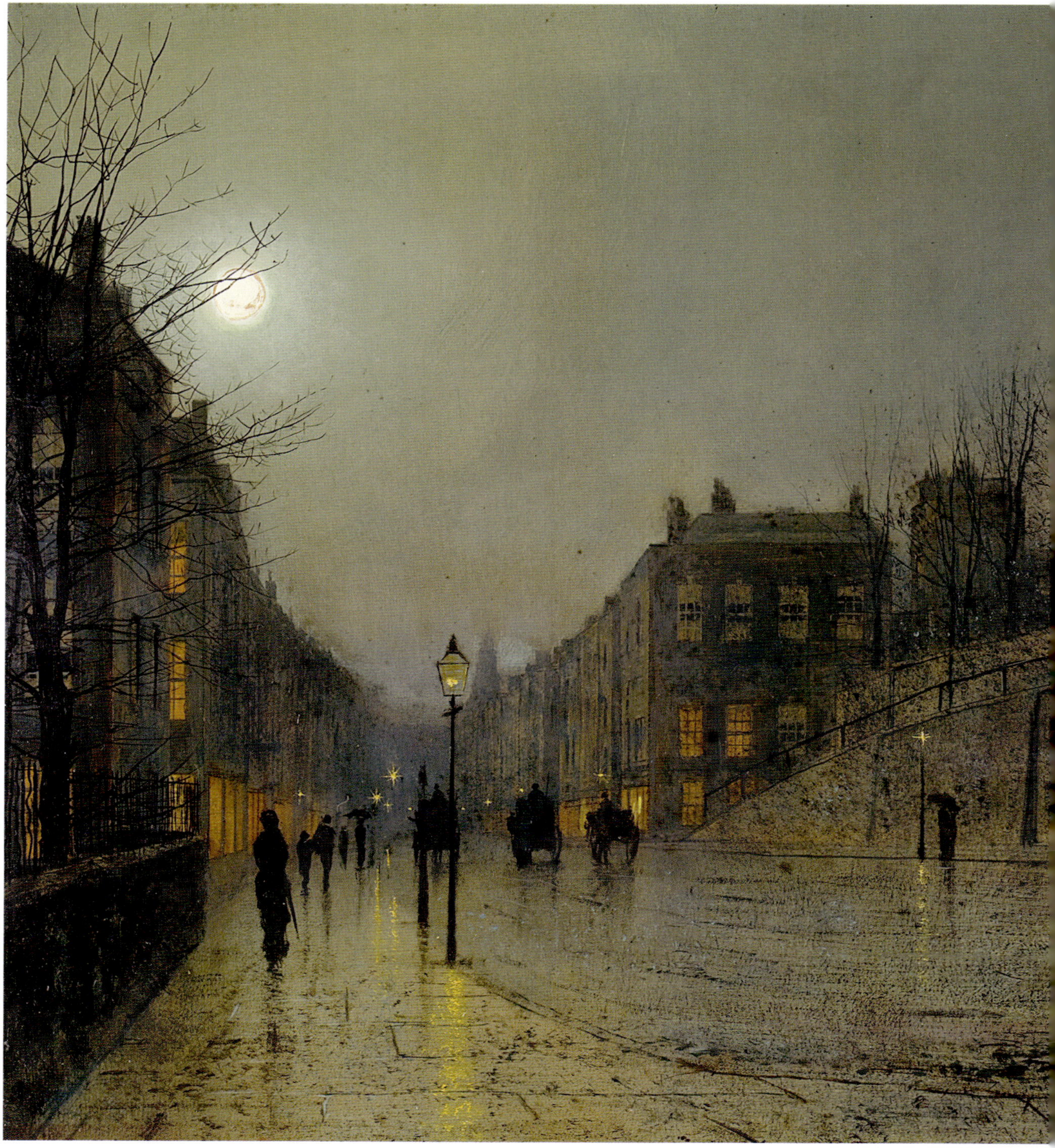

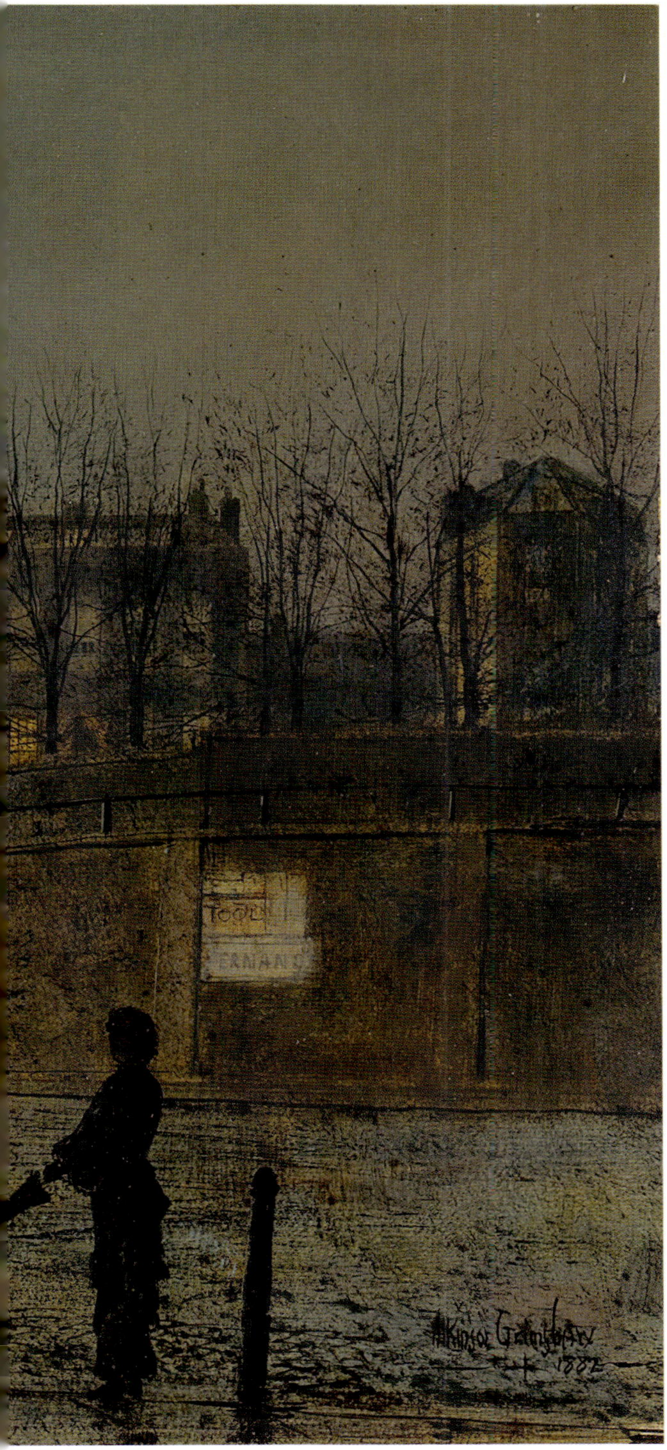

View of Heath Street by Night

Atkinson Grimshaw 1882

While already a well-established and sought-after place for wealthy Londoners to settle (see, for example, the painting of the large estate, p.22), Hampstead grew in earnest after the overground station opened in the 1860s, with many large houses being built in the following decades. Grimshaw pictures it during this boom – perhaps with an eye on sales to the prosperous middle classes moving in. Like much of his mature work, it is a moonlight scene, with mist and rain creating a mysterious atmosphere. The muted tones are relieved only by the white moon and yellow gaslights, emphasising the cosy warmness of the houses.

Like the Pether family (pp.172–3), Grimshaw specialised in moonlit city scenes. However, his work is not as picturesque or conventional, emphasising instead the fog-cloaked drama and romance of the city after sundown. Grimshaw had established himself as a successful painter in Leeds, coming to London regularly to sketch and to visit galleries. In the mid 1880s he moved to London full-time, where he came to the attention of Whistler, who is said to have remarked: 'I considered myself the inventor of Nocturnes until I saw Grimmy's moonlit pictures.'

Houghton Place

Spencer Gore 1912

The residential square – with neat Georgian or Victorian townhouses and private garden in the centre – is perhaps the archetypal London housing type. It was first seen in the elite schemes of Covent Garden and Lincoln's Inn Fields and ended up as *Eastenders'* Albert Square.

When Spencer Gore lived at 2 Houghton Place in Ampthill Square, it was on the slide slightly. Positioned just behind Euston Station and near his mentor Walter Sickert in Mornington Crescent, Gore moved to a flat here shortly after getting married. Ampthill Square was demolished in the 1960s and replaced by a trio of council tower blocks (which appear in some paintings by Frank Auerbach, see p.133). These are in turn under threat due to the proposed creation of the High Speed 2 railway line into Euston.

In 1913 Gore moved to Richmond, where he painted the views from his new windows and in the nearby Richmond Park. It was while doing the latter in winter weather that he caught pneumonia and died a few days later, at the age of only thirty-five.

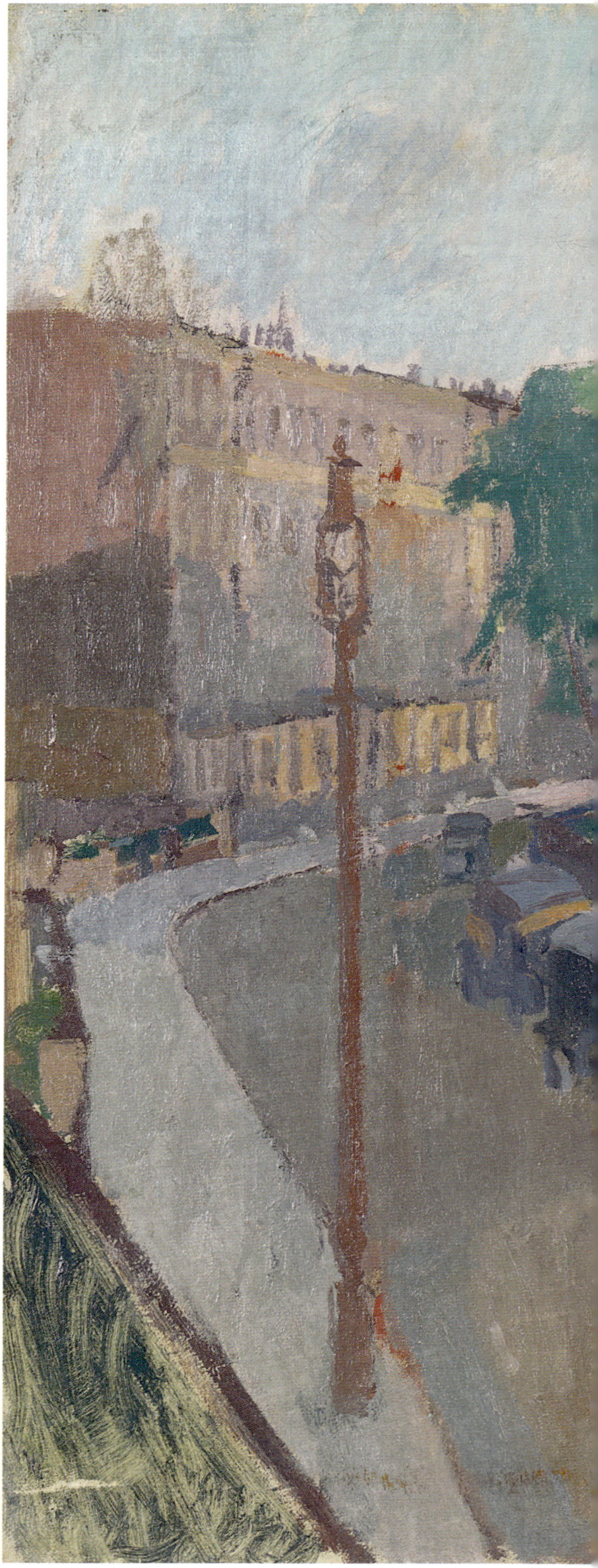

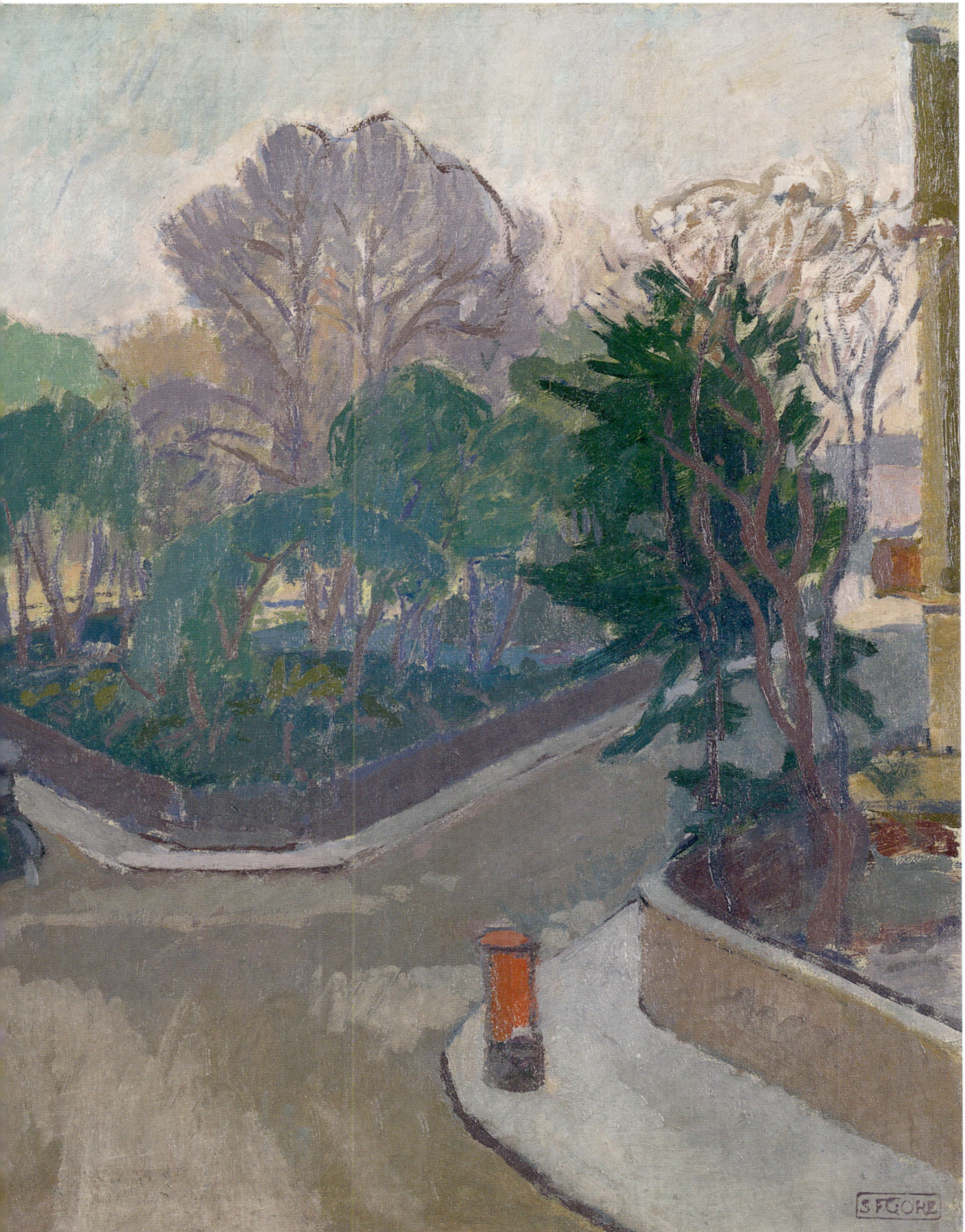
S.F.GORE

Hampstead Garden Suburb from Willifield Way

William Ratcliffe c.1914

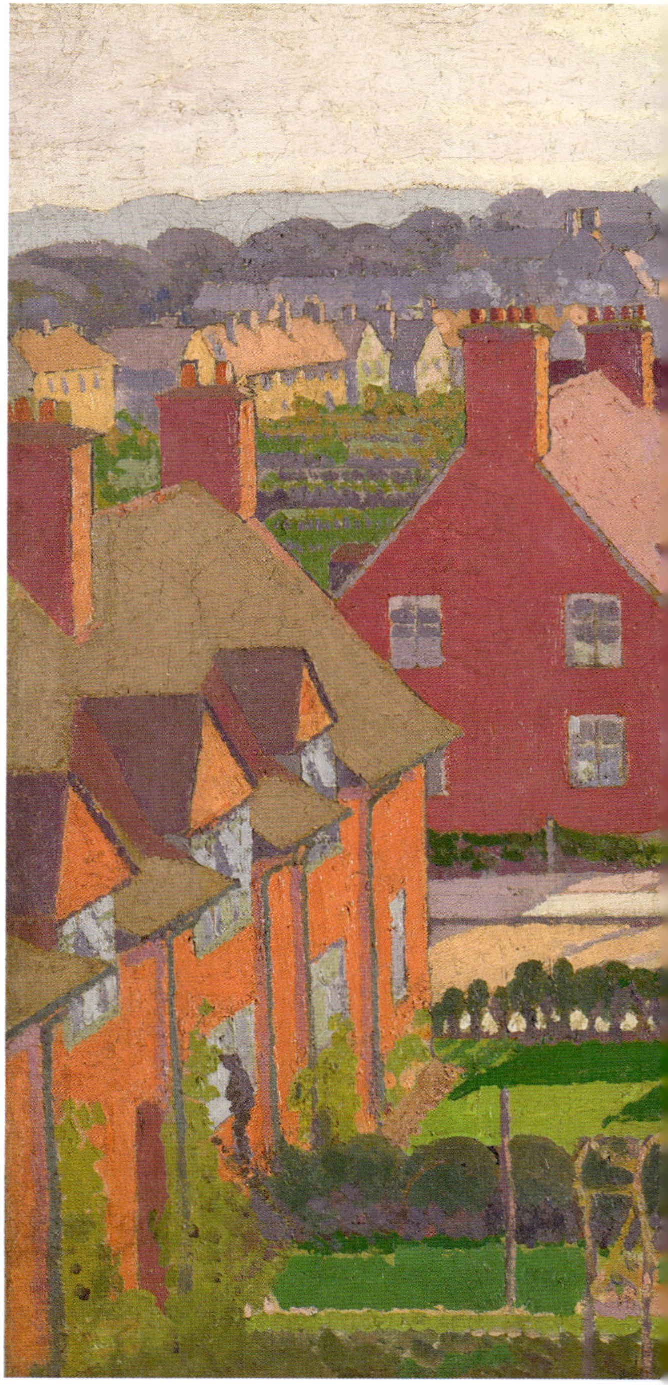

The role of the artist in regenerating and re-energising unfashionable areas of London has not gone unnoticed by property developers, who now often aim to get 'creatives' to support their projects by offering studio or workshop spaces, or by providing space for pop-up restaurants and cafes. But this is not a new trend. The arts and crafts-inspired developments of the early twentieth century – such as Letchworth Garden City or Hampstead Garden Suburb – were enthusiastically supported by artists.

Although today these suburbs might be considered boring or conservative, for artists such as William Ratcliffe – a long-standing but lesser-known member of the Camden Town Group – they were thrillingly modern in their utopian blending of the best of urban and rural living. The tree-lined avenues with their spacious well-designed houses provided a new, dignified way of life intended for a wide social spectrum. Born in Norfolk, Ratcliffe lived in Letchworth before moving to the street depicted here with his brother. His painting uses the vibrant colours of the Post-Impressionists to suggest the quiet end of a warm spring day.

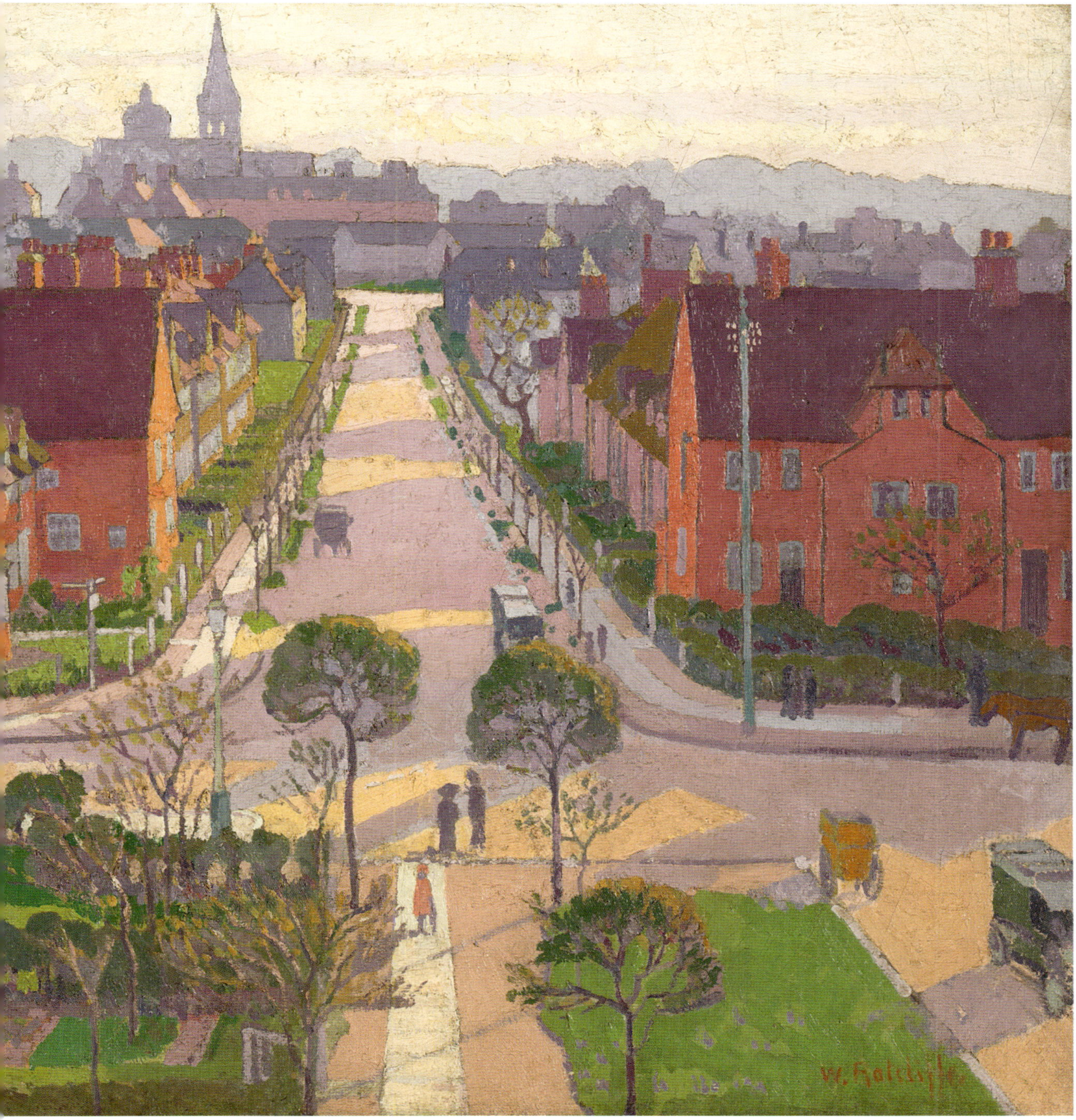
W. Ratcliffe

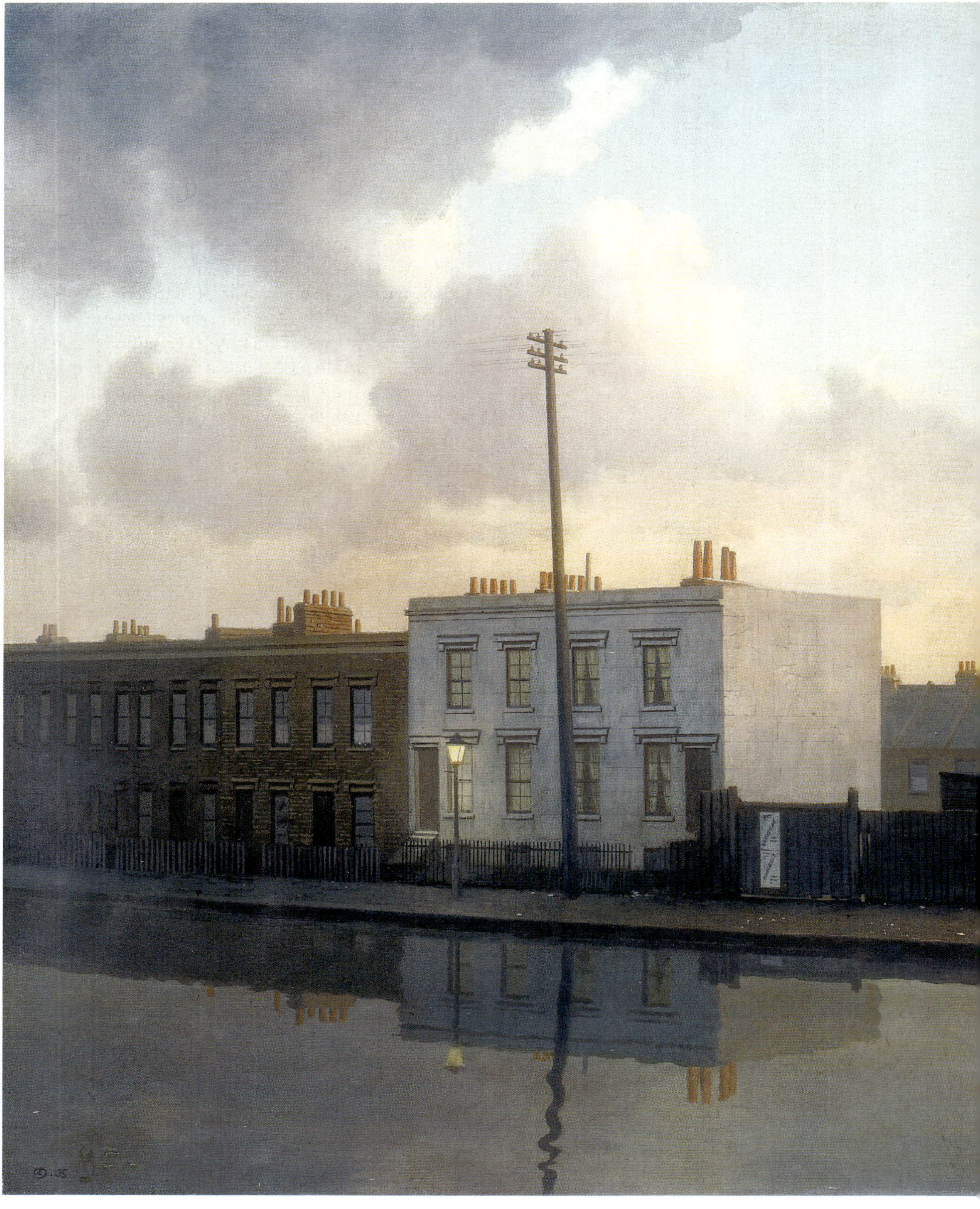

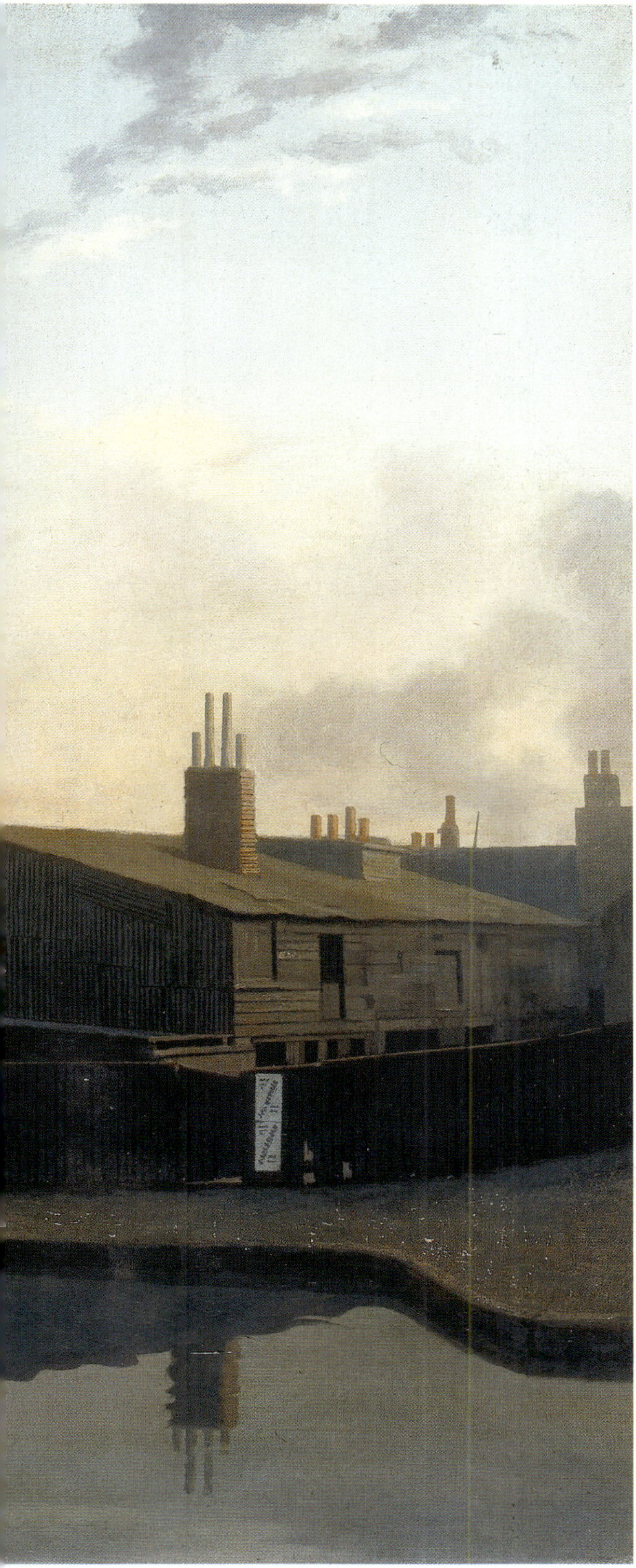

The Surrey Canal, Camberwell

Algernon Newton 1935

Algernon Newton's paintings show us a London without people. Newton spent much of his career painting canals or other bodies of water, showing forlorn Victorian housing reflected under a low sun. He once wrote: 'There is beauty to be found in everything, you only have to search for it; a gasometer can make as beautiful a picture as a palace on the Grand Canal, Venice. It simply depends on the artist's vision.' The exact location is hard to pinpoint – this part of the Surrey Canal in south London has since been filled in to form a linear park in Peckham and the lower half of Burgess Park.

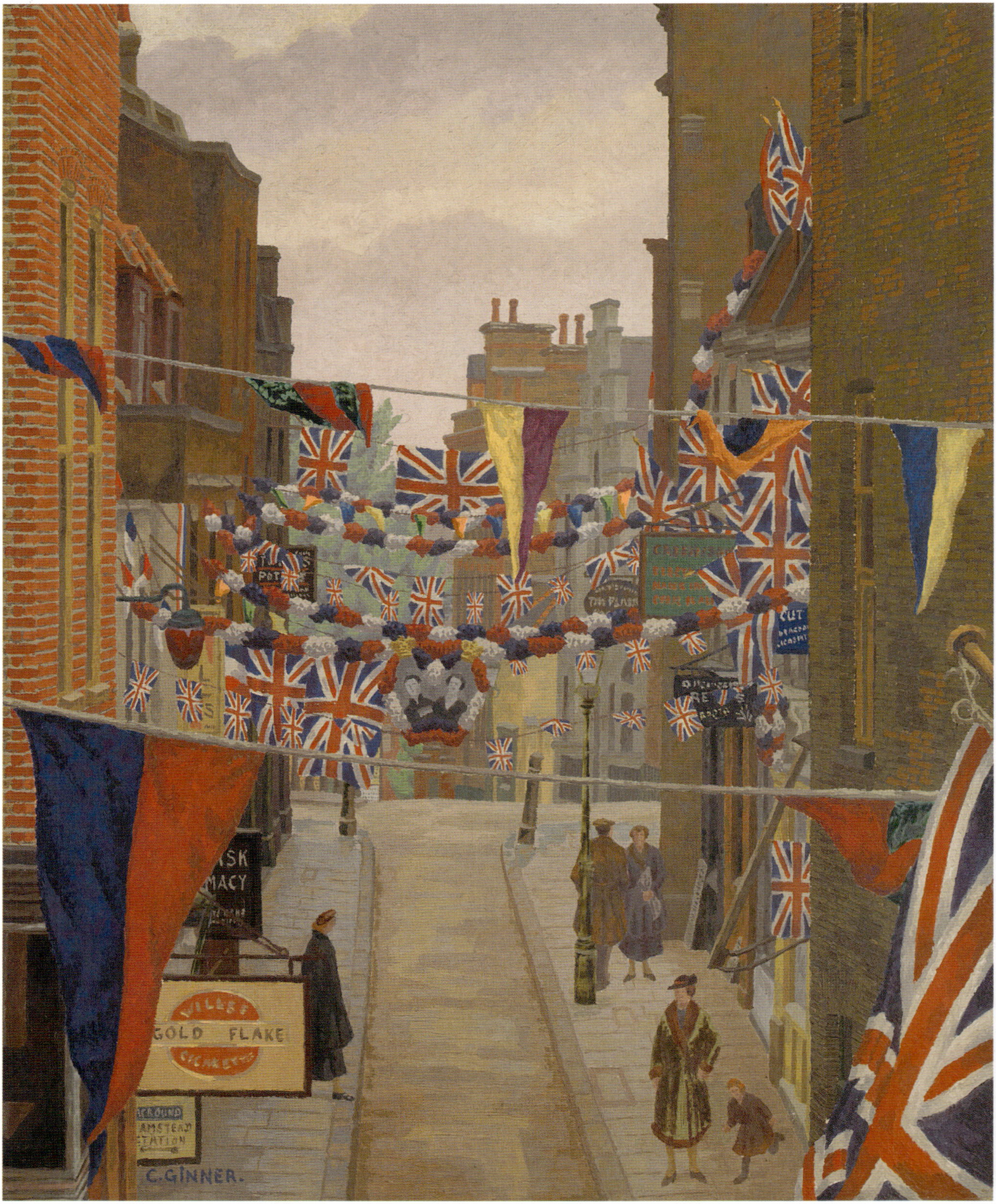
GOLD FLAKE
C.GINNER.

Flask Walk, Hampstead, on Coronation Day

Charles Ginner 1937

The 1930s were Hampstead's heyday as a meeting place for artists and intellectuals. Ginner lived at 61 Hampstead High Street from 1919 to 1938. In that time he could well have bumped into the likes of David Bomberg (1890–1957), Naum Gabo (1890–1977), Barbara Hepworth (1903–75), Piet Mondrian (1872–1944), Henry Moore (1898–1986), Paul Nash (1889–1946), Christopher Richard Wynne Nevinson (1889–1946) or Ben Nicholson (1894–1982). The last was described in a newspaper article as 'the complete bourgeois conception of a Hampstead artist, vivid scarf, beret and all.'

Like many artists of the time, Ginner regularly painted the views out of his windows, and did many variations of this scene of Flask Walk. The bunting is up for the coronation of George VI (r.1936–52). Ginner was not a noted royalist but was probably attracted by the colour and movement of the flags, creating a great sense of perspective as they recede down the alleyway.

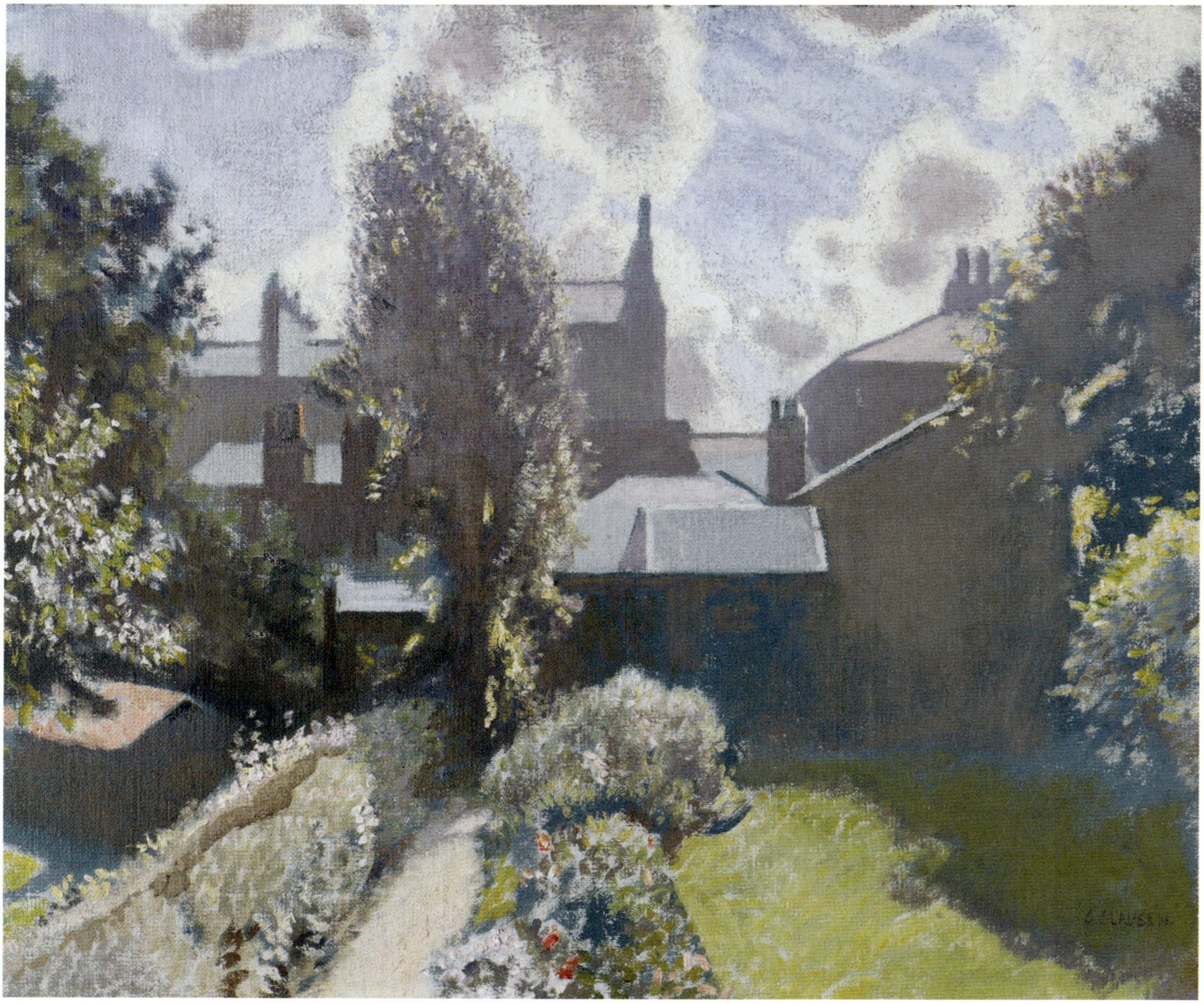

My Back Garden

Sir George Clausen exhibited 1940

'There will always be an England' went the patriotic song released the year before this painting was shown. And even though London was in the middle of the Blitz, there is a sense here of eternal peace. Surely nothing will disturb this sunny domestic idyll in a sleepy suburban street in north-west London's Maida Vale?

George Clausen was 88 when he painted this work. He had had a successful life, becoming Professor of Painting at the Royal Academy and receiving a knighthood in 1927. His work has a lot in common with that of the Impressionists, with its intense interest in the effects of light and a frequent focus on rural people and places. Despite the subject matter obviously being limited by circumstances, it fits into a tradition of garden painting by the likes of Monet and Pissarro. The backs of the houses silhouetted against the sky are reminiscent of the picturesque country cottages of his earlier work.

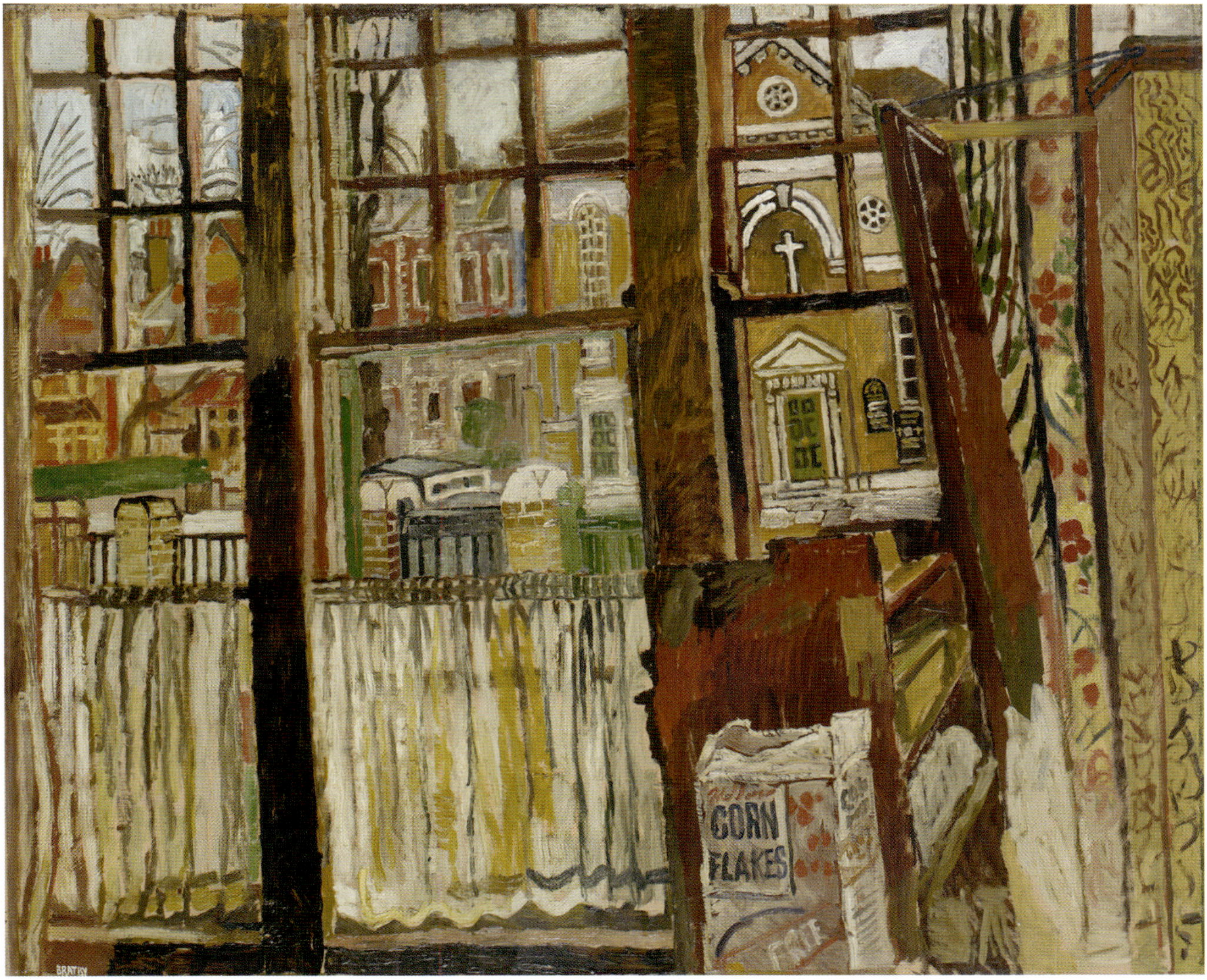

Window, Dartmouth Row, Blackheath

John Bratby c.1954–6

John Bratby was one of the four artists dubbed the Kitchen Sink school for their realist invocations of mundane domesticity. He worked in a deliberately crude style, painting ugly everyday things, including several portraits of a toilet. The art world was shocked by his raw new vision and he became a short-lived celebrity – the visual arts equivalent of theatre's 'angry young men'.

This view seems to be literally of a kitchen sink, or at least a kitchen counter, with a box of Corn Flakes and a low net curtain. The glimpses of the street outside, however, show us to be in a rather pleasant and expensive street on the edge of Blackheath, a wealthy south-east London suburb where Bratby bought a large house after his initial successes of the 1950s. His work includes several views of the area and neighbouring Greenwich.

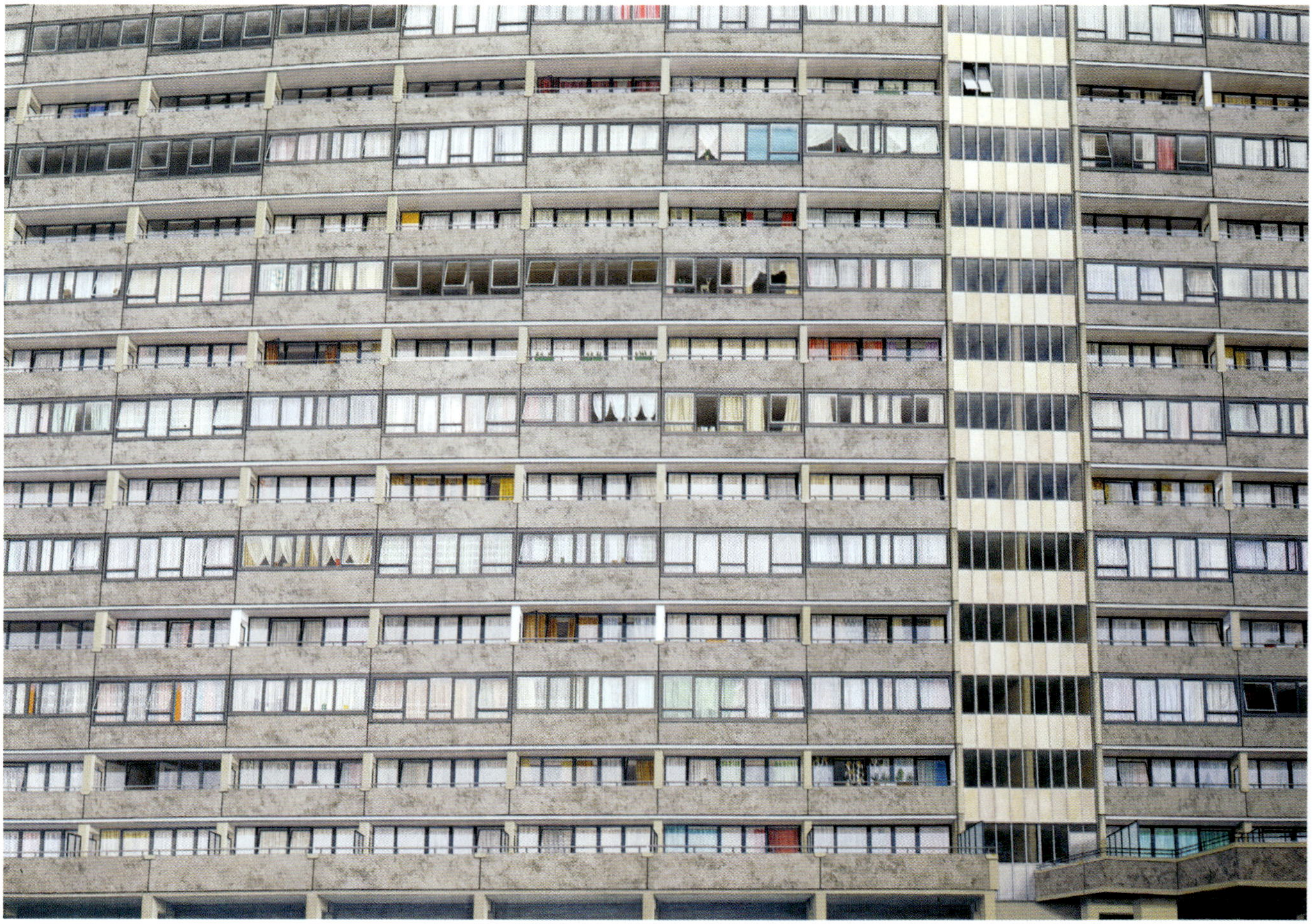

Albany Flats

David Hepher 1977–9

David Hepher started by painting close-up views of ordinary middle-class houses. By the late 1970s he had moved on to depicting council tower blocks. This is Bradenham, a block of flats on the Aylesbury Estate in south London. One of the largest council estates in Europe when it was built, it is at the time of writing being demolished and redeveloped by the local council. The last few residents of this block were forced to negotiate a maze of razor-wire-topped hoardings to get in and out of their homes.

Although he doesn't often feature people in his work, Hepher's paintings are carefully observed portraits of real places. He says: 'In many ways [a house] represents, particularly for the English, the face people present to the world, at the same time providing a refuge from too close a contact with other people. All the owner's personality is revealed in his home.' However, by cropping off the top, bottom and sides of the flats, the artist also recalls the abstract grids of Agnes Martin (1912–2004) or Piet Mondrian (1872–1944).

Mornington Crescent – Summer Morning

Frank Auerbach 2004

Although it might seem to be entirely abstract, as with much of Auerbach's work, this painting is closely based on his observations of the London cityscape within a close radius of the studio he has worked in since the 1950s. Auerbach works obsessively on his paintings, scraping the canvas back and repainting every day until he is satisfied with the result. He once said, 'I see no virtue in my laborious processes, I dare say that grander and more electric images have been made by some with less trouble.' Like the work of his friend Leon Kossoff (p.179), here Auerbach uses impasto, applying paint so thickly to the surface, it is almost sculptural.

Mornington Crescent – close to Camden Town in north London – must be the most painted ordinary street in London. Auerbach has painted it at all angles and in all seasons; Spencer Gore lived nearby and painted it often; Walter Sickert had a studio on the road, marked by a blue plaque metres from the location of this painting.

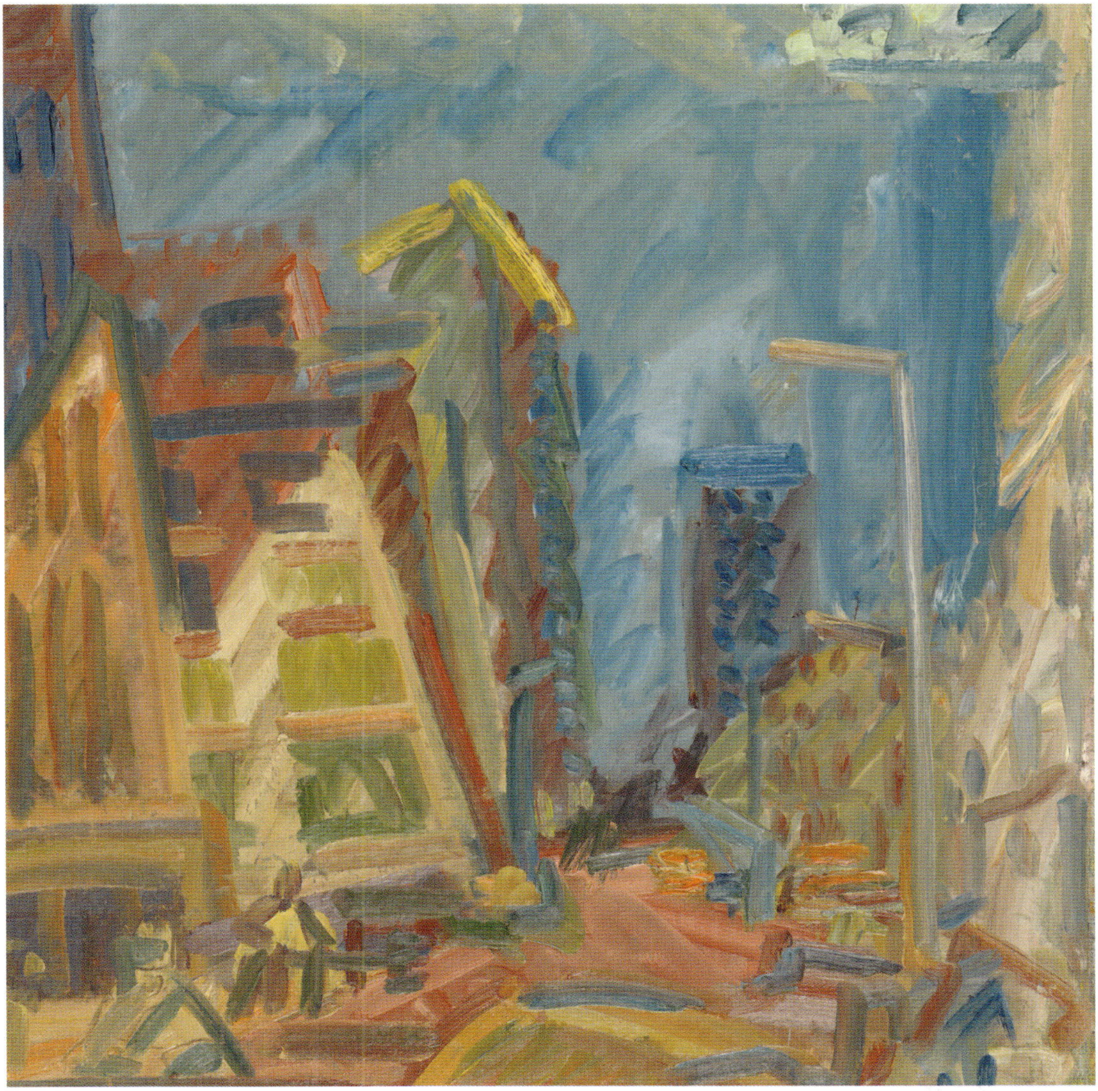

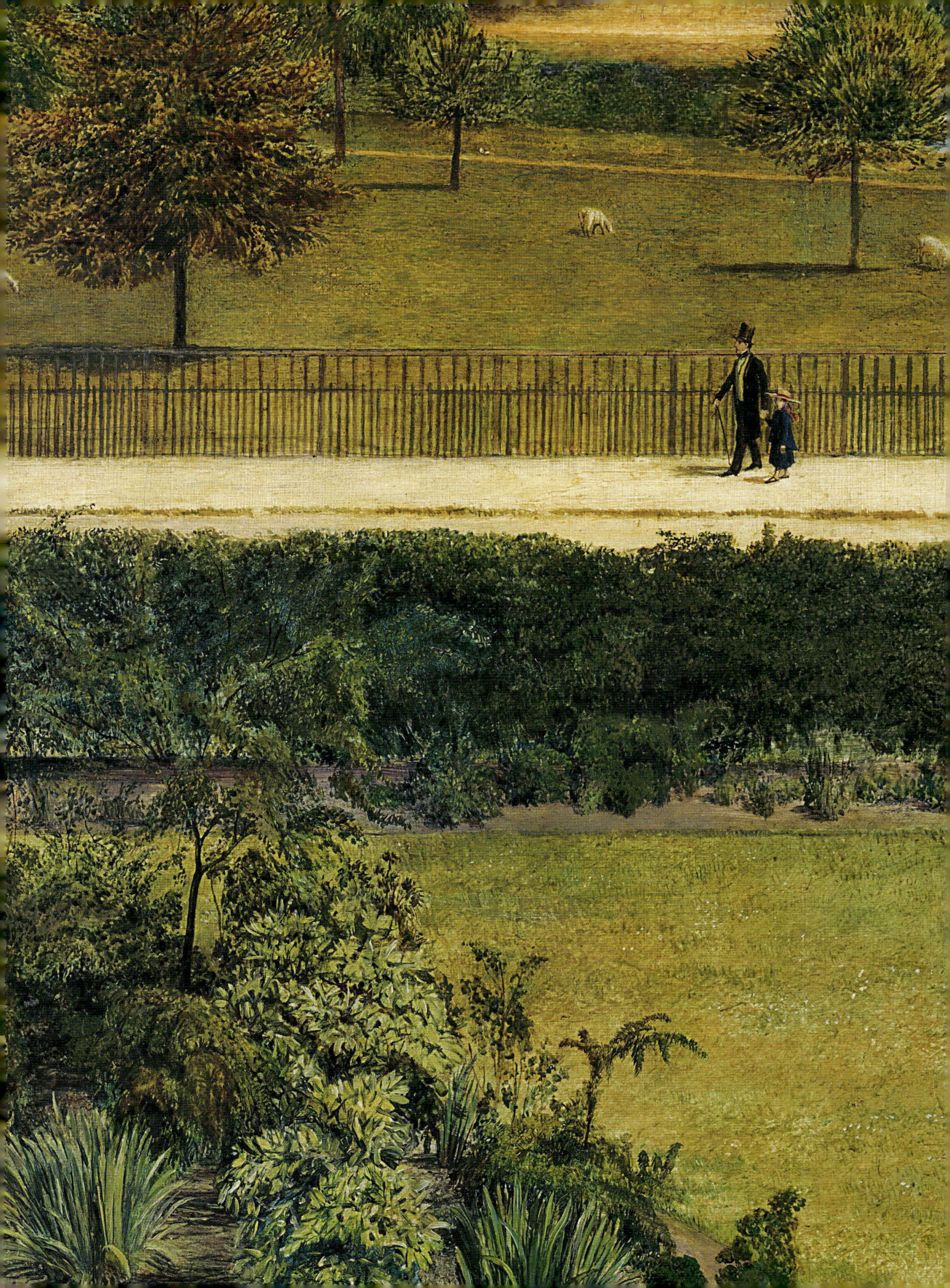

6

PEACE AND TRANQUILLITY

NON-LONDONERS, EVEN THOSE WHO are regular visitors, often imagine the city as an endless sweep of human flesh, a place full of pollution, traffic and unknowable chaos. And London is all of those things, or can be. But those who spend more time in the capital know that you can bypass the busy streets with quiet side roads, or escape the crowds into the many, many parks, and it's not unusual to find yourself quite alone when walking the river path or sitting in a forgotten square.

This side of London is one that has often found its reflection in art – perhaps for the overwhelming reason that it is far more straightforward to paint a static park or river view than a busy boulevard. But artists have also responded to the character of the city itself. London is one of the world's greenest major cities, with four times as much open space as Paris or New York. The eight famous Royal Parks – including Hyde Park, St James's Park and Regent's Park – were established by the royal family to allow them to continue their beloved rural pursuits of hunting and riding within their capital city. Painters have captured the changing fashions in garden design – from the formal French-inspired layouts of the seventeenth century to the romantic and picturesque designs pioneered by native gardeners.

The eighteenth century brought a rise in the popularity of landscape painting and a discovery of the sublime qualities of the British landscape. But while sketching trips to the rugged environs of the Lake District or North Wales were important, many painters also made use of the far more convenient rural landscape immediately surrounding central London in villages such as Hampstead and Richmond, which have now been absorbed into the metropolitan area. Even artists deeply associated with pastoral mysticism, such as William Blake (1757–1827)and Samuel Palmer (1805–81), trained their vision by observing Hampstead's hills and ponds.

Other artists have found beauty in the pollution, the choking smog creating the mysterious lighting effects which brought painters such as Claude Monet (1840–1926) and Victor Pasmore (1908–98) towards pure abstraction.

Charles Allston Collins *May, in the Regent's Park* 1851 (detail). See p.140

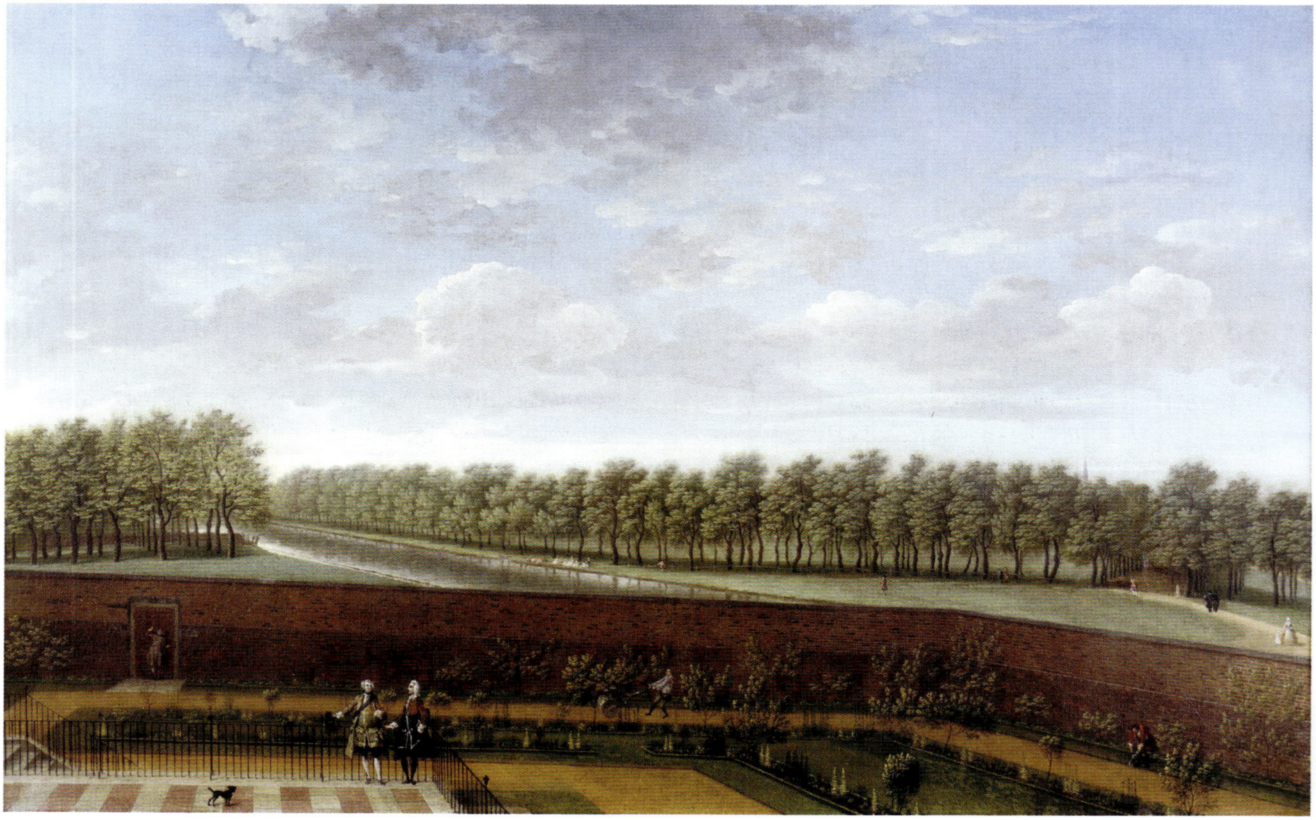

St James's Park from the Terrace of No. 10 Downing Street

British School c.1736–40

Who is this in the back garden of Number 10? The figure on the left is possibly Robert Walpole, the first prime minister, who was given the property by George II (r.1727–60). The garden terrace is here arranged in a neat geometrical pattern typical for the time. It has gone on to provide the location for many memorable moments in British political history, including in 1991, when a mortar shell fired by the IRA landed here, narrowly avoiding killing the cabinet.

Over the wall there is a sweeping view of St James's Park and a real sense of the rural feeling the park's designers were trying to invoke. The park was created by James I (r.1603–25) in the early seventeenth century; he kept exotic animals including an elephant and crocodiles here. It was reshaped by Charles II (r.1660–85) in the French style – you can see the long, straight canal which once ran through the park in imitation of Versailles. The park was a fashionable spot around this time for strolling and impromptu acts of lechery. Cows grazed and visitors could buy freshly-squeezed milk.

Kew Gardens: The Pagoda and Bridge

Richard Wilson 1762

Richard Wilson was a pioneer of British landscape art who influenced J.M.W. Turner (1775–1851) and John Constable (1776–1837). He began as a portrait painter but in the 1740s started painting landscapes, previously the preserve of Dutch painters and the likes of Claude Lorrain (1600–82). He may have been spurred on by seeing the latter's work in the collections of his patrons. Like Lorrain, Wilson played close attention to nature – the clouds, trees, streams and flowers – and rearranged and selected the topography to suit his composition.

Wilson's London paintings are concentrated on the still-rural reaches of the River Thames around Richmond. This one is unusual in that it includes a recognisable landmark – the then recently built Chinese pagoda at Kew Gardens. Tapping into a craze for Chinoiserie, the ten-story, tapering structure was unlike anything Londoners had seen before, and many doubted it would stay standing. The lake has been moved for effect and to show the rustic wooden bridge, which is said to have been built overnight to surprise Charles II's queen. Kew began life as an aristocratic estate and developed haphazardly from the early seventeenth century, before being adopted as the national botanical garden in 1840.

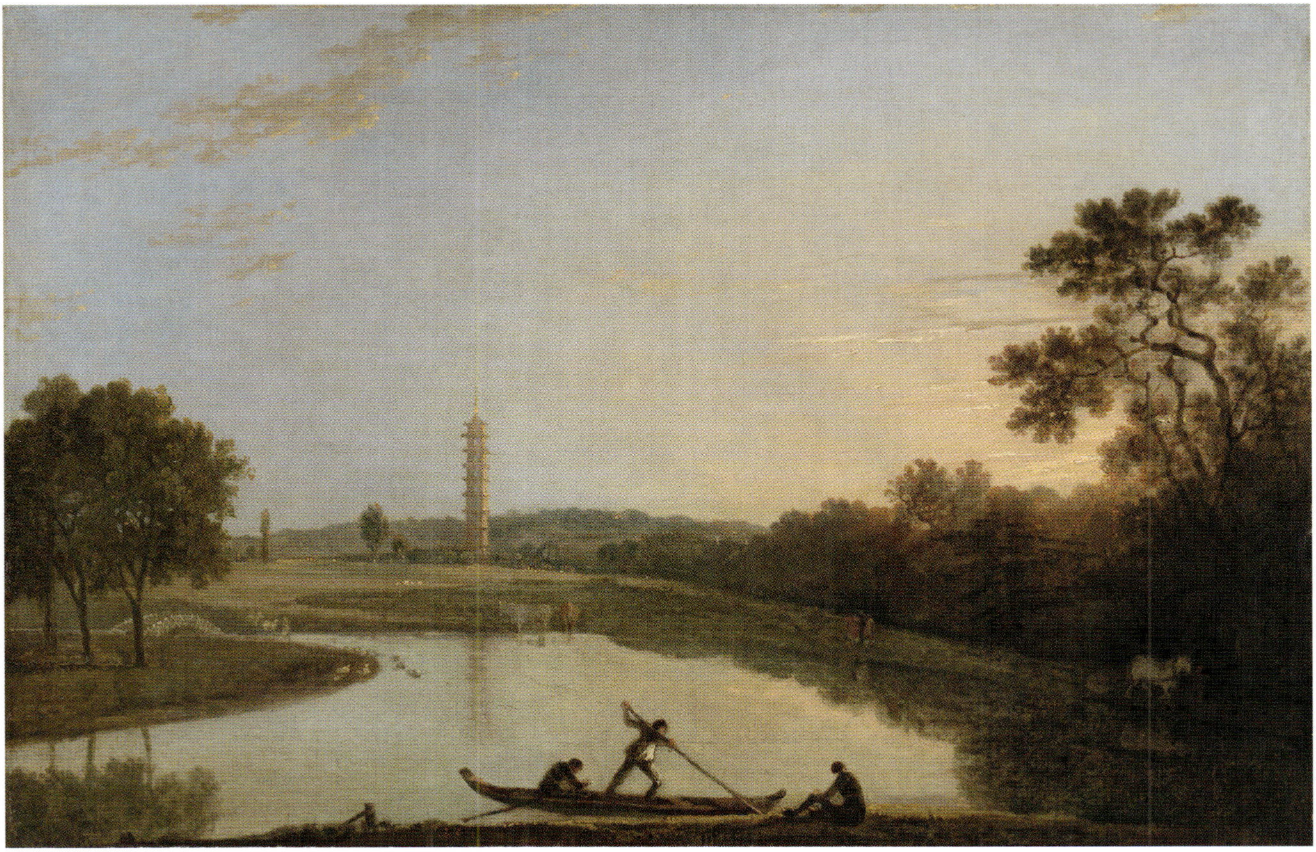

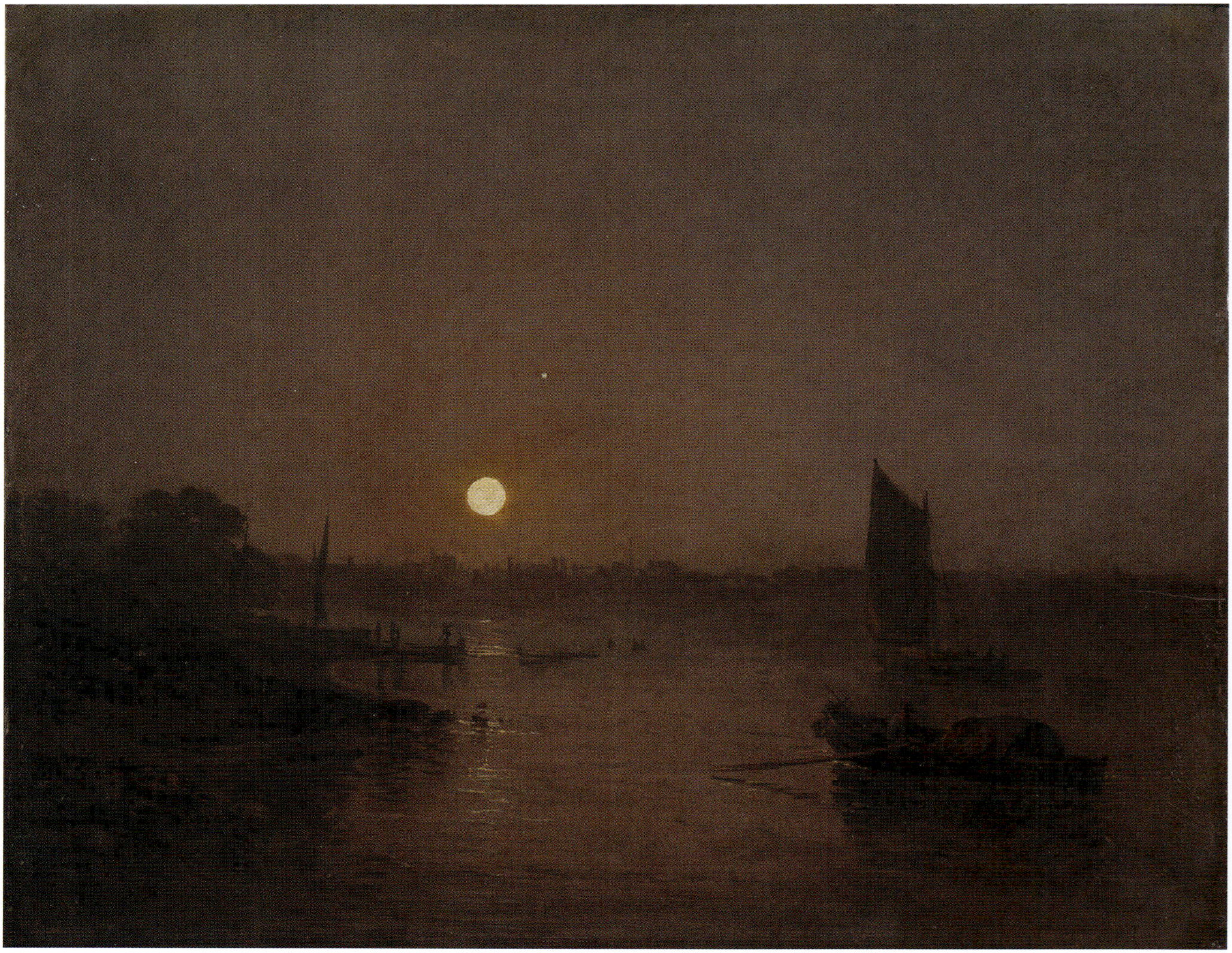

Moonlight, a Study at Millbank

J.M.W. Turner exhibited 1797

This was only the second oil painting that the young Turner submitted to the Royal Academy. He didn't go on to paint central London much in oil, preferring watercolour for such scenes. It is hard to tell exactly what this view shows but the title suggests it is looking north from the current location of Millbank pier, just outside the present site of Tate Britain. This painting predates Vauxhall Bridge, which now blocks the view. Moonlight effects were popular with collectors at the time, and a speciality of Dutch landscape painters and English artists such as Henry Pether (p.172).

Thomson's Aeolian Harp

J.M.W. Turner exhibited 1809

The view of the languidly winding River Thames from Richmond Hill is one of the most beautiful in England, and is protected by an act of Parliament. Although deep within London, evidence of the city has been carefully excluded from view, leaving a scene of timeless Arcadian splendour.

Turner lived nearby in Twickenham for a large part of his working life, and drew and painted this scene often. This painting sees him mid-career, in self-imposed competition with the classical landscapes of Claude Lorrain (1600–82), not yet ready to paint landscapes solely for their beauty. And so he has added an invented classical scene, inspired by James Thomson's poem *An Ode on Aeolus's Harp* (c.1748). The Three Graces and the Four Seasons dance around the titular harp, a divine instrument that played when touched by the wind.

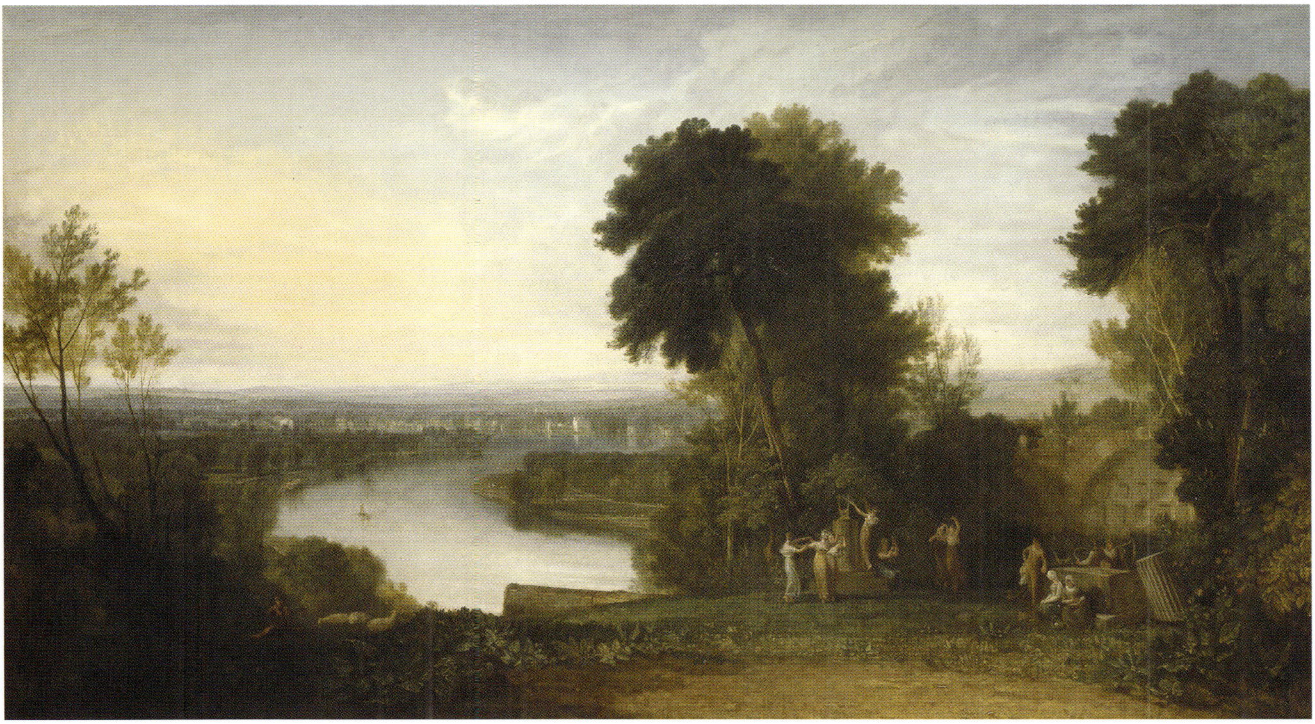

May, in the Regent's Park

Charles Allston Collins 1851

The Pre-Raphaelites were the leading lights of London's art scene in the mid nineteenth century, but they were largely uninterested in painting the city itself. They focused on figures rather than landscapes, and the location that appears most often is the Holy Land in their many Biblical scenes. Two important exceptions are John Roddam Spencer Stanhope's (1829–1908) *Thoughts of the Past*, exhibited 1859, which shows a view of Waterloo Bridge through a window, and Ford Madox Brown's (1821–93) *Work* 1852–65, which shows road builders in a Hampstead street. However, in both of these the topography is secondary to the narrative.

This painting by Collins is unusual, then, for its lack of central figures or moral payload. Collins was close to John Everett Millais (1829–96) but was never officially accepted into the Pre-Raphaelite Brotherhood. He ended up as a writer like his brother, Wilkie Collins, and his father-in-law, Charles Dickens. This painting of Regent's Park shows several Pre-Raphaelite traits, for which it was criticised when it was first exhibited. Critics complained about Collins's obsessive attention to detail, in his painting of the trees and shrubs, for example. They also disliked the lack of receding perspective, which makes the composition appear as flat horizontal strips.

Collins lived with his mother in 17 Hanover Terrace, one of the elegant and expensive white stucco terraces created by John Nash to surround the park. This view is the one out of his upper window across to the boating lake.

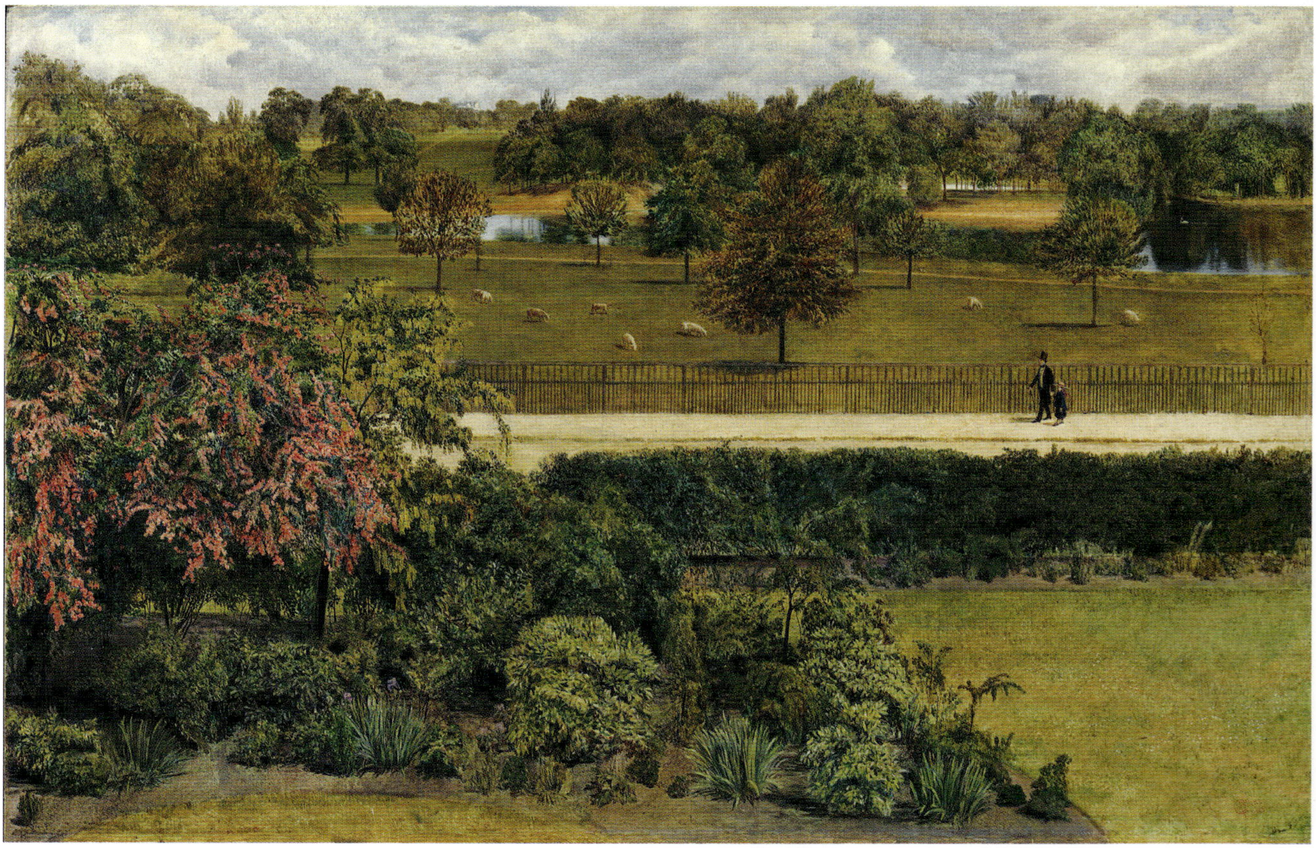

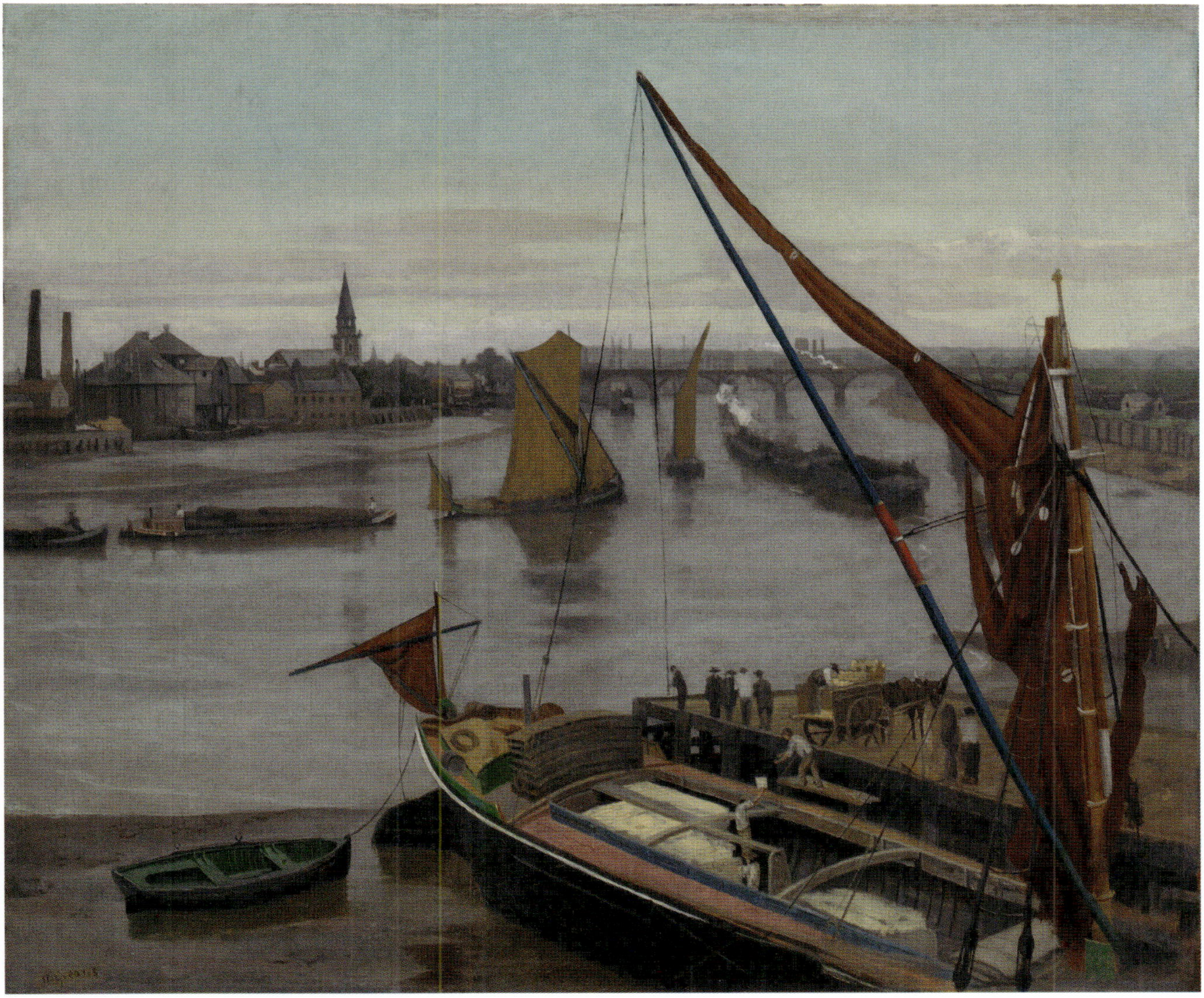

Battersea Reach

Walter Greaves c.1870

After Whistler moved to Chelsea, Walter Greaves became his assistant, student and friend, abandoning the characterful, untutored style of his earlier work (pp.94–5) for the more subdued atmospherics of the master.

The view shown here is south from around Cremorne Pleasure Garden. Battersea is to the left and to the right is the location of Chelsea Harbour. Dominant in the foreground is a Thames barge with its red sail. The high angle lends the scene a sense of picturesque charm rather than the bustling energy of William Lionel Wyllie's painting of a similar subject, painted from the water's level (pp.66–7). Unlike his teacher, Greaves was proud of the accuracy with which he depicted the river life he knew so well. 'To Whistler a boat was always a [colour] tone,' he later recalled. 'To us it was always a boat.'

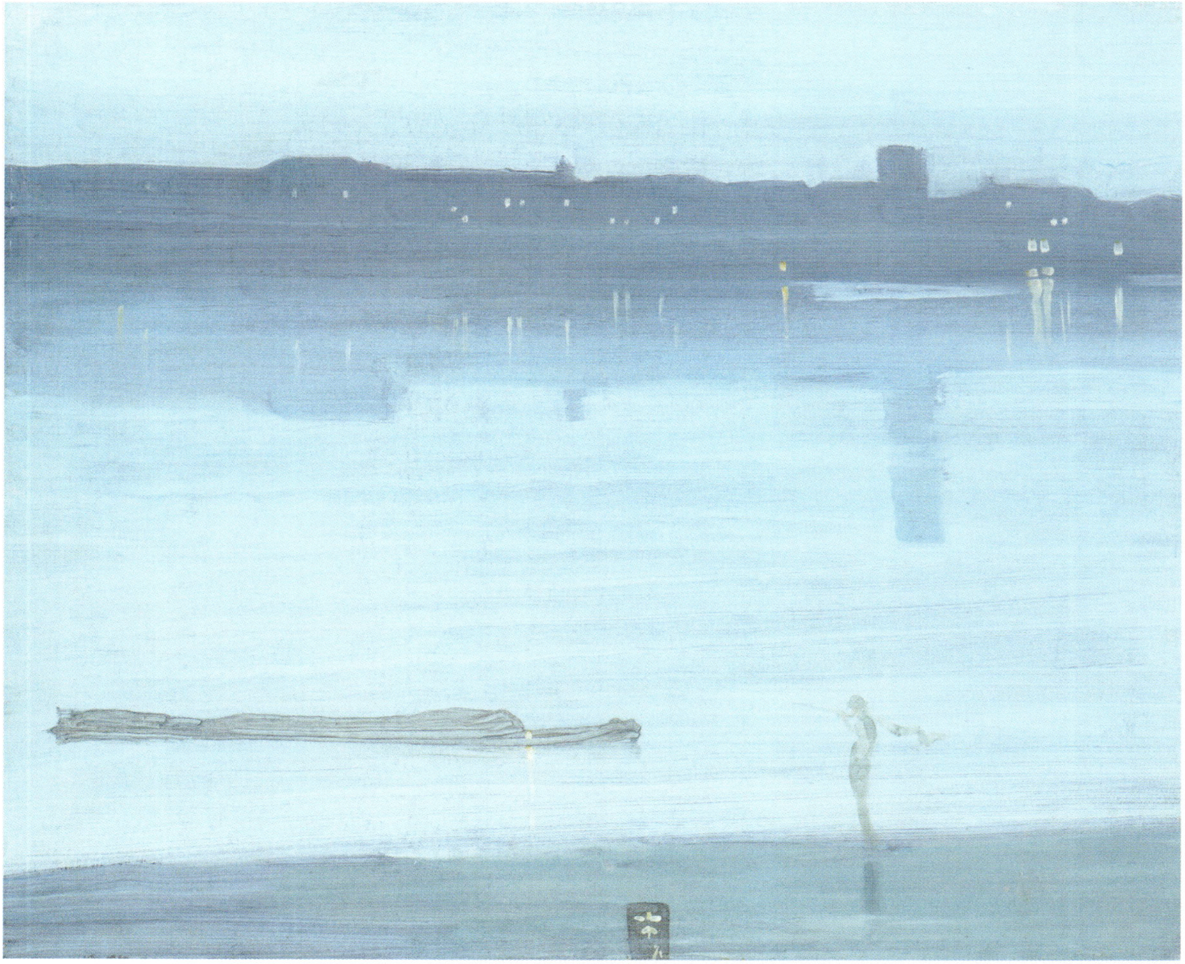

Nocturne: Blue and Silver – Chelsea

James Abbott McNeill Whistler 1871

In the second half of the nineteenth century, Chelsea was perfect for ambitious artists – vigorous, unpretentious and affordable, but still upmarket enough for the social climbers. Turner moved there in 1846 when it was little more than a fishing village. But it developed quickly, with the building of the Chelsea Embankment in 1874. Whistler lived in several addresses around Tite Street from 1863 onwards and was the social butterfly at the hub of a network of artists, poets and bon vivants.

Whistler didn't need to look far for subject matter – just outside his front door was the River Thames, with its beguiling, ever-shifting light and picturesque barges, and Old Battersea Bridge, the river's last surviving wooden bridge and a romantic tumble of crumbling beams.

This painting is the first of his famous Nocturnes, in which the Thames would dissolve into a near-abstract 'arrangement of line, form and colour', as he put it. Although he aimed to divest 'the picture of any outside anecdotal interest', his mother recalled he was inspired to paint it after returning home with her on a steamer (a passenger boat) from Westminster. The river was in a 'glow of rare transparency an hour before sunset' and he rushed home to set it down on canvas.

This moonlit view shows Chelsea from Battersea Bridge – the square bulk to the right is Chelsea Old Church. It is a similar stretch of river to that painted by Turner seventy years earlier (p.138), but Whistler's account of it belongs to a new era.

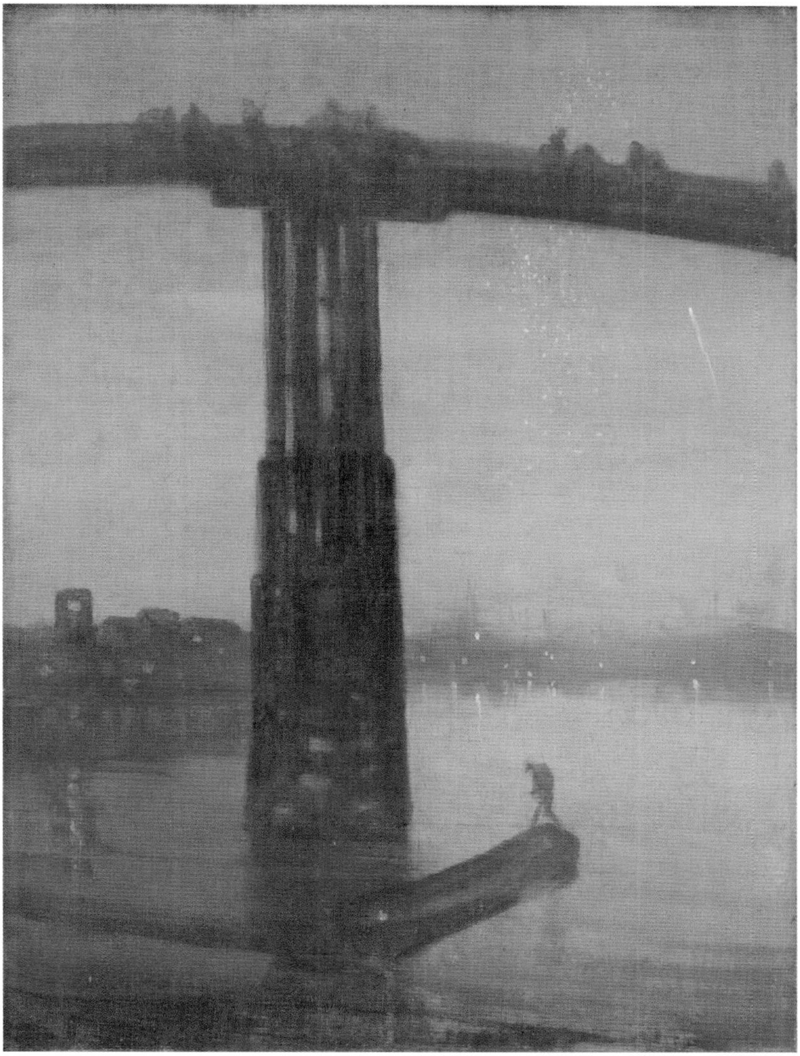

Nocturne: Blue and Gold – Old Battersea Bridge

James Abbott McNeill Whistler c.1872–5

In this Nocturne, Whistler turns the precarious wooden arc of Old Battersea Bridge into a shadowy form that is nearly impossible to read. Dark figures seem to scurry along the top and the pinpricks of light on the right-hand side come from a falling firework. It's likely he was inspired by his beloved Japanese woodcuts, such as those by Hiroshige (1797–1858), which show tightly cropped arched bridges.

In his notorious libel trial against the critic John Ruskin (1819–1900), Whistler explained that: 'I did not intend it to be a correct portrait of the bridge, but only a painting of a moonlight scene.' Nonetheless it is a fairly accurate depiction of the crossing, which was replaced by the less quaint but far more practical cast-iron structure in 1890.

Waterloo Bridge, Sunlight Effect

Claude Monet 1903

Houses of Parliament, Effect of Sunlight in Fog

Claude Monet 1904

A good London sunset is unforgettable – the grey, flat light that reigns most days is for half an hour replaced by searing orange and pink beams that illuminate dramatic clouds and twinkle off the River Thames. Claude Monet was the poet of these sunsets and sunrises, their beauty made manifold by the thick, foggy air of early twentieth-century London. He had a method of painting many views of the same subject simultaneously, capturing the changing effects of the light. In London, where one can often experience all four seasons in the space of twenty minutes, he nearly met his match.

'The weather is magnificent but unsettled,' he wrote to his wife about a day's work on the Thames. 'I can't begin

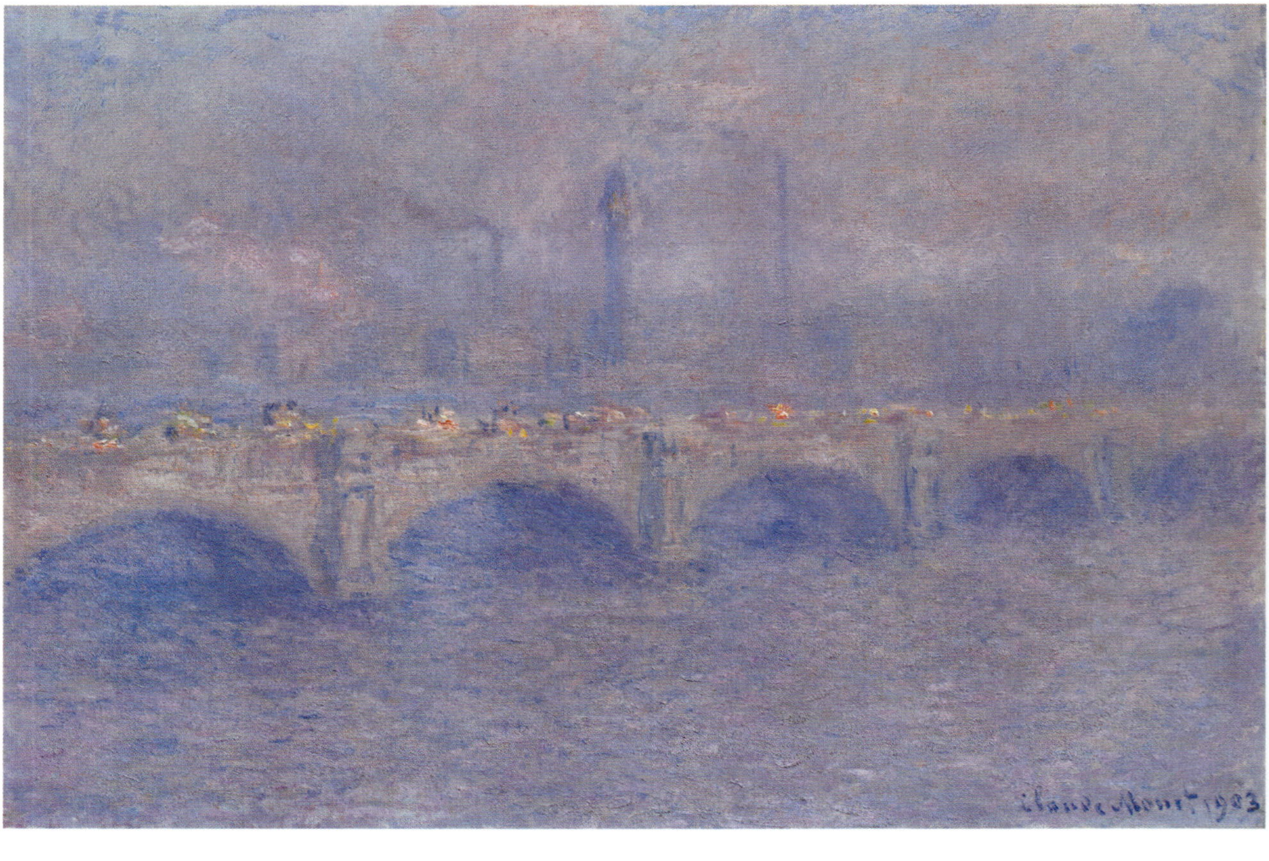

to describe a day as wonderful as this. One marvel after another, each lasting less than five minutes, it was enough to drive one mad. No country could be more extraordinary for a painter.'

Monet came on pilgrimages to London for three successive years in 1899, 1900 and 1901, returning to the subject of an early work: the Thames near the Houses of Parliament. Staying in the Savoy, he painted the view right towards Parliament (below) and left towards Waterloo Bridge (below left), executing dozens of versions of each.

This is the granite Waterloo Bridge whose opening was celebrated in paint by John Constable (pp.166–7). Monet usually painted it in the morning sun – here you can see the dense traffic travelling across it. When the finished paintings were exhibited in Paris in 1904, the catalogue described the bridge as like a 'carnival procession, a floral garland in the middle of this indeterminate space'.

In the afternoon Monet would move to a spot outside St Thomas' Hospital on the other side of the river and paint the sun setting behind the Palace of Westminster. Although premised in the fiery sky, its dappled reflections in the water and the looming silhouette of the neo-Gothic architecture, these paintings take leave of the earthly realm and rejoice in the sheer beauty of light and colour.

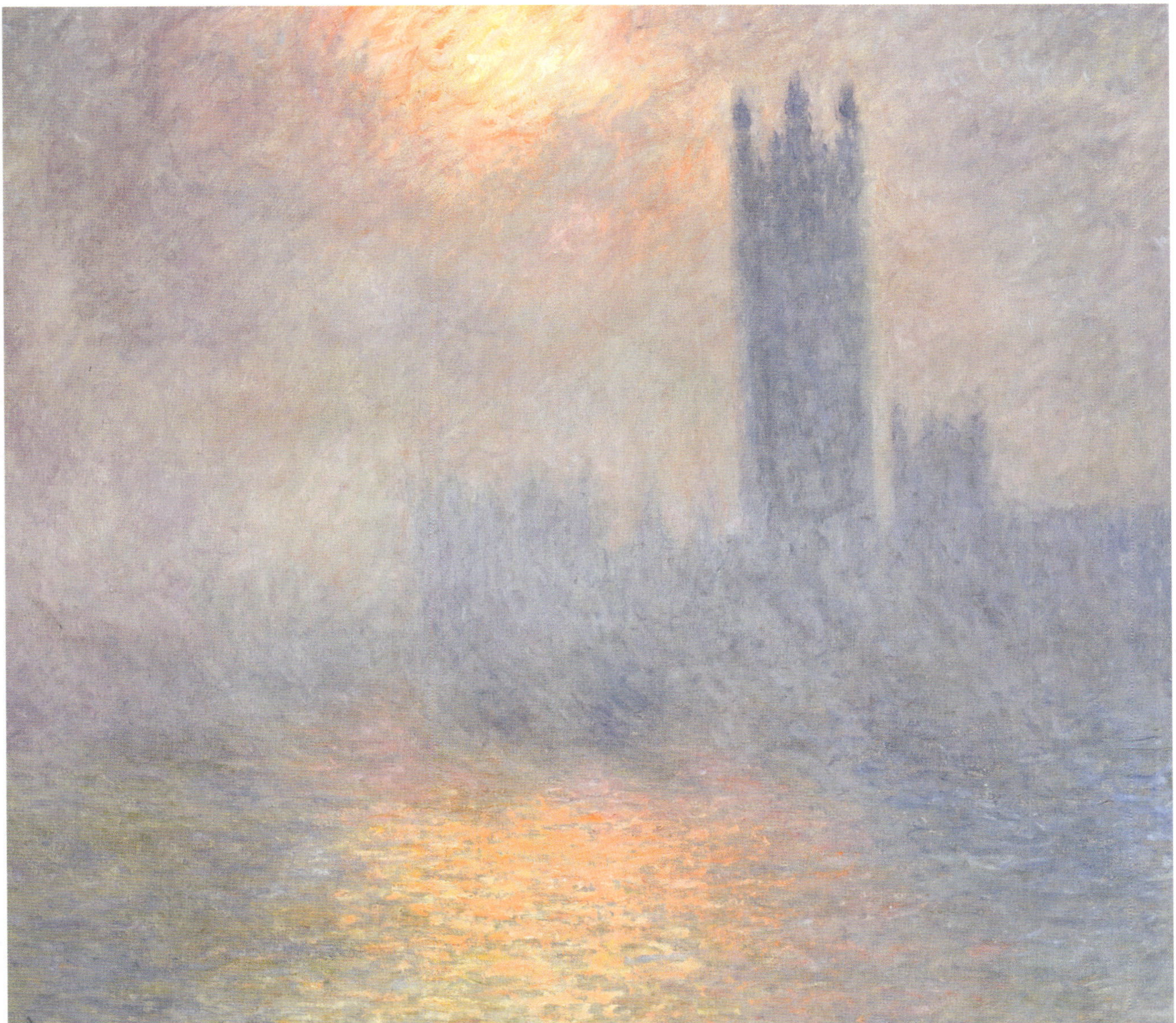

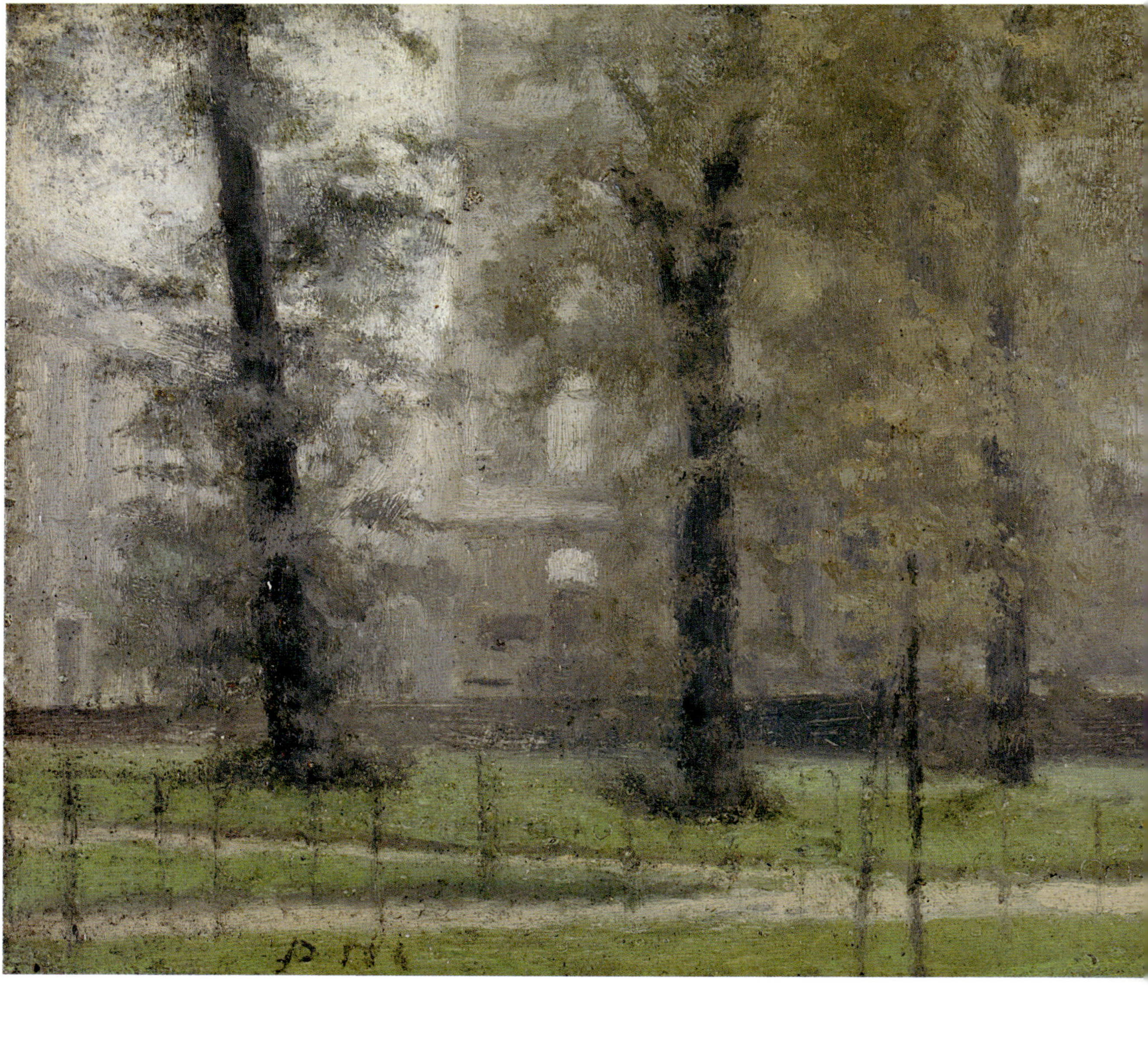
P H

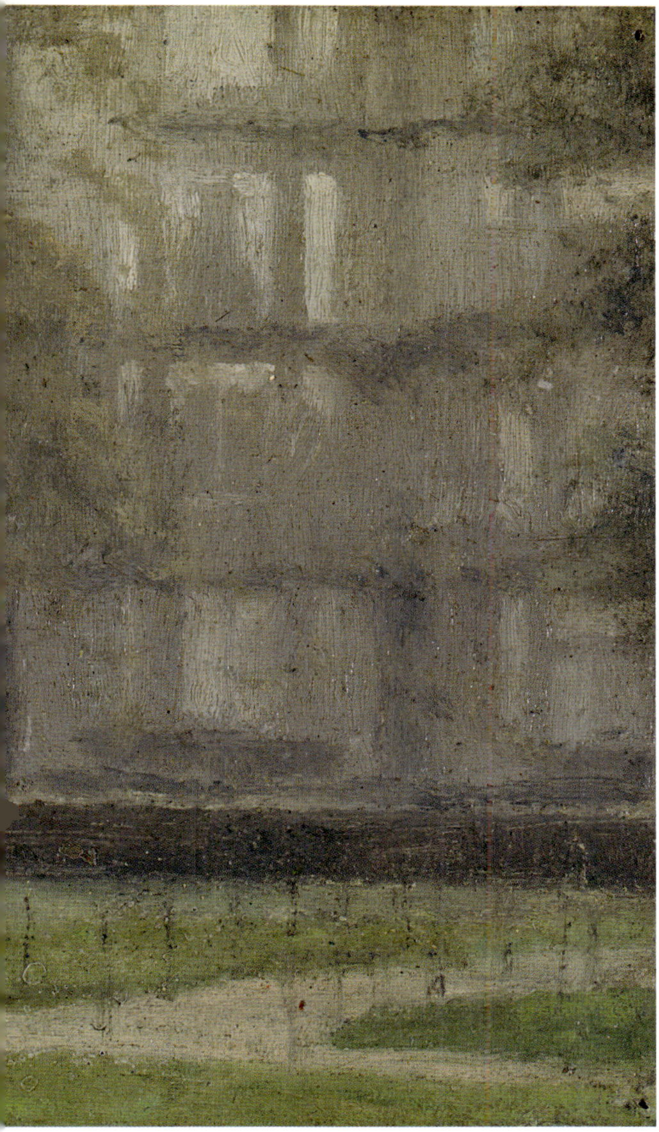

By Hyde Park Gate, Kensington Gardens

Paul Maitland c.1906

Paul Maitland was an isolated artist who in the last years of his life obsessively painted views of the southern half of Kensington Gardens. He had a spinal injury that got worse as he got older, restricting him to subjects near his home, south of Kensington High Street.

His earlier paintings focus on river scenes influenced by Whistler. The majority are like this, very small oil paintings on wooden panels, executed on the spot. Maitland was considered to be one of the 'London Impressionists', but his work has a grey, drizzly quality rather than the bright colours associated with the style. He resolutely avoids the specific – the Royal Albert Hall, the Albert Monument and Kensington Palace are just metres from this spot – instead capturing a universal sense of a big city park, hemmed in by large buildings.

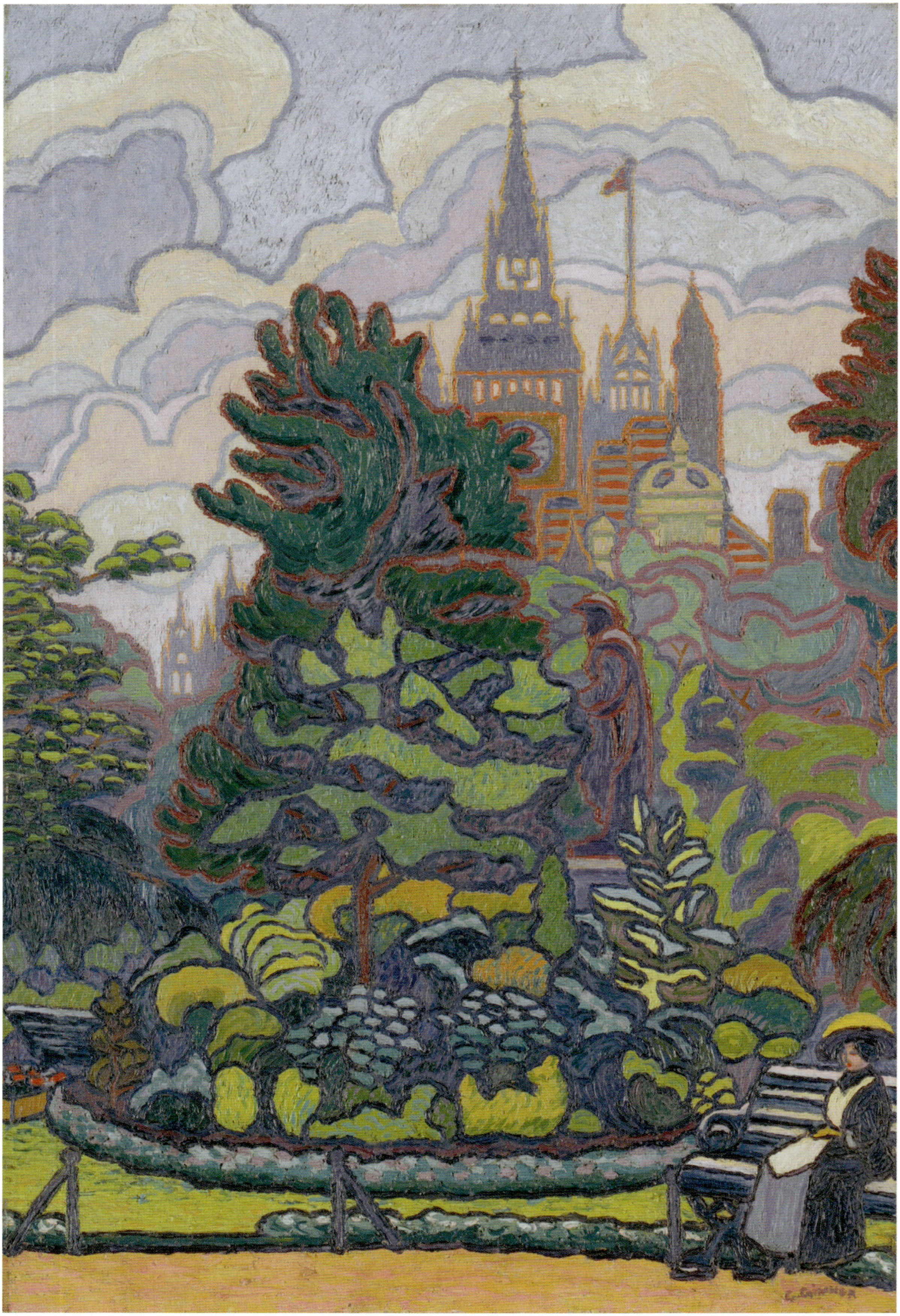

Victoria Embankment Gardens

Charles Ginner 1912

Part of the Camden Town Group, Ginner presents the happiest view of London, with bold, bright, jewel-like colours. He would usually make a detailed preparatory sketch, then apply the paint methodically, even planning out the order in which the colours would be added. Born in France, Ginner stayed in touch with the art scene there. This work shows the strong influence of Vincent van Gogh (1853–90) with its boldly outlined blocks of colour. The vivid, almost unnatural colours recall Henri Matisse (1899–1954) or André Derain (pp.68–9).

The scene is an unusual variant on the familiar view of the Palace of Westminster from the north – rather than painting it from the river, Ginner shows the clock tower peeking out behind the trees of Whitehall Gardens, a little known and therefore tranquil spot behind Charing Cross Station. The building in front of Parliament is New Scotland Yard, where the Metropolitan Police are once again based after a half-century absence.

The Quiet River: The Thames at Chiswick

Victor Pasmore 1943–4

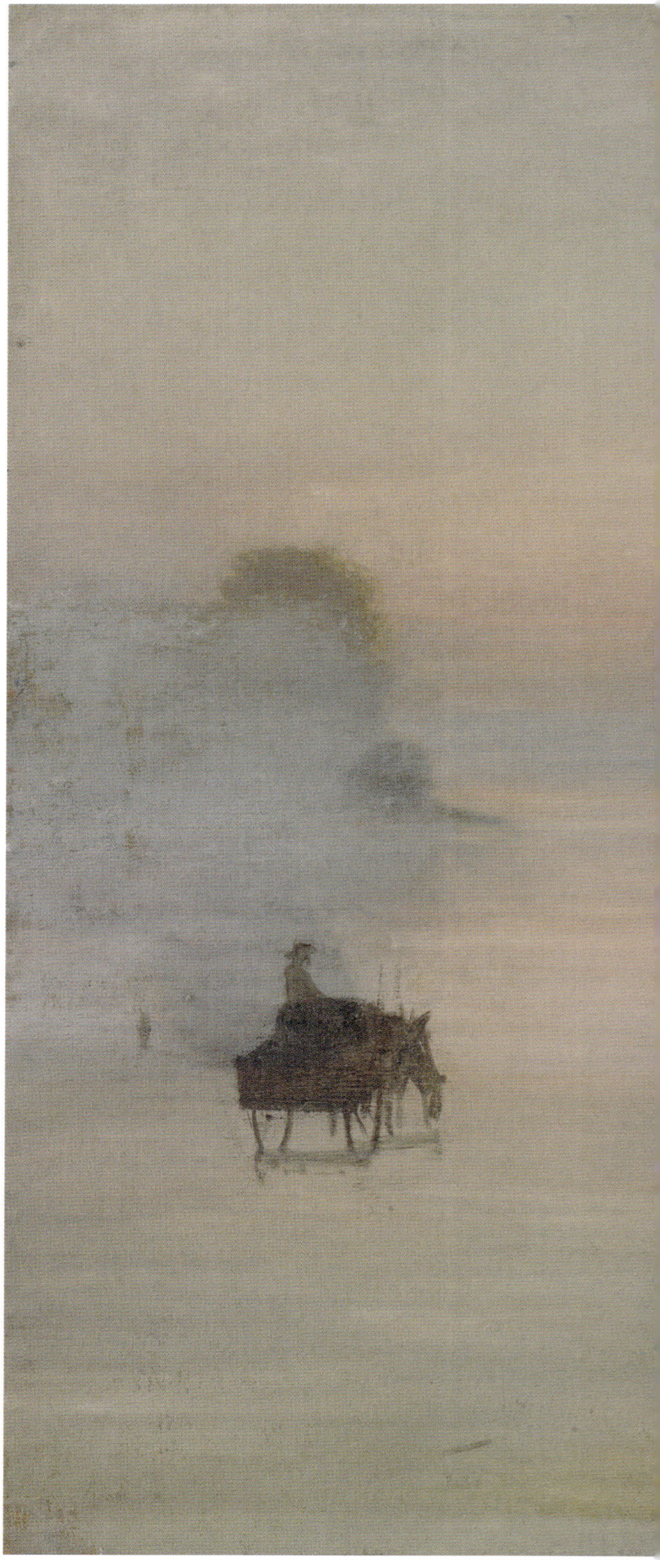

This dreamy painting of the river captures the early-morning London haze more honestly than Monet's theatrics, and looks back to Whistler and Turner. Pasmore was a founding member of the Euston Road School, who, like their predecessors in Camden Town, advocated painting realist views of the city. In their case they had a political goal to engage the general public in art. The School broke up at the beginning of the Second World War and Pasmore was imprisoned for being a conscientious objector.

This painting was part of series made near Pasmore's home on Upper Mall in Chiswick, a western suburb. The view west includes Chiswick Eyot and maybe the chimneys of the Fuller's brewery. However, Pasmore has invented elements such as the breakwater extending across the middle of the painting for compositional reasons. This work was the start of a move away from realism and after the war Pasmore emerged as one of England's leading abstract artists.

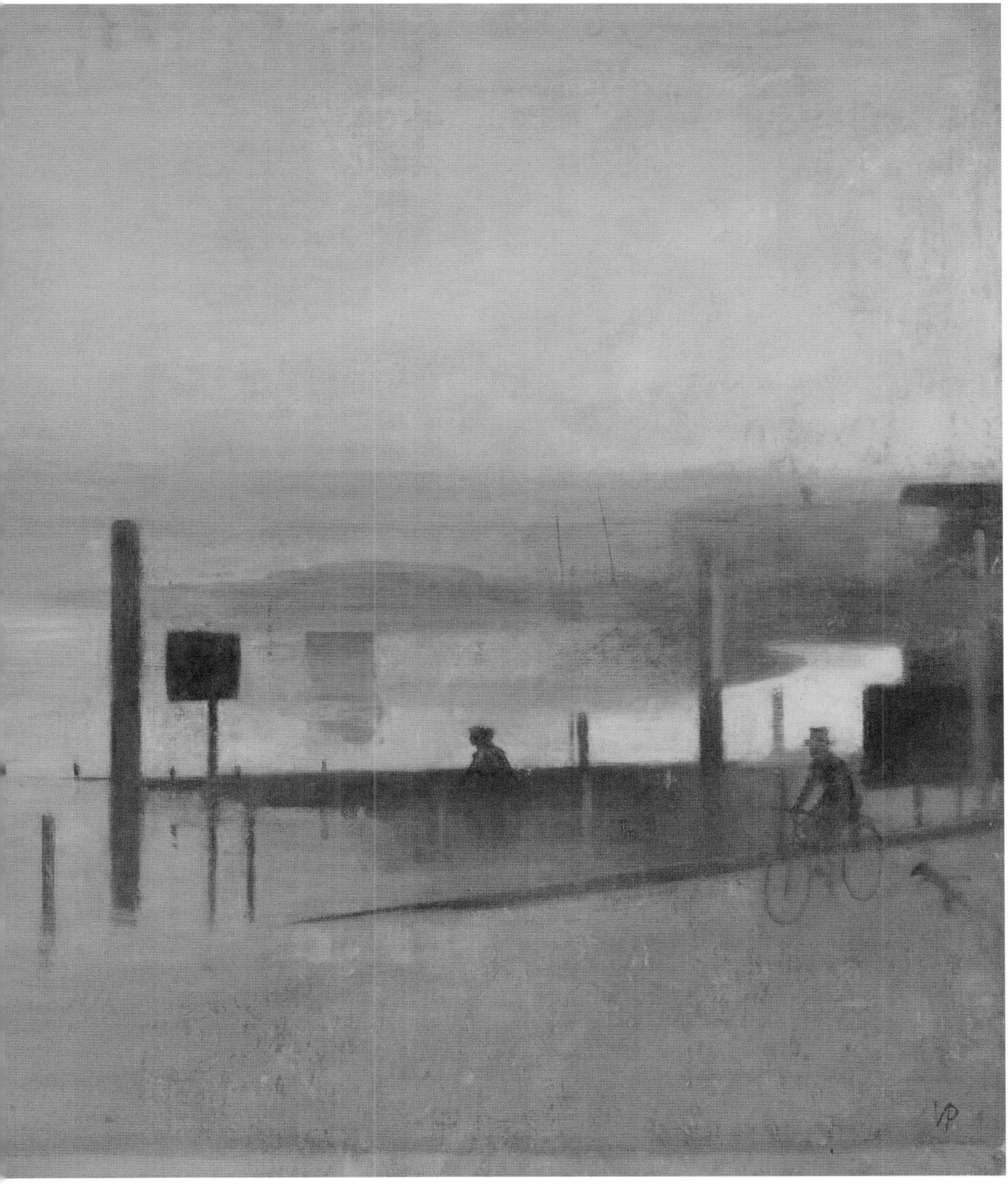

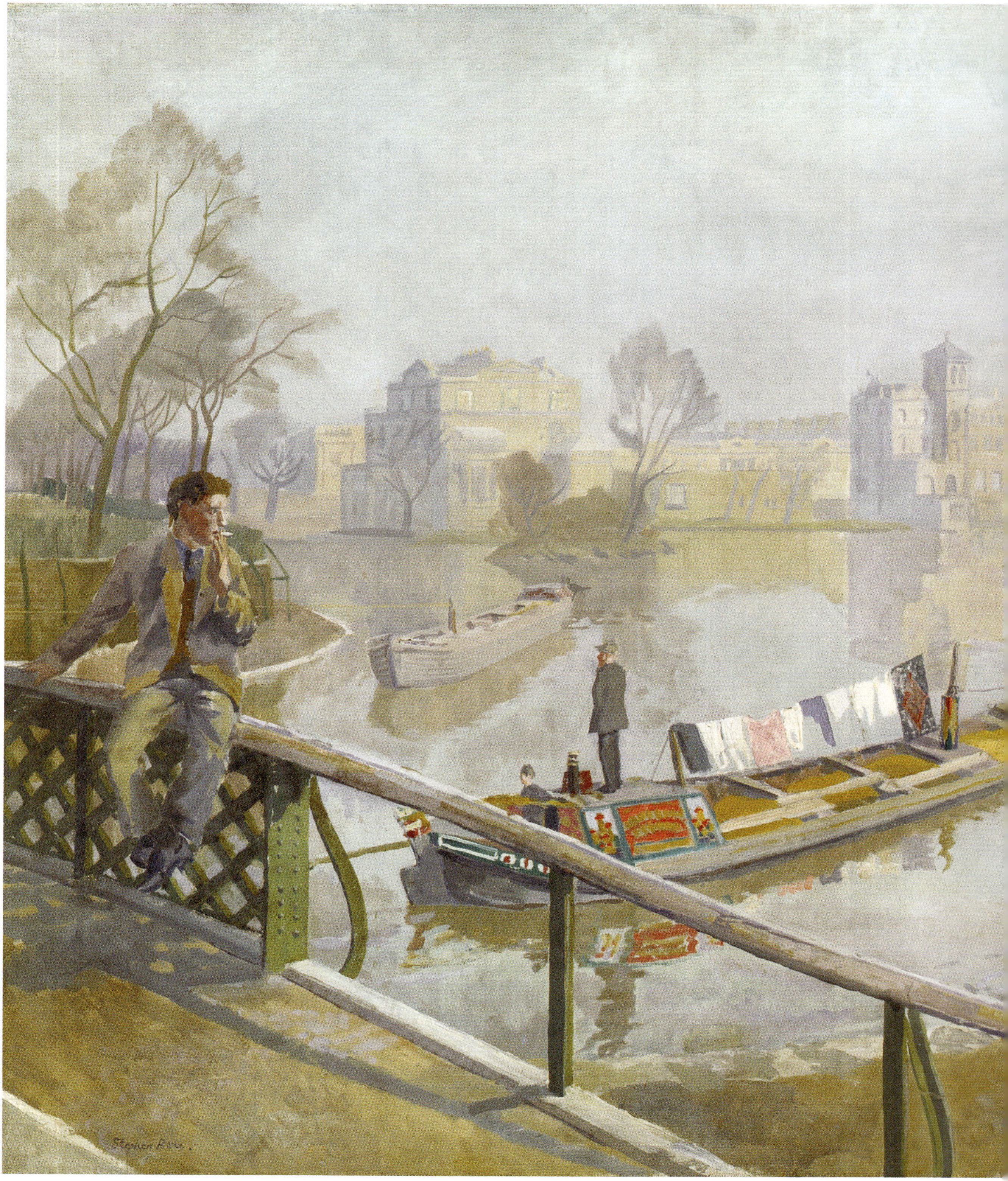

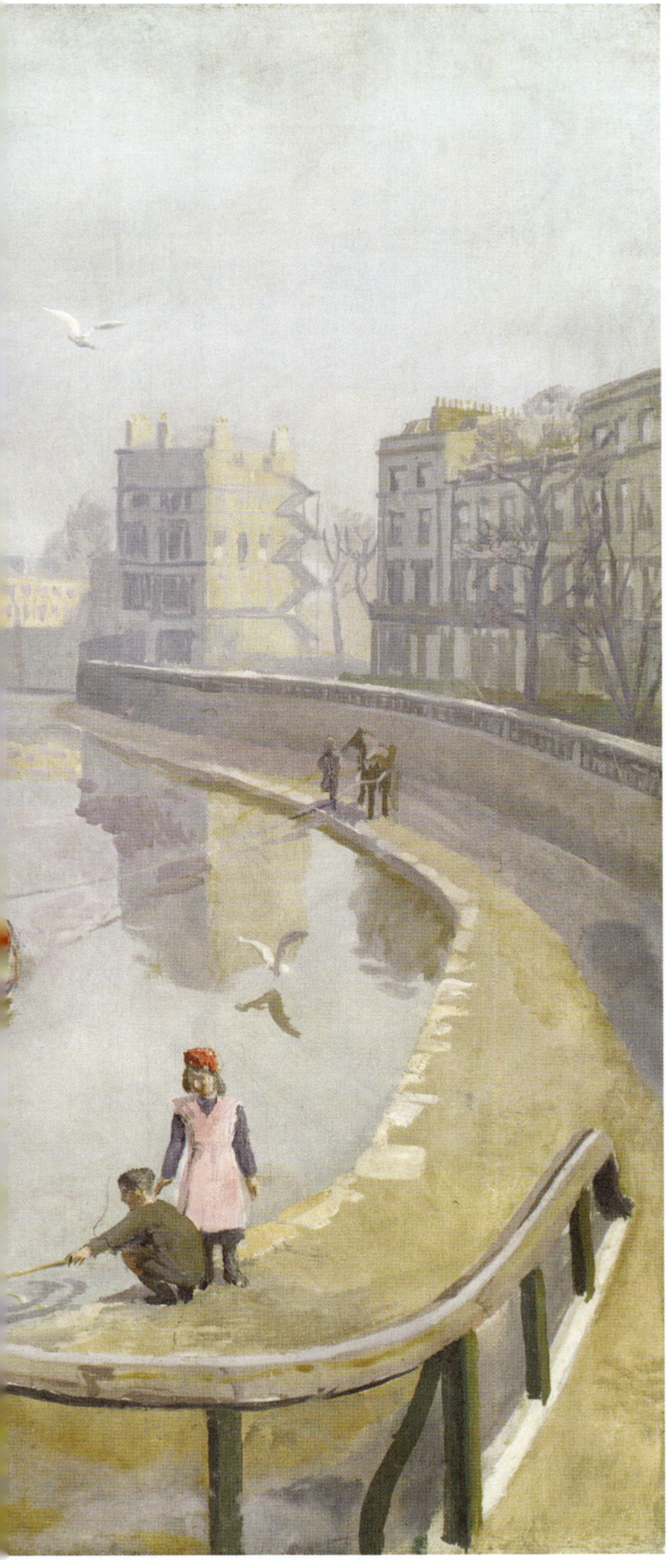

Little Venice

Stephen Bone 1952

Placid water merges into the cloudless sky; a man lolls on the railings while children play in the canal water. The Grand Union and Regent's Canals meet in this junction at the back of Paddington Station, giving the area its tongue-in-cheek name. No longer major transit routes, the canals are used mainly by pleasure boats to the nearby London Zoo and canal-barge dwellers, such as those pictured here. The houses shown at the back have since been replaced by Rembrandt Gardens, named in honour of the canal-filled city of Amsterdam.

Stephen Bone liked to paint water and its reflections, and during the Second World War he was attached to the Navy as an official war artist. His book *Albion: An Artist's Britain* (1939) includes landscapes from every part of the country. After the war, Bone found his style of painting out of fashion, and worked as an art critic, broadcaster and children's author.

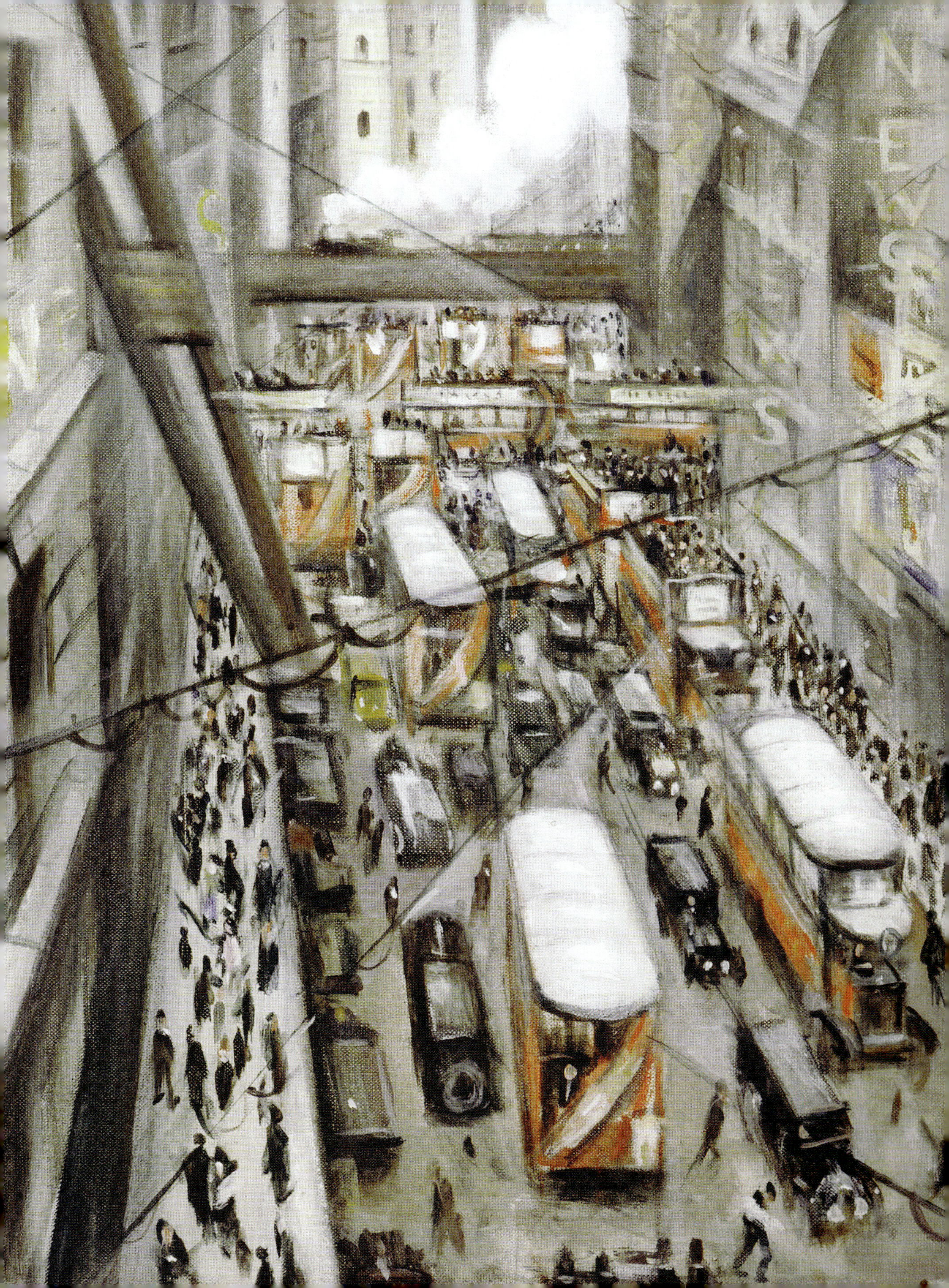
NEWS

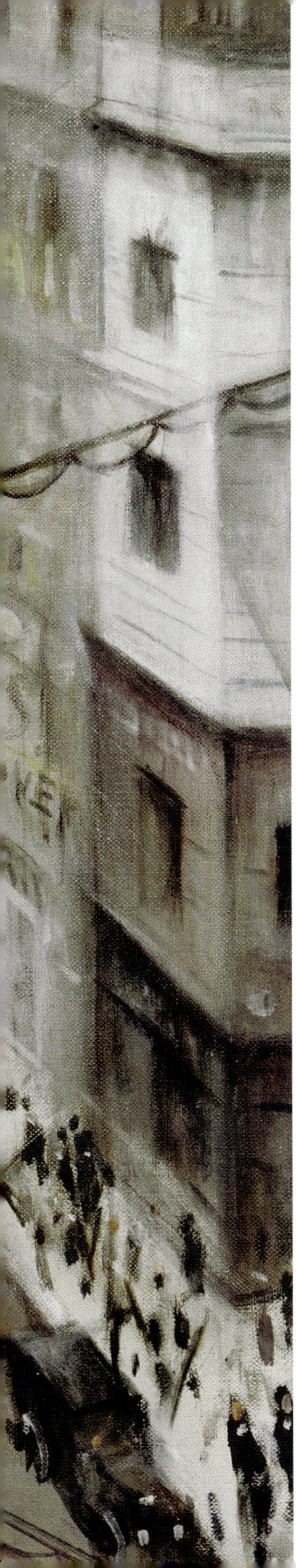

7

A CITY OF SPECTACLE

WHAT IS THE PURPOSE OF A CITY? To provide a place for people to live and work, certainly, and also somewhere they can find entertainment and education. But for a capital city such as London, that once was the most powerful in the world, there is a need for something more – to inspire, to impress, to intimidate.

This is not something London has ever found easy. The grand schemes that transformed cities like Paris or Vienna into bombastic imperial capitals have always foundered in pragmatic, democratic, unsentimental London. Even when the tightly wound streets of the medieval city were swept away by the Great Fire of 1666, Londoners chose to rebuild the city pretty much as it was, albeit in brick and stone rather than wood.

Yet, in whatever haphazard fashion, London has acquired a roster of sights that are famous around the world. Many of these landmarks, and the paintings made to glorify them, date from two periods in which the city was attempting to assert its ascendency.

In 1750, London had recently overtaken Paris as Europe's largest city. It had over 600,000 inhabitants and was about to undergo an unprecedented growth spurt, quadrupling in the next century to become the biggest city that had ever existed. St Paul's Cathedral had been completed in 1710 and now Westminster and the West End were being brought up to the standard set abroad. The arrival of Canaletto in 1746 helped Londoners to see their city as a rival in beauty to Venice, and stimulated a generation of local artists to paint their hometown.

A century later, the city ruled the world's largest empire and engineering marvels, such as the Embankment, the railways and the new Palace of Westminster, were symbols of power and prowess. Victorian painters, many now forgotten, took up the challenge to create new icons which could be distributed around the country and the world via the extensive new systems of transport and communication. They created a range of paintings which are beguiling despite their bombast.

Christopher Richard Wynne Nevinson *Amongst the Nerves of the World* 1930 (detail).
See p.176

An Arch of Westminster Bridge

Samuel Scott c.1750

Westminster Bridge was more than just a quick way to get across the River Thames. The first bridge to be created in central London since the Romans, it was a symbol of prestige, modernity and success. Painters of the period, from homegrown talents like Samuel Scott to international superstar Canaletto (1697–1768), captured its construction at every stage.

This view is similar to one by Canaletto, which famously shows a bucket dangling in silhouette. Scott also shows the workers on the bridge, enjoying a drink on a rudimentary wooden platform, perhaps celebrating its completion. However, it is hard to explain the presence of swimmers at the bottom right, surely a dangerous and unpleasant thing to do in the Thames.

Sometimes described as a follower of Canaletto, Scott was making topographical views of London before the Venetian artist's arrival in 1746. But the sudden growth in demand for such work may have encouraged him to switch from the marine paintings he had specialised in before. Scott lived in Covent Garden and was friends with William Hogarth (1697–1764) and the other artists who populated the area at that time. His views of Old London Bridge, the Tower of London and Westminster were much copied.

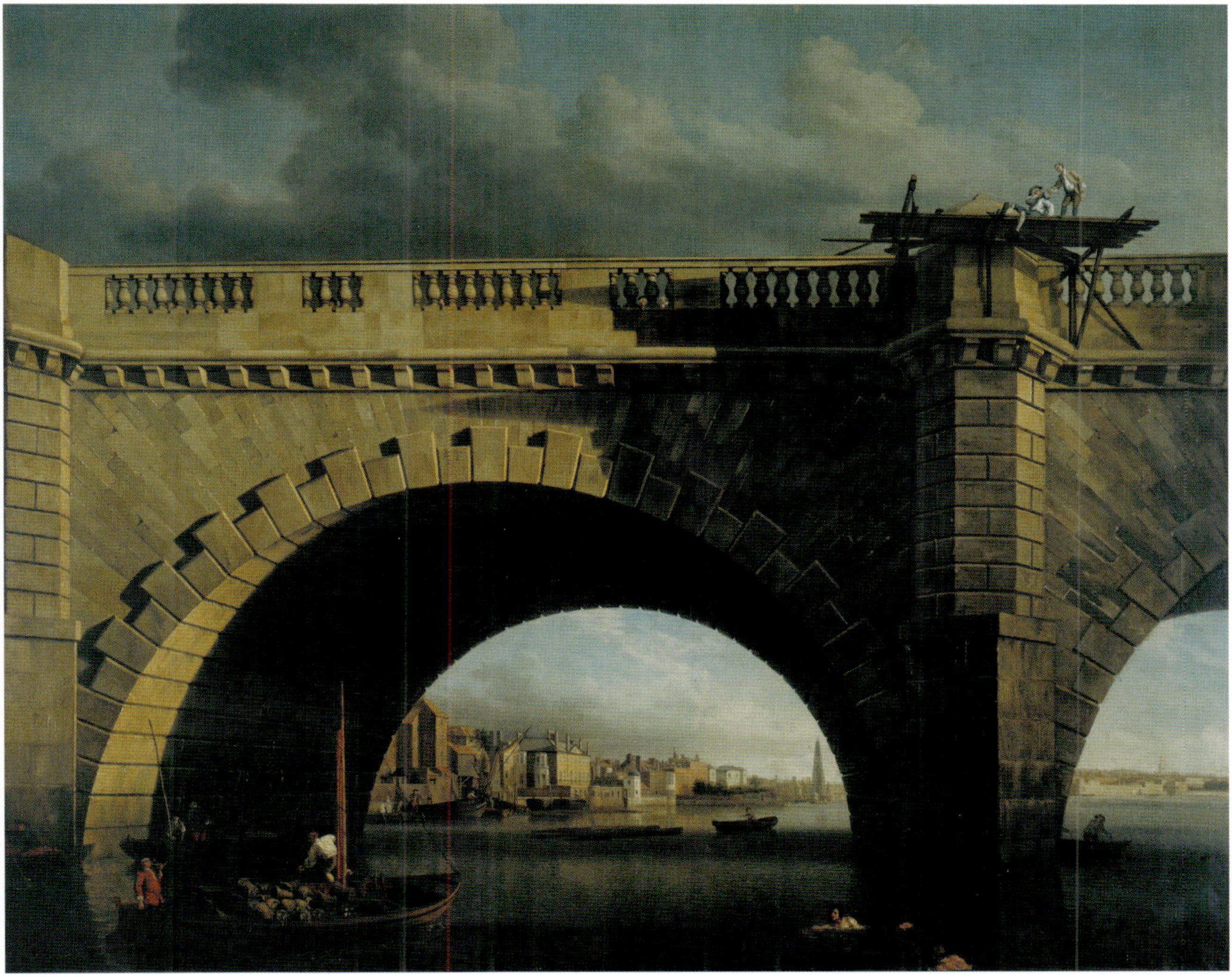

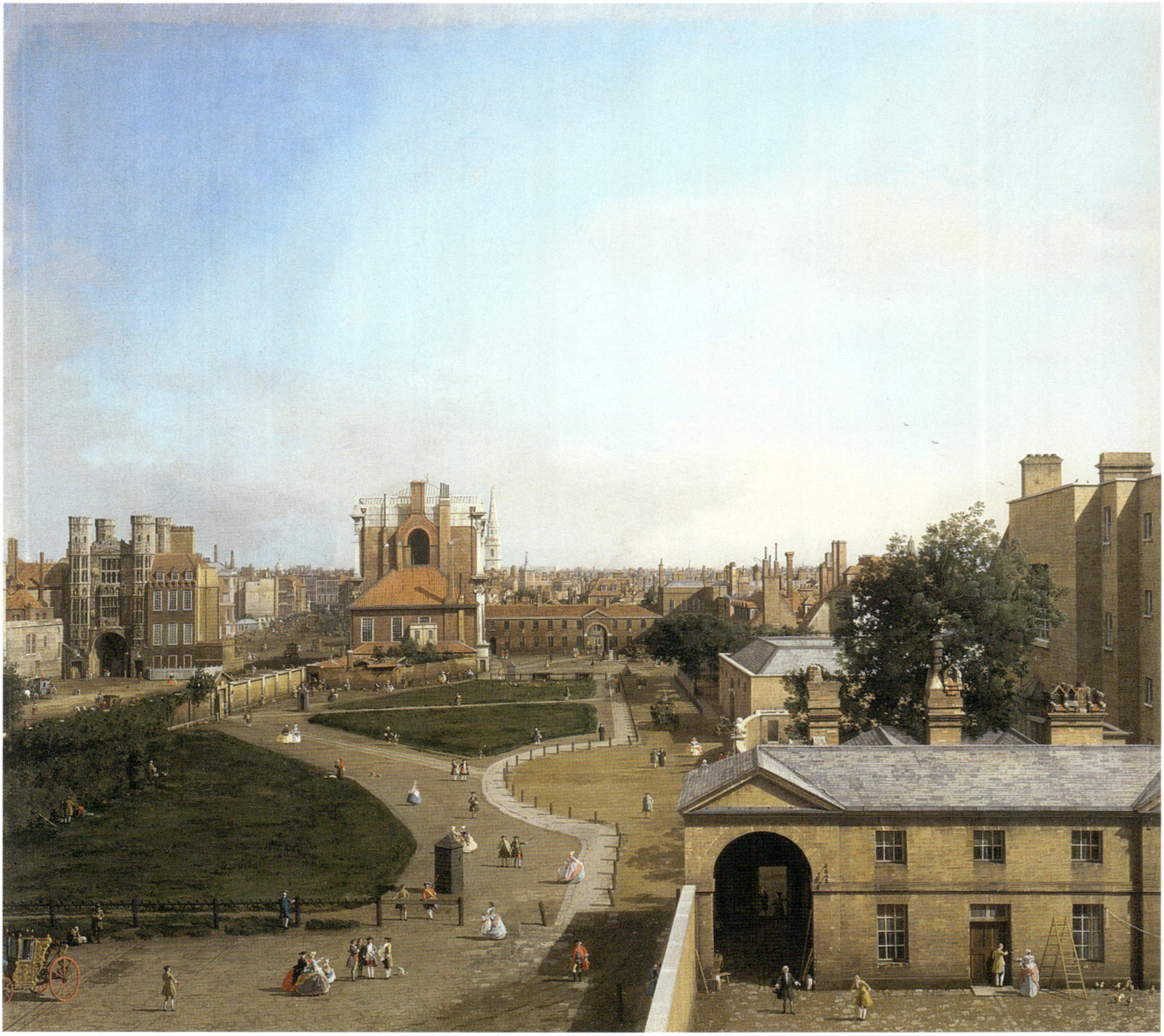

Whitehall and the Privy Gardens from Richmond House

Canaletto (Giovanni Antonio Canal) c.1746–7

The jewel-like paintings of Venice created by Canaletto and his contemporaries were favourite mementoes for British aristocrats on the Grand Tour of Europe. When war meant the flow of visitors dried up, Canaletto came to his clients, living and working in London from 1746 to 1755. He arrived in a city which was – as ever – a building site. An only partially successful attempt was underway to turn Whitehall into a grand processional avenue to connect to the nearly finished Westminster Bridge. He recorded this in a series of unusual pictures from the home of a patron, the Duke of Richmond.

This is a behind-the-scenes view – instead of the grand frontages you see the backyard of Richmond House. Inigo Jones's Banqueting House, the first British building in the Renaissance style, is shown side-on and partially obscured, with only a hint of its Palladian detailing. Just behind it is the spire of St Martin-in-the-Fields. To the left is the Holbein Gate, a remnant of the medieval Palace of Westminster, which was demolished in 1759.

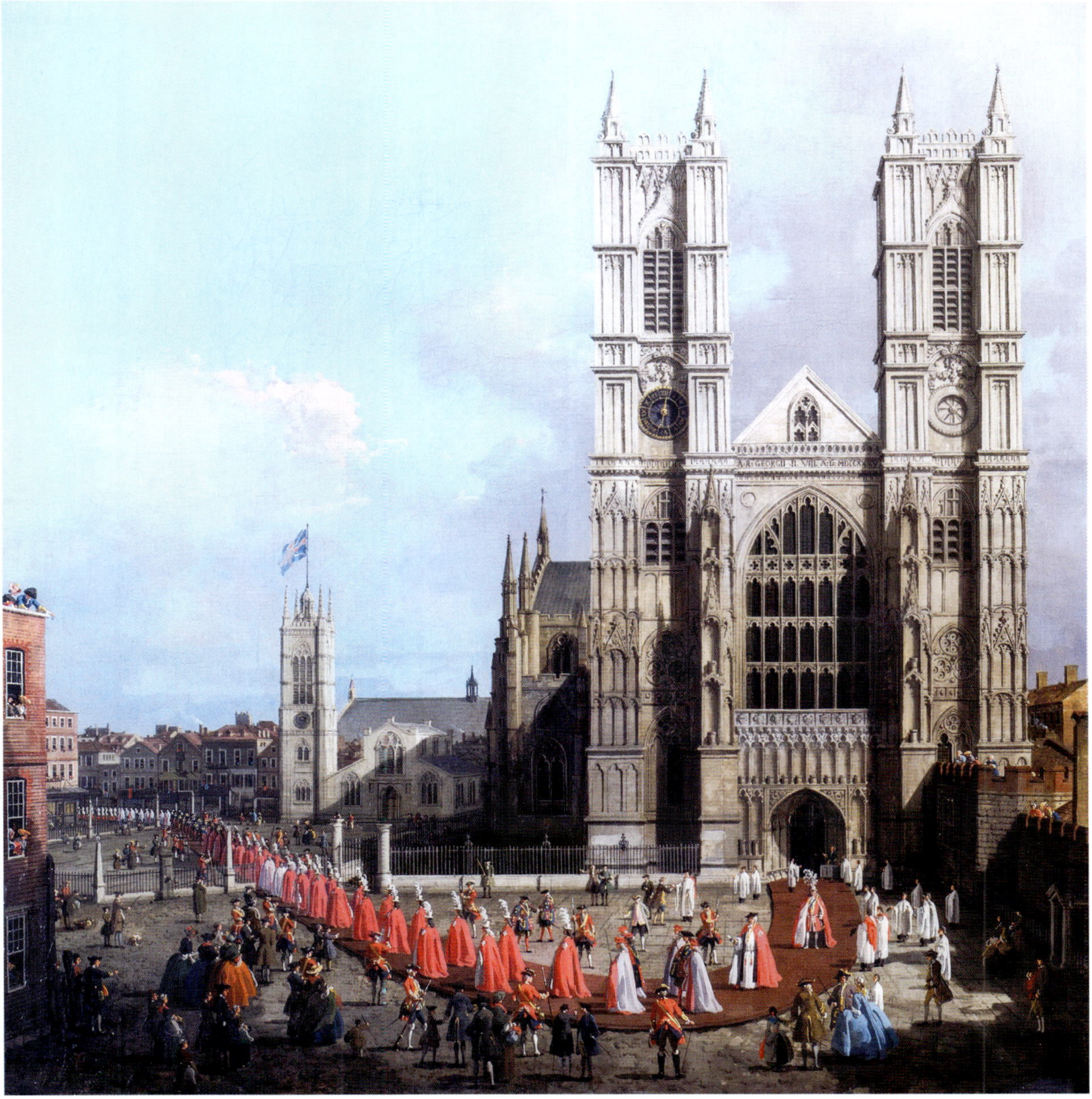

Procession of Knights of the Bath, Westminster Abbey

Canaletto (Giovanni Antonio Canal) c.1749

This shows Canaletto on typical picture-postcard form. He painted stunningly detailed views of key buildings, including St Paul's and Northumberland House (on the current site of Charing Cross Station). Here he depicts one of the arcane and ancient ceremonies the Abbey is known for: the installation of the Knights of the Bath. The western towers shown here had only recently been finished – designed by Nicholas Hawksmoor (1661–1736) to add some verticality to the otherwise squat building.

A View of Greenwich from the River

Canaletto (Giovanni Antonio Canal) c.1750–2

Canaletto didn't adapt his style much to the English climate. His river views have a limpid light never previously witnessed in the UK, and glistening blue water that the silty River Thames has never possessed. But this vista was made for him like no other, the one place where London threatens to out-Venice Venice. Built on the site of the Palace of Placentia, and palatial in appearance, Greenwich Hospital was actually a retirement home for sailors of the Royal Navy. It was designed by a supergroup of eighteenth-century architects, including Christopher Wren, John Vanbrugh and Nicholas Hawksmoor. The receding wings frame the Queen's House; the view is surmounted by the Royal Observatory. The view is little changed today and can be seen from a public park created for the purpose.

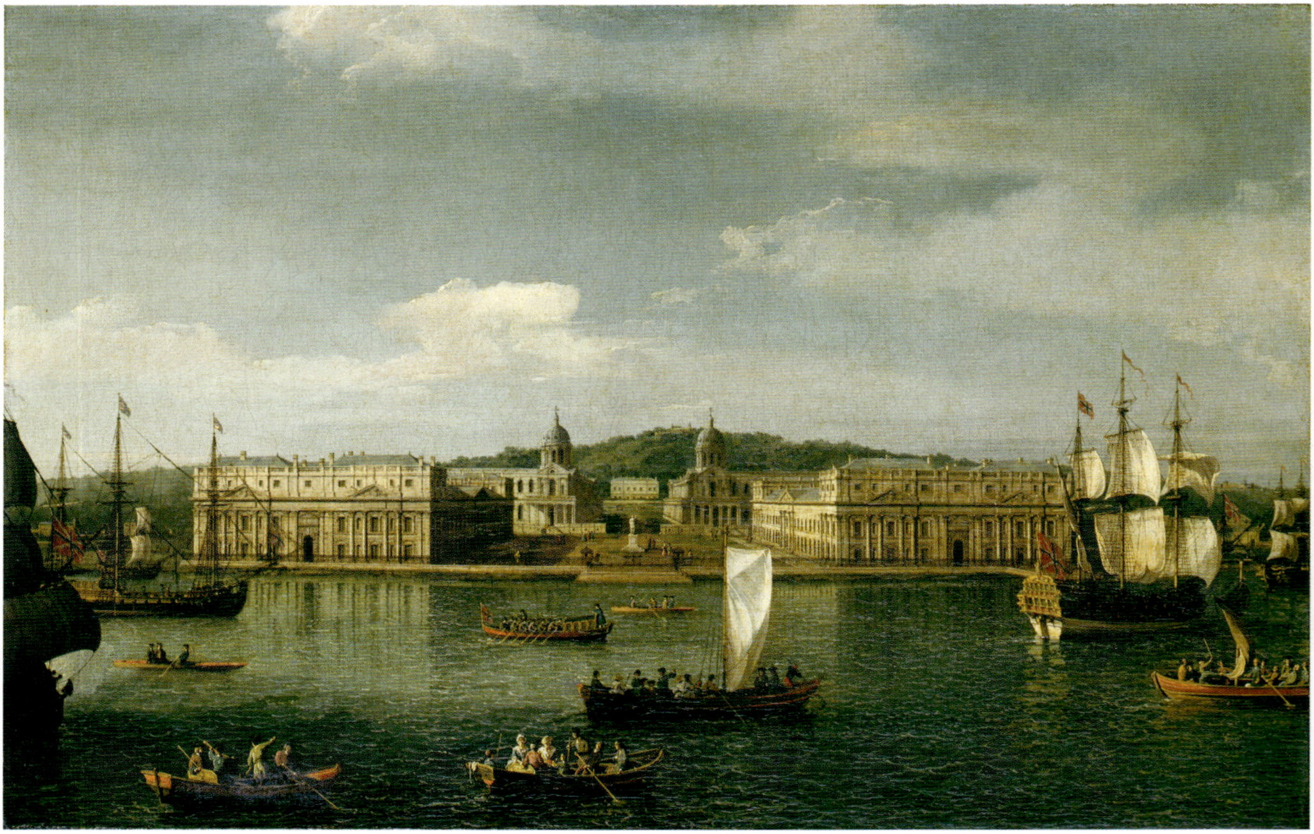

London: The Thames on Lord Mayor's Day, looking towards the City and St Paul's Cathedral

Canaletto (Giovanni Antonio Canal) c.1750

London could have hoped for no more spectacular advertisement than this. The stinking dyeworks and dusty warehouses that lined the river are transformed into Venetian palazzos by Canaletto's brush. Behind them rise the multitude of spires thrown up by Sir Christopher Wren, surmounted by St Paul's looking otherworldly in its magnificence and cream-white purity. At the far right can be seen the Monument, the Tower of London with an enormous flag and Old London Bridge.

The River Thames itself is thronged with rowboats nipping among the gilded barges belonging to the livery companies of the City of London. The pageant has been held annually for centuries and takes the new Lord Mayor to be presented to the monarch's representatives in Westminster – it is now a procession on land (pp.174–5).

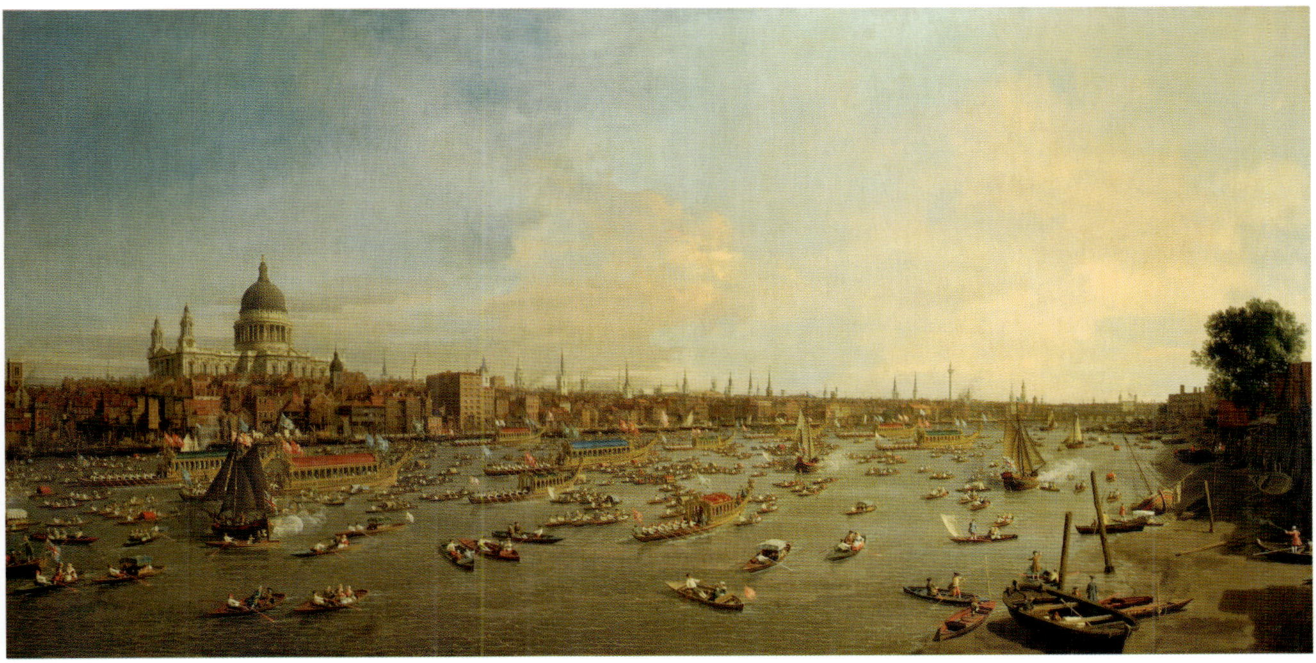

A View of the Thames with the York Buildings Water Tower

After Samuel Scott c.1760–70

Originally by Samuel Scott, this view of the completed Westminster Bridge was evidently popular as it was copied many times. The landmarks of modern Westminster are starting to appear, although it is not possible to see any of them from this position today, as the Hungerford Footbridge and the Charing Cross Railway Bridge block the entire view.

In the centre is Westminster Abbey with its newly acquired towers. Peeking out to the right is the Banqueting House, hardly noticeable today among the giant offices of Whitehall, but for much of its life it dominated its neighbours. Nearest to us on the right is the York Watergate, then a grand river entrance to one of the mansions that lined the Strand, now marooned far from the river thanks to the building of the Embankment. The obelisk-like structure next to it was the York Water Tower – a prominent landmark that appears in many paintings of the area, providing, as here, a strong vertical on which to base the composition.

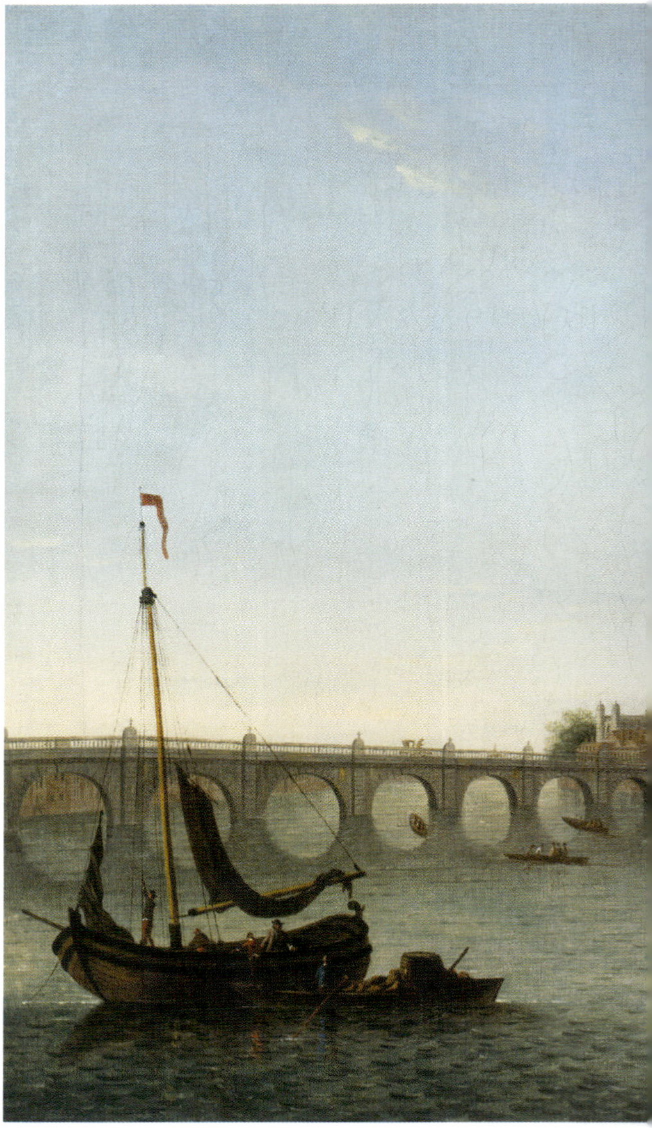

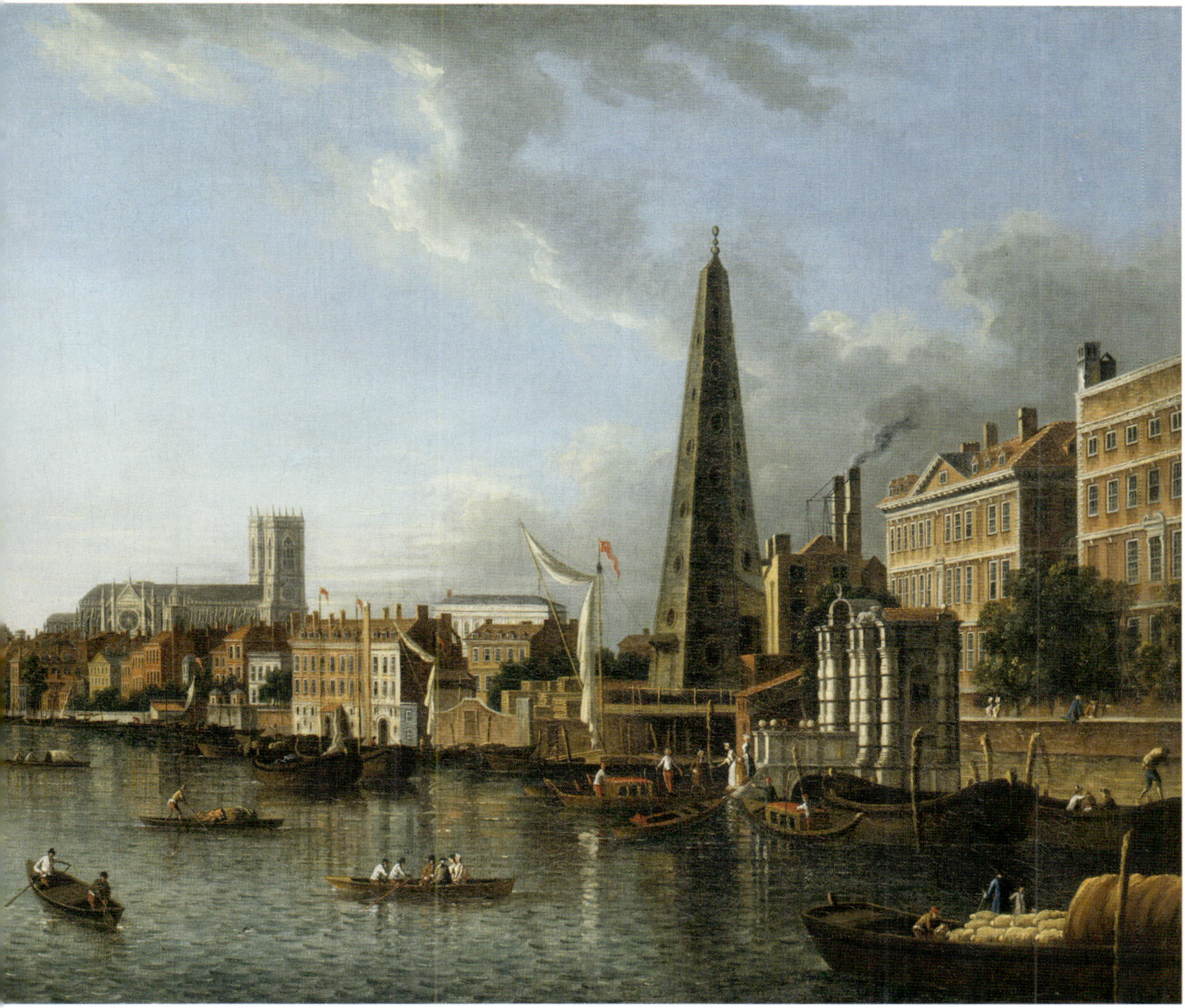

Capriccio: St Paul's and a Venetian Canal

William Marlow c.1795

Sir Christopher Wren's baroque dome-topped designs for St Paul's were considered at first to be too Catholic, too Italian for Protestant England, which is why this playful image is not as incongruous as it might be. William Marlow – a pupil of Samuel Scott – specialised in views of London and also travelled around France and Italy. He has simply grafted St Paul's on to the end of a typical Venetian canal scene, as if Ludgate Hill – which still follows the same streetline – has been filled with water. The *capriccio* – a light-hearted architectural fantasy – was a popular sub-genre of the time.

Marlow might have been inspired by the grand canals that were then being built to ship industrial products around the country – a scheme to extend the canals to London had been started a couple of years earlier. Perhaps this painting was intended to mark the moment London surpassed Venice as the world's greatest trading city.

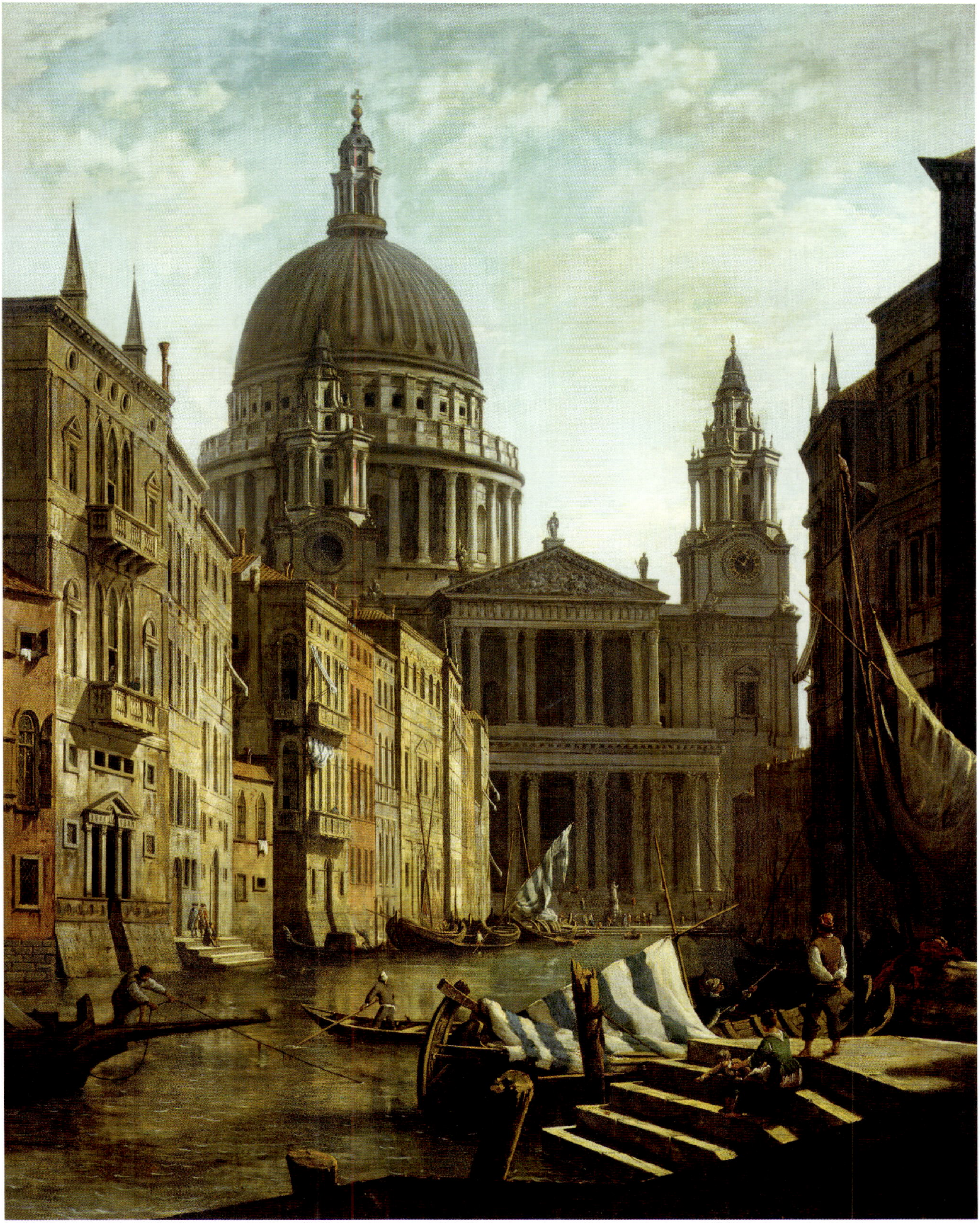

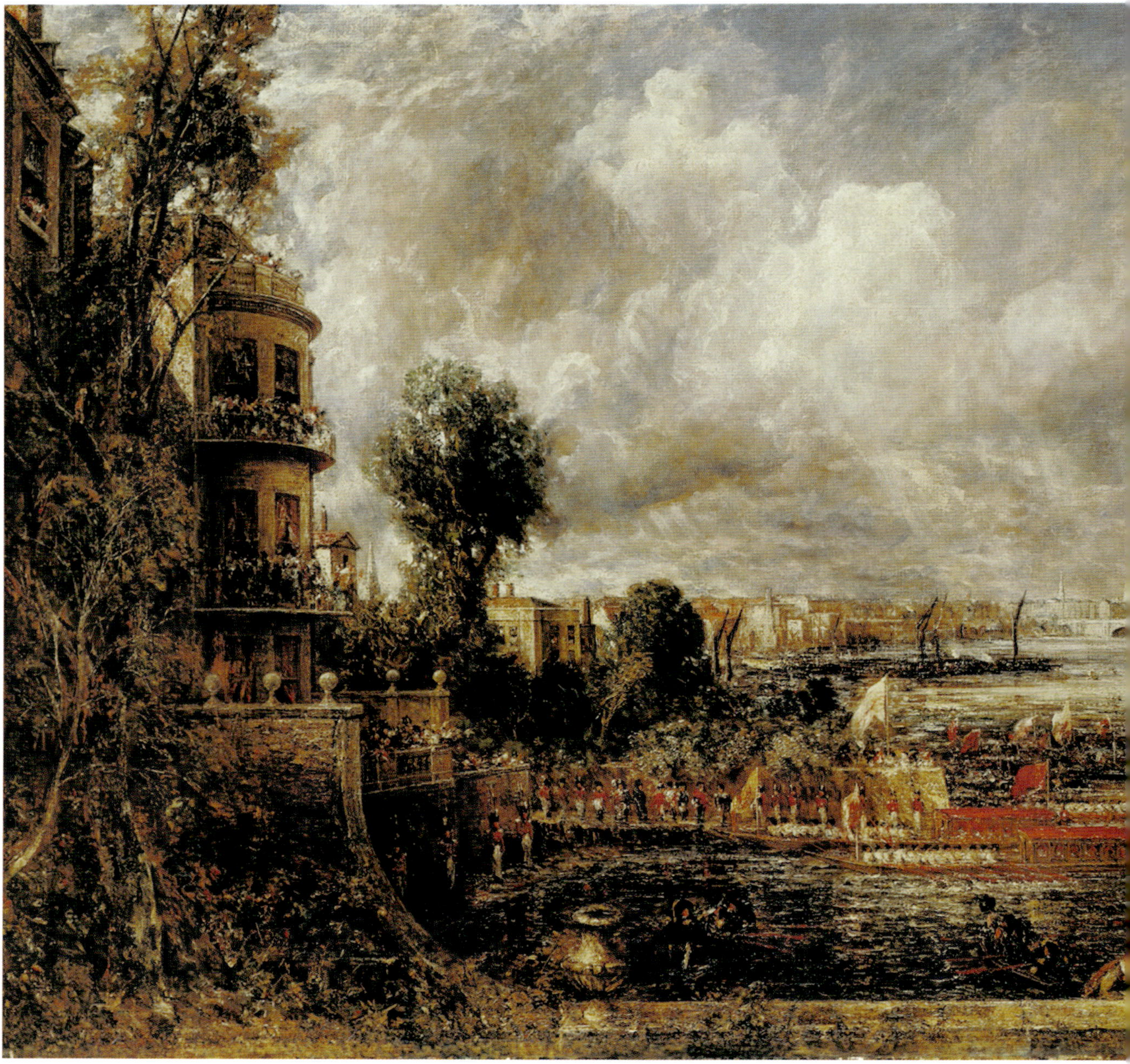

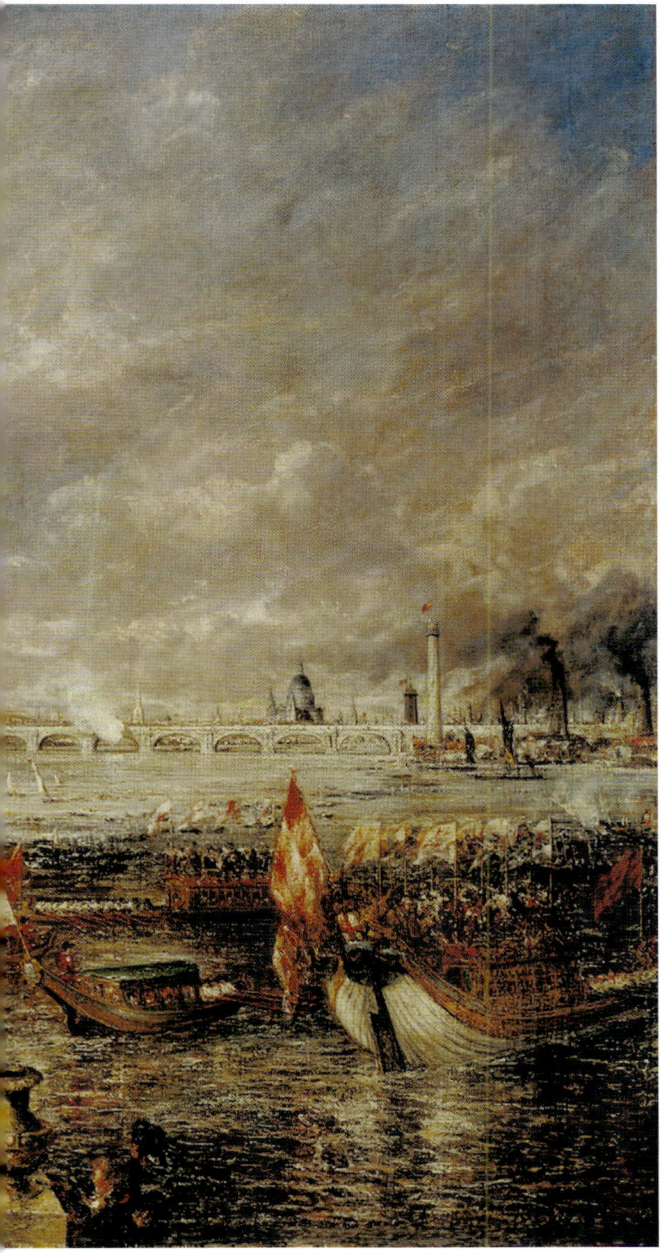

The Opening of Waterloo Bridge ('Whitehall Stairs, June 18th, 1817')

John Constable exhibited 1832

The fifteen-year gap between the events depicted and the exhibition of the finished painting are indicative of the trouble Constable had with it. Waterloo Bridge opened on 18 June 1817, the two-year anniversary of the battle it commemorates. Constable had just moved to London and would more than likely have witnessed it first-hand. The Prince Regent is waiting to board the royal barge which took him to the south side of the bridge, seen in the middle distance. He crossed the bridge, lined with veterans of the battle, before returning by barge.

Constable rarely painted cityscapes and this densely layered scene posed him a tough challenge. He made many sketches and experimented with different heights and angles before he was happy. As a result, the painting includes some buildings – such as the tall white shot tower on the far right – which didn't exist in 1817.

His miseries didn't end when it was exhibited at the Royal Academy in 1832 – then housed in Somerset House, visible on the far side of the bridge. Critics confused it with the new London Bridge which had just opened, and J.M.W. Turner infamously added a red buoy to his own painting in order to spoil Constable's delicately balanced colour tones.

The Houses of Parliament with Westminster Bridge and Abbey from South Side of the Thames

John Anderson 1872

The intricate Gothic traceries that cover the Palace of Westminster present a challenge to a painter akin to that of human hair. Generalise or simplify and you miss the richness that is clearly visible to the naked eye. Try to paint every detail, as the otherwise little-known landscape painter John Anderson has here, and the result feels fussy and overwrought. The fevered air to this painting is added to by the melodramatic moonlit sky.

Yet it succeeds in its aim to create an iconic image of Victorian power. Most of what is seen here was new: the current Westminster Bridge opened in 1862 and the Palace of Westminster and the Victoria Embankment in 1870. Portcullis House now hides the view of Westminster Abbey, but otherwise the view is little changed.

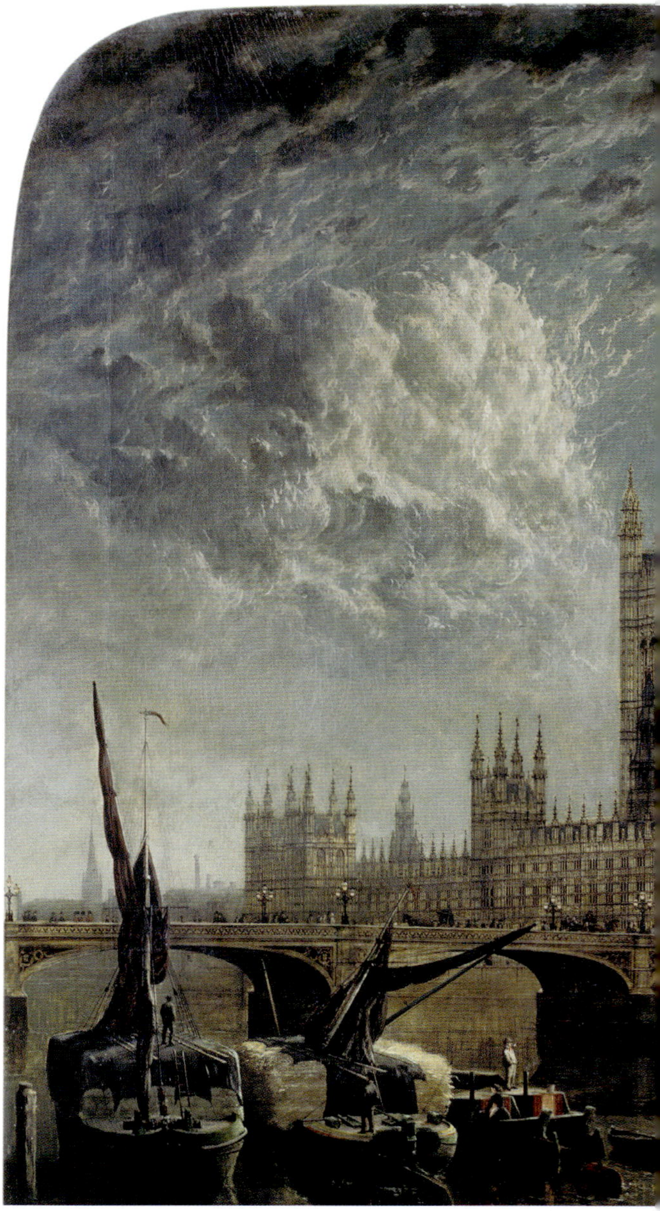

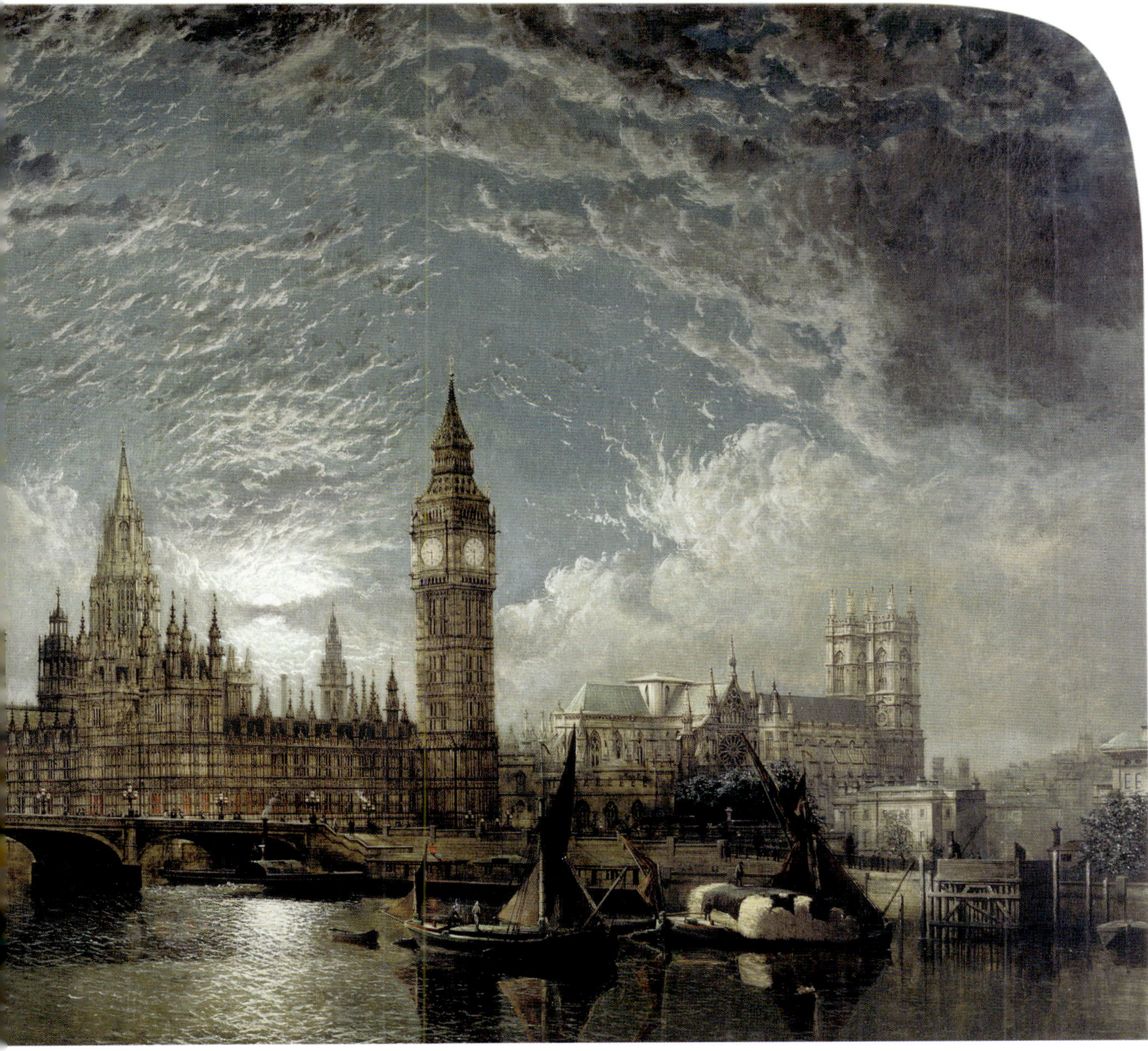

The Embankment

John O'Connor 1874

A marvel of nineteenth-century engineering, the Thames Embankment improved the river's flow, tidied up the mess of wharves and docks, created a sewer and an underground railway, and added this promenade atop.

John O'Connor rose to prominence as a scene painter at the Haymarket Theatre and was popular with the royal family, for whom he painted special events. This painting has a sense of occasion, although the troop of grenadier guards was probably just added for pictorial effect. The guards are watched by a woman from the terrace of Somerset House. In the distance the view is closed out by Blackfriars Bridge and Cannon Street Station, with its original roof.

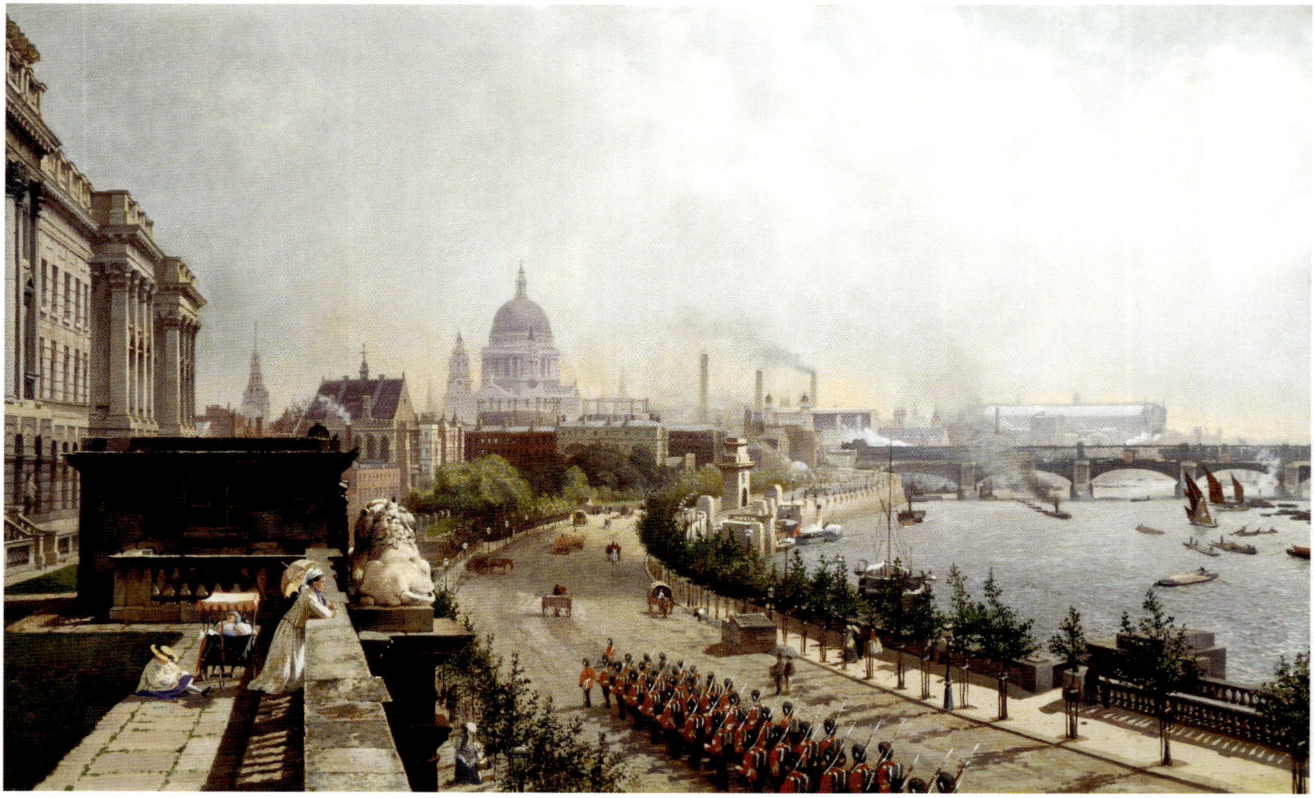

From Pentonville Road looking West: Evening

John O'Connor 1884

Reproductions of this painting can often be seen in London pubs. It clearly encapsulates a popular sense of Londoness with its charming combination of monumental architecture, credible street scenes and warm evening light. At first glance one might mistake the central building for the Palace of Westminster. Instead it is St Pancras Station, which adopted the neo-Gothicism which was to become the defining style of late Victorian London. It is sadly under-represented in art, unlike its riverside sibling. The enormous train shed reaching out behind it was the largest single-span structure in the world at the time.

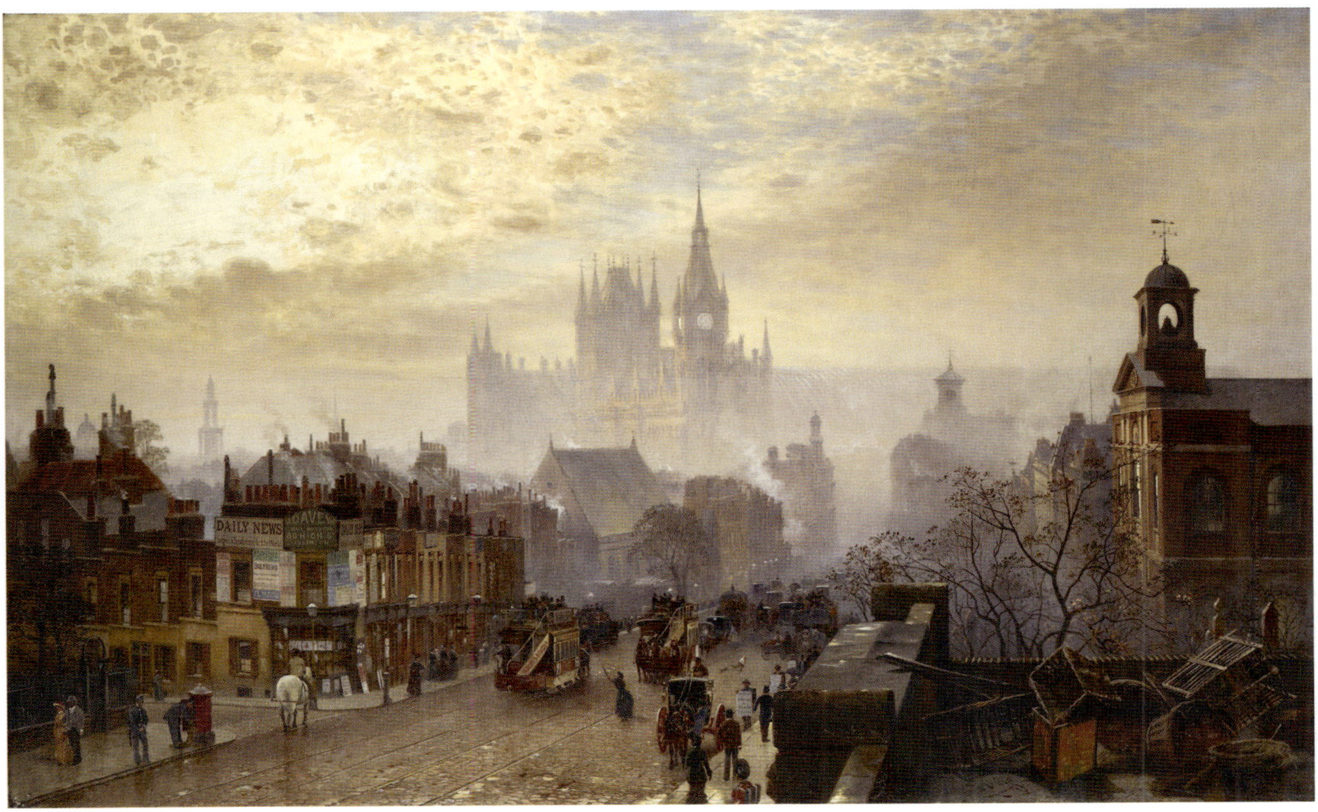

Trafalgar Square, by Moonlight

Henry Pether c.1862

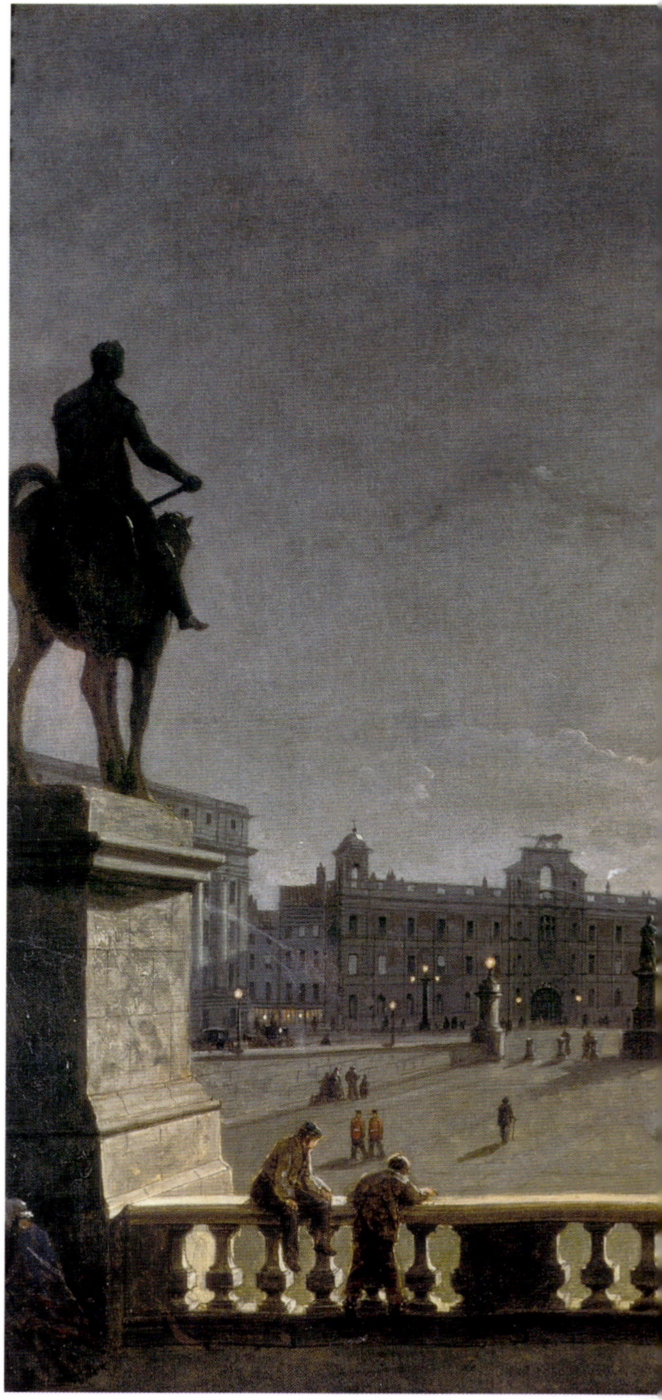

Here is the tourist-friendly view of Trafalgar Square that Tissot's painting (p.100) slyly denies us. Sometimes called 'London's Drawing Room', Trafalgar Square has been the location of riots as often as it has celebrations. Its strident imperial architecture, created as part of early-nineteenth century redevelopment, is softened by its typically British sense of compromise – it's really more of a misshapen pentagon than a square.

Henry was the son of Abraham Pether, who specialised in landscapes illuminated only by a bright full moon, for which he earnt the nickname 'Moonlight' Pether. His skill and deep scientific knowledge brought him success in the late eighteenth century, but not enough to provide for his large family. Despite this, his sons Henry and Sebastian continued the family trade – of the more than a hundred paintings in British public collections by the three, only a handful show daylight. While his father created many romantic imaginary views, Henry stuck to accurate depictions of London.

This is one of the last paintings of Northumberland House (in the left mid-distance), the grandest of the large aristocratic houses that used to line the Strand. Immortalised in paint by Canaletto and many copiers, it was demolished in 1874.

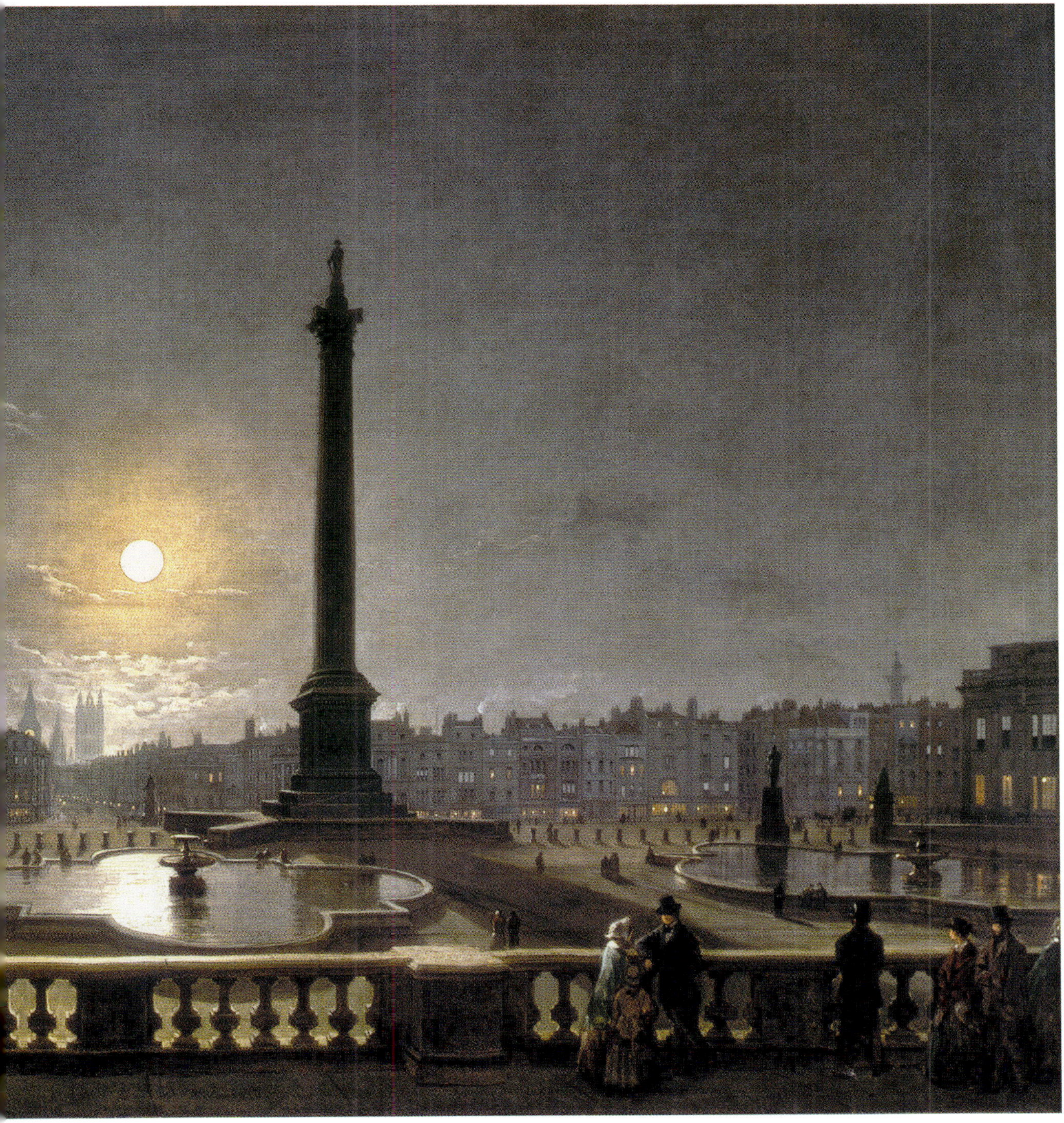

The Ninth of November, 1888

William Logsdail 1890

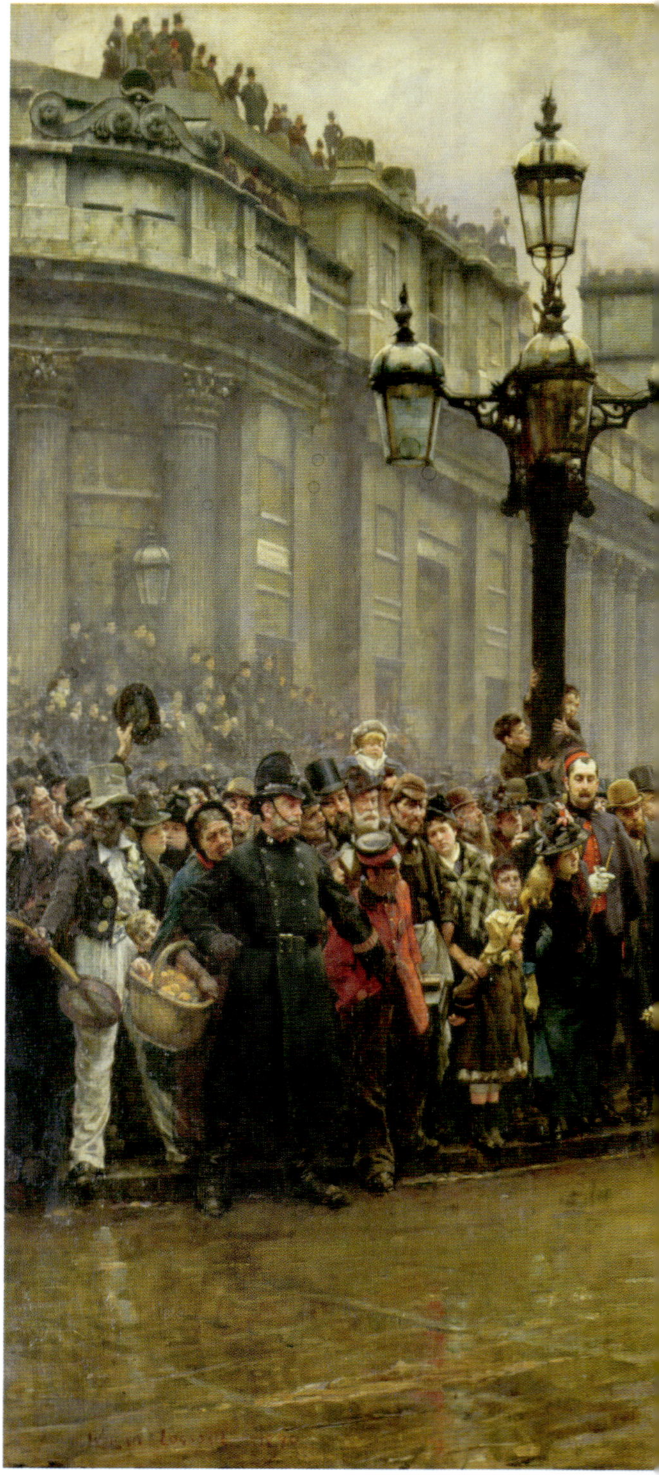

By the late nineteenth century, the Lord Mayor's Show, depicted as a Thames-borne regatta by Canaletto (p.161), had turned into the street procession we know today. By this time the event was seen as tawdry and anachronistic, pomp and ceremony put on for the benefit of tourists and the lower classes.

This is the last of Logsdail's series of London paintings, which did not find a warm reception. Critics, both conservative and avant-garde, found this work particularly hard to understand. One decried its 'brutal realism' – instead of transforming the scene into visual poetry, it is almost like a snapshot taken by one of the spectators. They struggled with its lack of a moral narrative. Are we supposed to be impressed by the parade? If Logsdail is critiquing the social hierarchy, why are the crowds resigned to the sides? For today's viewer, this ambivalence gives it its historical and sociological interest.

Like his *St Martin-in-the-Fields* (p.65), neo-classical architecture is as dominant as the figures – here in the shape of the Bank of England and the Royal Exchange.

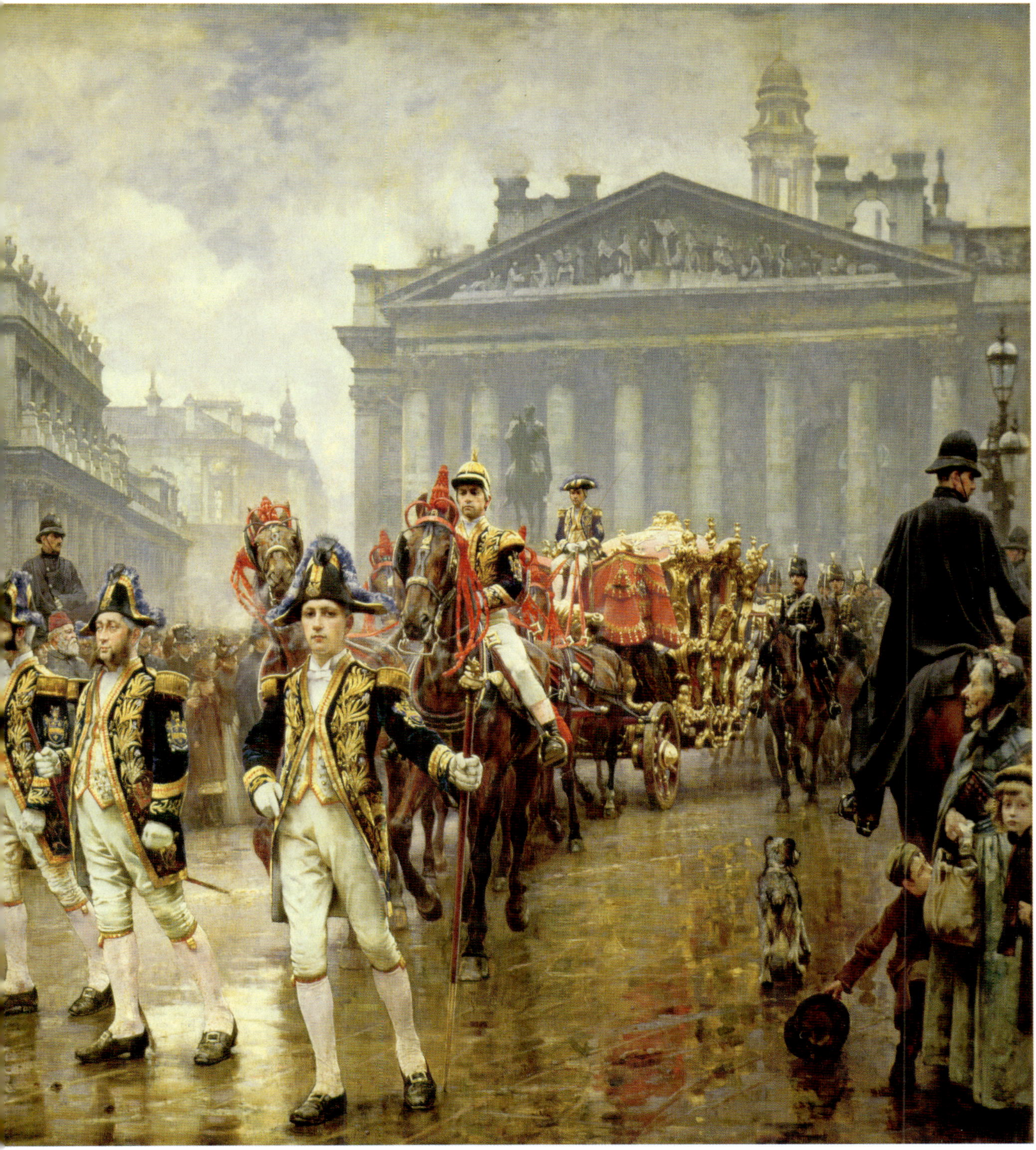

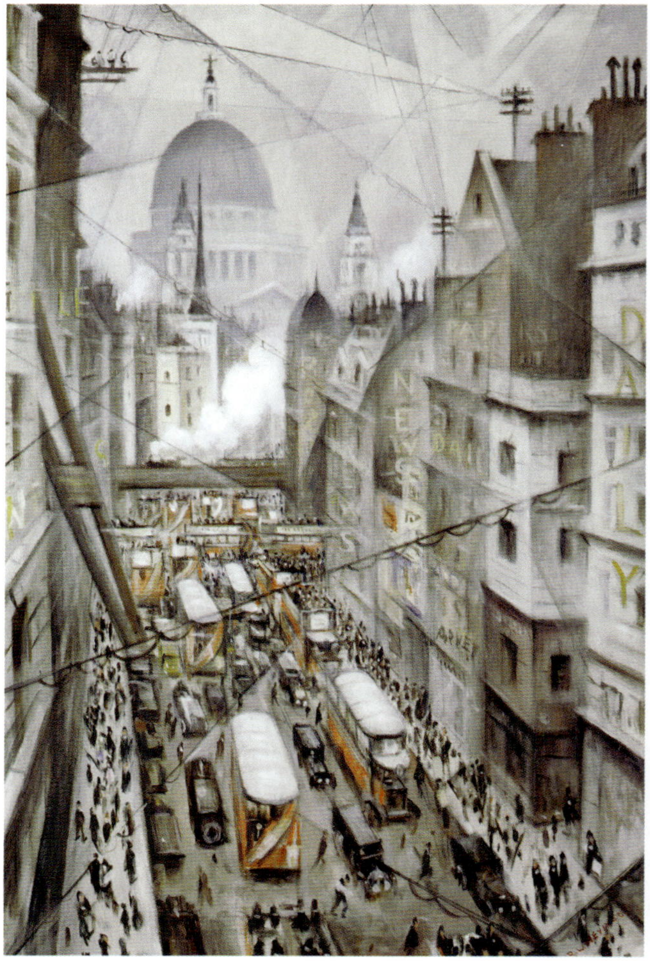

Amongst the Nerves of the World

Christopher Richard Wynne Nevinson 1930

London, Winter

Christopher Richard Wynne Nevinson 1928

After the First World War, Nevinson's hard-edged avant-garde style softened and became more realist. He painted London regularly in the interwar years, his work at times becoming as warm and soft as early impressionism. In 1930 he wrote: 'On the innumerable times that I have arrived back in London, I have been overwhelmed by its peculiar beauty, its exquisite, lingering twilight; the streets, shiny with rain, converted to canals more romantic than Venice...'

However, these two paintings hark back to his dalliance with abstraction to great effect. Painted a couple of years apart, it is hard not to see them as companion works, both anchored by the dome of St Paul's. In *Amongst the Nerves of the World* (above) the telegraph wires criss-crossing Fleet Street are reminiscent of Italian Futurist Umberto Boccioni's (1882–1916) 'lines of force', splintering the picture space into facets. In this case they really are lines of force: they are the conduits for the world's communications, as noted in the title. The British newspaper industry, which is still known by the name of this street despite leaving it decades ago, is visible in the loosely drawn signs on the buildings. It's a world Nevinson would have known from his father, a well-known writer for the *Daily Chronicle*.

At the top of the canvas is the oft-painted view of St Paul's from Ludgate Hill, with the now-demolished railway viaduct in front of it. The backs of the motor buses in the foreground look astonishingly like the new Routemasters introduced in 2012.

London, Winter (opposite) shows a different side to London's industry, with its cranes and barges. One of the two shot towers on the South Bank is shown prominently on the right-hand side. In this painting the arms of the cranes serve the function of fragmenting the picture space, which is further punctuated and articulated by a terrifyingly large flock of seagulls.

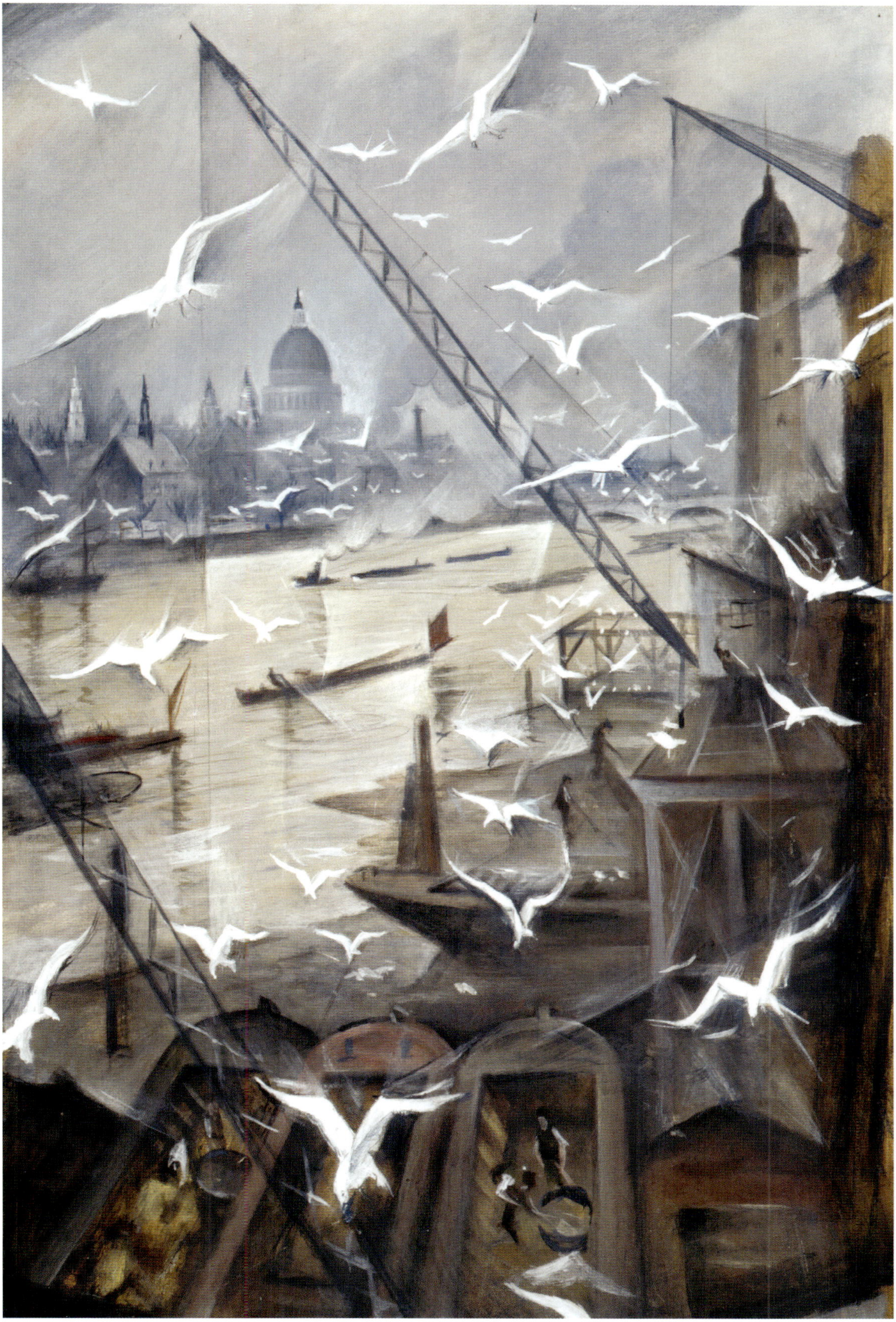

Christ Church, Spitalfields, Morning

Leon Kossoff 1990

Leon Kossoff grew up in the East End of London and here captures the ominous, looming mass of Nicholas Hawksmoor's church, which stands on the border of the City and Whitechapel. As the centre of the Ripper murders, it plays a key role in Alan Moore's graphic novel *From Hell* (1989) and Peter Ackroyd's novel *Hawksmoor* (1985), which both credit it with sinister occult power. Finished in 1729, the church's bombastic design was intended to impress on the local Huguenot community the supremacy of the Anglican Church. Kossoff adopts the view of a passerby straining up their neck, compressing the dizzying verticality of the structure into a square canvas.

Although he was intimately familiar with the church and painted it many times, Kossoff began working on this painting in his usual way, with a series of sketches and explorations. He described his motivation: 'The urgency that drives me to work is not only to do with the pressures of the accumulation of memories and the unique quality of the subject on this particular day but also with the awareness that time is short, that soon the mass of this building will be dwarfed by more looming office blocks and overshadowed. The character of the building will [then] be lost forever, for it is by its monumental flight into unimpeded space that we remember [it].'

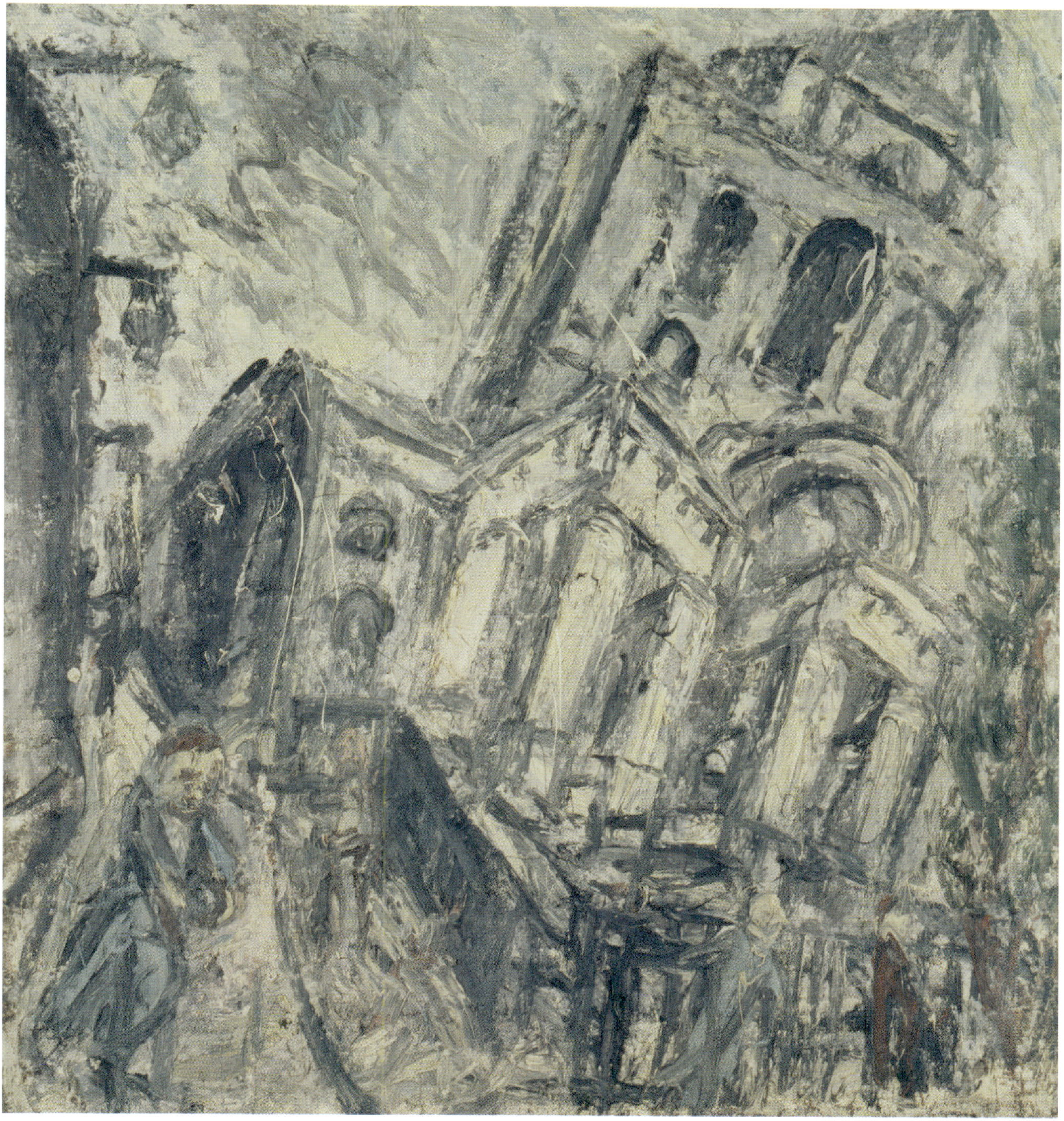

The below map highlights the locations depicted in the paintings illustrated in this book. The numbers provided refer to corresponding page numbers.

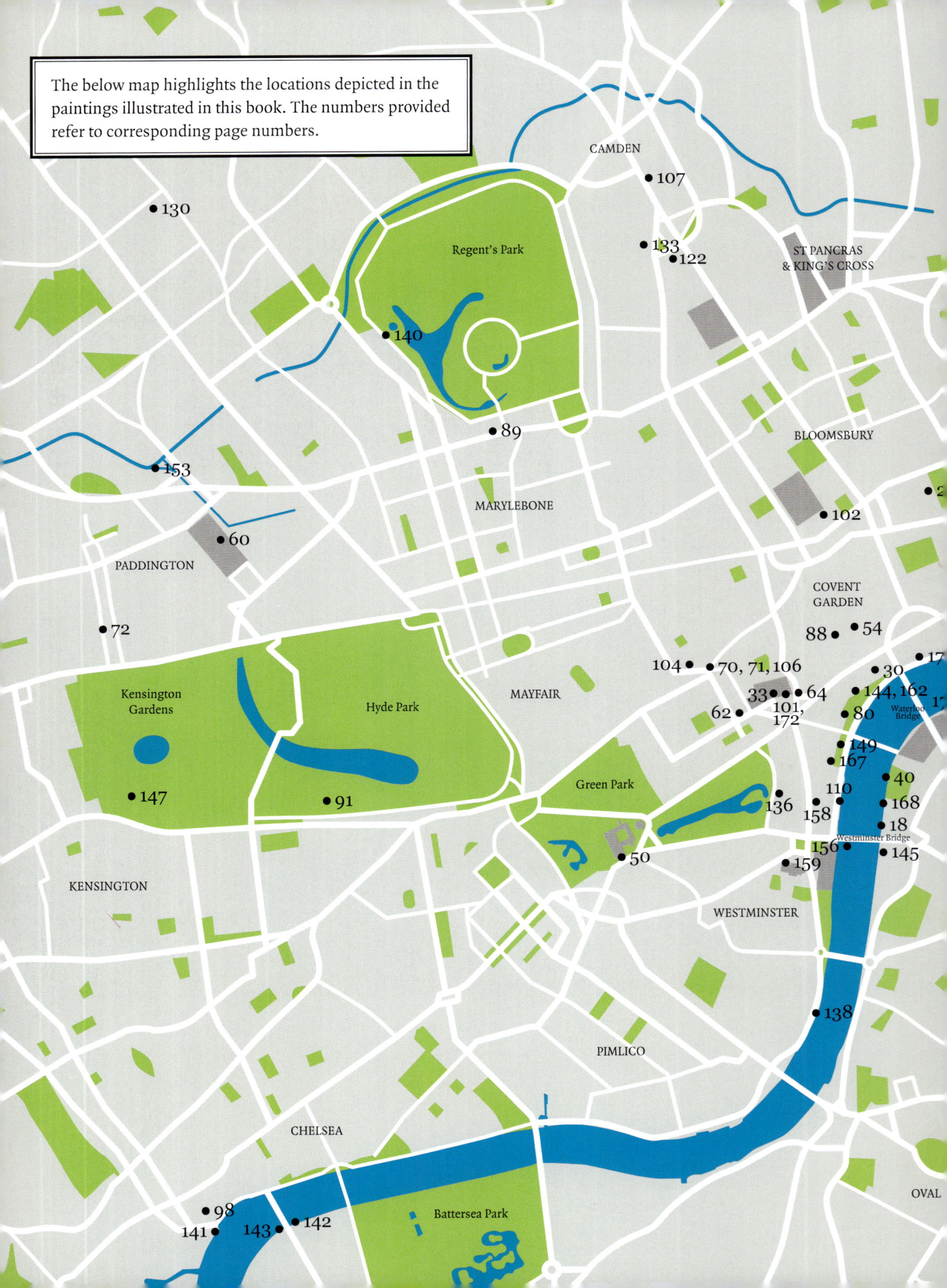

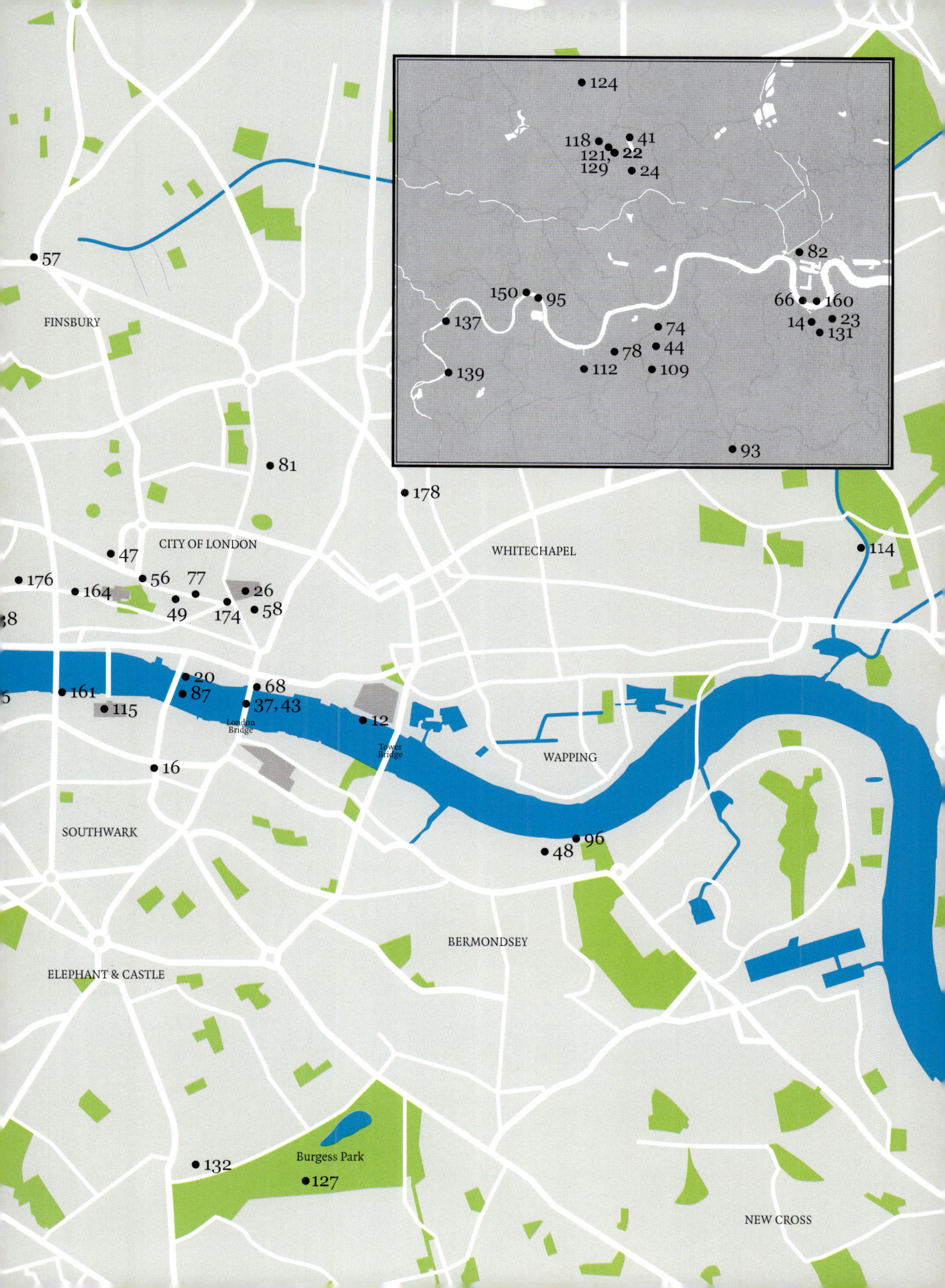

124
118
41
121,
22
129
24
82
150
95
66
160
137
14
23
131
74
44
78
112
109
139
93
57
FINSBURY
81
178
CITY OF LONDON
47
WHITECHAPEL
114
176
56
77
164
26
49
174
58
20
87
68
161
115
37,43
London Bridge
12
Tower Bridge
WAPPING
16
SOUTHWARK
96
48
BERMONDSEY
ELEPHANT & CASTLE
Burgess Park
132
127
NEW CROSS

LIST OF WORKS

Measurements of artworks are given in centimetres, height before width. Page references to the works are given at the end of the entries.

John Anderson
The Houses of Parliament with Westminster Bridge and Abbey from South Side of the Thames 1872
Oil on canvas 107 x 183
Museum of London
Illustrated pp.168–9

Frank Auerbach
Mornington Crescent – Summer Morning 2004
Oil on canvas 132.7 x 132.3
Tate. Accepted by HM Government in lieu of inheritance tax and allocated to Tate 2015
Illustrated p.133

Walter Bayes
Battle of Britain: Parachutists from an Enemy Aircraft Brought Down in an Apparent Attempt to Bomb Buckingham Palace 1942
Oil on canvas 119 x 140.9
Imperial War Museum, London
Illustrated p.51

Jacques-Emile Blanche
Ludgate Circus: Entrance to the City (November, Midday) c.1910
Oil on board 104.8 x 81.6
Tate. Presented by Georges A. Mevil-Blanche 1947
Illustrated p.6

David Bomberg
Evening in the City of London 1944
Oil on canvas 86.5 x 106.8 (framed)
Museum of London
Illustrated p.49

Stephen Bone
Little Venice 1952
Oil on canvas 76.2 x 102.2
Tate. Purchased 1997
Illustrated pp.152–3

Clive Branson
Selling the 'Daily Worker' outside the Projectile and Engineering Works 1937
Oil on canvas 40.6 x 50.7
Tate. Bequeathed by Noreen Branson 2004
Illustrated pp.74–5

Clive Branson
Blitz: Plane Flying 1940
Oil on canvas 61 x 50.9
Tate. Bequeathed by Noreen Branson 2004
Illustrated p.45

John Bratby
Window, Dartmouth Row, Blackheath c.1954–6
Oil on hardboard 122.5 x 150
Government Art Collection. Purchased from Mayor Gallery, October 1995
Illustrated p.131

British School
Curds and Whey Seller, Cheapside c.1730
Oil on canvas 127.3 x 102
Museum of London
Illustrated p.56

British School
St James's Park from the Terrace of No. 10 Downing Street c.1736–40
Oil on canvas 89.4 x 142.8
Museum of London
Illustrated p.136

Canaletto (Giovanni Antonio Canal)
Whitehall and the Privy Gardens from Richmond House c.1746–7
Oil on canvas 101.5 x 117
The Trustees of the Goodwood Collection
Illustrated p.158

Canaletto (Giovanni Antonio Canal)
Procession of Knights of the Bath, Westminster Abbey c.1749
Oil on canvas 100 x 100
Westminster Abbey
Illustrated p.159

Canaletto (Giovanni Antonio Canal)
A View of Greenwich from the River c.1750–2
Oil on canvas 59.1 x 94
Tate. Lent from a private collection 1997, on long term loan
Illustrated p.160

Canaletto (Giovanni Antonio Canal)
London: The Thames on Lord Mayor's Day, looking towards the City and St Paul's Cathedral c.1750
Oil on canvas 140.5 x 260.5
Lobkowicz Collections, Czech Republic
Illustrated p.161

Jesse Dale Cast
'The Windmill', Clapham Common 1934
Oil on canvas 43.2 x 54.6
Tate. Presented by David Cast 1983
Illustrated pp.108–9

Sir George Clausen
My Back Garden exhibited 1940
Oil on canvas 50.8 x 61
Tate. Presented by the Trustees of the Chantrey Bequest 1940
Illustrated p.130

Charles Allston Collins
May, in the Regent's Park 1851
Oil on mahogany 44.5 x 69.2
Tate. Purchased 1980
Illustrated pp.134–5, 140

Attributed to John Constable
Fire in London, Seen from Hampstead c.1826
Oil on paper laid on panel 9.5 x 15.2
Yale Center for British Art, Paul Mellon Collection
Illustrated p.41

John Constable
The Grove, Hampstead c.1821–2
Oil on canvas 35.6 x 30.2
Tate. Presented by Miss Isabel Constable 1888
Illustrated p.119

John Constable
The Opening of Waterloo Bridge ('Whitehall Stairs, June 18th, 1817') exhibited 1832
Oil on canvas 130.8 x 218
Tate. Purchased with assistance from the National Heritage Memorial Fund, the Clore Foundation, the Art Fund, the Friends of the Tate Gallery and others 1987
Illustrated pp.166–7

John Constable
Sir Richard Steele's Cottage, Hampstead 1831–2
Oil on canvas 21 x 28.6
Yale Center for British Art, Paul Mellon Collection
Illustrated pp.24–5

André Derain
The Pool of London 1906
Oil on canvas 65.7 x 99.1
Tate. Presented by the Trustees of the Chantrey Bequest 1951
Illustrated pp.68–9

Anthony Eyton
Bankside – The Turbine Hall 1995–6
Oil on canvas 151.4 x 126.8
Tate. Purchased with assistance from the Charlotte Bonham Carter Charitable Trust 1996
Illustrated p.115

William Powell Frith
The Railway Station 1862
Oil on canvas 116.7 x 256.4
Royal Holloway, University of London. Purchased by Thomas Holloway, 1883
Illustrated pp.60–1

Charles Ginner
Piccadilly Circus 1912
Oil on canvas 81.3 x 66
Tate. Purchased 1980
Illustrated p.70

Charles Ginner
Victoria Embankment Gardens 1912
Oil on canvas 66.4 x 46.1
Tate. Purchased 1984
Illustrated p.148

Charles Ginner
Flask Walk, Hampstead, on Coronation Day 1937
Oil on canvas 61 x 50.8
Tate. Purchased 1941
Illustrated p.128

Spencer Frederick Gore
Houghton Place 1912
Oil on canvas 51.5 x 61.4
Tate. Presented by the Contemporary Art Society 1927
Illustrated pp.122–3

Walter Greaves
Hammersmith Bridge on Boat-race Day c.1862
Oil on canvas 91.4 x 139.7
Tate. Presented by the Trustees of the Chantrey Bequest 1922
Illustrated pp.84–5, 94–5

Walter Greaves
Battersea Reach c.1870
Oil on canvas 64.1 x 76.8
Tate. Purchased 1940
Illustrated p.141

Atkinson Grimshaw
View of Heath Street by Night 1882
Oil on board 36.8 x 53.7
Tate. Purchased 1963
Illustrated pp.120–1

Arthur Hacker
A Wet Night at Piccadilly Circus 1910
Oil on canvas 71 x 91.5
Royal Academy of Arts, London. Diploma Work given by Arthur Hacker, R.A., accepted 1910
Illustrated p.106

Wilfred Stanley Haines
Night Raid over London Docklands c.1941
Oil on canvas 63.3 x 75.8
Museum of London
Illustrated pp.34–5, 48

Vilhelm Hammershøi
British Museum, Winter 1906
Oil on canvas 50.5 x 44.8
Fuglsang Kunstmuseum, Denmark
Illustrated p.103

Benjamin Robert Haydon
Punch or May Day 1829
Oil on canvas 150.5 x 185.1
Tate. Bequeathed by George Darling 1862
Illustrated p.89

David Hepher
Albany Flats 1977–9
Oil and sand on canvas 197.5 x 279.4
Tate. Purchased 1979
Illustrated p.132

William Hogarth
The Four Times of Day: Morning 1736
Oil on canvas 73.7 x 61
National Trust Upton House, Warwickshire
Illustrated p.88

Ken Howard
Cheapside 10.10 a.m., 10 February 1970 1970
Oil on canvas 183 x 152
Guildhall Art Gallery, City of London
Illustrated p.76

Claude de Jongh
The Thames at Westminster Stairs 1631
Oil on panel 46.4 x 80
Yale Center for British Art, Paul Mellon Collection
Illustrated pp.18–19

Claude de Jongh
View of Old London Bridge from the West 1650
Oil on oak panel 71 x 126 (approx.)
Victoria and Albert Museum, London
Illustrated pp.20–1

Ben Johnson
Looking Back to Richmond House 2011
Acrylic on canvas 183 x 274
Private collection
Illustrated pp.32–3

Lily D. Joseph
Roofs, High Holborn c.1937
Oil on canvas 1[illegible]4.6 x 147.3
Tate. Presented by the Trustees of the Chantrey Bequest 1937
Illustrated pp.28–9

Oskar Kokoschka
View of the Thames 1959
Oil on canvas 9[illegible].4 x 123.2
Tate. Presented by David Hellings 1970
Illustrated pp.30–1

Leon Kossoff
Christ Church, Spitalfields, Morning 1990
Oil on board 198.6 x 189.2
Tate. Purchased 1994
Illustrated p.179

Leon Kossoff
The Flower and Fruit Stalls, Embankment 19[illegible]5 1995
Oil on hardboard 182.8 x 203.1
Tate. Purchased 1997
Illustrated p.80

Carl Laubin
Canary Wharf 1991
Oil on canvas 200 x 150
Museum of London
Illustrated p.83

William Logsdail
St Martin-in-the-Fields 1888
Oil on canvas 143.5 x 118.1
Tate. Presented by the Trustees of the Chantrey Bequest 1888
Illustrated p.65

William Logsdail
The Ninth of November, 1888 1890
Oil on canvas 137 x 272
Guildhall Art Gallery, City of London
Illustrated pp.174–5

Philip James de Loutherbourg
The Great Fire of London c.1797
Oil on canvas 60 x 81.3
Yale Center for British Art, Paul Mellon Collection
Illustrated p.37

L.S. Lowry
Piccadilly Circus, London 1960
Oil on canvas 76.2 x 101.6
Private collection
Illustrated pp.52–3, 71

Niels Møller Lund
The Heart of the Empire 1904
Oil on canvas 137 x 183
Guildhall Art Gallery, City of London
Illustrated pp.26–7

William Macduff
Shaftesbury, or Lost and Found 1862
Oil on canvas 46.7 x 40.5 (framed)
Museum of London
Illustrated p.63

Paul Maitland
By Hyde Park Gate, Kensington Gardens c.1906
Oil on wood 9.9 x 18
Tate. Presented anonymously in memory of Sir Terence Rattigan 1983
Illustrated pp.146–7

William Marlow
Capriccio: St Paul's and a Venetian Canal c.1795
Oil on canvas 129.5 x 104.1
Tate. Purchased 1954
Illustrated p.165

Jack McFadyen
Canal Lovers 1993–4
Oil on canvas laid on board 94.5 x 78.3
Museum of London
Illustrated p.114

Lisa Milroy
Finsbury Square 1995
Oil on canvas 175.5 x 229.1
Tate. Presented by the Patrons of New Art (Special Purchase Fund) through the Tate Gallery Foundation 1996
Illustrated p.81

Claude Monet
Waterloo Bridge, Sunlight Effect 1903
Oil on canvas 65.7 x 101
The Art Institute of Chicago. Mr and Mrs Martin A. Ryerson Collection 1933.1163
Illustrated p.144

Claude Monet
Houses of Parliament, Effect of Sunlight in Fog 1904
Oil on canvas 81 x 92
Musée D'Orsay, Paris
Illustrated p.145

Balthazar Nebot
Covent Garden Market 1737
Oil on canvas 64.8 x 122.8
Tate. Purchased 1895
Illustrated pp.54–5

Christopher Richard Wynne Nevinson
Among the London Searchlights 1918
Oil on canvas 61 x 45.7
Private collection
Illustrated p.42

Christopher Richard Wynne Nevinson
London, Winter 1928
Tempera on board 73.7 x 48.7
Museum of London
Illustrated p.177

Christopher Richard Wynne Nevinson
Amongst the Nerves of the World 1930
Oil on canvas 97.7 x 72.5
Museum of London
Illustrated pp.154–5, 176

Algernon Newton
The Surrey Canal, Camberwell 1935
Oil on canvas 71.8 x 91.4
Tate. Presented by the Trustees of the Chantrey Bequest 1940
Illustrated pp.126–7

John O'Connor
The Embankment 1874
Oil on canvas 90.5 x 143.5 (framed)
Museum of London
Illustrated p.170

John O'Connor
From Pentonville Road looking West: Evening 1884
Oil on canvas 90.3 x 150.3
Museum of London
Illustrated p.171

Sir William Orpen
The Café Royal, London 1912
Oil on canvas 137.5 x 113.5
Musée d'Orsay, Paris
Illustrated p.105

Victor Pasmore
The Quiet River: The Thames at Chiswick 1943–4
Oil on canvas 76.2 x 101.6
Tate. Presented by the Trustees of the Chantrey Bequest 1958
Illustrated pp.150–1

Henry Pether
Trafalgar Square, by Moonlight c.1862
Oil on canvas 60.4 x 91
Museum of London
Illustrated pp.172–3

John Piper
Christ Church, Newgate Street 1941
Oil on canvas 75.6 x 63.1
Museum of London
Illustrated p.46

Camille Pissarro
The Crystal Palace, London 1871
Oil on canvas 47.2 x73.5
The Art Institute of Chicago. Gift of Mr and Mrs B.E. Bensinger 1972.1164
Illustrated pp.92–3

James Pollard
The Royal Mail Coaches for the North Leaving the Angel, Islington 1827
Oil on canvas 103.2 x 146.4
Tate. Presented by Paul Mellon through the British Sporting Art Trust 1979
Illustrated p.57

William Ratcliffe
Hampstead Garden Suburb from Willifield Way c.1914
Oil on canvas 51 x 76.3
Tate. Presented by Tate Members 2006
Illustrated pp.116–17, 124–5

Samuel Scott
An Arch of Westminster Bridge c.1750
Oil on canvas 135.7 x 163.8
Tate. Purchased 1970
Illustrated p.157

After Samuel Scott
A View of the Thames with the York Buildings Water Tower c.1760–70
Oil on canvas 60.3 x 109.5
Tate. Purchased 1891
Illustrated pp.162–3

Jan Siberechts
View of a House and its Estate in Belsize, Middlesex 1696
Oil on canvas 107.9 x 139.7
Tate. Purchased with assistance from the Art Fund and the Friends of the Tate Gallery 1995
Illustrated p.22

Walter Sickert
The New Bedford c.1914–15
Oil on canvas 91.4 x 35.6
Tate. Bequeathed by Sir Edward Marsh through the Contemporary Art Society 1953
Illustrated p.107

Walter Sickert
Queen's Road Station, Bayswater c.1916
Oil on canvas 62.3 x 73
The Samuel Courtauld Trust. The Courtauld Gallery, London
Illustrated pp.72–3

James Tissot
London Visitors c.1874
Oil on canvas 160 x 114.2
Toledo Museum of Art, Ohio. Purchased with funds from the Libbey Endowment, Gift of Edward Drummond Libbey, 1951.409.
Illustrated p.100

William Townsend
South Bank 1948
Oil on canvas 63.5 x 76.2
Tate. Presented by Dr Charlotte Townsend-Gault and Nicholas Townsend 2000
Illustrated pp.110–11

J.M.W. Turner
Moonlight, a Study at Millbank exhibited 1797
Oil on mahogany 31.4 x 40.3
Tate. Accepted by the nation as part of the Turner Bequest 1856
Illustrated p.138

J.M.W. Turner
London from Greenwich Park exhibited 1809
Oil on canvas 90.2 x 120
Tate. Accepted by the nation as part of the Turner Bequest 1856
Illustrated pp.10–11, 23

J.M.W. Turner
Thomson's Aeolian Harp exhibited 1809
Oil on canvas 166.7 x 306
Manchester Art Gallery. Gift from HM Treasury, 1979
Illustrated p.139

J.M.W. Turner
The Burning of the Houses of Lords and Commons, 16 October 1834 1835
Oil on canvas 92 x 123.20
Cleveland Museum of Art. Bequest of John L. Severance 1942.647
Illustrated p.40

Unknown artist
Charles d'Orleans in the Tower of London late fifteenth century
Vellum 36.5 x 27
British Library, London
Illustrated p.13

Unknown artist
Prospect of London and the Thames from above Greenwich c.1620–30
Oil on panel 29.4 x 92.2
Museum of London
Illustrated pp.14–15

Unknown artist
London from Southwark c.1630
Oil on wood 57.7 x 85.7
Museum of London
Illustrated pp.16–17

Unknown artist
Frost Fair on the Thames, with Old London Bridge in the distance c.1685
Oil on canvas 64.1 x 76.8
Yale Center for British Art, Paul Mellon Collection
Illustrated pp.86–7

Unknown artist, after Waggoner
The Great Fire of London 1666
Oil on canvas 47 x 72
Guildhall Art Gallery, City of London
Illustrated p.36

Edward Matthew Ward
The South Sea Bubble, a Scene in 'Change Alley in 1720 1847
Oil on canvas 129.5 x 188
Tate. Presented by Robert Vernon 1847
Illustrated pp.58–9

Carel Weight
Clapham Junction 1978
Oil on canvas 70.8 x 90.8
Tate. Presented by the Trustees of the Chantrey Bequest 1978
Illustrated pp.78–9

Carel Weight
The Dogs 1955–6
Oil on board 122.6 x 243.8
Tate. Presented by the Trustees of the Chantrey Bequest 1956
Illustrated pp.112–13

James Abbott McNeil Whistler
Wapping 1860–4
Oil on canvas 72 x 101.8
National Gallery of Art, Washington DC. John Hay Whitney Collection
Illustrated pp.96–7

James Abbott McNeil Whistler
Nocturne: Blue and Silver – Chelsea 1871
Oil on wood 50.2 x 60.8
Tate. Bequeathed by Miss Rachel and Miss Jean Alexander 1972
Illustrated p.142

James Abbott McNeil Whistler
Nocturne: Blue and Gold – Old Battersea Bridge c.1872–5
Oil on canvas 68.3 x 51.2
Tate. Presented by the Art Fund 1905
Illustrated p.143

James Abbott McNeil Whistler
Cremorne Gardens, No. 2 c.1870–80
Oil on canvas 68.6 x 134.9
Metropolitan Museum of Art, New York. John Stewart Kennedy Fund, 1912. Acc.n.12.32
Illustrated pp.98–9

Richard Wilson
The Inner Temple after the Fire of 4 January 1737 1737
Oil on canvas 64.8 x 95.2
Tate. Bequeathed by Richard and Catherine Garnons 1854
Illustrated pp.38–9

Richard Wilson
Kew Gardens: The Pagoda and Bridge 1762
Oil on canvas 47.6 x 73
Yale Center for British Art, Paul Mellon Collection
Illustrated p.137

James Digman Wingfield
The Opening Ceremony of the Great Exhibition, London 1851
Oil on canvas 139.7 x 106.7
Nottingham Castle Museum and Art Gallery
Illustrated p.90

William Lionel Wyllie
Toil, Glitter, Grime and Wealth on a Flowing Tide 1883
Oil on canvas 115.6 x 165.1
Tate. Presented by the Trustees of the Chantrey Bequest 1883
Illustrated pp.66–7

SELECTED SOURCES AND FURTHER READING

There are books on every aspect of London and London life – a selection of the most useful and enjoyable titles are listed here. Also listed are the many websites used in the preparation of this book, which now allow one to search through tens of thousands of paintings, and view London from impossible angles.

ART AND ARTISTS IN LONDON

Dana Arnold (ed.), *The Metropolis and its Image: Constructing Identities for London, c.1750–1950*, Oxford 1999

Simon Baker and Helen Delaney (eds), *Another London: International Photographers Capture City Life 1930–1980*, London 2012

Susan Doran (ed.), *Royal River: Power, Pageantry & the Thames*, London 2012

Mireille Galinou and John Hayes, *London in Paint: Oil Paintings in the Collection at the Museum of London*, London 1996

Nancy Rose Marshall, *City of Mud and Gold: Painting Victorian London*, New Haven and London, 2012

David Piper, *Artists' London*, London 1982

Harley Preston, *London and the Thames: Paintings of Three Centuries* (exh. cat.), London 1977

Kit Wedd, with Lucy Peltz and Cathy Ross, *Artists' London: Holbein to Hirst*, London 2001

LONDON HISTORY

Peter Ackroyd, *London: The Biography*, London 2001

Ken Allinson, *Architects and Architecture of London*, Oxford 2008

Craig Charles, Graham Diprose and Mike Seaborne, *London's Changing Riverscape: Panoramas from London Bridge to Greenwich*, London 2009

Simon Foxell, *Mapping London: Making Sense of the City*, London 2007

Ross Glinert, *The London Compendium* London 2012

Cathy Ross and John Clark, *London: The Illustrated History*, London 2008

Anthony Sutcliffe, *London: An Architectural History*, New Haven and London 2006

Russ Willey, *Chambers London Gazetteer*, Edinburgh 2006

GENERAL ART HISTORY AND ARTIST BIOGRAPHIES

Tim Barringer, Jason Rosenfeld and Alison Smith, *Pre-Raphaelites: Victorian Avant-Garde* (exh. cat.), London 2012

David Bindman (ed.), *The History of British Art* (3 vols), London 2008

Helena Bonett, Ysanne Holt and Jennifer Mundy (eds), *The Camden Town Group in Context*, Tate Research Publication, May 2012, www.tate.org.uk/art/research-publications/camden-town-group (accessed July 2016)

Penelope Curtis (ed.), *Tate Britain Companion: A Guide to British Art*, London 2013

David Dewing (ed.), *Home and Garden: Paintings and Drawings of English, Middle-Class, Urban Domestic Spaces, 1675 to 1914*, London 2003

David Dewing (ed.), *Home and Garden: Paintings and Drawings of English, Middle-Class, Urban Domestic Spaces 1914 to 2006*, London 2007

David Fraser Jenkins and Hugh Fowler-Wright, *The Art of John Piper*, London 2016

Susanne Keegan, *The Eye of God: A Life of Oskar Kokoschka*, London 1999

Margaret F. MacDonald, and Patricia de Montfort, *Whistler and the Thames* (exh. cat.), London 2013

Steven Parissien, *Celebrating Britain: Canaletto, Hogarth and Patriotism*, London 2015

Jane Sellars (ed.), *Atkinson Grimshaw: A Painter of Moonlight*, Harrogate 2011

Matthew Sturgis, *Walter Sickert: A Life*, London 2005

Gillian Tindall, *The Man Who Drew London: Wenceslaus Hollar in Reality and Imagination*, London 2003

Robert Upstone (ed.), *Modern Painters: The Camden Town Group* (exh. cat.), London 2008

ONLINE RESOURCES

www.tate.org.uk
– Includes detailed information on all works in the Tate collection, including excerpts from previously published catalogues.

www.artuk.org
– A catalogue of all oil paintings in public collections in the United Kingdom.

www.oxfordartonline.com
– Authoritative art encyclopaedia (subscription).

www.google.co.uk/maps

www.bing.com/maps
– Essential resource, especially the three-dimensional views which were invaluable in locating the locations of the paintings.

ARTIST BIOGRAPHIES

JOHN ANDERSON 1835–1919
Born in Annan, Scotland, Anderson trained in London at the Department of Science and Art, South Kensington. He painted several views of Westminster. He was Headmaster of Coventry School of Art (1863–1906) and exhibited at the Royal Academy, London.

FRANK AUERBACH b.1931
Born in Berlin to Jewish parents, Auerbach moved to Britain as a child to escape the Nazis. He studied at St Martin's School of Art, London, and with David Bomberg at night classes. He has worked from the same studio near Mornington Crescent in north west London since the 1950s. He is friends with Leon Kossoff, with whom he shares a style of thick application of paint.

WALTER BAYES 1869–1956
Bayes was born in St Pancras, central London, to an artistic family – his father Alfred Walter Bayes illustrated Hans Christian Andersen. After studying at the Westminster School of Art, London, and then in Paris, Bayes became a teacher, including at the Camberwell School of Art, south-east London, and an art writer. He became the art critic of the *Athenaeum* in 1906, was a founding member of the Camden Town Group and the London Group, and after the First World War he was appointed principal of the Westminster School of Art. He contributed to the Recording Britain scheme during the Second World War.

JACQUES-EMILE BLANCHE 1861–1942
Born in Paris, Blanche's father was a sought-after psychiatrist. He was self-taught as an artist, and became a successful portrait painter. He spent time regularly in London from 1870 onwards, where he was friends with Walter Sickert and John Singer Sargent. Blanche created a series of London views, sometimes working from a mobile studio on wheels. In later life, he wrote an unreliable and sensationalist autobiography.

DAVID BOMBERG 1890–1957
Bomberg was born in Birmingham to a family of Polish-Jewish immigrant leatherworkers – they moved to the East End of London when he was a child. He studied at the Westminster School of Art under Richard Sickert, and the Slade School of Art alongside C.R.W. Nevinson but was expelled for the radical nature of his abstract paintings. He exhibited with the Camden Town Group in 1913. After the Second World War, he taught at Borough Polytechnic (now South Bank University), where there is a hall of residence named after him. Frank Auerbach and Leon Kossoff were among his students. He died in London.

STEPHEN BONE 1904–58
Born in Chiswick, west London, Bone was the son of prominent artist Sir Muirhead Bone. He enrolled at the Slade School of Art in 1922 but left after a year to work as a book illustrator. During the Second World War he enlisted as a war artist, taking his father's post, and painted many naval scenes. After the war he became an art critic and worked in television and radio.

CLIVE BRANSON 1907–44
Artist and poet, Branson was also an active communist, a recruiter for the International Brigade and fought in the Spanish Civil War. He was captured and held as prisoner of war, where he painted and sketched the camp and inmates. He joined the British army and died in action in Burma.

JOHN BRATBY 1928–92
Born in Wimbledon, south-west London, Bratby studied at Kingston College of Art and the Royal College of Art. Considered a founder of the Kitchen Sink style in the 1950s, he later moved on to abstraction and a form of pop art, painting portraits of famous figures. He wrote a series of autobiographical novels in the 1960s.

CANALETTO (GIOVANNI ANTONIO CANAL) 1697–1768
Influential Italian painter and etcher of landscapes. Born in Venice, Canaletto spent the whole of his life there except for a sojourn in London from 1746 to 1755. Immensely popular with the British aristocracy, his finely detailed and luminescent paintings were highly prized mementoes of the Grand Tour of Europe. He moved to England after the War of the Austrian Succession reduced the number of tourists to Venice. During his time in London, some critics believed his work was becoming increasingly mechanical and formulaic, and even accused him of being an imposter.

JESSE DALE CAST 1900–76
Portrait and landscape painter who studied in London at the Camberwell School of Arts and Crafts and the Slade School of Art. During the Second World War, his south London home was hit by a bomb, killing his wife and destroying many of his paintings. After the war, he went into teaching, mainly at the Hornsey College of Art.

SIR GEORGE CLAUSEN 1852–1944
Born in London, the son of a Danish interior decorator. At 14 he was apprenticed to a firm of decorators but also attended evening classes at the National Art Training School, South Kensington. He was a founding member of the New English Art Club and became influential in the Royal Academy, where he was Professor of Painting for two years. Clausen was knighted after completing a mural for the Houses of Parliament in 1926.

CHARLES ALLSTON COLLINS 1828–73
Born in Hampstead, north-west London, the son of genre painter William Collins, Charles studied at the Royal Academy Schools. He was closely associated with the Pre-Raphaelite Brotherhood, especially John Everett Millais, but his nomination for membership was rejected. His older brother was the novelist Wilkie Collins and he married Charles Dickens's daughter Kate, later designing the cover for Dickens's unfinished novel *The Mystery of Edwin Drood* (1870). He abandoned painting in the 1850s, taking up a writing career. He is buried in Brompton Cemetery, west London.

JOHN CONSTABLE 1776–1837
One of the major British painters of the nineteenth century, Constable was born in Suffolk. His father was a wealthy corn merchant and John worked for the family business after leaving school. His amateur sketches of the local landscape were noticed and he persuaded his father to let him train as a painter. He moved to London to study at the Royal Academy Schools. He lived with his wife in Bloomsbury, central London, but from 1819 rented a house in Hampstead, north-west London. In 1829 he became a Royal Academician and made popular lectures to the students there. He is buried in the St John-at-Hampstead churchyard, north London.

ANDRÉ DERAIN 1880–1954
French painter best known for his invention of 'fauvism' with Henri Matisse. Derain visited London in 1906 at the behest of art dealer Ambroise Vollard. He turned towards classicism after the First World War and worked on set designs for the Ballet Russes.

ANTHONY EYTON b.1923
Born in Teddington, west London, Eyton studied at Reading University and, after the Second World War, at Camberwell School of Art, south London. He has taught at Camberwell, the Royal Academy Schools and in Canada.

WILLIAM POWELL FRITH 1819–1909
Born in Yorkshire, Frith's parents were in domestic employment and encouraged him to become an artist. He came to London to study at the Royal Academy Schools and elsewhere. He became part of the fashionable social scene, associating with artists including Richard Dadd and Edward Matthew Ward. He gained critical, popular and financial success with his large paintings of contemporary subjects including *Ramsgate Sands* 1854, *The Derby Day* 1856–8 and *The Railway Station* 1862. Frith married twice and had nineteen children. He is buried in Kensal Green Cemetery, west London.

CHARLES GINNER 1878–1952
Born in France to British parents, Ginner became an artist against his family's

wishes. After living in Paris for a decade, he moved to London in 1910 and remained there the rest of his life. He became close to Harold Gilman and Spencer Gore, and was a founding member of the Camden Town Group. He also joined the London Group and the Cumberland Market Group. In 1950 Ginner was made a CBE for his contribution to the arts. He died in London.

SPENCER GORE 1878–1914
Born in Epsom, Surrey, Gore attended Harrow School, then enrolled in the Slade School of Fine Art. He met Walter Sickert while travelling in France and persuaded the older artist to return to London. They became firm friends and together founded the Camden Town Group, of which Gore was the first president. Gore married in 1912 and moved to Richmond in 1913. Sadly he caught pneumonia while painting in Richmond Park and died aged thirty-five.

WALTER GREAVES 1846–1930
Born at 31 Cheyne Walk in Chelsea to Charles Greaves, a Chelsea boatbuilder who had rowed J.M.W. Turner on the River Thames. With his brother Henry, Greaves became friends with James Abbott McNeill Whistler when he moved to Chelsea in 1863. The Greaveses taught Whistler about the river and he taught them to paint. Whistler eventually abandoned Greaves for more sophisticated friends, and he was later accused of plagiarising Whistler's work. Greaves fell into obscurity and died in poverty.

ATKINSON GRIMSHAW 1836–93
John Atkinson Grimshaw was born in Leeds and gave up his job as a railway clerk to paint. He became successful and especially known for his moonlight scenes. He also pioneered an unusual technique of painting on to photographs. He spent time in London in the 1880s, taking a studio in Chelsea.

ARTHUR HACKER 1858–1919
Born in London, Hacker's father was an engraver and the registrar for births, deaths and marriages for Kentish Town, north London. Best known for classical portraits and religious scenes, Hacker studied at the Royal Academy, where he was elected an Academician in 1910. He is buried in Brookwood Cemetery in Surrey, also known as the London Necropolis.

WILFRED HAINES 1905–44
Born in Wimbledon, south London, Haines came from a family of weavers and became a textile designer himself. During the Second World War he served as a fireman and was killed by a flying bomb. He is buried in Wimbledon Cemetery.

VILHELM HAMMERSHØI 1864–1916
Hammershøi was born, studied, lived and died in Copenhagen, Denmark, and most of his exterior work depicts the city, although he is best known for his mysterious interiors. He travelled extensively in Europe visiting London several times.

BENJAMIN ROBERT HAYDON 1786–1846
Born in Plymouth, son of a printer. Haydon came to London to study at the Royal Academy, where he impressed others with his enthusiasm. After setting himself up as a history painter, some success followed but his insistence on working on a vast scale and his tendency to fight with his patrons led to money problems, and he was several times imprisoned for debt. He wrote an important autobiography and several lectures and articles on art. Eventually overwhelmed by his lack of success, Haydon took his own life aged sixty and is buried in St Mary's Gardens, Paddington.

DAVID HEPHER b.1935
Born in Surrey, Hepher studied in London at Camberwell and the Slade School of Art. He is best known for his paintings of buildings, especially brutalist tower blocks in London. He has lived in Camberwell, south London, since the 1960s.

WILLIAM HOGARTH 1697–1764
Extremely influential and popular, the British painter and engraver who pioneered sequential, comic-strip like art was born in London and apprenticed to an engraver in Leicester Fields (now Leicester Square) and also studied at the St Martin's Lane Academy. In 1724 he joined the academy run by James Thornhill in Covent Garden and later married his daughter. Hogarth gained fame and fortune from the success of his series of paintings and engravings *A Harlot's Progress* and *The Rake's Progress*, and moved to a home and studio in Leicester Square. In 1749 he bought a country house in Chiswick, west London, which is now a visitor attraction. He is buried nearby in Old Chiswick Cemetery.

KEN HOWARD b.1932
Born in London, Howard studied at Hornsey College of Art and the Royal College of Art. He has been president of the New English Art Club, and became a Royal Academician in 1991 and an OBE in 2010. He is known for his paintings of Venice, London and studio interiors.

BEN JOHNSON b.1946
Born in Llandudno, Wales, Johnson studied in London at the Royal College of Art, and has lived and worked in London since the 1960s. He is known for his large, detailed cityscapes of cities including Liverpool, London, Hong Kong and Jerusalem.

CLAUDE DE JONGH c.1600–1663
A Dutch Golden Age painter, little is known about him. He is recorded as a member of the Utrecht Guild of St Luke from 1627 and probably visited London several times to make sketches.

LILY D. JOSEPH 1863–1940
Born in Bermondsey, south London, Joseph studied at the Royal College of Art. Her brother was the painter Solomon J. Solomon and her husband was an architect, Delissa Joseph; they occasionally exhibited together. She was an active member of the women's suffrage movement, on one occasion missing a private view of an exhibition due to being jailed.

OSKAR KOKOSCHKA 1886–1980
Born in Pöchlarn, Austria, Kokoschka studied in Vienna. Badly wounded in the First World War, he travelled Europe in the 1920s, painting views of its great cities, including London. After the war he lived in Dresden, Germany, then moved to Prague after the rise of the Nazis. In 1938 he fled to the United Kingdom, and gained British citizenship in 1946. However, he found London a poor base from which to travel and in the 1950s relocated to Switzerland, where he died.

LEON KOSSOFF b.1926
Born in Islington, north London, to Russian Jewish parents, Kossoff studied at St Martin's School of Art and Borough Polytechnic (now London South Bank University). At Borough he was taught by David Bomberg and became friends with fellow student Frank Auerbach, whose use of heavy impasto was an influence. He has had studios in Mornington Crescent and Willesden, both in north-west London, and Bethnal Green, East London, often painting the surrounding areas.

CARL LAUBIN b.1947
Born in New York, Laubin studied architecture at Cornell University. In 1973 he moved to London and began painting views of buildings yet to be constructed. He turned to painting full-time in 1986 and now specialises in large-scale imagined views constructed of dozens of real buildings.

WILLIAM LOGSDAIL 1859–1944
Born in Lincoln, Logsdail studied at the Lincoln School of Art and in Antwerp, Belgium. He lived for many years in Venice, painting many scenes of the city, and in London 1887–92, during which time he produced an ambitious series of city views. He settled in west London with his wife in 1902, predominantly painting portraits for the rest of his career. He moved to Oxfordshire in the 1920s, where he died.

PHILIP JAMES DE LOUTHERBOURG 1740–1812
Born and educated in Strasbourg, France, Loutherbourg moved to Paris, where he became a fashionable figure and was elected to the French Academy despite

being below the required age. In 1771 he settled in London, where he designed scenery, costumes and stage machinery at the Drury Lane Theatre. He invented the *Eidophusikon*, an elaborate mechanical theatre. He also painted many maritime scenes. He was made a member of the Royal Academy in 1781. He died in Chiswick, west London, and is buried at Old Chiswick Cemetery.

L.S. LOWRY 1887–1976
Born in Lancashire, in the north of England, after leaving school Lowry worked as a clerk for a firm of chartered accountants, studying art in the evenings at Manchester's Municipal College of Art and Salford School of Art. He worked as a rent collector until his retirement in 1952. His fame grew during the 1950s and 1960s and he was elected as a Royal Academician in 1962. He is best known for his paintings of the area around his home in Pendlebury, Greater Manchester, but Lowry also made several views of London, usually when coming to visit his gallerist.

NIELS MØLLER LUND 1863–1916
Born in Faaborg, Denmark, Lund grew up in Newcastle-upon-Tyne and studied in Paris. He made impressionist paintings of London and north-east England.

WILLIAM MACDUFF 1824–81
Genre painter, particularly of country scenes. Little is known about his life.

PAUL MAITLAND 1863–1909
Born in Chelsea, Maitland studied at the Royal College of Art and under Theodore Roussel. He injured his back as a baby, resulting in poor health throughout his life. Influenced by Whistler, and most of his work depicts Chelsea Embankment or, towards the end of his life, Kensington Gardens.

WILLIAM MARLOW 1740–1813
Born in London, Marlow was a pupil of Samuel Scott and also studied at the St Martin's Lane Academy. He travelled extensively in France and Italy and throughout Britain, which provided material for his paintings which are close in style to Scott and Canaletto. Commercially successful, he moved to Twickenham in 1885 in semi-retirement, where he died.

JOCK MCFADYEN b.1950
Born in Paisley, Scotland, McFadyen studied at Chelsea School of Art. His paintings focus on the urban experience and his early work focuses on the pre-gentrification of London's East End. He lives and works in a converted industrial building in the East End, and Edinburgh.

LISA MILROY b.1959
Born in Vancouver, Canada, Milroy spent time as a student in Paris before moving to London in 1978. She then studied at St Martin's School of Art and Goldsmiths College. Milroy is known for her paintings of everyday objects arranged into grids. She became a Royal Academician in 2005.

CLAUDE MONET 1840–1926
One of the central figures of the impressionist movement, Monet was born and studied in Paris. After the outbreak of the Franco-Prussian War, he moved with his family to London in September 1870. He studied the work of J.M.W. Turner and John Constable, met Camille Pissarro and painted views of the River Thames. He left London in May 1871, eventually returning to France. His first impressionist exhibition was held in 1874. He visited London in 1899, 1900 and 1901, painting his famous series of Thames views exhibited in Paris in 1904.

BALTHAZAR NEBOT active 1730–65
Painter of urban scenes and part of the Covent Garden Group. Little is known about his life; he is assumed to be of Spanish descent and married in London about 1729.

CHRISTOPHER RICHARD WYNNE NEVINSON 1889–1946
Son of the war correspondent Henry Nevinson and suffrage campaigner and writer Margaret Nevinson, he was born in Hampstead, north London. He attended the Slade School of Art where he met Mark Gertler, Stanley Spencer, Paul Nash and Dora Carrington. After spending time in Paris, he met Pablo Picasso and the futurist Filippo Tommaso Marinetti. He became an official war artist during the First World War and his resulting works brought him fame and notoriety. He suffered a stroke during the Second World War and died in Hampstead.

ALGERNON NEWTON 1880–1968
Born in Hampstead, north London, Newton was a grandson of one of the founders of art supplies company Winsor & Newton. He mainly painted unoccupied scenes of canals and back streets in London, Cornwall and Yorkshire. He became a Royal Academician in 1943.

JOHN O'CONNOR 1830–89
Born in Londonderry, Ireland, O'Connor was orphaned at the age of 12. His uncle provided him with work as a scene painter in a Belfast theatre. He moved to London in 1848 to work at the Theatre Royal, Drury Lane, and was the principal scene painter at the Haymarket Theatre from 1863. He began exhibiting paintings and became a favourite of the royal family, whom he depicted during special events.

WILLIAM ORPEN 1878–1931
Born in County Dublin, Ireland, Orpen was a precocious painter, enrolling at the Dublin Metropolitan School of Art at the age of thirteen. He came to London to study at the Slade School of Art in 1897. After leaving he ran his own art school with Augustus John and divided his time between London and Dublin. He became a sought-after and fashionable portrait painter, and used his personal connections to secure himself the role of official war artist during the First World War – he made 138 works in all. He died in London and is buried at Putney Vale Cemetery, south-west London.

VICTOR PASMORE 1908–98
Born in Surrey, Pasmore moved to London to work in an administrative job, studying painting at the Central School of Art and Design in the evenings. He was one of the founders of the Euston Road School, which advocated representational painting. They held an exhibition titled *15 Paintings of London* in 1938. During the war, Pasmore was imprisoned for being a conscientious objector. Upon his release, he moved towards pure abstraction and expanded his practice into sculpture and architecture.

HENRY PETHER 1800–80
Son of the painter Abraham Pether (1756–1812), Henry took up his father's speciality of moonlit scenes, as did his brother Sebastian.

JOHN PIPER 1903–92
Born in Epsom, Surrey, Piper moved to London to work at his father's law firm. He refused to become a partner, sacrificing his inheritance, and instead attended Richmond School of Art, then the Royal College of Art. During the Second World War he worked as an official war artist, recording military and historic sites and damaged churches. After the war he created fabric designs and wrote books and articles as well as continuing to paint.

CAMILLE PISSARRO 1830–1903
A Danish-French painter and one of the founders of the impressionist movement, Pissarro moved to Norwood, now a southern suburb of London, in 1870, to avoid the Franco-Prussian war. His paintings were not popular but he met the influential dealer Paul Durand-Ruel, who put him in touch with Claude Monet, who was also in London. He returned to Paris after the war but visited London again in 1890, 1892 and 1897, painting central London, Kew and Chiswick. His son Lucien was also a painter and settled in London in 1890, later joining the Camden Town Group and influencing Spencer Gore.

JAMES POLLARD 1792–1867
Born in Islington, north London, the son of a successful painter and publisher, Robert Pollard. Pollard specialised in paintings of mail coaches and hunting scenes, many of which were turned into popular prints. However, his subject

matter was outmoded by the arrival of the railways and he died in poverty in Chelsea, south-west London.

WILLIAM RATCLIFFE 1870–1955

Born in Norfolk, Ratcliffe trained as a designer in Manchester. He worked as wallpaper designer and lived in London briefly for work around 1901, before moving to the new town of Letchworth Garden City around 1906. He met the painter Harold Gilman, who encouraged him to enrol at the Slade School of Art, which he did in 1910. Ratcliffe was a member of the Camden Town and London groups. He spent the latter part of his life living with family and friends and died in a relative's house in Hampstead.

SAMUEL SCOTT c.1702–72

Born in Covent Garden, the son of a barber-surgeon, Scott began painting maritime scenes. He started making paintings of London in 1746, the year Canaletto arrived, probably spurred on by the Italian artist's popularity. Scott's works were successful and frequently copied. Like other prominent artists of the time, such as his friend William Hogarth, Scott was involved in the foundation of the Foundling Hospital for 'deserted young children'. William Marlow was among his students. Scott retired to Twickenham in 1758 and then to Bath, where he died.

JAN SIBERECHTS 1627–c.1700

Born in Antwerp, Belgium, the son of a sculptor, Siberechts was one of the many Dutch and Flemish painters who came to England, feted by the aristocracy for their innovative landscape paintings. He arrived around 1672 and lived in London. Siberechts travelled widely, painting major country homes including Longleat, Chatsworth and Wollaton. His work is some of the earliest depicting the British landscape. He died in London.

WALTER SICKERT 1860–1942

One of the most influential British artists of the late nineteenth and early twentieth centuries, Sickert led a complex and cosmopolitan life. Born in Munich to a German artist father and an Anglo-Irish mother, he moved to London at the age of eight. He studied at University College and Kings College, London, before a stint at the Slade School of Art. He became a pupil of James Abbott McNeill Whistler, before travelling to Paris and meeting impressionist painter Edgar Degas. Sickert spent time in Dieppe and Venice, before returning to London in 1906. He lived around the Camden Town area, which gave the name to the group of artists he founded, including Spencer Gore and William Ratcliffe. Sickert taught at Westminster School of Art, where David Bomberg was among his pupils. He continued to be successful and influential in later life, becoming a member of the Royal Academy. He died in Bath.

JAMES TISSOT 1836–1902

Born in Nantes, France, Jacques Tissot anglicised his name to James due to his interest in English culture. He studied in Paris and was involved in the revolutionary Paris Commune. He fled to London in 1871 where he already had connections. His paintings of the upper-class social scene were instantly popular and he became wealthy, with a house in St John's Wood, north-west London. He was invited to participate in the first impressionist exhibition in 1874, but declined. Towards the end of his life Tissot moved towards religious works, depicting scenes from the Bible. He died in France.

WILLIAM TOWNSEND 1909–73

Born in London, Townsend studied at the Slade School of Art. He was associated with the Euston Road School and the London Group. After the Second World War he spent his career in education, teaching at Camberwell School of Art, the Slade and the University of London.

J.M.W. TURNER 1775–1851

Along with William Hogarth, Turner was one of the greatest painters to be born in London. He was born in Maiden Lane, Covent Garden, the son of a barber, and baptised at the local church, St Paul's Covent Garden (much depicted in earlier art). He spent his childhood in various places, including the seaside town of Margate, but returned to London to study at the Royal Academy Schools at the age of 14. By 1802, he was a Royal Academician and recognised as the outstanding painter of his generation. He opened his own gallery off Harley Street in central London and built a home in Twickenham, a leafy area of south-west London. Turner retained his Cockney accent and 'rough' manners throughout his life despite moving in aristocratic circles. In 1819 and 1828 he visited Italy, which provided a new impetus to his work. In later life Turner moved to Cheyne Walk, Chelsea, where he lived incognito with his lover, Sophia Booth. Locals called him 'Admiral Booth', and it was rumoured he was a great man who would be buried in St Paul's Cathedral, as he was on his death in 1851.

EDWARD MATTHEW WARD 1816–79

Born in Pimlico, central London, Ward gained renown as an illustrator in his youth, before entering the Royal Academy Schools. He joined The Clique along with William Powell Frith, who looked up to William Hogarth and David Wilkie, whose work they considered to express the British character. Ward specialised in history painting and won the commission to paint eight scenes for the corridor of the Houses of Parliament. He fell in love with Henrietta Ward (no relation) when she was eleven; their elopement five years later was helped by novelist Wilkie Collins, brother of Charles Allston Collins. Ward suffered depression later in life and took his own life at home in Windsor.

CAREL WEIGHT 1908–97

Born in Paddington, central London, to a bank worker and a chiropodist, Weight spent most of his childhood with his godmother in Fulham, south-west London. He studied at Hammersmith School of Art and Goldsmiths College, where he developed his imaginative, unexpected and often lighthearted paintings. He spent time during the Second World War as an official war artist in Italy and began to teach afterwards, while continuing to paint scenes of south and west London. He became Professor of Painting at the Royal College of Art, a CBE and a Royal Academician. He died in London.

JAMES ABBOTT MCNEILL WHISTLER 1834–1903

Whistler was born in the United States to a prominent civil engineer, who was employed to build a railroad from Moscow to St Petersburg, and thus spent part of his childhood in St Petersburg, studying at the Imperial Academy of Fine Arts. As a teenager he joined the West Point military academy, where he learned mapmaking, but was dismissed for his insolent attitude. He spent time in bohemian Paris before settling in London in 1859, gaining fame for his etchings and notoriety for his experimental paintings. He became the hub of a social circle that included Oscar Wilde and in 1877 sued the critic John Ruskin for libel. He spent most of the rest of his life in Chelsea, living at seven different addresses around Cheyne Walk and Tite Street. He is buried in Old Chiswick Cemetery, west London.

RICHARD WILSON c.1714–82

Born in Wales, the son of a clergyman, Wilson moved to London in 1729 to become an apprentice to a portrait painter. He lived for three years at Samuel Scott's house in Covent Garden. From 1750 to 1757 he lived in Italy, and on his return became the first major British painter to concentrate on landscapes. In 1768 he became a founding member of the Royal Academy. He died in Wales.

JAMES DIGMAN WINGFIELD 1800–72

English painter and Royal Academician known for his historical subjects and scenes from literature. Little is known about his life.

WILLIAM LIONEL WYLLIE 1851–1931

Born in Camden, north London. Wyllie's father and brother were also painters. He studied at Heatherley's independent art school and at the Royal Academy Schools. He had a passion for sailing and began to specialise in maritime subjects. He became a member of the New English Art Club in 1887 and a Royal Academician in 1907. Wyllie died in Primrose Hill, north London, and was buried with full naval honours in Portsmouth in recognition of his marine work.

PICTURE CREDITS

The publishers have made every effort to trace all the relevant copyright holders and apologise for any omissions that may have been made.

References are to page numbers.

COPYRIGHT

© Frank Auerbach, courtesy Marlborough Fine Art p.133
© The Estate of Walter Bayes p.51
© The Estate of David Bomberg. All Rights Reserved, DACS 2017 p.49
© The Estate of Stephen Bone. All Rights Reserved, DACS 2017 pp.152–3
© John Bratby Estate/ Bridgeman Images p.131
© The Estate of Jesse Dale Cast pp.108–9
André Derain © ADAGP, Paris and DACS, London 2017 pp.68–9
© Anthony Eyton/ Bridgeman Images p.115
Charles Ginner © reserved pp.70, 148
© David Hepher p.132
© Ken Howard/ Bridgeman Images p.76
© Ben Johnson. All Rights Reserved, DACS 2017 pp.32–3
© Fondation Oskar Kokoschka/ DACS 2017 pp.30–1
© Leon Kossoff pp.80, 179
© Carl Laubin p.83
© The Estate of L.S. Lowry. All Rights Reserved, DACS 2017 pp.52–3, 71, cover
© Joch McFadyen p.114
© Lisa Milroy p.81
© The Piper Estate/ DACS 2017 p.46
© The Estate of William Ratcliffe pp.116–7, 124–5
© Tate pp.126–7, 128, 150–1
© The Estate of William Townsend pp.110–11
© Carel Weight Estate/ Bridgeman Images pp.78–9, 112–13

PHOTOGRAPHIC

Ole Akhøj p.103
© The Art Institute of Chicago pp.92–3, 144
© British Library Board/ Bridgeman Images p.13
© Christie's Images/ Bridgeman Images pp.42, 52–3, 71, cover
© The Cleveland Museum of Art p.40
The Samuel Courtauld Trust, The Courtauld Gallery, London pp.72–3
By permission of the Trustees of the Goodwood Collection p.158
Guildhall Art Gallery, City of London/ Bridgeman Images pp.26–7, 36, 174–5
© IWM (Art.IWM ART LD 2514) p.51
© Lobkowicz Collections, Czech Republic p.161
Manchester Art Gallery, UK/ Bridgeman Images p.139
Courtesy Manya Igel Fine Arts, London/ Bridgeman Images p.76
© The Metropolitan Museum of Art/ Art Resource/ Scala, Florence pp.98–9
© Museum of London pp.14–15, 16–17, 34–5, 46, 48, 49, 56, 63, 83, 114, 136, 154–5, 168–9, 170, 171, 172–3, 176, 177
Courtesy National Gallery of Art, Washington D.C. pp.96–7
© National Trust Images/ John Hammond p.88
Photography Incorporated, Toledo p.100
© RMN-Grand Palais (musée d'Orsay)/ Hervé Lewandowski pp.105, 145
© Royal Academy of Arts, London p.106
Royal Holloway, University of London/ Bridgeman Images pp.60–1
© Tate 2017 pp.6, 10–11, 23, 54–5, 68–9, 70, 74–5, 80, 81, 84–5, 94–5, 110–11, 119, 120–1, 126–7, 128, 130, 132, 133, 134–5, 140, 141, 142, 143, 148, 150–1, 152–3, 157, 160, 162–3, 165, 166–7, 179
© Tate 2017. Photo: Samuel Cole and Mark Heathcote pp.146–7
© Tate 2017. Photo: Mark Heathcote pp.28–9, 30–1, 38–9, 45, 57, 58–9, 66–7, 78–9, 107, 108–9, 112–13, 115, 116–17, 122–3, 124–5, 138
© Tate 2017. Photo: Joe Humphrys pp.2, 22, 65, 89
© UK Government Art Collection p.131
© Victoria and Albert Museum, London pp.20–1
© Dean and Chapter of Westminster p.159

INDEX

Note: page numbers in **bold** refer to information contained in captions.